WOMEN IN POLITICS:

OUTSIDERS OR INSIDERS?

A Collection of Readings

Lois Lovelace Duke, Editor
Clemson University

PRENTICE HALL, Englewood Cliffs, New Jersey 07632

Library of Congress Cataloging-in-Publication Data

Women in politics : outsiders or insiders? / edited by Lois Lovelace
 Duke.
       p.   cm.
    Includes bibliographical references.
    ISBN 0-13-969221-5
    1. Women in politics--United States. 2. Feminism--United States.
 I. Duke, Lois Lovelace.
 HQ1236.5.U6W663 1993
 320'.082--dc20
                                                         92-23113
                                                            CIP

Editorial/production supervision and
  interior design: Shelly Kupperman
Acquisition editor: Julie Berrisford
Copy editor: Judy Ashkenaz
Prepress buyer: Kelly Behr
Manufacturing buyer: Mary Ann Gloriande
Editorial assistant: Nicole Signoretti
Cover designer: Lucille Paccione
Cover photo: AP/Wide World Photos

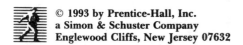

© 1993 by Prentice-Hall, Inc.
a Simon & Schuster Company
Englewood Cliffs, New Jersey 07632

Printed in the United States of America
10 9 8 7 6 5 4 3 2 1

ISBN   0-13-969221-5

PRENTICE-HALL INTERNATIONAL (UK) LIMITED, *London*
PRENTICE-HALL OF AUSTRALIA PTY. LIMITED, *Sydney*
PRENTICE-HALL CANADA INC., *Toronto*
PRENTICE-HALL HISPANOAMERICANA, S.A., *Mexico*
PRENTICE-HALL OF INDIA PRIVATE LIMITED, *New Delhi*
PRENTICE-HALL OF JAPAN, INC., *Tokyo*
SIMON & SCHUSTER ASIA PTE. LTD., *Singapore*
EDITORA PRENTICE-HALL DO BRASIL, LTDA., *Rio de Janeiro*

CONTENTS _____

PREFACE

This book is designed to provide a supplemental reader on the topic of women and politics to accompany a basic American government text, as well as for use in women and politics courses. We begin with a feminist theoretical framework, examine some gender differences in political attutides and voting, explore how women have fared in competing for public office, and then look at the various branches of government and how women are (and in some cases are not) participating in the functions of government. Each chapter has been written with the college undergraduate in mind.

ORGANIZATIONAL FRAMEWORK

The book is organized into eight chapters, divided into four parts. Part I includes an analysis of "Women, Equality, and Feminist Theory." Part II explores the topic of "Women and Politics," including women as participants, women and political parties, and women running for elective office. Part III, "Gender and Governments," examines women and their role as policymakers in political institutions; this topic includes women as state legislators, women in the U.S. Congress and projections for their future role, and the courts' differential treatment of women and men in the law. Part IV looks at "Women and National Policy" in such public policy areas as family and medical leave, affirmative action, and women in combat; it concludes with a chapter on female activists and their contributions to change. The following is a brief summary of the chapters included in the book:

CHAPTER 1   THE STUDY OF WOMEN: THE NEW FRAMEWORK

Feminist Theory and the Politics of Empowerment
Iva E. Deutchman

This study critically evaluates feminist theories about power. The concept of power has long fascinated not only political analysts, but political activists as well. Among many reasons to support an increase in the number of women officials, one overriding reason has been based on the belief that women feel differently about power and use power differently than men. Men, it is argued, see power as *power over*, an ability to influence or dominate, whereas women see power as *power to*, or empowerment. Thus, power for women can be seen as less confrontational and more cooperative than power for men. Deutchman critically examines the claim that women and men are different in both their concept of power and their use of power.

The Riddle of Consciousness: Racism and Identity in Feminist Theory
Nancie E. Caraway

Utilizing the poltical and epistemological contributions of contemporary Black feminist theory, Nancie E. Caraway points up the intersections of gender, race, and class as determinants of oppression. She argues that the texts of Black feminists teach us that feminist theory and politics should address this "multiple jeopardy." She cautions that feminists need to be wary of the damaging consequences of conceptions like identity and self, which have set up white norms. In her discussion of identity politics, Caraway questions many of the assumptions of mainstream white feminism. She proposes instead multicultural goals in which the themes of racism and identity come together in a configuration that can address the theoretical issues about the female subject. She argues that a critical identity politics cautions us not to become too comfortable too long in one spot with one identity lest we forget and stifle the ways in which we change, contradict, and grow in history.

CHAPTER 2   GENDER DIFFERENCES IN POLICITAL ATTITUDES AND VOTING

The Gender Gap 1988: Compassion, Pacifism, and Indirect Feminism
Janet Clark/Cal Clark

Studies have shown that women tend to be more liberal than men on issues relating to social programs and economic security; that is, women have shown more humanitarian, social welfare–oriented attitudes. Women have also tended to be less supportive of militarist or aggressive action in foreign affairs and have tended to oppose the use of nuclear energy as a power source, perhaps as a manifestation of their more environmentalist or pacifist views. This article evaluates this gender gap between men and women in how they vote and in their attitudes about a wide range of political issues.

Changing Views about Gender Equality in Politics: Gradual Change and Lingering Doubts
Linda L. M. Bennett/Stephen E. Bennett

This article examines gender differences and similarities in political behavior and attitudes. Even while some attitudes are changing, women continue to be more politically passive than men. The authors conclude that the sex-role socialization process still tends to define a less politically active role for women than men.

The Generations of Feminism
Elizabeth Adell Cook

Previous research has found that younger women are more likely to hold feminist attitudes than are older women. There is also some evidence, however, that young women in the 1980s are less supportive of feminism than were older women. This suggests there may be some generational influences at work. Cohort analysis of the 1972 to 1984 American National Election Studies indicates that women who came of age during the period of social activism of the 1960s and the growth of the women's movement in the 1970s exhibit higher levels of politicized feminist consciousness than do women of earlier generations, but that women who came of age during the more conservative late 1970s and early 1980s exhibit lower levels of feminist consciousness than do women of the Sixties and Women's Liberation cohorts.

Gender, Partisanship, and Background Explain Differences in Grass-Roots Party Activists' Political Attitudes
Anne E. Kelley/William E. Hulbary/Lewis Bowman

The authors report the importance of gender as a variable in accounting for political attitudes among party activists in Florida. Using data from a 1984 survey, the authors develop a political ideology scale, which they then relate to gender, party, and social characteristics. They find that partisanship is the major discriminating variable but that, regardless of party affiliation, gender often is related to ideological differences among the party activists. Several social characteristics offer explanations about which of the women and men, representing Florida's precinct committeepersons, are more liberal or conservative than would be expected on the basis of partisanship alone.

More than Pink and Blue: Gender, Occupational Stratification, and Political Attitudes
Gertrude A. Steuernagel/Thomas A. Yantek

Women's lives are changing, and these changes are not without implications for political life in the United States. One of the most significant changes in women's lives during the twentieth century has been in relation to their roles as workers. A number of researchers have established the importance of understanding the relationship between employment and women's political behavior. Since it has been established that work force participation is linked to women's political behavior, there is a need to focus on the realities of women's employment and the details of the kind of workplace environment in which women find themselves. This study is concerned with the effects of occupational segregation on women's political attitudes. Using data from the 1984 University of Michigan National Election Study as well as statistics on occupation segregation and integration from the U.S. Bureau of the Census, the authors examined the attitudes of workers in three census occupational categories. The conclusions suggest a need to go beyond the sex of respondents in order to comprehend the significance of gender and its relationship to political attitudes.

CHAPTER 3   WOMEN AND ELECTIONS: THE UPHILL STRUGGLE

On the Eve of Transition: Women in Southern Legislatures, 1946–1968
Joanne V. Hawks/Carolyn Ellis Staton

Many scholars considered the post–World War II era a quiescent time for white middle-class American women. After a period of wartime involvement, many women supposedly retreated into a more traditional lifestyle. Yet, between 1946 and 1968, almost 100 women entered legislatures in the South, a particularly traditional region. Data indicate that they were predominantly women who were already involved in the public sphere in one or more ways. Even though many were serious legislators, the press emphasized their domesticity and femininity instead of their legislative achievements.

Women on Southern City Councils: Does Structure Matter?
Susan A. MacManus/Charles S. Bullock III

This article examines the influences of governmental structural variables (single-member district election systems, council size, incumbency return rate, length of term, staggered terms, and majority vote requirements) in assessing female representation on Southern city councils. The research data were drawn in the spring of 1986 from the 211 cities with 1980 populations over 25,000 in eleven Southern states. Although the researchers occasionally observed variations across the structural variables considered, the overwhelming thrust of their findings is that structural features are not associated with whether women serve as council members.

John Bailey's Legacy: Political Parties and Women's Candidacies for Public Office
Barbara Burrell

This essay reviews the relationship between political party organizations and women's candidacies for public office in the United States. Its theme is that the women and politics literature has developed a static and negative perspective on the role of parties in the recruitment of female candidates and has not carefully incorporated the changing nature of party organization as chronicled in the parties' literature into its research. The essay discusses various scenarios regarding the parties' impact on women's campaigns, the possible positive and negative effects of party decline, and the possible transformation of party leadership into more supportive organizations.

CHAPTER 4   LEGISLATURES, WOMEN, AND POLICYMAKING

Women in Congress
Marcia Lynn Whicker/Malcolm Jewell/Lois Lovelace Duke

In recent years, women have made some inroads in obtaining elected political office. Those inroads, however, have not included gains in female representation in Congress. Across the more than seventy years since women secured the right to participate politically with the passage of the Nineteenth Amendment, female representation in Congress has increased from a minuscule 0.2 percent of total membership in 1922 to only 5.2 percent in 1988. At that rate of increase, women will not achieve equality in representation until the year 2582. Women who do obtain congressional office do so at an older age than their male counterparts, serve significantly fewer terms, and are more likely to decline to seek reelection. The gap between democratic rhetoric and representational reality for women is great, despite a significant narrowing in the experiential backgrounds of men and women who are elected to Congress.

Why Are More Women State Legislators?
Wilma Rule

This research analyzes why women's recruitment in the fifty state assemblies and senates increased 100 percent in the decade from 1974 to 1984. Findings show that women's recruitment to state legislatures has doubled because of two trends occurring simultaneously in the last decade.

One was a building on the gains in the Republican-moralistic states most favorable to women in the 1960s and 1970s. At the same time, women's dramatic legislative increases in the "new wave" states show that the Democratic party no longer constitutes a barrier.

CHAPTER 5   THE EXECUTIVE BRANCH: WOMEN AND LEADERSHIP

The Maleness of the American Presidency
Marcia Lynn Whicker/Todd W. Areson

The authors explore why the U.S. presidency has been a bastion of maleness. They identify factors that account for the unlevel presidential "playing field" that women candidates face: the presidential system of direct, popular election; the paucity of women who have gained experience in the three presidential "launching roles"; the difficulty women face in securing campaign funding for national and subnational races; and long-standing public images of a conflict for women—but not for men—between familial and political roles.

CHAPTER 6   THE COURTS: WOMEN AND DECISIONS

Views from the State Bench: Gender Roles and Judicial Roles
Elaine Martin

This study represents a new area of research in which the author attempts to establish some dimensions to the different, gender-based perspectives male and female judges might bring to the bench. Three areas of potential attitudinal differences between women and men are examined: perceptions of the role of female judges, perceptions of gender bias in the courts, and decisions on five hypothetical cases raising women's rights issues. A major underlying question in the study is whether gender or feminist ideology is a more important influence on judicial attitudes. Controlling for feminism reveals statistically significant variations between genders on almost every attitudinal variable tested. The influence of gender and feminism was less apparent in respondents' votes in the hypothetical cases.

On Credibility: Differential Treatment of Women and Men in the Law
Victor F. D'Lugin

This research indicates that one key variable in understanding the treatment of women in law is the differential awarding of credibility. The hypothesis: Regardless of rule, men are assumed to possess credibility, whereas women must earn credibility. Women's treatment as victims, expert witnesses, and professionals is examined. Credibility is shown to possess an intrinsic contradiction that permits courts to rely on sexist assumptions in exercising discretionary authority. The resulting action of courts is advantageous to men and detrimental to women.

CHAPTER 7   PUBLIC POLICY: THE FEMINIST PERSPECTIVE

The Handmaid's Tale and *The Birth Dearth*: Prophecy, Prescription, and Public Policy
Diane D. Blair

This chapter deals with the politics of reproduction. It compares and analyzes Margaret Atwood's *The Handmaid's Tale* (1986) and Ben Wattenberg's *The Birth Dearth* (1987). Blair argues that Atwood, writing from a feminist perspective, posits a dystopia in which women have been reduced to the function of breeders. By contrast, Wattenberg, writing from what Blair describes as a "nationalistic perspective," deplores the current American "birth dearth," attributes it primarily to "working women," and proposes a variety of pro-natalist remedies. Blair maintains that among the significant implications of these two books, especially when they are read in tandem, are the following: that pro-natalism, justified by the United States' relatively low fertility rate, has climbed high on many conservative agendas; that this movement seriously jeopardizes many of the gains achieved by feminists in recent years; and that the contemporary pro-natalist drive has long and powerful historical precedents.

The Family and Medical Leave Act: A Policy for Families
Joan Hulse Thompson

Exclusion of males has been a policy of the women's liberation movement for ideological, symbolic, and pragmatic reasons. Therefore, the transformation of the Congresswomen's Caucus into the Congressional Caucus for Women's Issues raised questions about the viability of a political organization founded on gender and the optimal future strategy for the women's movement. Relying on extensive interviewing and participant observation, the author examines the benefits and challenges that come from forging a partnership with congressmen. The diversity of congresswomen formed an insurmountable obstacle to unity and effectivness for the Congresswomen's Caucus. Sharing credit with the men has created tensions, but the expansion gave the caucus far more members in positions of power and a better media presence. Because their goals were legislative and reformist rather than revolutionary, partnership with men was the logical course for the caucus congresswomen.

Sex at Risk in Insurance Classifications? The Supreme Court as Shaper of Public Policy
Ruth Bamberger

Although numerous laws have been passed prohibiting sex discrimination in a variety of public policy areas, the insurance industry has retained the practice of discriminating by gender in determining coverage and premium rates. The industry argues its position on cost-efficiency and actuarial grounds. Civil rights and feminist groups have criticized such discrimination on grounds of fairness and prevailing social policy. Although they have pursued their cause through multiple channels of government, the Supreme Court is perceived to be the primary agent of policy change. The Court has signaled that sex may be at risk as a classification, but its role as shaper of policy on this issue has been incremental at best.

Affirmative Action as a Woman's Issue
Roberta Ann Johnson

This reading offers a generic definition of affirmative action and then does three things. First, it raises the development of the federal affirmative action policy from the issuing of Executive Orders by Presidents Roosevelt, Kennedy, and Johnson to its full implementation in the Department of Labor. Second, the paper summarizes and evaluates all the affirmative action cases decided by the Supreme Court, starting with the Bakke decision. Finally, using Census Bureau and Department of Labor statistics and secondary sources, the study considers the ways in which affirmative action increases opportunities for women. Throughout the paper, the author recognizes affirmative action for its redistributive thrust.

Affirmative Action and Combat Exclusion: Gender Roles in the U.S. Army
Richard D. Hooker, Jr.

The women's movement has resulted in the removal of many obstacles for women—obstacles that crossed political, economic, social, cultural, and legal boundaries. One significant change, and one that elicits emotional arguments on both sides, extends to the role of women in the military. Specifically, this debate centers around the question of whether the military should permit women in combat. With the intervention of U.S. forces in the activities of other countries, this issue has become even more salient to the U.S. public. This article reviews the current policy of the U.S. Army with respect to the role of women, examines court cases brought about as a result of this issue, and evaluates the arguments for those who would favor full participation of women in all aspects of military life versus those who take a traditional approach to the role of female soldiers.

CHAPTER 8   WOMEN ACTIVITST: ATTITUDES, TACTICS, AND CHANGE

Virginia Foster Durr: An Analysis of One Woman's Contributions to the Civil Rights Movement in the South
Lois Lovelace Duke

This research explores Virginia Foster Durr's contributions to the civil rights movement in the Deep South, using the theoretical framework of leadership as outlined by James MacGregor Burns. For many years Durr worked behind the scenes in efforts to eliminate the poll tax and bring about the right to vote for all Americans. She also supported the civil rights movement by giving aid and encouragement to many civil rights activists, including Rosa Parks and the Montgomery, Alabama, bus boycotters. Durr worked as her husband's legal secretary in support of many civil and human rights cases. She opened her home in Montgomery, Alabama, to many civil rights workers who traveled to and from Alabama, and provided them with room, board, and support. Those who stayed in the Durr home included the Kennedys, Tom Hayden, and C. Vann Woodward.

American and British Trends in Gender Differences: A Comparison of Anti–Nuclear Weapons Activists
Glen Sussman

This research examines the extent to which gender-based differences are in evidence among one set of political actors involved in a salient contemporary issue—nuclear weapons. On the basis of cross-national survey data gathered from anti–nuclear weapons activists in the United States and the United Kingdom, the author compares political attitudes and policy preferences. Consideration of participation levels is also analyzed, with attention directed at both conventional and unconventional political action. The findings are discussed against the backdrop of the "gender gap," which has received much publicity in recent political literature.

A Grassroots Approach to Change: Anarchist Feminism and Nonheirarchical Organization
Kathleen P. Iannello

This study analyzes systems of power within the framework of organizations. The author argues that it is from the notion of power as a type of energy or "empowerment" that a feminist framework for organizations emerges. Three feminist organizations were selected for in-depth study, identified as follows: (1) the feminist peace group, (2) the women's health collective, and (3) the business women's association. Findings reveal that in both the peace group and the health collective, critical decisions are reserved for the entire membership of the organization, whereas routine decisions are delegated horizontally. The business women's association did not provide a model of collectivist organization; it was found to be clearly hierarchical both on paper and in operation. The author concludes that whereas examples of male-value-linked hierarchical organization abound, female-value-linked forms of organization are more difficult to find.

ACKNOWLEDGMENTS

This book is specifically dedicated to the more than seventy scholars, female and male, who responded to the call for papers for a special edition of *The Journal of Political Science* published at Clemson University on the theme of "Women in American Politics," Volume 17, Numbers 1 and 2, Spring 1989. The response was overwhelming and pointed up the need for this book.

Thanks also go to Sarah Snyder and Jo Traweek at the University of Alabama and to Marianne Blair and Kathlyn Harbin at Clemson University for their excellent secretarial support in this endeavor. I would also like to thank the Women's Caucus for Political Science for their encouragement and assistance. Finally, I would like to thank Senior Editors Karen Horton and Julie Berrisford and Dolores Mars and the staff at Prentice Hall.

Lois Lovelace Duke

THE STUDY OF WOMEN: THE NEW FRAMEWORK

Until the 1960s, most of the research about movements for women's rights centered on women's suffrage in the nineteenth and early twentieth centuries. Since the 1960s, however, an enormous number of studies on women and politics have been added to the scholarly literature. Even a superficial review of the wealth of books, journal articles, and other publications analyzing the relationship between gender and politics reveals that the field of research in this area has grown substantially.

Over the past twenty-five years, scholars who wished to research the influence of women's political behavior in the American political process experienced numerous "growing pains." These included limited financial support for research on the topic, initial efforts to study a field that had established norms identified and defined from a male perspective and male-shaped understanding of the political world, and a tendency to view gender-related research as a "special-interest" focus, "outside" the normal theoretical framework. For all these reasons, many studies on women and politics turned out to be simply descriptive narratives drawn from traditional concepts, as opposed to empirically driven research studies.

The early pioneers of scholarly research on gender and politics, however, may currently reflect on a significant legacy of contributions. These include the present solid body of literature analyzing gender socialization, women's political behavior (at both the individual and the group level), and women's role (to include officeholding) in the political sector. As we enter the 1990s, however, it appears that the early scholars analyzing the issue of women in American politics have passed along to the next generation of researchers on this topic a clear challenge: to ascertain why it is that women are still represented in such small numbers in both elective and appointive political offices. Clearly there is a need to use the previously researched information to provide a new agenda in which findings on the role and performance of females in the public sector can be more conclusive. Why are more women not serving as elected and appointed officials in politics? Why are more issues of concern to women not being addressed in our public policies? Why are women still being discriminated against and still suffering sexual harassment?

The next research agenda to explore further this issue of women and politics should address these questions, thereby leading the way in putting equal rights for women into practice. We begin this book by considering the issue of equality for women from the perspective of feminist theory. We will then move to an examination of gender differences in political attitudes and voting. We will look at women in U.S. government and continue with an analysis of women and national policy. We will conclude with a look at female activists who have themselves moved from theory to practice. Along the way we hope to provide some insight into the questions raised herein. First, however, let us consider several issues of concern to women from a theoretical feminist framework. For our purposes here, we define *feminist framework* as an overall analysis of the nature and causes of female inequality and an accompanying alternative or proposal for ending women's discrimination.

In our first reading, Iva Ellen Deutchman critically evaluates feminist theories about power. The concept of power has long fascinated not only political analysts but political activists as well. Among the many reasons to support an increase in the number of women officials, one overriding reason has been based on the belief that women feel differently about power and use power differently from men. Men, it is argued, see power as *power over*, an ability to influence or dominate, whereas women see power as *power to*, or empowerment. Thus, power for women is seen as less confrontational and more cooperative than power for men. Deutchman critically examines the claim that women and men are different in their concept of power and their use of power.

Nancie E. Caraway uses the political and epistemological contributions of contemporary Black feminist theory to point up the intersections of gender, race, and class as determinants of oppression. She argues that the texts of Black feminists teach us that feminist theory and politics should address this "multiple jeopardy." She cautions that feminists need to be wary of the damaging consequences of conceptions like *identity* and *self* that have set up white norms. In her discussion of identity politics, Caraway questions many of the assumptions of mainstream white feminism. She proposes instead multicultural goals in which the themes of racism and identity come together in a configuration that can address the theoretical issues about the female subject. She argues that a critical identity politics cautions us not to become too comfortable too long in one spot with one identity, lest we forget and stifle the ways in which we change, contradict, and grow in history.

Feminist Theory and the Politics of Empowerment

Iva Ellen Deutchman

INTRODUCTION

Power is often seen as one of the most important concepts for political analysis. Indeed, many political scientists would define _politics_ as concerned primarily with the allocation and distribution of power.[1] It is perhaps surprising, then, that there is so much disagreement about how to define, let alone measure, power.

Most contemporary scholars define _power_ as a relationship rather than a property or quality. In other words, power is not something an actor has or possesses. Rather, it is an ability to influence another actor or actors. Someone can exercise power in a proactive manner, meaning that he or she engages in a behavior designed to influence another actor or actors. Alternatively, someone can choose _not_ to act when he or she might be expected to do so; that, too, is an exercise of power.

Consider, for example, that you are an unseen witness to an important conversation. If you make your presence known and stop the conversation, that would be an exercise of power. But if you remain hidden and learn information you aren't supposed to know, that, too, would be an exercise of power.

The concept of power has long fascinated not only political analysts but political activists as well. In the twenty years or so since the so-called second wave of feminism, many female political activists have argued that we need more women in politics. Among the many reasons to support an increase in the number of women officials, one overriding reason has been based on the belief that

Iva Ellen Deutchman is a professor of political science at Hobart and William Smith Colleges.

I would like to thank Professors Peter Beckman, Ilene Nicholas, Lee Quinby, and William Waller, as well as my former honors students Susan Fletcher and John Monahan, for their careful attention to an earlier version of this paper.

women feel differently about power and use power differently from men. Men, it is argued, see power much as I have described it here. Women, by contrast, see power as less confrontational and more cooperative. From this it follows that we will have a more humane government with better policies if we elect more women to political office.

Before we come to such conclusions, however, it is wise to examine critically the claim that women and men are very different in their concept of power and their use of power. It is to this task that I now turn my attention.

While offering important critiques of more traditional theories, some feminist theories about power are themselves deeply problematic in their under-standing of power. The particular difficulties in these theories include a tendency toward essentialism (seeing men and women as inherently different in their natures), an ahistorical understanding of some nonfeminist theories of power, and some unresolved contradictions in implementing a feminist approach to power. What is needed is a feminist approach to power that is nonessentialist, structural, and historical.

POWER AS GENDER-RELATED

Although there are a variety of approaches to the treatment of power within feminist scholarship, feminist analysis insists that to talk about power is to discuss gender; in other words, power relations are themselves gendered. Holding per-haps the most extreme position, Jean Lipman-Blumen considers gender roles as "the model for power relationships between generations, socio-economic classes, religious, racial and ethnic groups, as well as between imperial powers and their colonies, and between less developed and post-industrial societies."[2] Gender as model implies that the dominance–submission roles that men and women play are the basis for power relations of all kinds.

Other feminist theorists hold that it is difficult and perhaps impossible to sever gender from power. As Joan Scott reminds us, "gender is a primary way of signifying relationships of power. It might be better to say, gender is a primary field within which or by means of which power is articulated."[3] Because men and women do not have the same access to resources that are associated with power and because they are socialized to use power differently, "gender becomes impli-cated in the conception and construction of power itself."[4] That is, women do not have (much) power because their gender has denied them access to resources (such as inheritance) that often yield power.

Power as gender-related goes beyond discussions that consider authority and wealth as primary attributes. Many feminist theorists hold that conditions of oppression often reveal real strength in the oppressed, challenging traditional notions that women are perpetual victims. Jean Lipman-Blumen and Elizabeth Janeway,[5] among others, speak of the reciprocal relationship between influencer and influencee. As Elizabeth Janeway says, "the two members of the power relationship—we can call them the powerful and the weak, or the governors and governed, rulers and ruled, leaders and followers—do not interact at the ultimate level of total dominance and utter subordination."[6] Linda Gordon, in her brilliant social history of family violence, argues the need to recognize women victims' "bravery, resilience, and ingenuity, often with very limited resources, in trying to protect and nurture themselves and their children."[7] To argue that gender relations are power relations, as much feminist theory does, is not to argue that women are perpetual victims.

Feminist theory argues not only that power is gendered but also that women both define power and use power differently than men do. Feminist theorists such as Janet Flammang[8] and Nancy Hartsock[9] argue that women define power as empowerment or *power to*, whereas men see power as domination or *power over*. Certainly, as Jeffrey Isaac states, "[e]mpiricist power theorists have confined themselves to one particular locution, 'power over,' corresponding to their belief that a proper social science is a science of behavioral regularities."[10] These empiricist theorists have clearly monopolized the power debate,[11] and hence their definitions of power have predominated. Power as gender-related thus forces us to reconsider our everyday relationships as models of power.

For a better understanding of the power debates, it is useful to know that traditional social science has often made a distinction between what is called empirical and normative theory. *Empirical theory* refers to theory about what is or what exists—in other words, "is"-based theory. *Normative theory* refers to "shoulds" or "oughts"—what *should* exist in a prescriptive sense. Although this duality is extreme in that it is arguably impossible to separate what is from what should be, many theorists have seen themselves as representative of one position and sometimes hostile to the other. This is certainly true regarding conflicting theories of power, both feminist and nonfeminist.

The concept of empowerment or "power to" suggests a broadness that "power over" lacks. "Power over" only captures the ability to act or compel actions, whereas, "power to" is more inclusive, comprising both the ability to act and the ability to refrain from action. However, the power to refrain from action, when exercised, is never quantifiable.[12] Hence, empirical theorists cannot fully capture the feminist concept of "power to" or empowerment.

EMPOWERMENT AS A FEMINIST CONCEPT

Some feminist theorists have argued that empowerment is a particularly feminist concept which stands in striking opposition to masculinist ideologies of power. Such theorists argue that empirical differences in women's and men's power behaviors are apparent. Lipman-Blumen asserts that "men and women engage in the gender power relationship with notably distinct styles."[13] Janet Flammang asserts that whereas "[f]eminists recognize that women have been denied power . . . women do not want power if what that means is business as usual, 'getting yours at someone's expense,' a zero-sum game where one person's gain is another's loss."[14] Feminist theory thus calls for women's empowerment without calling for men's subordination. As Flammang notes, "the best way to put an end to the theory and practice of masculinist 'power over' is to bring into being the theory and practice of feminist 'power to.' "[15]

Nancy Hartsock emphasizes the benefits to community that empowerment brings when she says that "women's stress on power not as domination but as capacity, on power as a capacity of the community as a whole, suggests that women's experience of connection and relation have consequences for understandings of power and may hold resources for a more liberating understanding."[16] Sarah Lucia Hoagland suggests:

> "Power-over" is a matter of dominance, of forcing others, of bending them to our will through a variety of overt and covert methods. It is the power of control, and our attention is riveted on those who blatantly exercise it, because it is backed by coercion, threats, and instances of destruction.
>
> "Power-from-within," on the other hand, is a matter of centering and remaining steady in our environment as we choose how we direct our energy. . . . "Power-from-within" is the power of ability, choice and engagement. It is creative and hence it is an affecting and transforming power, but not an imposing power.[17]

Hilary Lips displays again the despair some women feel at conforming to androcentric power structures:

> Many people who are trying to restructure the relationships between women and men in the direction of greater equality find the issue of power problematic. While trying to break free of sexual stereotypes, they are torn between the desire to increase their power and the distaste they feel for the idea of imposing their will on others. Those involved in the women's movement, for instance, often question the ethics of building up power that can be exerted over others, sometimes fear and mistrust powerful individuals within their own ranks, and are wary of becoming part of powerful institutions.[18]

Flammang and other feminist scholars envision power as essentially social and cooperative. Rather than argue that one person's gain necessitates another's loss, these feminist critics of power argue that everyone can win. Jane Jaquette reminds us, however, that as long as the male model of power is the only one accorded any legitimacy, women's cooperative vision of power is easily and effectively discounted.[19]

RESULTS OF EMPOWERMENT

Feminist theory thus argues that power is gendered, that a particularly feminist alternative to traditional definitions of power has emerged, and that this concept of empowerment is not only a theory but also a way of describing and analyzing women's actual power behavior. Women, it is argued, not only should use power differently from men; in fact they do.

Because power is so intimately connected to political participation, the argument follows that women's increased political participation opens up the possibility that both politics and policy would change substantially in the future. The way in which one sees power—as empowerment (a shared or cooperative effort) or domination (a zero-sum game with clear winners and losers)—is a critical determinant of one's political behavior. For example, it is often argued that women delegate or share authority whereas men prefer a hierarchical model of power with one (white) male in control.

The feminist vision of power, as a cooperative non-zero-sum relationship called empowerment, is heralded as better than the masculinist view it opposes. By "better than," feminist theorists mean more humane, less destructive, more fully human. For many feminist theorists, women's cooperative vision of power will have a salving, if not saving, political effect. To understand this better, it is helpful to examine in more detail the male model of "power over" which these feminist theorists reject.

"POWER TO" VERSUS "POWER OVER"

Feminist theory defines itself in opposition to what it labels male-based theories of power, which range from antifeminist to nonfeminist. The initial impulse of post-1968 feminist theory was in opposition to overtly misogynist (or antiwoman) theories. The vigorous debate about power that has occurred over the last twenty years has not addressed feminist concerns. Part of the reason is simply historical: Feminist theory has had its transformative impact in the social sciences after the early debates about power that took place in the 1960s.

The zero-sum, masculinist model of power that feminist theory opposes sees power as a causal relationship of domination: One agent causes another agent to perform some act he or she would not otherwise perform.[20] This understanding of power is clearly in the empiricist tradition to which Jeffrey Isaac earlier referred, and it is a conception of power that predominated for many years. This definition was later challenged by Peter Bachrach and Morton Baratz, who claimed that it excluded nondecisions.[21] In other words, by focusing only on observable activity, theorists like Robert Dahl ignored the mobilization of bias,[22] which prevents some interests from being heard. Hence, they discount or overlook examples of power that can prevent issues from becoming issues. This understanding of power, as suggested earlier, is not sensitive to the idea of "power to," or the ability to refrain from acting.

Steven Lukes extends the argument of Bachrach and Baratz even further.[23] He suggests that power can and does involve the shaping of preferences so that an issue might not reach the policy agenda because one agent's preferences have already been thoroughly shaped by another's. No conflict between these parties may be observed because the power was exercised long before the analyst could observe it.

I would argue that this debate about power is more nonfeminist than antifeminist. The "genderedness" of power, which feminist theorists take as their starting point, is clearly missing. The male critics of Dahl and others, who are clearly sensitive to the way in which the political system shapes and manipulates preferences, do not see gender as a critical aspect of power relations.

Even recent articles on power, which have the benefits of fifteen years or more of feminist theory, still do not foreground gender in their understanding of power. For example, Jeffrey Isaac argues that power must be understood in terms of actors' "enduring, socially structured relationships,"[24] a claim to which many feminist theorists would subscribe. He defines social power as deriving from "enduring structural relationships in society and exercised by individuals and groups based on their location in a given structure,"[25] but only acknowledges in a footnote that this view is being argued by some contemporary feminist theorists of patriarchy. Gender is thus a footnote or an incidental rather than a place from which to begin the analysis of power. Thus, feminist theory counterposes itself against a theory of power that does not see gender as critical.

PROBLEMS WITH THE FEMINIST TREATMENT OF POWER

Feminist theorists have leveled important charges against traditional theorists in their exposition of the gendered nature of power. Before adopting separate power models for men and women, however, let us examine some aspects of feminist theory that do not enable us to generalize and thus can be considered weak at this point in time.

Feminist theory associates empowerment ("power to" or "power-from-within") with feminism. In other words, it posits that empowerment is a particularly *feminist* alternative to the zero-sum model of power. Many nonfeminist thinkers, however, have also promoted this model. Certainly E. E. Schattschneider, Bachrach and Baratz, and Michel Foucault, among others, are sensitive to the nonhierarchical, empowerment model.[26] As Sara Evans recounts, the early social movements of the 1960s embraced this notion of power.[27] Clearly, however, neither Schattschneider, Bachrach and Baratz, nor the New Left leaders of the 1960s were *feminists*. (In fact, as Evans among others argues, the opposite is the case concerning the New Left.) When feminists argue that empowerment is particularly feminist, they need to be aware that the concept itself has a prefeminist history and has in fact been attractive to activists (like those of the New Left) whose commitment to feminism is indeed questionable.

Therefore, in reading scholars like Janet Flammang or Jane Jaquette, it is difficult to understand what they see as distinctly feminist about empowerment. If they mean that the women's movement embraces this theory, although it is not the first to do so, they need to be clearer in telling us that. If they mean to associate empowerment exclusively with feminism, they are making a historical error.

There are, however, more substantial problems with these feminist theories of power. To claim, as some feminist theorists do, that woman define and use power differently than men do, is to make an essentialist argument—that is, an argument that posits that men and women are somehow inherently different from one another. Sandra Morgen and Ann Bookman suggest:

> Essentialist theory has once again taken root today and has found receptive audiences among many feminists. Unlike traditional or nineteenth-century feminist theories, current perspectives rarely explicitly endorse a biological essentialism. "Difference" is often conceived in more psychosocial terms, with the link to biology implicit, and sometimes denied. Nevertheless, essential male and female natures are posited.[28]

Linda Alcoff concurs, noting the tendency within many radical and cultural feminist theories "toward setting up an ahistorical and essentialist conception of female nature."[29] She goes on to suggest an "essentialist definition of woman makes her identity independent of her external situation."[30] Gender differences are thus seen to be fixed, permanent, innate because they are ultimately connected to, if not rooted in, biology.[31] On the basis of her reading of Nancy Hartsock, Sondra Farganis suggests that "a 'feminist theory of power' would no longer speak of 'power as dominance or domination,' but would build on the particularities of a feminist standpoint that comes out of feminine contributions to human subsistence and to mothering."[32]

Thus, the argument that men see power as domination while women see power as cooperation has an essentialist component, making it both politically and philosophically problematic. Politically, it is a partial resurrection of the nineteenth-century doctrine of separate spheres,[33] a doctrine with both antifeminist and feminist potential. The separate spheres doctrine argues that women are of a higher moral caliber than men. Because of their better natures, women would purify public life. Alternatively, because of their more delicate natures, women should retreat to the relative "safety" of the home. Some strands of modern-day feminist theory have thus, in effect, breathed life into this possibly dangerous doctrine. As Alcoff remarks, "belief in women's innate peacefulness and ability to nurture has been common among feminists since the nineteenth century and has enjoyed a resurgence in the last decade, most notably among feminist peace activists."[34]

Philosophically, essentialism underlies the claims of both many radical and cultural feminists and their historical and contemporary antifeminist opponents. It is critical that feminist theorists appreciate the antifeminist potential of essentialist arguments because of our inability to control the direction of the debate. In other words, in arguing for women's unique and missing voice, an antifeminist, rather than feminist, position may be the result. Ruth Milkman says that "feminist scholars must be aware of the real danger that arguments about 'difference' or 'women's culture' will be put to uses other than those for which they were originally developed."[35] Milkman suggests that, given the political posture of the patriarchal state, the likelihood is great that essentialist arguments made by feminists will lead to antifeminist policies. The demise of the nineteenth-century woman suffrage movement should alert us to the genuine political dangers of employing essentialist arguments.

Historical, political, and philosophical problems mandate moving beyond essentialism. Such a move, however, does not mean denying the reality of gender differences. Rather, we need a theory that acknowledges the complex relationship between gender and social structure. Mary Poovey suggests an anti-essentialist, feminist position in her argument:

> We must recognize that what [most] women now share is a positional similarity that masquerades as a natural likeness and that has historically underwritten oppression, *and* we must be willing to give up the illusory similarity of nature that reinforces binary logic even though such a move threatens to jeopardize what is "special" about women. My argument is that the structural similarity that pretends to reflect nature masks the operation of other kinds of difference (class and race, for example) precisely by constructing a "nature" that seems desirable, because it gives women what seems to be (but is not) a naturally constructive and politically subversive role.[36]

Similarly, Joan Scott reminds us:

> An insistence on differences undercuts the tendency to absolutist, and in the case of sexual difference, essentialist categories. It does not deny the existence of gender difference, but it does suggest that its meanings are always relative to particular constructions in specified contexts. In contrast, absolutist categorizations of difference end up always reinforcing normative rules.[37]

Feminist theory about power needs to reject essentialist implications, grounding itself, as Scott and Poovey argue, in the specific and real-life conditions of our existence.

EMPIRICAL DIFFERENCES IN GENDER-BASED POWER BEHAVIOR

Feminist theorists who deny essentialist claims believe we must confront gender differences in designing political theories about power. It is first necessary to discover whether or not gender-based behavioral differences exist and to uncover their causes and assess their importance. To agree that significant gender-based behavioral differences exist in general does not necessarily mean there are gender-based differences in power behavior or, in fact, that power behavior is politically relevant. The empirical questions, in the case of gender-based differences and gender-based power differences, are as difficult as the normative questions.

Many of us would like to believe that women and men have different power behaviors, and that women's methods of exercising power would be less violent, less hierarchical, less destructive than men's. Virginia Sapiro suggests:

> [t]here is also reason to believe that women and men may have different orientations toward political processes (as opposed to policy issues); they may, for exam-

ple, deal with conflict in different ways. . . . They seem to react to human association differently. . . .[38]

However, she aptly cautions that "when we find differences such as these in social psychological or developmental literature, however, it is necessary to establish empirically their relationship to politics and political process."[39]

Most of the research on gender-based differences in power behavior comes from social psychologists.[40] These scholars have primarily investigated power drive (need for power) and power style (the way in which one customarily exercises or blocks influence attempts). Although the corpus of this research suggests a similarity in male and female orientations toward power, the relationship between access to power resources, one's position in the power structure, and actual use of power is more complex than gender-only accounts of power behavior might suggest. It is therefore a high-risk strategy to assert the existence of gender-based differences in power behavior in the face of evidence, which, though inconclusive, tends to suggest the absence of such differences.

EMPOWERMENT AND THE EXERCISE OF POWER

The empowerment model, though arguably more comprehensive than the "power over" locution, faces several substantial problems. In particular, I am concerned that the coming into being of empowerment involves several contradictions that are either ignored or finessed by the model's supporters. Janet Flammang has noted that her position on empowerment "is naive wishful thinking in a world of scarce resources and tight budgets."[41] Frederick Frey has argued that a power vacuum, or a situation where no one exercises power, cannot exist indefinitely.[42] Sooner or later someone will "take charge." An ideal of power devoid of domination (or at least hierarchical leadership) may thus be impossible to attain.

As Frey suggests, power is not given up voluntarily; rather it is taken. If men have more access to structural power and the resources that translate into power than do women, and if men benefit from their power superiority, we should not expect them suddenly to cede power to women. Groups with access to political and economic power rarely undergo a consciousness-raising experience culminating in their renunciation of privilege. Thus, feminists who wish to replace "power over" with "power to" may never be in a position to enforce such a choice.

Moreover, in order to enforce such a choice, feminists would be in the contradictory position of using "power over" in order to make the world safe for "power to." Were feminists able to exercise that kind of power—that is, the power necessary to redefine power—it is quite likely they would lack the consciousness to thus redefine it. Another way of saying this is to suggest that "power to" is not distinctly feminist; rather, it is distinctly "outsider." When outsider status no longer applies, the ideology supporting it is transformed to conform with the new (insider) status.

Flammang asserts that women do not want power if it means obtaining power at someone else's (presumably men's) expense. This surely implies that either there is no serious opposition to women's empowerment or that women will graciously concede defeat in the face of opposition rather than use "power over." Clearly, the cooperative vision of power will have enough serious and dedicated opponents that it would not be instituted cooperatively. As the zero-sum model suggests, feminists would thus need to defeat their "power over" opponents or be defeated themselves.

It is difficult to know whether Flammang thinks that most feminists should wish to be on the winning or the losing side. Assuming, however, that most feminists would prefer to win, a second problem arises. Once they have used "power over" in order to win, it is not clear in what form the feminist consciousness of empowerment would survive. Ends and means are connected in such a way that to use any means to achieve desirable ends may clearly compromise the ends themselves. Feminists who use "power over" in order to achieve power to may, in the final analysis, no longer have a feminist consciousness. But if they do not use "power over" they are going to be political losers, in no position even to articulate alternative political frameworks. It is this contradiction that is particularly ignored in the relevant literature. How long an outsider consciousness remains uncorrupted by praxis is a perennial question in political analysis and a crucial one, which needs to be considered in arguing for an alternative conception of power.

The tendency toward essentialism, which I argued earlier undergirds the women and empowerment debate, further complicates the question of how empowerment could come into being. If women's nature is responsible for their conception of power as shared and cooperative (as male nature, presumably, results in seeing power as domination and hierarchy), then women would be unable to adopt a zero-sum model of power because it would not be in their nature to do so. If, however, Frey is correct that power must be taken, as the zero-sum model suggests, then women would never be able to seize power.

If we reject essentialism and argue that women could adopt a zero-sum orientation toward power in order to replace it later with "power to," we still confront the argument that the feminist vision of power as cooperative and non-zero-sum could only work in a situation where everyone shared a conception of a common (and probably self-evident) public good. In such a world, power might well consist of cooperative, non-zero-sum relationships based on mutual support in realizing desired goals. Obviously, that is not the existing state of political affairs, where issues are won and lost. Clearly, the current choice is not whether we will have "power over" or "power to": It is, rather, who wins and who loses.

Some feminist theorists may dismiss my critique of empowerment because they perceive it to be male-centered. Hilary Lips expresses this uneasiness very well:

> Feminist groups constitute a good example of what happens when power is viewed with suspicion. Initially, many such groups actively avoided having formal

leaders in order to avoid the negative effects of power. After a time, however, a more sophisticated approach gained ground, and it was recognized that a lack of structural leadership can sometimes pave the way for unchecked tyranny by informal "leaders." . . . However, some feminists still voice skepticism about those in power, even when the powerful are also of feminist persuasion.[43]

Lips suggests, however, that "it is questionable whether the transforming power can be attained without, in some sense, power over others."[44]

In arguing that the empowerment model poses substantial problems, theoretically and in its potential for realization, I am not suggesting that women do not have a substantial claim to exercise power, politically or otherwise. Quite the opposite. It is dangerous to base women's claims to political power on the argument that they would use power differently (read: better than) men. Men's claim to power is not, after all, based on their ability to use power in particularly beneficial ways. Perhaps all such claims to power should be so argued, but that is another issue. What I am saying is that the empowerment model is as deeply problematic, albeit in different ways, as the androcentric "power over" model it opposes. Moreover, it is not necessary to argue that women use power differently from men in order to make the case for women's increased political power.

SUMMARY

Feminist theory thus suffers from a lack of clarity as to what is distinctively feminist about empowerment. More important, it exhibits a tendency toward essentialism in its insistence that women think about and use power differently than men do. That women think about or use power differently than men has not been sustained by the empirical social psychological studies that have attempted to quantify power behavior. Finally, feminist thinking about power runs into a series of contradictions when confronting the implementation of "power to" in a zero-sum world of "power over."

If we are to evaluate subsequent feminist theories of power, at least three criteria must be considered. A feminist theory of power that is both normative and empirical and that does not lend itself to antifeminist uses must be historical, structural, and nonessentialist.

It must confront and account for the (limited) empirical evidence that argues for a convergence in men's and women's power behavior. It must delineate what is specifically feminist about empowerment in light of that model's appeal to nonfeminist thinkers. It must address the questions of how nonhierarchical, nonmasculinist behaviors will or can come to replace the zero-sum politics of winners and losers. The questions that should shape such a feminist discourse about power cannot be answered here. Until we begin to be more responsive to these questions, however, we cannot hope to replace "power over" with "power to."

NOTES

1. A citation of the relevant literature on power would be enormous. Many scholars have argued for the centrality of power in political analysis, beginning as far back as Plato and finding more recent expression in works such as Jeffrey Isaac's *Power and Marxist Theory* and the feminist literature cited herein.

2. J. Lipman-Blumen, *Gender Roles and Power* (Englewood Cliffs, NJ: Prentice-Hall, 1984), p. 5.

3. J. Scott, "Gender: A Useful Category of Historical Analysis," *American Historical Review*, 91, 1986, p. 1069.

4. Scott, "Gender," p. 1069.

5. E. Janeway, "Women and the Uses of Power," in H. Eisenstein and A. Jardine (Eds.), *The Future of Difference* (New Brunswick, NJ: Rutgers University Press, 1980), pp. 327–344.

6. Janeway, "Women and the Uses of Power," p. 328.

7. L. Gordon, *Heroes of Their Own Lives*, (New York: Viking, 1988), p. 251.

8. J. A. Flammang, "Feminist Theory: The Question of Power," in S. G. McNall (Ed.), *Current Perspectives in Social Theory*, Vol 4 (Greenwich, CT: JAI Press, 1983), pp. 37–83.

9. N. Hartsock, *Money, Sex and Power: Toward a Feminist Historical Materialism* (Boston: Northeastern University Press, 1983).

10. J. Isaac, "Beyond the Three Faces of Power: A Realist Critique," *Polity*, 10, 1987, pp. 20–21.

11. Ibid.

12. P. Bachrach and M. Baratz, "The Two Faces of Power," *American Political Science Review*, 56, 1962, pp. 947–952.

13. Lipman-Blumen, *Gender Roles and Power*, p. 21.

14. Flammang, "Feminist Theory," p. 71.

15. Ibid., p. 74.

16. Hartsock, *Money, Sex and Power*, p. 253.

17. S. Hoagland, "Lesbian Ethics: Some Thoughts on Power in Our Interactions," *Lesbian Ethics*, 2, 1986, p. 7.

18. H. M. Lips, *Women, Men and the Psychology of Power* (Englewood Cliffs, NJ: Prentice-Hall, 1981), p. 10.

19. J. Jaquette, "Power as Ideology: A Feminist Analysis," in J. H. Steihm (Ed.), *Women's Views of the Political World of Men* Dobbs Ferry, NY: Transnational, 1984), pp. 9–29.

20. R. Dahl, "The Concept of Power," *Behavioral Science*, 2, 1957, pp. 201–215.

21. P. Bachrach and M. Baratz, "Decisions and Non-Decisions: An Analytic Framework," *American Political Science Review*, 1963, Vol. 57, pp. 632–642,

and "The Two Faces of Power," *American Political Science Review*, 1962, Vol. 56, pp. 947–952.

22. E. E. Schattschneider, *The Semisovereign People* (Hinesdale, IL: Dryden Press, 1960).

23. S. Lukes, *Power: A Radical View* (London: Macmillan, 1974).

24. Isaac, "Beyond the Three Faces of Power," p. 21.

25. Ibid., p. 28.

26. M. Foucault, *Power/Knowledge: Selected Interviews and Other Writings, 1972–1977* (New York: Pantheon, 1980).

27. S. Evans, *Personal Politics: The Roots of Women's Liberation in the Civil Rights Movement and the New Left* (New York: Random House, 1980).

28. S. Morgen and A. Bookman, "Rethinking Women & Politics: An Introductory Essay," in A. Bookman and S. Morgen (Eds.), *Women and the Politics of Empowerment* (Philadelphia: Temple University Press, 1988), p. 21.

29. L. Alcoff, "Cultural Feminism versus Post-Structuralism: The Identity Crisis in Feminist Theory," *Signs*, 1988, Vol. 13, p. 411.

30. Ibid., p. 433.

31. Ibid.

32. S. Farganis, *The Social Reconstruction of the Feminine Character* (Totowa, NJ: Rowman and Littlefield, 1986), p. 160.

33. C. Degler, *At Odds: Women and the Family in America from the Revolution to the Present* (New York: Oxford, 1980).

34. Alcoff, "Cultural Feminism versus Post-Structuralism," p. 413.

35. R. Milkman, "Women's History and the Sears Case," *Feminist Studies*, 1986, Vol. 12, pp. 394–395.

36. M. Poovey, "Feminism and Deconstruction," *Feminist Studies*, 1988, Vol. 14, p. 63.

37. J. Scott, "Deconstructing Equality-versus-Difference: Or, The Uses of Post-Structuralist Theory for Feminism," *Feminist Studies*, 1988, Vol. 14, p. 47.

38. V. Sapiro, "Reflections on Reflections: Personal Ruminations," *Women and Politics*, 1987, Vol. 7, p. 25.

39. Ibid.

40. A review of the relevant literature would make a good-sized book. Important empirical studies on gender differences in power behavior include: D. Buss, H. Gomes, D. Higgins, and K. Lauterbach *et al.*, "Tactics of Manipulation," *Journal of Personality and Social Psychology*, 1987, Vol. 52, pp. 1219–1229; I. E. Deutchman, "Socialization to Power: Questions about Women and Politics," *Women and Politics*, 1985–1986, Vol. 5, pp. 79–91; A. Eskilson and M. G. Wiley, "Sex Composition and Leadership in Small Groups," *Soci-*

ometry, 1976, Vol. 39, pp. 183–194; P. Johnson, "Women and Power: Toward a Theory of Effectiveness," *Journal of Social Issues*, 1976, Vol. 32, pp. 99–110; D. C. Jones, "Power Structures and Perceptions of Power Holders in Same-Sex Groups of Young Children," *Women and Politics*, 1983, Vol. 3, pp. 147–164; C. Koberg, "Sex and Situational Influences on the Use of Power: A Follow-up Study," *Sex Roles*, 1985, Vol. 13, pp. 625–638; P. Kollock *et al.*, "Sex and Power in Interactions: Conversational Privileges and Duties," *American Sociological Review*, 1985, Vol. 50, pp. 34–46; B. F. Meeker and P. A. Weitzel-O'Neill, "Sex Roles and Interpersonal Behavior in Task-Oriented Groups," *American Sociological Review*, 1977,

Vol. 42, pp. 91–104; L. Molm, "Gender and Power Use: An Experimental Analysis of Behavior and Perceptions," *Social Psychology Quarterly*, 1985, Vol. 48, pp. 285–300; M. E. Thompson, "Sex Differences: Differential Access to Power or Sex-Role Socialization," *Sex Roles*, 1981, Vol. 7, pp. 413–424. This list is only suggestive and not intended to be exhaustive.

41. Flammang, "Feminist Theory," Vol. 4, p. 71.

42. F. W. Frey, "The Motivation to Power," unpublished paper presented at the American Political Science Association, 1984.

43. H. M. Lips, *Women, Men and the Psychology of Power*, p. 13.

44. Ibid.

FURTHER READING

ALCOFF, L. Cultural feminism versus post-structuralism: The identity crisis in feminist theory. *Signs*, 13 (Spring 1988), pp. 405–436.

BACHRACH, P., and BARATZ, M. The two faces of power. *American Political Science Review*, 56 (December 1962), pp. 947–952.

BACHRACH, P., and BARATZ, M. Decisions and non-decisions: An analytic framework. *American Political Science Review*, 57 (September 1963), pp. 632–642.

DAHL, R. The concept of power. *Behavioral Science*, 2, (July 1957), pp. 201–215.

DEGLER, C. *At odds: Women and the family in America from the revolution to the present*. New York: Oxford, 1980.

EISENSTEIN, Z. *The radical future of liberal feminism*. New York: Longman, 1981.

EVANS, S. *Personal politics: The roots of women's liberation in the civil rights movement and the New Left*. New York: Random House, 1980.

FARGANIS, S. *The social reconstruction of the feminine character*. Totowa, NJ: Rowman and Littlefield, 1986.

FLAMMANG, J. A. Feminist theory: The question of power. In S. G. McNall (Ed.), *Current perspectives in social theory* (Vol. 4, pp. 37–83). Greenwich, CT: JAI Press, 1983.

FOUCAULT, M. *Power/knowledge: Selected interviews and other writings, 1972–1977*. New York: Pantheon, 1980.

FREY, F. W. The motivation to power. Unpublished paper presented at the American Political Science Association, 1984.

GORDON, L. *Heroes of their own lives*. New York: Viking, 1988.

HARTSOCK, N. *Money, sex and power: Toward a feminist historical materialism*. Boston: Northeastern University Press, 1983.

HOAGLAND, S. Lesbian ethics: Some thoughts on power in our interactions. *Lesbian Ethics*, 2 (1986), pp. 5–32.

ISAAC, J. Beyond the three faces of power: A realist critique. *Polity*, 10 (Fall 1987), pp. 4–31.

ISAAC, J. *Power and Marxist theory: A realist view*. Ithaca, NY: Cornell University Press, 1987.

JAGGER, A. *Feminist politics and human nature*. Totowa, NJ: Rowman and Allanheld, 1983.

JANEWAY, E. Women and the uses of power. In H. Eisenstein and A. Jardine (Eds.), *The future of difference* (pp. 327–344). New Brunswick, NJ: Rutgers University Press, 1980.

JAQUETTE, J. Power as ideology: A feminist analysis. In J. H. Steihm (Ed.), *Women's views of the political world of men* (pp. 9–29). Dobbs Ferry, NY: Transnational, 1984.

LIPMAN-BLUMEN, J. *Gender roles and power*. Englewood Cliffs, NJ: Prentice-Hall, 1984.

LIPS, H. M. *Women, men and the psychology of power*. Englewood Cliffs, NJ: Prentice-Hall, 1981.

LUKES, S. *Power: A radical view*. London: Macmillan, 1974.

MILKMAN, R. Women's history and the Sears case. *Feminist Studies*, 12 (Summer 1986), pp. 375–400.

MORGEN, S., and BOOKMAN, A. Rethinking women & politics: An introductory essay. In A. Bookman and S. Morgen (Eds.), *Women and the politics of empowerment* (pp. 3–32). Philadelphia: Temple University Press, 1988.

POOVEY, M. Feminism and deconstruction. *Feminist Studies*, 14 (Spring 1988), pp. 51–66.

SAPIRO, V. Reflections on reflections: Personal ruminations. *Women and Politics*, 7 (Winter 1987), pp. 21–27.

SCHATTSCHNEIDER, E. E. *The semisovereign people*. IL: Dryden Press, 1960.

SCOTT, J. Gender: A useful category of historical analysis. *American Historical Review*, 91 (December 1986), pp. 1053–1075.

SCOTT, J. Deconstructing equality-versus-difference: Or, the uses of post-structuralist theory for feminism. *Feminist Studies*, 14 (Spring 1988), pp. 33–50.

The Riddle of Consciousness:
Racism and Identity
in Feminist Theory

Nancie E. Caraway

INTRODUCTION

Feminist scholarship offers both an intellectual and political stimulus to under-graduate students in political science. It may fruitfully be called syncretic because it "brings together" so many threads about knowledge, political action, and power—and the implications of scholarship in general. Formally, it is akin to African-American studies, gay studies, and other moments in ethnic studies (Chicana, Latina, Asian, Arab, Native American) because it crosses disciplines and introduces students to historical, theoretical, empirical, and interpretive modes of inquiry. And, importantly, these academic initiatives recognize their ties to grass-roots constituencies and movements for social justice. Being explicitly tied to social movements belies the claims of "neutrality" and "objectivity" professed by much social science conventional wisdom.

The increasing encounter of feminist scholarship with traditional concerns of political science (such as the Constitution, the judiciary, and electoral politics) has been challenging and revitalizing. It has displaced naturalized taboos (as in, "It's not natural for women/Blacks to participate in the nation's civic life") and exposed as riddles what were considered universal truths (as in, "We all know that politics is about state and national security, not sexual double standards, parenting, or housework"). It has resulted in the inclusion of courses in feminist theory in most political science departments at U.S. universities. This inclusion, however, carries with it the important caveat that one can't "just add women and stir."

Nancie E. Caraway is a political theorist and feminist scholar from Hawai'i who is living and working in Washington, D.C. Currently she is an assistant professor of government at the American University.

The feminist imperative expands knowledge because it requires that we rethink old categories and accepted truths that have excluded women and women's experiences. What this means is that the concept of gender (the socially constructed "masculine" and "feminine" meanings attached to our biological plumbing) is now considered along with political authority, freedom, democracy, justice, race, and class as one of the important markers of political experience. The challenge requires as well new explanatory theories of "how things came to be this way" and new agendas for stimulating critical consciousness and account-ability for oppression—whether oppression is practiced by the state, men, corpo-rations, whites, *or* women.

The history of feminism itself is crucially a history of theory. Feminist scholarship has worked to demystify theory's abstractions by insisting, not only that the personal is political, but that the very meanings of the political and what counts as political experience are open to radical reinterpretation. This rethinking of traditional categories such as democracy, citizenship, and con-sciousness has enabled feminist theorists to ask subversive questions of the "can-ons" of political science: Which actions and experiences are considered political? How has the liberal public–private split rendered invisible women's contributions to culture? Who benefits from a social and political structure that subjugates women? What processes of identity and consciousness "produce" female and male political actors? And, importantly, how have traditional concepts of citizen-ship excluded women of all races?

So, although traditional concerns of political science remain legitimate, the perspectives from which they are examined are radicalized by feminist the-ory. Feminist political theorists have also turned to their own practices. They are attempting to examine the interlocking oppressions based on sex, gender, race, class, sexual preference, national origin and ethnicity—and to devise strategies for overcoming those oppressions. Feminist theory describes (never unproblem-atically) the world from the perspectives of women by asking what kinds of political power and actions contribute to a more egalitarian society. This probing critique of traditional theories of citizenship and democracy has highlighted women's alternative political practices and the masculinist thought that has rele-gated women to inferior positions in the public world.

An analysis of grass-roots activism of diverse women in the United States and other parts of the world historically has redefined the way "politics" is often thought of in our culture—as the actions of male elected officials. By making the activities of previously invisible women central, feminist scholars are helping to write both them and a new conception of democracy into the history of social change.

One of the most compelling turns in contemporary feminist theory is the emphasis on racism within feminism and the ways in which "women's oppres-sion" has reflected the concerns of middle-class white women. This affords many new voices and feminisms the opportunity to negotiate community. Feminist women of color have insisted on articulating their own identities and experiences. In response, white feminists are working to contribute to this expanded understanding of "women" by interrogating their own racism, privilege, and the need for historical accountablity for American apartheid and white supremacy. This is a painful but potentially liberating process, which views racism and sexism not solely as "problems" but as textured ways of defining reality and living our lives. White feminists have learned that they too are "racialized."

The emphasis in feminist theory on identity politics, ethical commitments to creating coalitions of diverse women, and reflections on critical consciousness itself sets a new agenda for students of politics. These new configurations inhabit a challenging world of social theory to which I hope to introduce female and male political science students. A gentle warning to readers: Theoretical language provokes and often frustrates newcomers. But try to work with it. Think of theory's often technical terminology as an occasion for high-spirited translation (of the type required when we strain to "understand" the riffs of a Dylan concert)—and intellectual growth.

Multicultural feminist theory (the name for the dynamics I've been discussing) has its own mode of communicating—like rap, blues, jazz, or African-American gospel testifying. The language of theory, however, does pose problems: It's dense, and it may ask that we read against the grain, follow the flow a bit while it teases us into a new coded way of thought. Much of these sentiments derive from something called postmodernism or poststructualism—an intellectual attitude that offers skeptical insights, some of which are helpful to thoughtful feminists, some obfuscatory. This essay tries to sort out the criteria. Think of your frustration with theory-talk not as a declaration of verbal warfare, but as a meeting place of thought and spirit, a process of riddle solving.

As you travel the sometimes demanding terrain of this essay, remember the goal of creating a more robust "woman-friendly polity."[1] Toward this end, I employ two symbolic images of identity and consciousness in this essay as an entrée to these issues in current feminist theory: Toni Morrison's narrative in her novel of slavery, *Beloved*, and the autobiographical essay "Identity: Skin Blood Heart" by the white feminist Minnie Bruce Pratt.

KNOWING AND BEING: RACISM AND QUESTIONS OF FEMINIST THEORY

> *Here, she said, in this place we flesh; flesh that weeps, laughs; flesh that dances on bare feet in grass. Love it. Love it hard. Yonder they do not love your flesh. They despise it. They don't love your eyes; they'd just as soon pick em out. No more do they love the skin on your back. Yonder they flay it. And O my people they do not love your hands. Those they only use, tie, bind, chop off and leave empty. Love your hands! Love them. Raise them up and kiss them. Touch others with them, pat them together, stroke them on your face 'cause they don't love that either. *You* got to love it, *you!*[2]

*Source: Toni Morrison, *Beloved* (New York: Knopf, 1987), pp. 88–89.

With this extraordinary declaration from her novel of enslavement,[3] Toni Morrison's "unchurched preacher" Baby Suggs articulates the passion of collective self-affirmation to her congregation of ex-slaves. Morrison's narrative speaks to the symbolic project that has defined the African-American quest for agency and free space in the world the "whitethings" created.

This white world condemned by Morrison's text is a world in which African-Americans have had their stories, identities, and very being defined by hegemonic white culture. I, as a white feminist, inhabit a similarly hegemonic terrain, that of the community of feminist scholars and activists whose legacy, too often, has been one of "whitethings" defining feminist life and aspirations for women of color. Fortunately, for our ethical health and our political direction, new stories, theories, and strategies voiced by feminist women of color are retooling feminist thought in penetrating and passionate modes to transform a deracinated "whitething" feminism. In this article, I want to chart some contours of this new multicultural direction, situate them within certain themes of identity politics, and provide a pedagogy about accountability for overcoming racism and developing critical consciousness, themes that come to us from Minnie Bruce Pratt.

As a political theorist, not a literary critic, I began to engage the coda of subjectivity and identity not through a technical philosophical discourse, but from the sheer emotional pull of Morrison's exhortation about the flesh of Black slaves—that is, the *identity* project of African-Americans. The graphic physicality of Baby Suggs' statement concretizes for us that theory is truly never removed from the power-laden context of specific historical lives. When intellectuals consider utterances such as "deconstruction of the subject"—a provocative but often tediously hollow postmodernist challenge to certainties that we can truly "know" our "selves"—we need only return our thoughts to Morrison's prayerful *subjects* in the sun-dappled forest clearing to remember what social analysis is "about." This focus alerts us to the contributions of Black feminist theory to "our" (all women's) sense of the female subject. What can we learn about a revitalized polity and a newly committed series of feminisms if we look for the theoretical issues entangled within the arc narrated by Morrison?

Morrison's statement "*You* got to love it. *You!*" rejects the stigmas of otherness and difference inculcated by white supremacist culture, and validates, albeit tenuously, subjectivity and identity. This statement thus intersects in important ways with current epistemological debates—debates over "how we know what we know"—in feminist theory.[4] In particular, it demonstrates the creative challenges of Black feminism to feminist theory and politics.[5]

I have used Morrison's words to call attention to white racism within feminism and to validate feminist efforts at ending racist oppression as the central goal of feminist politics today. Let me note that the militant voices and courage of African-American women were first to insist on the important task of decentering "whiteness" as the norm in feminist politics. In many historical moments, they have served as the conscience of feminist practice, the spirit that drives the movement back to the essential commitment feminist scholars ought to have toward enhancing the lives of marginalized women.

Contemporary Black feminist theory arises from the same spirit of affirmation and specificity reflected in Morrison's exhortation to the nineteenth-century Black community. The analysis that I will develop here characterizes such a project as "identity politics." But how do we reconcile this concern with agency and identity, given the red flags postmodernism sends up? The cultural power of our symbolic systems to seduce, delude, and encourage conceits about "self" and "authenticity" bear the footprints of metaphysics and take us away from the social and historical moorings in which such needs are produced. I want to think of identity politics as a contextual, not essentialist, process evolving out of political commitments and struggles for justice in multicultural feminist coalitions.[6] Identity is in the etched details of mediated lives and struggle. The reflective and reflexive political biography of the white feminist Minnie Bruce Pratt, to which I will return, is a luminous example of such a justice-seeking identity. Pratt's story is a chronicle of the fits and starts of seeking to know "who" one "is," a crucible of how a white feminist in a racist movement can be politicized through identity politics into a deeply personal interrogation of her own historical and racial roots.

What I hope to suggest in this essay is that questions about the self, about knowing and being, are not mutually exclusive. I am arguing that we must be able to articulate *some experiential foundation*, some notion of self, before we may act in the world. Rather than polarize antagonisms between feminists who "think" and feminists who "act," we need to see reflection and resistance as equally valid requirements of political and civic experience. Questions about and strategies for experiencing "identity" are crucial in this process. The perspectives derived from identity politics seek to emphasize the deep context, the "situated knowledges" (to use Donna Haraway's term), of our connected lives. Such a foundation is powerfully rendered in Morrison's preacher Baby Suggs's commentary: "In this place we flesh . . . *You* got to love it, *you*!" As Black feminist Cheryl Townsend Gilkes has pointed out, questions of identity have both historical and spiritual resonance for Black women *and* men. Black women's life experiences are grounded in a context that derives personal identity collectively, from a larger racially oppressed community "bound together by common interest, kinship, and tradition."[7] In charting the heroic and courageous activism of Black women in their struggle for dignity and equality ("uplift of the entire race") throughout American history, contemporary Black feminist historians *assume* the necessity of political agency, subjectivity, and identity as the very condition for social change.[8]

As a corollary to this understanding of the self as an entity that *is*, but is always in process, under seige, evolving as persons and events touch and change, African-American women insist that for feminist discourse and politics to be relevant to their daily concerns, they must acknowledge the intersections of gender, race, and class as determinants of oppression, and not view gender as the *primary* form of oppression. This revolutionary paradigm shift is transforming feminism; we all are emerging from a new feminist "text" freshly educated about redefining the boundaries and connections of otherness. One need only observe the spectrum of contemporary feminist communities and activities to see the impact of such thinking. The writings of Black feminists are teaching us, in this regard, that feminist theory and politics should address the "multiple jeopardy" and "multiple consciousness" of Black women, in Deborah King's formulation.[9]

IDENTITY POLITICS: POSITIONAL RESISTANCE TO WHITE RACISM

As articulated by the Black feminist Combahee River Collective in a 1977 manifesto, "Our politics evolve from a healthy love for ourselves, our sisters, and our community. . . ." Their first commitment was to the cultural center they shared as women within the Black community.

> Even our Black women's style of talking, testifying in Black language about what we have experienced, has a resonance that is both cultural and political. We have spent a great deal of energy delving into the cultural and experiential nature of our oppression out of necessity because none of these matters have ever been looked at before. No one before has ever examined the multilayered texture of Black women's lives.[10]

The collective determined to align with progressive Black men in solidarity to resist racist oppression—struggling with them against sexism—and to frame their own oppression within the overlapping networks of family and community ties. More recently, Deborah King has spelled out these webbed commitments of Black feminists to the "special circumstances of our lives in the United States: the commonalities that we share with all women, as well as the bonds that connect us to the men of our race." King acknowledges the "distinctive context for Black womanhood," which she insists be defined and interpreted by Black women themselves: "While drawing on a rich tradition of struggle as blacks and as women, we continually establish and reestablish our own priorities."[11]

These statements argue for a politics of identity that is embodied in experiences and cultural spaces whose meanings are determined by those who live their daily lives in the tissue of interwoven contradictions. Alliances, priorities, and interpretations of self are relational and not responses to any set of given objective needs. Identity politics here finds affinity with a conceptualization of Donna Haraway in her explication of a feminist "objectivity" grounded in "partial local knowledges": "Feminism is about the sciences of the multiple subject with (at least) double vision. Feminism is about a critical vision consequent upon a critical positioning in unhomogeneous gendered social space."[12]

The operative phrase here is "critical positioning." For homophobes and chauvinists along with racists may well lay claim to a particular locus of cultural groundings and alliances that teach intolerance and racial and sexual revanchism. One might envision a mythologizing of David Duke as a Southern populist, white male grass-roots expression of Arcadian-inspired public will, or even "white male, ex-Klansman and neo-Nazi"—that is to say, Duke's "identity." But it is not enough to issue a cultural-demographic schemata of one's identity-defining characteristics. In order to meet the politicized and justice-seeking criteria of identity politics, a fully articulated resistance and a critical positioning to oppression must be present. The multiple "subject" or shifting self that often comes to life in "nonfeminist" settings—as the women of the Combahee River Collective recognized—provides a more democratized terrain for feminist civic potential.

One colloquial way of stating this principle is to say that, as feminists, we need to "start where people are at," not insisting that feminist identity be based on shedding familial, regional, or religious local skins. How is it then that Black feminism's embodiment of identity politics demonstrates a *critical* and thus valorized stance?

One would be on dangerous ground in projecting a romanticized image of "the oppressed" as beyond criticism. We diminish our critical edge if we dismiss postmodernist admonitions about the human potential for culpability in projecting illusions, of adopting institutionalized discourses of truth, reason, and certainty as foundations for political life. At the same time, however, we can look to the political *knowledge* that comes from the oppositional world view Black feminist bell hooks locates in living "on the edge" of white society.[13]

Such a critical and protean version of identity politics advances a space for political action and collective transformation. All feminists need to see value in the experience of those "on the edge" because such a vantage point embodies a negative moment, inherently attuned to flesh and blood deprivation and pain as central to political attention. As one feminist theorist has conceputalized such a stance, the knowledge gained by living "on the other side of the tracks" is justified by the critical positioning of those persons on the margins of societies.[14] The struggle against hierarchies of power is the substance that merits our allegiance to the practices and knowledge of the marginalized.

Toni Morrison in *Beloved* makes clear that "stories" and "identities" in America's apartheid have been far from reciprocal, far from the bridges of empathy and human understanding that ethical consciousness demands of human commerce. The "other" may indeed be alien and murderous. And one "identity" has not been as good as another. Morrison gives us a story about "subjects" struggling to wrest definition of what human beings are supposed to be from white masters. It is their *critical position* vis-à-vis the dominant racist society that must be endorsed, their determination to re-vision an "other" that does not annihilate, rather than their essence as "pure" petitioners.

BE THE RIGHT THING: POSITIONING WHITE FEMINIST IDENTITY AND RACIAL IMPERATIVES

This emerging portrait of identity politics tantalizes the theoretical imaginations of feminist scholars in its bonding of epistemological considerations with imperatives for historical political action. Feminist thinkers/activists may embrace knowledge about the "fluid" and unfixed construction of identity—albeit described in specific, historic local narratives. Such portraits need not be racially (or otherwise) specific; they surely fulfill the intertextual criteria of the most provocative multicultural feminist scholarship by speaking to "us all." Collectivities of multicultural, multiracial, sexually diverse feminists may find empowerment in the resources of identity politics about the shared and differentiated faces of female oppression.

Identity politics is the terrain of social outlaws.[15] It militantly asserts who "we" are and what "we" mean (this holds, especially so, for white feminists given the history of white assumptions in much feminist theory) and engages the potential for those explorations in coalition or affinity venues. It demands accountability for correcting the racism of everyday life which the expanded vision of multicultural feminism reveals to us. I want to briefly explore one of the most penetrating and transformative instances of identity politics work by a non-Black, non–person-of-color (to reverse the white solipsistic linguistic norm "nonwhite")—Minnie Bruce Pratt's 1984 essay "Identity: Skin Blood Heart."[16]

Pratt's text, an intensely probing meditation on her own shifting selves, is a powerful model for other white feminists to follow in order to question our own complicity in and accountability for correcting the myriad racist practices existing in the world around us—a precondition for successful coalition building. Pratt, a white, Southern-born, Christian-raised, lesbian woman, takes her reader inside an exploration of a divided consciousness, demonstrating the postmodernist feminist thesis that the "wholeness" of the self involves an inescapably protean encounter with others. The manner in which Pratt frames her experiential/ political project of struggling to derive an "identity" from which the various layers of her life "fit," empowering her to act, foregrounds questions of otherness and accountability. Pratt uses her feminism, a politics of everyday life, as a springboard from which to investigate self-consciously those many "edges" on which she stands: ". . . I will try to be at the edge between my fear and outside, on the edge at my skin, listening, asking what new thing will I hear, will I see, will I let myself feel, beyond the fear."[17] Pratt is able to let her multiple experiences of otherness float in an uneasy alliance, allowing them to open her eyes to other scenarios of domination and oppression. Her own outsider status as a lesbian alerts her to the marginalization of others with whom she attempts to ally, without collapsing them all into one "grand polemics of oppression."[18]

Central to Pratt's articulation of her search for self and identity are two important metaprocesses that are important tools for white feminists' antiracist efforts. She has the ability to problematize, to evaluate reflectively, every encounter with another and to take nothing for granted in interracial relationships. These displacements provide a valuable corrective to status quo attitudes. Pratt encourages white women to scrutinize the historical and ideological layers attendant to encounters with "others"—paying particular attention to the concealments and exclusions, the buried "holes in the text,"[19] that submerge and mystify the violations of race, class, and gender.

Pratt frustrated and doubtful of overcoming the chasm of racism. But Pratt keeps on keeping on. These painful incidents become challenges to overcome, not paralyzing dead ends in Pratt's story; they stand as markers of the quotidian signs of racism. As Pratt assays the costs to those whom her own protection and privilege as a Southern white woman has disadvantaged, she is able to "free" herself from the poisonous racism by acknowledging her own family's participation in its system. She is empowered to locate the harm, to identify the victims that the vision of the society of her white childhood excluded. By seeking the absences, she may now "gain truth" when she expands her constricted eye, "an eye that has only let in what I have been taught to see."[20]

Revelation and psychological unpeeling continue when Pratt's professor husband takes her and their children to a new town, a Southern "market town." Geography and history again stimulate her questioning of the town whose center, tellingly, is not a courthouse, but a market house. With complacent, middle-class white friends at dinner in a private club overlooking the town's central circle, she queries them about the marketplace. They chat about the fruits and vegetables, the auctioned tobacco that was sold at the market. "But not slaves," they said. It is left to the Black waiter—a silent figure who boldly breaks through "the anonymity of his red jacket"—to assume the role of educator, disrupting white historical amnesia to tell them of the men, women, and children who were sold at the market near where they now dine.

> *What he told me was plain enough: This town was a place where some people had been used as livestock, chattel, slaves, cattle, capital, by other people; and this use had been justified by the physical fact of a different skin color and by the cultural fact of different ways of living. The white men and their families who had considered Black people to be animals with no right to their own children or to a home of their own still did not admit that they had done any wrong, nor that there had been any wrong, in *their* town. What he told me was plain enough: Be warned: they have not changed.[21]

The narrative of Pratt's identity journey is a useful feminist teaching precisely because her project does not become a study in narcissism, a withdrawing from political reality. Her newfound knowledge of racist history through a probing of her own personal history serves as a spur toward further inquiry and action. Her ability to approach the world and structures of domination as interlocked, as "overlapping circles," elicits knowledge of other traditions of struggle whose experiences she might draw upon. And importantly in the framework of coalition politics, Pratt perceives scenarios of persons in whose service she might present herself as an ally in their struggles.

*Source: Minnie Bruce Pratt, "Identity: Skin Blood Heart," in *Yours in Struggle: Three Feminist Perspectives on Anti-Semitism and Racism* (Minnie Bruce Pratt, Elly Bulkin and Barbara Smith, Eds.) (Ithaca, New York: Firebrand Books, 1984), pp. 17, 18, 21, 29, 35, 39, and 40.

*I knew nothing of these or other histories of struggle for equality and justice and one's own identity in the town I was living in: not a particularly big town, not liberal at all, not famous for anything: an almost rural eastern North Carolina town, in a region that you, perhaps, are used to thinking of as backward. Yet it was a place with so many resistances, so much creative challenge to the powers of the world: which is true of every county, town, or city in this country, each with its own buried history of struggle, of how people try to maintain their dignity within the restrictions placed around them, and how they struggle to break those restrictions.[22]

The potency of Pratt's story at this point in her account of the accumulated identities that she wrestles to incorporate has to do with her own connection to Southern racism. When she sought to find out what had been or was being done "in her name," the knowledge was shattering. "I had set out to make a new home with other women, only to find that the very ground I was building on was the grave of the people my kin had killed, and that my foundation, my birth culture, was mortared with blood."[23] The cracking and heaving and buckling Pratt experienced in what she describes as "the process of freeing myself" afforded no relief, no sanctimony. "This breaking through," she admits, "did not feel like liberation but like destruction." Her expanded sense of political accountability; her endeavors to locate a new "home," a chosen political community of women committed to justice; and her confession of loss are the flashpoints of Pratt's journey toward political conscience. This voice does not mute the pain and alienation such a process entails. Feel the drama in her telling:

*I think this is what happens, to a more or less extreme degree, every time we expand our limited being: it is upheaval, not catastrophe: more like a snake shedding its skin than like death: the old constriction is sloughed off with difficulty, but there is an expansion: not a change in basic shape or color, but an expansion, some growth, and some reward for struggle and curiosity. . . .

As I try to strip away the layers of deceit that I have been taught, it is hard not to be afraid that these are like wrappings of a shroud and that what I will ultimately come to in myself is a disintegrating, rotting *nothing*: that the values that I have at my core, from my culture, will only be those of negativity, exclusion, fear, death. And my feeling is based in the reality that the group identity of my culture has been defined, often, not by positive qualities, but by negative characteristics: by the *absence of*: "no dogs, Negroes, or Jews"; we have gotten our jobs, bought our houses, borne and educated our children by the negatives: no niggers, no kikes, no wops, no dagos, no spics, no A-rabs, no gooks, no queers [emphasis in original].[24]

Pratt's essay resonates in so many ways with wisdom and warnings vital to struggling antiracist feminists. The integrity with which she describes her story

*Source: Minnie Bruce Pratt, "Identity: Skin Blood Heart," in *Yours in Struggle: Three Feminist Perspectives on Anti-Semitism and Racism* (Minnie Bruce Pratt, Elly Bulkin and Barbara Smith, Eds.) (Ithaca, New York: Firebrand Books, 1984), pp. 17, 18, 21, 29, 35, 39, and 40.

encourages our own probings. Her identity project can stand as a document of feminist politicization precisely because Pratt resists those self-destructive urges that are anathema to enacting social change: the reactionary extreme of abandoning her own complexly vexing Southern culture, the paralyzing guilt and fear that come with the knowledge of the enormity and barbarity of white privilege. Throughout this powerful essay, Pratt reveals herself determined to understand the volatile psychic hold of home, childhood, and patriarchal "protection" of white women in her class. There is no denouement in Pratt's search for "identity," only continued working-through. Hers, and ours, entails a long-term commitment, a meditation on consciousness that is grounded in daily actions that allow us to connect with or bypass the "others" with whom we seek community. This seeking is the riddle of consciousness to be grappled with through political struggle.

Pratt also shows her readers the psychic dangers of denial and its opposite, absorption into the other: the desire to cover her "naked, negative [self] with something from the positive traditions of identity which have served in part to help folks survive our people."[25] Finally Pratt can come to an awareness and acceptance of her own *whiteness*—while resisting the culture of white supremacy, on the one hand, and, on the other, avoiding the condescending trap of "cultural impersonation," of attempting to "become Black." We come to see such gestures for what they are—sentimental balms of political quietism.

In the language of postmodern thought, Pratt's essay provides a "genealogy," a deep sifting through of the ideological and historical practices that render the tangle of "self." She asks how the contradictions that regulate her life came to be—in discourse, in history, in region, in family. Pratt offers a response to the issues of racism within feminism that takes us to the other side of paralyzing white guilt. In the "knowing and being" philosophical frame of feminist thought, Pratt's example ties reflection with the crucial next step of political engagement and activism for justice. She offers us the gift of openness to begin again each day that struggle to turn our received "identities" upside down.

CONCLUSION

The conception of identity politics I have attempted to sketch questions many of the troubling assumptions of mainstream white feminism. It brings to life the need for white feminists not only to endorse a call for *inclusion* and *diversity* within feminist organizations, but to go "beyond the inclusion of persons and texts," as Sandra Harding has recently argued, and ask "what should *we* be doing in order to be desirable allies from *their* perspectives?"[26] Identity politics with a postmodern tilt, then, facilitates such a commitment by rejecting the possibility of a common "woman's experience" that can be objectively derived. This reading follows Minnie Bruce Pratt's example in cautioning against the tendency to substitute a critical consciousness, or therapy, or other premises that assume we have an unchanging "essence." We are encouraged to focus instead on strategic discourse, by asking under which conditions we may work together democratically, and on political action toward common goals.

Feminists interested in multicultural goals may employ these ideas with the model of political action in strategic coalitions of diverse women. The themes of racism and identity come together in a configuration that can address the theoretical issues about the female subject so vital to current feminist thought. I hope my epigrammatic beginning, with Toni Morrison's searing accomplishment in *Beloved* of textually imparting the criminal genealogy of Black flesh in America, reminds us all just what is at stake in questions of identity and racial memory.

We ought not forget how the construction of a "self" that sees its own reflection in those "semiotic technologies"[27] created by the culture that creates us, can still feel injustice and endure pain. At the same time, a critical identity politics cautions us not to become too comfortable too long in *that spot* with *that identity*, lest we forget and stifle the ways in which we change, contradict, and grow in history. The achievement of identity itself must be viewed as one moment of political struggle, a struggle that precludes our standing, innocent, on the other side of our cultural mediations.

Identity politics calls for practices of deep contextualization, with accounts of persons that are always explicitly described, colored, gendered, situated—that, to borrow from Louis Althusser, resist simplification in the last instance. And, more importantly, it gives us grounds for politics and coalitions in the renegade terrain of that "real" world of shared struggle in feminist community.

NOTES

1. Kathleen B. Jones, "Citizens in a Woman-Friendly Polity," *Signs*, 15 (4) (Summer 1990), pp. 781–812.

2. Toni Morrison, *Beloved* (New York: Knopf, 1987), pp. 88–89.

3. Although most critics have characterized Morrison's novel as a novel "of slavery," I wish to adopt the term *enslavement*. Black feminist and long-time civil rights activist Ruby Sales has made a strong case for rejecting the word *slavery* in favor of *enslavement*. In her analysis, the former term suggests a passivity and renders the process of enslavement benign. Using the word *slavery* diminishes the moral and political responsibility demanded of the one who enslaves. If there's enslavement, there's an enslaver and an enslaved person. The term *enslaved*, according to Sales, doesn't mean a person is passive; it implies coercive force was used against that person. Further, importantly, the term implies that the enslaved person is resisting. See Ruby Sales, "In Our Own Words: An Interview with Ruby Sales," *Woman's Review of Books*, 7 (5) (February 1990), p. 24.

4. The problematic has been identified in these debates as one of "subject-centered discourse" and is occasioned by currents in what is intellectually framed as "postmodernist skepticism" of the founding categories of Western Enlightenment thought—truth, objectivity, the coherent self, agency, identity—all constructs from which feminism itself derived. For lucid discussions of these issues and feminism's encounter with postmodernism, consult Kathy Ferguson, "Interpretation and Genealogy in Feminism," Paper presented at the Western Political Science Association, San Francisco, March 1988; Kathy Ferguson, "Subject-Centeredness in Feminist Discourse," in Kathleen B. Jones and Anna G. Jonasdottir (Eds.), *The Political Interests of Gender* (pp. 66–78) (London: Sage Publications, 1985); Linda J. Nicholson (Ed.), *Feminism/Postmodernism* (New York and London: Routledge, 1990); Jane Flax, "Postmodernism and Gender Relations in Feminist Theory," *Signs*, 12 (4) (Summer 1987), pp. 621–643; Linda Alcoff, "Cultural Feminism versus Post-Structuralism: The Identity Crisis in Feminist Theory," *Signs*, 13 (3) (Spring 1988), pp. 406–436; Leslie Wahl Rabine, "A Feminist Politics of Non-Identity," *Feminist Studies*, 14 (2) (Spring 1988), pp. 11–31; the entire volume on "Feminism and Epistemology: Approaches to Research in Women and Politics," in *Women & Politics*, 7 (3) (Fall

1987); Donna Haraway, "A Manifesto for Cyborgs: Science, Technology, and Socialist Feminism in the 1980s," in Nicholson, *Feminism/Postmodernism*, pp. 190–233; Donna Haraway, "Situated Knowledges: The Science Question in Feminism and the Privilege of Partial Perspective," *Feminist Studies*, 14 (3) (Fall 1988), pp. 575–599.

5. See bell hooks, *Feminist Theory: From Margin to Center* (Boston: South End Press, 1984); bell hooks, *Ain't I a Woman* (Boston: South End Press, 1989); bell hooks, *Yearning: Race, Gender, and Cultural Politics* (Boston: South End Press, 1990); Audre Lorde, *Sister Outsider* (Trumansburg, NY: Crossing Press, 1984).

6. I am persuaded by Judith Butler's reading of the identity problematic in postmodern thinking that the deconstruction of identity need not lead to the deconstruction of politics. Through the dynamic of political confrontation and coalition politics, we understand who we are and what we mean in our explication of feminist common differences. Butler argues the case "that there need not be a 'doer behind the deed,' but that the 'doer' is variably constructed in and through the deed." Butler does not, but I will, tip my voluntarist hat to Marx for the originary seeds of the insight about the self-defining character of political struggle. Judith Butler, *Gender Trouble: Feminism and the Subversion of Identity* (New York: Routledge, 1990), pp. 148, 142.

7. Cheryl Townsend Gilkes, "Dual Heroisms and Double Burdens: Interpreting Afro-American Women's Experience and History," *Feminist Studies*, 14 (3) (Fall 1989), pp. 573–590, esp. p. 573.

8. In reviewing Paula Giddings's excellent history of Black feminist activism, *When and Where I Enter: The Impact of Black Women on Race and Sex in America* (New York: William Morris, 1984), Cheryl Townsend Gilkes states clearly that self-definition has historically been a major theme in Black feminist thought. Gilkes, "Dual Heroisms," p. 589, n. 4.

9. Deborah H. King, "Multiple Jeopardy, Multiple Consciousness: The Context of a Black Feminist Ideology," *Signs* 14, (3) (Autumn 1988), pp. 42–72.

10. "A Black Feminist Statement: The Combahee River Collective," in Gloria T. Hull, Patricia Bell Scott, and Barbara Smith (Eds.), *But Some of Us Are Brave* (Old Westbury, NY: Feminist Press, 1982), p. 17.

11. King, "Multiple Jeopardy," pp. 42, 72.

12. Haraway, "Situated Knowledges," p. 579.

13. hooks, *Feminist Theory*, Preface.

14. Linda Alcoff has developed a related conceptual framework of positionality as a basis for feminist activism that does not depend on an identity that is "essentialized"—that is, on an identity that is idealized as "transcendent" and "pure," without fault. Positionality, as she defines it, is a contextual strategy of achieving one's subjectivity. Positionality views woman's identity "relative to a constantly shifting con-

text, to a situation that includes a network of elements involving others, the objective economic conditions, cultural and political institutions and ideologies, and so on.... The position of woman is relative and not innate, and yet neither is it 'undecidable.' " Alcoff, "Cultural Feminism," pp. 433–434.

15. See Shane Phelan's highly original study of the political and theoretical dimensions of lesbian identity politics, *Identity Politics: Lesbian Feminism and the Limits of Community* (Philadelphia: Temple University Press, 1989).

16. Minnie Bruce Pratt, "Identity: Skin Blood Heart," in *Yours in Struggle: Three Feminist Perspectives on Anti-Semitism and Racism* (Minnie Bruce Pratt, Elly Bulkin, and Barbara Smith, Eds.), (Ithaca, New York: Firebrand Books, 1984).

17. Ibid., p. 18.

18. I don't wish to replicate here the emphasis on the subjectivity question in Pratt's project taken up by Chandra Talpade Mohanty and Biddy Martin in their essay, "Feminist Politics: What's Home Got to Do with It?," in Teresa de Lauretis (Ed.), *Feminist Studies/Critical Studies* (Bloomington: Indiana University Press, 1986), p. 206. My approach in considering Pratt is to understand the powerful symbol of political transformation she represents vis-à-vis white racism and multicultural feminist politics. But I do want to acknowledge Mohanty and Martin's skepticism about the potential of identity politics to be incorporated into feminist work for social change. The translation of discourses of self-revelation into strategic grassroots work is not axiomatic; we need to insist that the achievement of critical consciousness is a political, not solely a psychological, achievement. In this sense, a heightened consciousness leads to and requires moving from the local to the global, moving from psychic transformation to concrete acts in the material world to subvert systematic forms of oppression.

19. This is the phrase Friedrich Nietzsche employs in his critique of representation. Friedrich Nietzsche, *The Dawn of Day*, section 523 in Oscar Levy (Ed.), *The Complete Works of Friedrich Neitzsche*, Vol. 9 (New York: Gordon, 1974).

20. Pratt, "Identity: Skin Blood Heart," p. 17.

21. Ibid., p. 21.

22. Ibid., p. 29.

23. Ibid., p. 35.

24. Ibid., p. 39.

25. Ibid., p. 40.

26. Sandra Harding, "The Permanent Revolution," *Women's Review of Books*, 7 (5) (February 1990), p. 17.

27. Eloise Buker offers an incisive path through the dense thicket of semiotic discourse. She argues that feminists need not be "put off" by its technical jargon nor should they fall into a depoliticized passivity in the face of its abstractions. "In fact," Buker

argues, "we may well find [postmodernism's skepticism of Enlightenment notions of truth] liberating because we do not have to pretend that we have found THE universal laws, or even patterns that characterize all persons for all times. We can figure out what we think best in our own limited worlds. We will not defer our decisions until we know for sure what to do since we will understand that we always act in the midst of both our knowledge and our ignorance. Putting-off politics is not possible." Eloise Buker, "Rhetoric in Postmodern Feminism: Put-offs, Put-ons and Political Plays," Paper presented at the annual meeting of the American Political Science Association, San Francisco, August 30–September 2, 1990, p. 7.

2

GENDER DIFFERENCES IN POLITICAL ATTITUDES AND VOTING

Socialization partly explains our attitudes about politics and how politically active we later become as adults. For example, we know that women who have grown up in households in which their mothers took a relatively active role in politics are more likely themselves to vote and become active politically. Thus, even though the Nineteenth Amendment to the Constitution was ratified more than seventy years ago, it is only recently that comparable numbers of women and men are voting in national elections.

This raises the question of whether men and women are becoming more alike in other aspects of political behavior as well. For example, some studies have shown that women tend to be more liberal on issues relating to social programs and economic security; that is, women have shown more humanitarian, social welfare–oriented attitudes. Women have also tended to be less supportive of militarist or aggressive action in foreign affairs. Similarly, women have tended to oppose the use of nuclear energy as a power source—perhaps a manifestation of their more environmentalist or pacifist views. Janet Clark and Cal Clark evaluate this "gender gap" between men and women in how they vote and in their attitudes about a wide range of political issues.

We next examine gender differences and similarities in political behavior and attitudes. Are younger Americans coming to greater agreement than their parents or grandparents on the issue of gender equality in the political arena? Linda L. M. Bennett and Stephen E. Bennett find that even while some attitudes are changing, women continue to be more politically passive than men. Thus, in their research, the authors conclude that the sex-role socialization process still tends to define a less politically active role for women than men.

Previous research has found that younger women are more likely to hold feminist attitudes than are older women. There is also some evidence, however, that young women in the 1980s were less supportive of feminism than were older women, suggesting there may be some generational influences at work. Elizabeth Adell Cook explores this question using a technique called *cohort analysis*. Cohort (or generational) analysis of the 1972 to 1984 American National Election studies indicates that women who came of age during the period of social activism of the 1960s and the growth of the women's movement in the 1970s exhibit higher levels of politicized feminist consciousness than do women of earlier generations. Women who came of age during the more conservative late 1970s and early 1980s exhibit lower levels of feminist consciousness than women of the Sixties and Women's Liberation cohorts.

The next essay, by Anne E. Kelley, William E. Hulbary, and Lewis Bowman, reports the importance of gender as a variable in accounting for political attitudes among party activists in Florida. Utilizing data from a 1984 survey, the three authors develop a political ideology scale, which they then relate to gender, party, and social characteristics. They find that partisanship is the major discriminating variable but that, regardless of party affiliation, gender often is related to ideological differences among the party activists. Several social characteristics offer explanations about which of the women and men, representing Florida's precinct committeepersons, are more liberal or conservative than would be expected on the basis of partisanship alone.

Women's lives are changing—and these changes are not without implications for U.S. politics. One of the most significant changes for women during the twentieth century has been in their roles as workers. There has been a major social restructuring as large numbers of married women and women with preschool-aged children have become wage earners. What have women found in their work environment?

The final essay in this chapter, by Gertrude A. Steuernagel and Thomas A. Yantek, delves into some of the consequences for women and attitudes about employment. They study the issue of occupational segregation. Among their findings, they conclude that occupational segregation is one of the factors in explaining why women on the whole earn less than men. Their study then examines the effect of occupational segregation on women's political attitudes. The authors argue that if we want to understand the significance of gender and its relationship to political behavior, we need to examine the relationship between the specific circumstances of employment and politics. For example, the authors point up how sex-role socialization, life-cycle demands, and discrimination result in women being clustered in what they refer to as female-segregated jobs. There are indications that the experiences these women have in these jobs affect their political attitudes.

The Gender Gap 1988: Compassion, Pacifism, and Indirect Feminism

————————————————————————————————— *Cal Clark*

————————————————————————————————— *Janet Clark*

As illustrated by the other chapters in this book, the role of women in U.S. politics is in the process of fundamental change. An important part of this overall transformation has been the sudden development over the 1980s of a significant "gender gap" between men and women in their voting patterns and attitudes about a wide range of political issues. The emergence of this gender gap is important for several reasons. It implies that women have become more participant and assertive in U.S. political life, it underlines the need for the improvement of their woeful underrepresentation in public office, and it seemingly marks the culmination of several important socioeconomic and political trends in the United States.

This reading, then, examines the nature of the gender gap at the close of the 1980s based on the political attitudes of Americans that were expressed at the end of the 1988 campaign. It asks: How large is the gender gap? What are the political attitudes that are seemingly at its core? What does this portend for politics in the United States? The first section describes how the gender gap developed over the 1980s and summarizes the basic reasons that have been put forward to explain it. Building on this discussion, the second part of the essay considers the nature of the gender gap in 1988 and how it relates to the various explanations that have been adduced for the diverging political perspectives of men and women. Finally, the conclusion briefly considers the broader implications of the gender gap for U.S. politics.

Cal Clark is a professor of Political Science at the University of Wyoming; Janet Clark is a professor of Political Science at the University of Wyoming.

DEVELOPMENT OF THE GENDER GAP

Through the mid-1970s, the voting behavior and most political attitudes of men and women appeared to be remarkably similar. Table 1, for example, presents the gender gap in presidential and congressional voting and in party identification over the last four decades. For most of this period, there was little systematic difference between the sexes in terms of their voting or party preference; if anything, women leaned toward the Republicans during the Eisenhower era. In the 1980s, in sharp contrast, women became substantially less supportive of Republicans than men; by 1984, a gender gap of almost 10 percent had opened up between men and women in terms of both their voting for and approving the presidential performance of Ronald Reagan.[1] Thus, it appeared that a permanent gender gap had been formed in which women were more supportive of Democrats and men of Republicans.

This gender gap in voting and partisan affiliation seemingly reflected important changes in the way men and women viewed the central issues in American politics. Until the 1970s, women and men had had remarkably similar attitudes on most political issues, but with a few notable exceptions, such as women's greater concern for morality issues and opposition to policies that

Table 1   Gender Gap in Voting and Party Identification

	PRESIDENTIAL VOTE (PERCENTAGE REPUBLICAN)			GENDER GAP CONGRESSIONAL VOTE (PERCENTAGE REPUBLICAN)	GENDER GAP PARTY IDENTIFICATION (PERCENTAGE DEMOCRATIC)
Year	Male	Female	Gender Gap*		
1952	53%	58%	5%	−1%	1%
1954	—	—	—	—	−4%
1956	55%	61%	6%	9%	−3%
1958	—	—	—	2%	1%
1960	48%	51%	3%	−2%	4%
1962	—	—	—	6%	−4%
1964	40%	38%	−2%	0%	3%
1966	—	—	—	8%	0%
1968	43%	43%	0%	0%	4%
1970	—	—	—	2%	2%
1972	63%	62%	−1%	1%	6%
1974	—	—	—	3%	6%
1976	45%	51%	6%	1%	6%
1978	—	—	—	2%	3%
1980	53%	49%	−4%	4%	7%
1982	—	—	—	−5%	11%
1984	64%	55%	−9%	−5%	6%

Note:

*A positive gender gap means that women were more supportive; a negative one shows that men were more supportive.

Source: Henry C. Kenski. "The Gender Factor in a Changing Electorate," in Carol M. Mueller (Ed.), *The Politics of the Gender Gap: The Social Construction of Political Influence* (Beverly Hills, CA: Sage, 1988), pp. 44, 50, 55. Reprinted with permission.

threatened to involve the United States in violent conflict. Since the early 1970s, in contrast, significant differences in political attitudes between the sexes have emerged or expanded in such areas as "social compassion," support for minority rights, protection of the environment, and basic economic issues to augment greatly the initial limited attitudinal gap concerning peace and morality.[2]

Conventionally, it was implicitly assumed that women and men voted alike because the few issues on which they differed were generally unimportant for making a final choice between parties and candidates. As Emily Stoper persuasively argues, however, this interpretation is simplistic.[3] Women did have a consistent and distinct position on three issues (peace, personal morality, and political corruption), but this political perspective was not consistent with either traditional liberalism or conservatism and has never been adequately represented by either Republicans or Democrats. Thus, women may well have voted similarly to men, not because they did not have important positions of their own but because they were "cross-pressured" by the incomplete political menus with which they were presented. Assuming this, one might then argue that the gender gap erupted in the 1980s because the additional issue cleavages that emerged between the sexes tipped the balance in the "women's position" much more strongly in a liberal and Democratic direction.

This interpretation, however, raises the question of why women have different political attitudes than men do and why this attitudinal gender gap widened greatly in the 1980s. Carol Gilligan provides an answer to the first question with her theory that, psychologically, women react to the world *In a Different Voice*. According to this theory, women, compared to men, place more emphasis on "connectiveness" in personal and community relations rather than on abstract issues and power considerations, and on personal collaboration and issue resolution rather than on competition and confrontation.[4] These basic psychological orientations, in turn, can explain the three original issue differences between men and women noted before. If women were more concerned with protecting "home and hearth," they would naturally be more sensitive to the dangers of war and to the social costs of "immorality."

The explanation of why the gender gap suddenly widened to include a substantial number of other issues, however, needs further clarification. Until the 1970s, women in the United States were less interested in politics than men and less likely to engage in political activities, such as voting, discussing issues, or participating in campaigns. Conventionally, this participation gender gap was tied to basic patterns of socialization which made women more passive and home-oriented and, thus, less concerned with the public sphere than men.[5] This emphasis on childhood socialization into differentiated sex roles was then extended by Virginia Sapiro's "adult socialization" theory. She argued that childhood socialization experiences are mediated and reinforced by the adult roles that women assume, especially family and work roles, some of which are congruent with political activities while others are overwhelmingly privatized.[6] This is also consistent with explanations focusing on women's "structural position" in society. That is, concentrating on homemaking prevents women from entering the professions from which most politicians emerge (the law and broker-type businesses).[7]

During the 1970s and 1980s, however, the differences between the sexes in political interest and many types of "mass" political participation (e.g., voting) narrowed and even vanished, although preadult gender differences in political orientations continued. These basic changes were evidently stimulated by women's increased education and entrance into professional occupations, which produced "countersocialization," and by the activities of the women's movement, which sensitized women to the importance of political issues.[8] This change over a relatively short time, furthermore, provided support for the "adult socialization" and "structural position" perspectives.

Thus, as women became more involved in politics, they began to realize that their basic values applied to a broader range of issues, such as helping the less fortunate, supporting racial equality, protecting the environment, and most especially demanding equal rights for women. For example, Susan Carroll has explicitly argued that women's increased economic and psychological independence from men is a major cause of the gender gap.[9] Furthermore, the basic socioeconomic and political changes that have occurred in the United States over the last several decades, such as rising divorce rates and falling welfare expenditures, have contributed to a "feminization of poverty" that has given women an additional "self-interest" in being liberal on social welfare issues.[10]

This research on women's political attitudes, therefore, predicts that there will be a significant gender gap in each of the following seven areas:

1. Women's rights issues, such as the Equal Rights Amendment (ERA), abortion, and women's social roles
2. Issues of war and peace, such as defense spending, relations with the USSR, and aggressive foreign policy initiatives
3. Human compassion, such as help for the needy and support for minority rights
4. Self-interest in certain issues, such as child care and welfare aid for poor women and their families
5. Moral issues, such as substance abuse, school prayer, and feelings about "alternative lifestyles"
6. Political corruption, such as opposition to graft and influence peddling
7. Partisan affiliation and voting patterns

In terms of the direction of the gender gap, women would be expected to take the liberal position on the first four issues, the conservative one on the fifth, and an "antiestablishment" stance on the sixth. Thus, the Reagan administration's attack on welfare policies, more aggressive foreign policies (at least during its first term), and seeming lack of concern over lapses of business and political ethics provide a ready explanation for the burgeoning of the gender gap during the early 1980s. Consequently, the partisan balance for women's loyalties has seemingly been tipped in a liberal direction.

In addition to the partisan gender gap depicted in Table 1, survey data from the mid-1980s reported in Table 2 are consistent with almost all of these

Table 2 Gender Differences in American Public Opinion, Mid-1980s

	MEN	WOMEN	GENDER GAP*
Agree that U.S. should take military action against nations supporting terrorism	61%	44%	−17%
Oppose U.S. aid to Contras in Nicaragua	49%	61%	12%
Oppose the return to the military draft	48%	61%	13%
Approve the U.S. invasion of Grenada	68%	48%	−20%
Favor stricter regulation of hand guns	53%	66%	13%
Favor the death penalty for murderers	76%	69%	−7%
Favor relaxing environmental protection laws to improve the economy	58%	48%	−10%
Favor building more nuclear power plants	50%	24%	−26%
Favor cutting back on operation of nuclear power plants until better safety regulations	55%	76%	21%
Agree that government should work to reduce the income gap between rich and poor	61%	73%	12%
Favor increased spending for Social Security	43%	56%	13%
Favor federal aid to relocate unemployed to areas with job opportunities	47%	55%	8%
Favor preference to blacks in hiring and promotion where past discrimination	34%	49%	15%
Favor busing to achieve better racial balance in the public schools	24%	32%	8%
Newsstands should not be allowed to sell pornography	46%	73%	27%
Favor legalizing the possession of small amounts of marijuana for personal use	35%	25%	−10%
Favor the national law raising the legal drinking age in all states to 21	75%	82%	7%
Have a lot of confidence in the future strength and prosperity of the nation	39%	27%	−12%
Believe it possible now to start out poor and work hard to become rich	65%	55%	−10%
Satisfied with the way things are going in the United States	52%	42%	−10%

Note:

*A positive gender gap means that women were more supportive; a negative one shows that men were more supportive.

Source: "The Gender Gap Fact Sheet," Center for the American Woman and Politics (CAWP), National Information Bank on Women in Public Office (NIP), Eagleton Institute of Politics, Rutgers University, July 1987, pp. 3–4. Reprinted with permission.

hypotheses about the gender gap in American public opinion. This table shows that there is a consistent gender gap of 7 to 15 percent for women to be less supportive of military adventurism and harsh criminal penalties, more supportive of protecting the environment and using government to promote social and economic equality, and less confident in the "American dream" (for data on the women's rights and corruption issues, see the Stoper study). Thus, in the middle of the Reagan administration significant differences had clearly emerged between the political attitudes of men and women over a wide array of issues.

One should also ask what factors might exacerbate or attenuate this gender gap. First, exposure to "countersocialization" (i.e., experiences that help women overcome their socialization into traditional roles)[11] should make women more likely to favor women's rights, social compassion, and pacifism. Thus, the gender gap on these issues should be particularly pronounced among groups such as the young and the highly educated, for whom countersocialization for women should be greatest. Second, a wide gender gap should also be expected where most women have a special "self-interest" in an issue, such as child care. Third, where some men and women have a common economic interest in an issue (e.g., welfare programs for the poor), the gender gap should primarily be the result of "compassion," not "self-interest." Thus, it should be greatest among groups not directly affected by these policies (i.e., middle-class people with higher incomes). Finally, the gender gap on issues of war and peace might be especially wide among people with traditional values because such men would define these questions in terms of their conservative values, whereas such women would be more likely to see a threat to "home and hearth."[12]

These findings and hypotheses suggest two possible perspectives on the gender gap in the late 1980s. First, if it had been politically stimulated by the conservative Reagan administration, it should have decreased significantly for several reasons. George Bush's campaign for a "kinder, gentler America" should have defused the perceived threats of "raw conservatism"; Reagan's break-through in relations with the Soviet Union should have erased any image of his administration as "war-mongering"; and the involvement of both administration officials and prominent Democratic members of Congress in political scandals should have prevented the blame for corruption falling entirely upon either party. Alternatively, if the gender gap reflected deeper "structural changes" in U.S. society, the end of the Reagan administration should have had little impact.

The next section, therefore, examines the gender gap in the United States with data from a national survey conducted at the end of the 1988 presidential campaign. The extent of the differences between men and women is evaluated for each of the seven areas enumerated above, and the four potential explanations for the gender gap are tentatively tested. These results, then, should tell us something both about women's evolving perspectives on U.S. politics and about whether they are more influenced by transient political events or deeper social change.

THE GENDER GAP IN 1988

Constitutional limitations meant that 1988 marked the end of the Reagan era; and although his vice-president, George Bush, became the frontrunner as election day approached in November, he clearly represented a less strident conservatism than the outgoing president. Thus, although there was little reason to believe that the gender gap would change on many specific issues, the impact of these opinions on partisan divisions was more problematic.

Thus, we examined the nature of the gender gap both in terms of issue areas (women's rights, war and violence, social compassion, women's self-interest, traditionalism versus morality, and political corruption) and in terms of partisanship (1988 presidential and congressional vote, party identification, ideology, evaluation of President Reagan and the Congress, and perceptions of the two presidential candidates). Table 3 presents the percentage of men and women in the United States who held these various attitudes; the gender gap is simply the difference between these two figures. The data were taken from a national survey of voter attitudes conducted by the Survey Research Center of the University of Michigan.[13]

The results for women's rights issues in Table 3 are surprising in two regards. First, there was a surprising degree of support for them. Over two-thirds of all Americans believed that women should have an equal role in running the economy and government, rather than staying "in the home"; and slightly over half favored a liberal abortion policy and scored highly on an index of support for equality for all people (including women). Second, the presumption that the gender gap should be very pronounced for these issues because they are the ones stressed by feminists is clearly false. The gender gap was almost nonexistent (1.1 percent) for the key item of women's role in U.S. society; in fact, men were even slightly more likely than women to support abortion, so that there was a moderate gender gap in the expected direction only for the equal rights index (6 percent).

These results fit together with several previous findings to suggest that the impact of the feminist movement on the gender gap has changed fundamentally between the late 1970s and the late 1980s. During the 1970s, feminist issues and mobilization by the women's movement appeared central to the gender gap.[14] As a result, it was primarily confined to the most educated segment of the U.S. public because highly educated women formed the core of the feminist movement.[15] By 1984, however, the impact of women's rights had largely vanished,[16] foreshadowing the 1988 situation described previously. This change evidently occurred because, whereas gender consciousness first rose among women in the 1970s, men began to develop similar attitudes in the 1980s.[17] Thus,

Table 3 Gender Gap in 1988

	MEN	WOMEN	GENDER GAP*
Women's rights			
Liberal abortion policy	56.7%	52.8%	−3.9%
Equal role for women	68.3%	69.4%	1.1%
Equal rights for all people	47.0%	52.8%	5.8%
War and violence			
U.S. power and security important	48.6%	45.8%	−2.8%
More cooperation with USSR	46.2%	42.0%	−4.2%
Increase defense spending	36.8%	30.3%	−6.5%
Use military forces to protect oil in Middle East	70.1%	59.3%	−10.8%
Increase Stars Wars spending	25.2%	11.0%	−14.2%
Increase Contra spending	16.8%	8.2%	−8.6%
Support death penalty	85.7%	75.5%	−10.2%

	MEN	WOMEN	GENDER GAP*
Social compassion			
Social welfare most important problem for U.S.	16.5%	26.3%	9.8%
More government services	33.8%	41.4%	7.6%
Government guarantee job	24.3%	29.3%	5.0%
Government health insurance	39.5%	44.4%	4.9%
More Social Security spending	49.9%	65.1%	15.2%
More spending on homeless	58.8%	72.2%	13.4%
More food stamp spending	17.9%	24.3%	6.4%
More spending on schools	63.0%	67.0%	4.0%
More college aid	40.7%	49.6%	8.9%
Government help minorities	24.1%	28.2%	4.1%
Support affirmative action	16.8%	22.8%	6.0%
Self-interest and need			
More child care spending	52.3%	62.0%	9.7%
Personal finances improve	47.1%	38.0%	−9.1%
Traditionalism/morality			
Active school prayer	31.5%	38.7%	7.2%
Church almost weekly	33.0%	44.5%	11.5%
Alternative life-style tolerated	42.9%	36.4%	−6.5%
Patriotism index	53.4%	56.9%	3.5%
Political corruption			
Many officials crooked	38.1%	44.6%	6.5%
Partisanship			
Vote Bush 1988	56.5%	50.0%	−6.5%
Vote Democratic for Congress	58.7%	59.1%	0.4%
Republican identification	45.8%	38.7%	−7.1%
Conservative ideology	50.5%	46.2%	−4.3%
Republicans best party for solving main U.S. problems	27.2%	17.6%	−9.6%
Approve Reagan	71.9%	64.8%	−7.1%
Reagan made U.S. more secure	59.2%	41.9%	−17.3%
Reagan made economy better	49.9%	33.9%	−16.0%
Approve Congress	54.7%	65.3%	10.6%
Candidate personality			
Bush compassionate	62.3%	60.8%	−1.5%
Bush inspiring	37.8%	39.2%	1.4%
Bush strong leader	55.0%	52.8%	−2.2%
Bush intelligent	80.4%	77.6%	−2.8%
Dukakis compassionate	73.2%	74.9%	1.7%
Dukakis inspiring	41.6%	53.4%	11.8%
Dukakis strong leader	49.5%	61.6%	12.1%
Dukakis intelligent	88.7%	88.7%	0.0%

Note:

*A positive gender gap means that women were more likely than men to hold a particular attitude; a negative one shows that men were more likely than women to have the attitude in question.

Source: Computed from the data set for SETUPS analysis of *The 1988 Election*, distributed by the Interuniversity Consortium for Political and Social Research. Reprinted with permission.

the impact of the women's movement on the gender gap has changed over time. Initially, it had the direct effect of sensitizing women to women's rights issues, thereby broadening the gender gap. Later, however, these basic values became accepted by many men, which resulted in a shrinking of the gender gap in statistical terms. However, this "indirect effect" can be considered a political advantage because it means that a broader coalition now exists in support of women's rights.[18]

The gender gap on peace and violence issues still existed in 1988, but its extent on particular issues was somewhat variable. Women clearly were considerably more sensitive to the dangers of war than were men, as they were 9 percent to 14 percent less likely to support increased spending for the Nicaraguan Contras or the Star Wars program and the use of U.S. forces to protect oil supplies in the Middle East. There was also a significant gender gap of 6.5 percent on defense spending; and on another issue concerning "violence," women were 10 percent more reluctant than men to impose the death penalty on convicted murderers. However, women were only slightly less likely to believe that the power and security of the United States were important, and they were even less supportive than men of increasing cooperation with the USSR. These latter findings probably derive from the fact that women rated higher than men on all four "traditional" values included in Table 2 (church attendance, support for school prayer, patriotism, and views on "alternative" lifestyles). Still, even though such traditionalism meant that women did not conform to all the values normally associated with "pacifism," the gender gap on war and threats of violence is clearly pronounced.

The gender gap also continued to be quite visible in the area of social compassion, as women were 5 percent to 8 percent more liberal than men on a wide variety of issues concerning government services, welfare, education, and support for minority groups. The homeless and the elderly appeared to be special targets for women's "compassion" in that the gender gap on increasing spending for the homeless and for Social Security was almost 15 percent. In addition, a moderate gender gap of 6 to 7 percent continued in the area of women's greater concern about political corruption. To some (though unfortunately not a directly measurable) extent, these differences between the sexes derived from women's "self-interest." Women were significantly less likely than men (38 percent versus 47 percent) to have believed that their personal financial situations had improved over the last year. Thus, their greater financial stress can explain their comparative liberalism on social spending and cynical views toward public officials. On another dimension of self-interest, women were 10 percent more likely than men to support increased government spending on child care, an issue of obvious importance to their sex.

As would be expected, therefore, the gender gap on most political attitudes appeared to be little affected by the passing of the Reagan administration. It was more problematic, however, whether the partisan gender gap would diminish with the coming of George Bush's "kinder, gentler" America. In fact, the data in Table 3 demonstrate that the gender gap in partisanship continued apace as well. Michael Dukakis did 6.5 percent better among women than men; and there was a 7 to 10 percent difference between the sexes on most of the voting, partisan loyalty, and political approval items in this table (the only exception was voting for Congress in 1988). The gender gap in 1988 presidential voting was especially striking because men and women differed little in most of their personal evaluations of the two candidates. In addition, public opinion polls that were conducted in 1989 showed a fairly stable gender gap of about 7 percent in approval of President Bush's performance, although this may have narrowed a little at the end of the year (see Table 4). Thus, the gender gap in partisan matters is evidently more deep-seated in basic political orientations than it is a response to passing political personalities.

It is also interesting to estimate the relative contribution of different issues to the overall gender gap. We did this by applying an advanced statistical technique called multiple discriminant analysis, which computes the ability of a group of variables to differentiate between two or more items. In this case, we used 11 representative items from Table 3 to "discriminate between" men and women. The results are presented in Table 5. The canonical correlation of .32 indicates that in combination the 11 variables had only a fairly moderate ability to separate men from women.

What are more important, though, are the discriminant coefficients for each variable, which measure each one's relative explanatory effect. Clearly, the biggest difference between men and women was on peace issues since the strongest coefficients were for the Star Wars and Contra items (the negative coefficients show that men were more likely than women to want budget increases here). Women were more likely than men to support all of the social issues (Social Security, the homeless, child care, and overall government services), and women

Table 4 Approval of President Bush's Job Performance, 1989

	GALLUP POLL			CBS/NYT POLL		
	Men	Women	Gender Gap*	Men	Women	Gender Gap*
January	53%	49%	−4%	—	—	—
March	66%	59%	−7%	64%	58%	−6%
April	63%	54%	−9%	64%	59%	−5%
May	56%	57%	1%	66%	56%	−10%
June	74%	66%	−8%	—	—	—
July	72%	61%	−9%	71%	64%	−7%
August	75%	64%	−9%	—	—	—
September	73%	62%	−9%	73%	68%	−5%
October	72%	64%	−8%	—	—	—
November	70%	68%	−2%	67%	60%	−7%

Note:

*A positive gender gap means that women were more likely than men to hold a particular attitude; a negative one shows that men were more likely than women to have the attitude in question. Reprinted with permission.

Source: "Different Groups Rate the President," *The American Enterprise*, 1 (1) (January–February 1990), p. 84.

Table 5 Discriminant Analysis of Gender Gap Components

Canonical correlation	.32
*Discriminant coefficients**	
Increase Star Wars spending	−.51
Increase Contra spending	−.43
Vote for George Bush	.36
Increase Social Security spending	.29
Many officials crooked	.27
Increase homeless spending	.24
Increase child care spending	.20
Increase government services	.19
Favor liberal abortion policy	−.19
Favor school prayer	.14
Favor equal role for women	.01

Note:

*A positive coefficient means that women were more likely than men to hold a particular attitude; a negative one shows that men were more likely than women to have the attitude in question. Reprinted with permission.

Source: Computed from the data set for SETUPS analysis of *The 1988 Election*, distributed by the Interuniversity Consortium for Political and Social Research.

were also more concerned than men about political corruption. In perhaps surprising contrast, once these other attitudes were controlled, men and women differed little on women's rights (in fact, men were slightly more supportive of abortion than women), again suggesting that a cross-gender "coalition" has emerged concerning the centerpiece of the women's movement. Finally and most strikingly, once their political attitudes were controlled, women had a higher voting rate for George Bush than men. This implies that, if anything, the partisan gender gap might be expected to expand in the future as women increasingly apply their political values at the polls.

The first section also introduced several potential explanations for the gender gap: (1) that it would be greatest among women experiencing the most countersocialization (i.e., those who are younger and college-educated), (2) that the gender gap would be widest on "compassion" issues among the middle class, whereas the reverse might be true for "self-interest" ones, and (3) that "traditional" women might be atypically sensitive to violence issues. We tested these hypotheses in a rough fashion by computing the gender gap for six selected issues within different subgroups of the population based on age, education, income, and church attendance. The six issues were Bush vote, role of women, government services, the homeless, Contra aid, and child care.

The results from this analysis are presented in Table 6 and lend considerable support to our basic hypotheses, although a few caveats are suggested as well. First, there are several indications of the importance of countersocialization. The hypothesis that the gender gap would be the widest among the college-educated holds for all six of the items being examined. Thus, higher education

Table 6 Gender Gap* Among Subgroups

	BUSH VOTE	ROLE OF WOMEN	GOVERNMENT SERVICES	HOMELESS	CONTRAS	CHILD CARE
Age						
18–34	−2.5%	1.7%	17.1%	16.3%	−4.4%	6.3%
35–54	−6.8%	4.8%	5.5%	13.9%	−8.5%	14.6%
Over 55	−9.8%	−2.3%	0.6%	10.3%	−12.0%	6.1%
Education						
Under college	−1.7%	1.4%	0.7%	6.3%	−5.3%	8.3%
College	−9.4%	3.4%	12.8%	15.2%	−11.9%	10.4%
Family income						
Under $15,000	−5.5%	7.4%	3.5%	10.7%	−7.0%	5.5%
$15,000–35,000	−0.6%	3.2%	7.1%	9.6%	−10.0%	6.4%
Over $35,000	−8.3%	5.4%	7.3%	14.3%	−12.1%	14.6%
Church attendance						
Low	−5.0%	3.4%	6.2%	9.3%	−5.9%	9.0%
Almost weekly	−10.6%	0.4%	7.4%	17.6%	−13.5%	17.1%

Note:

*A positive gender gap means that women were more likely than men to hold a particular attitude; a negative one shows that men were more likely than women to have the attitude in question. Reprinted with permission.

Source: Computed from the data set for SETUPS analysis of *The 1988 Election*, distributed by the Interuniversity Consortium for Political and Social Research.

evidently provides an important countersocialization experience that affects women's attitudes. In addition, the gender gap for women's sociopolitical role was smallest (or even negative) among the groups for whom countersocialization about equal role models should be the least—people who were over 55 and who attended church regularly. However, the other countersocialization hypothesis— that the gender gap would be largest among the young—holds only for the government services and homeless items. In direct contradiction to our anticipations, the gender gap increased considerably with age for both Bush vote and support for the Contras. The latter probably reflects greater concern with anti-war norms among the young, but the results for presidential vote are admittedly hard to explain.

Second, the other predictions are generally supported as well. The gender gap on "compassion" (i.e., support for more government services and spending on the homeless and on child care) followed predictions in that it was greatest among the most affluent and the most educated. Moreover, "traditional" women, as indicated by almost weekly church attendance, did appear particularly concerned with war and peace issues, as the gender gap on support for the Contras was over twice as great (− 13.5 percent to − 6 percent) among regular churchgoers than among the less faithful. More traditional women also appeared to extend disproportionately strong compassion for the homeless and for child care (but not for increased public services in general), and these issue orientations evidently carried over into the voting booth since the gender gap in Bush support was twice as high (11 percent versus 5 percent) among those who went to church almost weekly or more often. Finally, one indication of self-interest can be found in the fact that the gender gap on child care (unlike the other two social issues) was almost the same for the 18 to 34 and over-55 age groups, whereas it was over twice as great among the middle-aged. Thus, the strong gender gap that would have been expected among the young was attenuated by the special interest of this age group in child rearing.

IMPLICATIONS

This short analysis has examined the nature of the gender gap in U.S. politics at the end of the 1980s. The growing gender gap that was associated with the mobilization of the women's movement and the conservative policies of the Reagan administration has continued unabated even after both of these stimulants have waned. Women continue to differ from men on a wide range of issues, and advanced if mysterious "number crunching" suggests that this difference in issue positions has yet to be fully translated into voting patterns. In particular, women hold quite distinct attitudes on issues related to pacifism and compassion. The current political scene holds mixed implications for these "women's issues." The recent movement toward the end of the Cold War can only be welcomed, but the budget crisis almost inevitably means that there will be little gain in government support for social compassion in the foreseeable future.

Turning to women's rights issues per se, our findings suggest an ironic conclusion about the women's movement—by seeming to fail, it has succeeded. Initially, the feminist movement tried to mobilize women in support of these issues; so that its success was marked by a burgeoning gender gap on them. In fact, the women's movement highlighted the gender gap in voting and attitudes in the early 1980s as a conscious strategy of applying pressure on politicians to support its agenda. From this perspective, the narrowing of the gender gap on its central issues would appear an embarrassing failure. As Carol Mueller cogently argues, however, feminist leaders overlooked a
nomenon—a growing coalition of both men an
changing to favor feminist attitudes on these issi
the values it endorses may well be expected to
generations take over the levers of the U.S. gov

NOTES

1. For data on presidential approval, see Henry C. Kenski, "The Gender Factor in a Changing Electorate," in Carol M. Mueller (Ed.), *The Politics of the Gender Gap: The Social Construction of Political Influence* (Beverly Hills, CA: Sage, 1988), pp. 47–49.

2. Sandra Baxter and Majorie Lansing, *Women and Politics: The Invisible Majority* (Ann Arbor: University of Michig... ...ess, ...), Chaps. 3, 4. Ethel Klein, *Gender Politics: From Consciousness to Mass Politics* (Cambridge, MA: Harvard University Press, 1984), Chap. 9; Keith T. Poole and L. Harmon Zeigler, *Women, Public Opinion, and Politics: The Changing Political Attitudes of American Women* (New York: Longman, 1985), Chaps. 2, 3.

3. Emily Stoper, "The Gender Gap Concealed and Revealed: 1936–1984," *Journal of Political Science*, 17 (1, 2) (Spring 1989), pp. 50–62.

4. Carol Gilligan, *In a Different Voice: Psychological Theory and Women's Development* (Cambridge, MA: Harvard University Press, 1982).

5. Barbara Deckard Sinclair, *The Women's Movement: Political, Socioeconomic, and Psychological Issues*, 3rd ed. (New York: Harper & Row, 1983), Chaps. 2–4; Fred I. Greenstein, *Children and Politics* (New Haven: Yale University Press, 1965), Chap. 6.

6. Virginia Sapiro, *The Political Integration of Women: Roles, Socialization, and Politics* (Urbana: University of Illinois Press, 1983).

7. Anthony M. Orum, Robert S. Cohen, Sherri Grasmuck, and Amy W. Orum, "Sex, Socialization, and Politics," *American Sociological Review*, 39 (2) (April 1974), pp. 197–209; Susan Welch, "Women as Political Animals? A Test of Some Explanations for Male–Female Participation Differences," *American Journal of Political Science*, 21 (4) (November 1977), pp. 711–730.

8. Baxter and Lansing, *The Invisible Majority*; Klein, *Gender Politics*; Vicky Randall, *Women and Politics: An International Perspective*, 2nd ed. (Chicago: University of Chicago Press, 1987), Chaps. 5, 6.

9. Susan J. Carroll, "Women's Autonomy and the Gender Gap: 1980 and 1982," in Carol M. Mueller (Ed.), *The Politics of the Gender Gap: The Social Construction of Political Influence* (Beverly Hills, CA: Sage, 1988), pp. 236–257.

10. Steven P. Erie and Martin Rein, "Women and the Welfare State," in Carol M. Mueller (Ed.), *The Politics of the Gender Gap: The Social Construction of Political Influence* (Beverly Hills, CA: Sage, 1988), pp. 173–191.

11. Diane L. Fowlkes, "Developing a Theory of Countersocialization: Gender, Race, and Politics in the Lives of Women Activists," *Micropolitics*, 3 (2) (1983), pp. 181–225.

12. For a case study supporting this hypothesis, see Cal Clark and Janet Clark, "Wyoming Women's Attitudes towards the MX: The 'Old' v. 'New' Gender Gap," *Journal of Political Science*, 17 (1, 2) (Spring 1989), pp. 127–140.

13. See Charles Prysby and Carmine Scavo, *Voting Behavior: The 1988 Election* (Washington, DC: American Political Science Association, 1989).

14. Klein, *Gender Politics*.

15. This explains the paradoxical fact that, overall, men and women were about equally supportive on many women's issues. In a 1976 Gallup study of "women in America," for example, among the college-educated, women were significantly more supportive of the Equal Rights Amendment than men (68 percent versus 62 percent), but among those with only a grade school education, women were less supportive of the ERA to a surprising extent (45 percent versus 56 percent). This suggests that many women in "traditional roles" saw the ERA as threatening their status. For these and other results of this study, see George H. Gallup, *The Gallup Poll: Public Opinion, 1972–1977*, Vol. 2 (Wilmington, DE: Scholarly Resources, 1978), pp. 684–710.

16. Arthur Miller, "Gender and the Vote: 1984," in Carol M. Mueller (Ed.), *The Politics of the Gender Gap: The Social Construction of Political Influence* (Beverly Hills, CA: Sage, 1988), pp. 264–268.

17. Patricia Gurin, "Women's Gender Consciousness," *Public Opinion Quarterly*, 49 (2) (Summer 1985), pp. 143–163.

18. Carol M. Mueller, "The Empowerment of Women: Polling and the Women's Voting Bloc," in Carol M. Mueller (Ed.), *The Politics of the Gender Gap: The Social Construction of Political Influence* (Beverly Hills, CA: Sage, 1988), pp. 25–26.

19. Mueller, "Empowerment of Women," pp. 25–26.

Changing Views about Gender Equality in Politics: Gradual Change and Lingering Doubts

Linda L.M. Bennett
Stephen E. Bennett

INTRODUCTION

An important difference between women and men in the United States disappeared in the 1980s. Since ratification of the Nineteenth Amendment in 1920, women had voted in national elections in smaller proportions than men. But in the 1988 presidential election, the U.S. Census Bureau estimated that 58.3 percent of women 18 years old and older turned out, compared to 56.4 percent of similarly aged men.[1] The turnout gap between women and men also disappeared in local elections.[2]

Exercising the franchise is but one way a citizen can participate in this political system, and profound gender differences remain in other modes of participation (for example, running for political office). The end of turnout differences is significant, however, because it calls into question some of the ways researchers have explained gender differences in political behavior and attitudes. Do we need to revise our thinking about the different factors that affect women and men and their involvement in politics? Are women and men becoming more alike in how they view politics? Are younger Americans coming to greater agreement than their parents or grandparents on the issue of gender equality in the political arena?

These are the questions we hope to answer in this essay. We begin with a review of explanations for gender differences in political behavior and

The data utilized here were originally collected by the University of Chicago's National Opinion Research Center and the University of Michigan's Center for Political Studies and were made available by the Interuniversity Consortium for Political and Social Research. We are responsible for all analyses and interpretations.

Linda L. M. Bennett is an associate professor of political science at Wittenberg University, and Stephen E. Bennett is a professor of political science at the University of Cincinnati.

46

attitudes. We will describe three basic explanations for gender differences: (1) *sex-role socialization* (how girls and boys learn "gender-appropriate" attitudes and behavior that affect how they view politics); (2) *structural* (the impact of education, occupation, income); and (3) *situational* (marital status, motherhood, homemaking). We create a way to measure what people think about political gender equality and describe those who still hold traditional conceptions of a "woman's place" in politics and society, and those who are taking on a more "modern" perspective that allows for full participation regardless of gender.

Even while some attitudes are changing, women are far from full participation in the political arena. The sex-role socialization process continues to encourage political passivity among women, although its effects are clearly weakening in areas such as voting. Socialization remains an important factor that can help us to understand the lingering differences between women and men on a host of political attitudes and behaviors.

THREE EXPLANATIONS FOR GENDER DIFFERENCES

Sex-role Socialization

In 1960 researchers defined sex-role socialization as "that portion of expectations about behavior proper for a male or female that involves political responses."[3] The study went on to explain that the "role definitions" between women and men, and women's willingness to "leave politics to men," was the source of gender differences in attitudes during the 1950s. Socialization literature of the 1960s and early 1970s supported research from the 1950s and argued that the passive role learned by young girls was a significant reason they avoided politics later in life.[4] Studies in the 1980s asserted that girls were still learning passivity from their mothers and that this learning process accounted for their political passivity as adults.[5] Political roles are learned not only from parents, but also at school, in church, from peers, and from the media. In other words, four decades of research concluded that as a result of exposure to a number of socializing agents, many women and men grow up believing that politics is a "man's world."

The problem with sex-role socialization research is that much of it was developed from studies of children, with little evidence offered of a conclusive link between childhood experience and adult attitudes or behavior. Attempts to bridge the period between childhood and adult years depended on researchers eliminating the influence of as many other factors as possible (some of which are discussed under structural and situational factors) and then concluding that only socialization was left as a reasonable explanation for gender differences in political thought, feelings, and actions.[6]

Structural Factors

Socioeconomic factors such as education, occupation, and income have long been known to be important in shaping a variety of attitudes. Education has been one of the strongest predictors of women's involvement and participation. In a study comparing brothers and sisters differentiated only by college attendance, the sibling with college exposure was consistently more politically interested, informed, and participatory than the one without the benefit of a college education.[7]

Along with education, women's employment status has been found by some to have an impact on political participation. In a study from the early 1970s, Kristi Andersen found a combined effect of employment and holding feminist opinions on women's willingness to participate. Working women who were supportive of an equal role in society for their sex were more participatory than their working sisters who did not back gender equality in society.[8] Still others found no differences in voting turnout between working and nonworking women and attributed gender differences to the greater political passivity of older women, who were more likely to be socialized into the notion that politics was a "man's business."[9] Tapping into the paycheck reality of work, Ellen McDonagh emphasized that work is not "liberating" if it is low-paid drudgery.[10]

Situational Factors

The number of women who become wives and/or mothers or who remain at home in the traditional role of homemaker has changed tremendously in recent years.[11] For this reason, recent research on situational factors disputes the conclusions of earlier studies. Studies from the 1950s argued that the duties of motherhood depressed women's political participation. It was assumed that women adopted the political attitudes of their husbands and looked to them for guidance when voting.[12] Lower levels of participation were most evident among less educated, low-socioeconomic-status women. The assumption was that women's absortion with the "private sphere" of the home created a major obstacle to their participation in the "public sphere" of politics.

Older, untested assumptions about women's political participation do not always hold up to empirical scrutiny. Later studies challenged the tendency of earlier studies to focus only on national elections and urged more attention to participation in state and local politics. Recent research offers more complex descriptions of the impact of motherhood and uncovered an increased likelihood to participate in local politics among women with school-aged children.[13] Virginia Sapiro found that a complex joint effect of motherhood and education was linked to higher levels of community participation among women. She also argued that educational achievement is more important than marital status, homemaking, or motherhood in leading women to a general interest in politics.[14] On the other hand, Nancy Romer found that young women who were politically active while in high school *expected* to be less politically active if they took on the roles of wife and mother.[15]

In reviewing the three explanations that have been offered for gender differences in political attitudes and participation, it should be evident that it is difficult to keep each explanation distinct. Researchers have tried to separate the effects of socialization from those of socioeconomic status and role choices such as being a wife and mother, but it is less clear that most women could separate them as easily. Even those who have argued for the impact of structural and situational factors find themselves returning to the key factor of how roles are learned, or socialization. As one set of researchers note, "socialization into the traditional feminine role in our culture produces a sense of self which is relatively more dependent on the definitions of others and a concern with homes and families, and matters related to them, over more 'distant' matters."[16] Structural and situational factors have been easier to study because there are clearer indicators by which their impact can be measured. Education, occupation, marital status, number of children—these are all simple questions on any public opinion survey, whereas socialization, a slow process of learning, is more difficult to uncover with surveys. Still, it remains a compelling explanation for how women and men view politics.

Having outlined the three explanations for gender differences, it is easy to see that socialization could be related to how much women strive to achieve in education and work, as well as their choices of marriage, motherhood, and whether they stay at home as caretakers to others.[17] Are there empirical indicators that can help us to measure attitudes developed from the socialization process? We find there are such indicators, although they are far from perfect, and we turn next to how sex-role socialization shows up in attitudes about women's "proper place" in the political world. If socialization does have an impact on how interested and involved people are in politics, then we need to understand how those views are shaped. Have opinions about where women belong in the political arena changed in recent years?

MEASURING OPINIONS ABOUT GENDER ROLES IN POLITICS

The next section will present data on how much involvement in the political arena people feel is appropriate for women. Before presenting those data, we offer a brief section on where the data come from and how attitudes are being measured.

The five time periods covered in this analysis are: 1974–1975, 1977–1978, 1982–1983, 1985–1986, and 1988–1989. Beginning in 1974, the National Opinion Research Center (NORC) at the University of Chicago included a series of questions on its General Social Survey asking a national sample of voting-age Americans about women's roles in business, industry, and politics. These questions have been asked on most General Social Surveys since. Three of the questions focus on gender roles and politics:

1. Do you agree or disagree with this statement? Women should take care of running their homes and leave running the country up to men.
2. If your party nominated a woman for president, would you vote for her if she were qualified for the job?
3. Tell me if you agree or disagree with this statement: Most men are better suited emotionally for politics than are most women.

For this study, these items were combined to form a "Political Gender Roles Index."[18] An index allows the combination of several narrower items into a single indicator measuring a more general concept. The Political Gender Roles Index groups responses to the three items on a scale ranging from "very modern" (disagrees that women should leave running the country up to men, would vote for a woman for president, and disagrees that men are better suited emotionally for politics) to "very traditional" (agrees the country should be run by men, would not vote for a woman, and agrees that men are more emotionally suited for politics). Those with a mix of responses were labeled "slightly modern" or "slightly traditional." The few people who said they "didn't know" what to think about any of the questions were placed in a middle "neutral" category. As you will see, there are very few people who take a neutral position on what women's political roles should be.

TRENDS IN OPINIONS ABOUT GENDER ROLES IN POLITICS

We begin with a general overview of what people think about women's appropriate roles in politics. Table 1 shows how much change there has been from 1974–1975 to 1988–1989. There has been a sharp increase in the percentage of people adopting "very modern" responses to the three items comprising the Gender Roles Index. The largest increase occurs in the period from 1977–1978 to 1982–1983. By the time Representative Geraldine Ferraro (D-NY) was selected by Walter Mondale as his vice presidential running mate in the 1984 presidential election, a majority of Americans were claiming to have a very modern orientation towards gender roles in politics.

The percentage of those expressing a very traditional orientation towards gender roles in politics was cut in half between 1974–1975 and 1988–1989. As recently as 1988–1989 almost one in five respondents favored more traditional roles for women (combine the "very" and "slightly" traditional categories).

Table 1 Public Opinion about Political Gender Roles for Various Years, from 1974–1975 to 1988–1989, in Percentages

	1974–1975	1977–1978	1982–1983	1985–1986	1988–1989
Very modern	41	42	53	51	57
Slightly modern	23	23	22	23	21
Neutral	3	3	3	2	3
Slightly traditional	20	20	15	16	13
Very traditional	13	12	8	8	6
(N)	(2,237)	(3,053)	(2,498)	(2,980)	(1,975)

Source: NORC's General Social Surveys.

That is less than the one-third with traditional notions in 1974–1975, but still a sizable group. Given the prominence achieved by women in government at all levels during the 1970s and 1980s—including city mayors, governors, members of Congress, U.S. senators, a United Nations ambassador, cabinet secretaries, and a vice-presidential candidate from a major party—the persistence of traditional ideas about political gender roles is intriguing.

Do women and men differ in their views about the roles that are appropriate for women to take in the political arena? Figure 1 shows that there are more similarities than differences in what women and men think about gender roles in politics. There is a sizable gap between the percentage of women and that of men who hold very modern views compared with those who hold very traditional views. By 1988–1989 only 6 percent of both sexes were steadfast in the belief that women should stay out of politics. The percentage of women subscribing to very modern views increased by almost 20 percentage points from 1974–1975 to 1988–1989. The percentage of men adopting a modern view of gender roles also increased during the same period, though not as sharply as that for women. Furthermore, between 1985–1986 and 1988–1989 the percentage of men expressing modern views remained stable, while 11 percent more women voiced modern views. By 1988–1989 women clearly outdistanced men in expressing very modern views about political gender roles. Even with that difference, three-quarters of women *and* men could be placed in the very modern or slightly modern categories by 1988–1989. If we are to understand why some people hold very modern views about political gender roles while others hold very traditional views, factors other than sex will have to be considered.

Figure 1 Women's and Men's Opinions about Gender Roles in Politics, for Various Years from 1974–1975 to 1988–1989

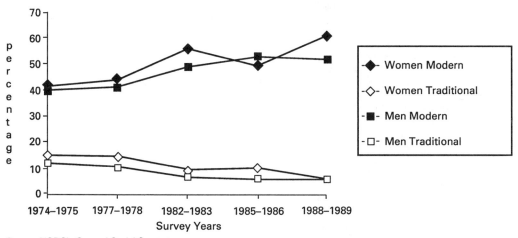

Source: NORC's General Social Surveys.

A MULTIVARIATE ANALYSIS OF THE SOURCES
OF POLITICAL GENDER ROLE OPINIONS

A better understanding of who holds modern opinions about political gender roles and who holds traditional opinions is possible by using a statistical technique called *multiple regression*, which allows a researcher to gauge the relative impact of several factors, or variables, on a phenomenon—in this case, beliefs about women's proper roles in politics. Several variables were included in this analysis for each survey year: structural factors such as years of schooling (an imperfect but usable measure of education), family income, and occupational prestige (the social status connected with the respondent's occupation);[19] situational factors such as marital status and whether the respondent had children; and, finally, additional factors said to be related to how people view politics, such as race, age, a measure of religious fundamentalism, political party identification, political ideology (liberal to conservative), whether or not the respondent's mother worked when the respondent was a child (an attempt to provide an empirical link in experience between childhood and adult years), region of the country the respondent lived in (the Southern states are noted for harboring a more conservative culture), whether the respondent read newspapers with any regularity, and the survey year to see if the passage of time had any impact on opinions.

From 1974–1975 to 1988–1989, what factors help to explain people's opinions about the appropriate roles for women in the political arena? Table 2 lists in order of importance the significant variables. The most important predictor of opinions about political gender roles is age. Younger people are far more likely to express modern views than are older people. In fact, younger women are more likely than younger men to express modern views. The education a respondent's father received comes in as a surprisingly strong predictor

Table 2   Significant Factors Affecting Opinions on the Political Gender Roles Index, in Rank Order, for All Survey Years from 1974–1975 to 1988–89

Respondent's age
Father's level of education
Respondent's level of education
Region where respondent lives (South vs. non-South)
Year survey was conducted
Religious fundamentalism
Mother's level of education
Respondent's political ideology (liberal or conservative)
Family income level
Respondent's political party affiliation (strength)
Did respondent's mother work?

$$R^2 = .18$$

Source: NORC's General Social Surveys.

(more educated fathers encourage more modern views), suggesting the lingering impact of one of the most important socializing agents: parents. How many years of education the respondent received enters as the third most important predictor, followed by the region variable measuring whether or not one lived in a Southern state. Even as the South is changing, the region's cultural conservatism continues to have an impact on its residents. The variables listed after region are statistically significant predictors but are weaker in their impact on opinions about political gender roles.

On the other hand, the variables *not* included in Table 2 are interesting as well. An example of such a variable is sex. From 1974–1975 to 1988–1989, sex does not serve as a significant predictor of whether a person will hold modern or traditional views. Does this mean that the process of sex-role socialization is no longer occurring in American families? No. The absence of sex as a predictor means that women and men have not disagreed fundamentally about their appropriate gender roles in politics. The perception of political gender roles still exists, and there has been more agreement than disagreement between the sexes about those roles. There is no guarantee, however, that this agreement will continue, and we will return to the point made earlier that between 1985–1986 and 1988–1989 a stable percentage of men professed modern views about political gender roles, whereas the percentage of women holding modern views rose sharply.

Almost as important is the absence of other factors thought to influence opinions about political gender roles. Among such factors are race, marital and parental status, family income, occupational prestige, whether the respondent's mother had worked, and partisanship. Although it would be risky to say that situational and, except for education, structural factors should be ignored in studies of gender and politics, they are clearly less important than previous literature would suggest.

Analyzing all the survey years together, as Table 2 does, can tell us about significant factors affecting opinion during that entire period, but it can hide changes that occur between the survey years included. With that in mind, notice that the survey year does enter as a significant predictor of gender roles in politics, suggesting that the passage of time is having an impact on the development of more modern orientations.

Although sex does not enter the regression analysis as a significant predictor of political gender role opinions, there are some subtle differences in the factors that predict these opinions among women and men. Table 3 shows that age, education, and religious fundamentalism are the three most important predictors for both women and men, but the order of the first two factors differs, with age more important to women and educational attainment more important to men. A separate percentage analysis comparing the various survey years (not shown here to save space) revealed an irony about the impact of education and age on the opinions of women and men. At all levels of formal schooling, women who were under age 30 in the mid-1980s were either more in favor of modern

Table 3   Significant Factors Affecting Women's and Men's Opinions on the Political Gender Roles Index, in Rank Order, for All Survey Years, 1974–1975 to 1988–1989

WOMEN	*MEN*
Respondent's age	Respondent's level of education
Respondent's level of education	Respondent's age
Religious fundamentalism	Religious fundamentalism
Year of survey	Family income level
Frequency of church attendance	Respondent's political ideology
Respondent's political ideology	Region where respondent lives
Family income level	Year of survey
Region where respondent lives	
$R^2 = .22$	$R^2 = .15$

Source: NORC's General Social Surveys.

gender roles in politics or at least equally so with women between 30 and 44 years old. But men, particularly those with college backgrounds who were on university campuses in the 1960s and early 1970s, are slightly more committed to equal gender roles in politics than are younger men who have been on college campuses in the 1980s. Furthermore, by 1988–1989 the gap between women and men appears to be widening, particularly at the lower levels of educational attainment.

Finally, the injection of religious fundamentalism into these regression models is consistent with the expectation that religious conservatism (be it Protestant, Catholic, or Jewish) holds to more traditional roles for women in the private and public spheres of life. Women are more frequent church attenders than men, and hence it is not surprising that this important socializing factor should help to predict opinions about gender roles for a certain percentage of women.

How successful are the regression models in explaining opinions about political gender roles? Success is defined as the cumulative ability of significant predictors to explain changing opinions on the Political Gender Role Index. No social science model we know is able to explain 100 percent of any phenomenon. Our models are able to explain from 15 to 22 percent of change on the index. Although we can point to previous studies that have relied on regression models of similarly modest capacity,[20] that is cold comfort.

There are two reasons for the modest explanatory power of the regression models. First, given the limits of secondary survey analysis, the models probably leave out key factors accounting for opinions about gender roles in politics because there are no variables in the data sets tapping respondents' relationships with parents and how parents passed on their political views. Recall that one reason some researchers have favored structural and situational factors to explain gender differences has been their ease of measurement. Second, the items making up our Political Gender Role Index are too few and too imprecise to capture the entire range of opinions about political gender roles.

CONCLUSIONS

Does it make a difference for grass-roots political behavior if people have traditional views of political gender roles? Yes, if data from the University of Michigan's Center for Political Studies' 1984 National Election Study can be believed. When a Political Gender Role Index was created using two of the items described here,[21] those with traditional views were less likely to vote, less likely to have been active in the campaign, less likely to report having joined an organization trying to deal with a national problem, and more likely to be politically apathetic. Although some of these differences wash out when education is controlled, there is still a residual impact of traditional opinions about political gender roles and willingness to participate in the political system.

The disappearance of the turnout gap between women and men is only in part a result of increased voting among women. It is also the result of a sharp decline in turnout among men. Women remain less politically interested and less likely to follow media accounts of campaigns, even when education is taken into account.[22] Behind women's continuing tendency to be less politically interested in their greater likelihood to agree that "sometimes politics and government seem so complicated that a person like me can't really understand what's going on." According to data from the University of Michigan's Center for Political Studies' National Election Surveys, between 1972 and 1984, 73 to 77 percent of women said they did not feel competent to understand public affairs, compared to 59 to 61 percent of men. Controlling for education does not eliminate gender differences on this item.

With the passage of time allowing less educated, traditionally socialized Americans to leave the voting-age public, and increased exposure to higher education among the young, support for modern views of gender equality in politics will probably increase. Still, the process will not be automatic. Recall that younger men on college campuses in the 1980s were less likely to express modern views than men who were on college campuses in the late 1960s and 1970s. The differences are not large enough to speak of a transformation in well-educated young men's opinions, but they remind us that the momentum toward acceptance of gender equality in politics can be lost, even among the well educated, unless continual effort is made to overcome older notions of where women "belong." The sex-role socialization process endures, and its impact is still felt in the political arena.

NOTES

1. U.S. Bureau of the Census, *Voting and Registration in the Election of November 1988*, Current Population Reports, Series P-20, No. 440 (Washington, DC: U.S. Government Printing Office, 1989), pp. 4–5.

2. Closure in the "turnout gap" is evident in data from the National Opinion Research Center (NORC).

In 1967 NORC reported that 27 percent of women said they *never* voted, compared to 22 percent of men. Even this gap was smaller than it would have been in the 1920s and 1930s, immediately after the Nineteenth Amendment's ratification. By 1987 NORC data revealed women and men equally likely to report having voted (68 percent versus 68 percent).

3. Angus Campbell, Philip Converse, Warren E. Miller, and Donald Stokes, *The American Voter* (New York: Wiley, 1960), p. 484.

4. Robert D. Hess and Judith V. Torney, *The Development of Political Attitudes in Children* (Chicago: Aldine, 1967); Fred I. Greenstein, *Children and Politics* (New Haven: Yale University Press, 1969).

5. Ronald B. Rapoport, "The Sex Gap in Political Persuading: Where the 'Structuring Principle' Works," *American Journal of Political Science*, 25 (1) (February 1981), pp. 32–48; "Sex Differences in Attitude Expression: A Generational Explanation," *Public Opinion Quarterly*, 46 (1) (Spring 1982), pp. 86–96; "Like Mother, Like Daughter: Intergenerational Transmission of DK Response Rates," *Public Opinion Quarterly*, 49 (2) (Summer 1985), pp. 198–208.

6. Anthony Orum, Roberta S. Cohen, Susan Grassmuck, and Amy W. Orum, "Sex, Socialization, and Politics," *American Sociological Review*, 39 (2) (April 1974), pp. 197–209.

7. Kent L. Tedin, David W. Brady, and Arnold Vedlitz, "Sex Differences in Political Attitudes and Behavior: The Case for Situational Factors," *Journal of Politics*, 39 (2) (May 1977), pp. 448–456; Ethel Klein, *Gender Politics* (Cambridge, MA: Harvard University Press, 1984).

8. Kristi Andersen, "Working Women and Political Participation," *American Journal of Political Science*, 19 (3) (August 1975), pp. 439–454.

9. Raymond E. Wolfinger and Steven J. Rosenstone, *Who Votes?* (New Haven: Yale University Press, 1980).

10. Ellen L. McDonagh, "To Work or Not to Work: The Differential Impact of Achieved and Derived States upon the Political Participation of Women," *American Journal of Political Science*, 26 (2) (May 1982), pp. 280–297.

11. Klein, *Gender Politics*.

12. Robert E. Lane, *Political Life* (New York: Free Press, 1965); Campbell et al., others, *The American Voter*.

13. M. Kent Jennings, "Another Look at Politics and the Life Cycle," *American Journal of Political Science*, 23 (4) (November 1979), pp. 755–771.

14. Virginia Sapiro, *The Political Integration of Women* (Urbana: University of Illinois Press, 1983), pp. 89–90, 136–138.

15. Nancy Romer, "Is Political Activism Still a 'Masculine' Endeavor?" *Psychology of Women Quarterly*, 14 (2) (June 1990), pp. 229–243.

16. Kristi Andersen and Elizabeth Cook, "Women, Work, and Political Attitudes," *American Journal of Political Science*, 29 (3) (August 1985), pp. 606–622.

17. Cal Clark and Janet Clark, "Models of Gender and Political Participation in the United States," *Women and Politics*, 6 (1) (Spring 1986), pp. 5–25.

18. Before summing the three items, it was first determined if they belonged in a composite index. When all survey years were combined and the three items were fed into SPSS[x]'s RELIABILITY routine, the value of .6960 for Cronbach's coefficient *alpha* was obtained. The items have an average interitem correlation of $r = .52$. Although the Political Gender Roles Index contains some measurement error, it is a satisfactory device for tapping opinions about gender roles in politics.

19. The NORC codebook describes the occupational prestige rating process as one guided by "the respondents' estimation of the social standing of occupations." The respondents' ratings generally range along a nine-point scale and are useful in assigning some order to the thousands of occupation codes in U.S. Census Bureau data.

20. See esp. Sapiro, *The Political Integration of Women*.

21. In 1984 the CPS did not ask the question "If your party nominated a woman for president, would you vote for her if she were qualified for the job?"

22. M. Margaret Conway, *Political Participation in the United States* (Washington, DC: Congressional Quarterly Press, 1985); Linda L. M. Bennett and Stephen E. Bennett, "Enduring Gender Differences in Political Interest: The Impact of Socialization and Political Dispositions," *American Politics Quarterly*, 17 (1) (January 1989), pp. 105–122.

The Generations of Feminism

Elizabeth Adell Cook

It is often observed that young people have different political values and beliefs than older people. On many issues, such as abortion, gender equality, and the willingness to allow atheists to teach in college, young people are more liberal than their parents, and much more liberal than their grandparents. Some of these differences will endure over time, and others will diminish. These differences can occur as the result of (1) generational effects and (2) life-cycle effects.

Generational effects refer to differences in the political values and behaviors of two different generations; these are the result of the different social and political context in which each generation grew up or came of age. Thus, members of a generation bear the imprint of a particular period even as they age and times change. Think about the attitudes of Americans toward Japan. We would not expect Americans who grew up with the phrase "Remember Pearl Harbor" (and who in fact do) to feel as warmly toward Japan as Americans who learned about World War II in history class. Most likely, these younger Americans grew up thinking of the United States and Japan as allies. Therefore, we would expect them to view Japan more warmly than older Americans, and we would not expect the views of younger Americans to change as a result of growing older.

Life-cycle effects are defined as those differences in the political values and behaviors of two different generations resulting from different lifestyles and responsibilities as a function of age. When we compare the young to the middle-aged, the young are less likely to be married, to have children, to own homes, to be saving for retirement, and to be concerned about elderly parents. Although a generation may marry later than preceding generations, or have fewer children,

Elizabeth Adell Cook is a visiting assistant professor of government and politics at George Mason University.

eventually all young generations will become middle-aged and assume many of the trappings of middle age. ("Just wait until you have children of your own.") When a younger generation becomes more like an older generation as it ages and its lifestyle changes, we refer to this as the life-cycle effect. The original differences observed between younger and older people were primarily the result of the differing life circumstances of the two generations. Thus, as the younger generation matures and experiences the changes in lifestyle usually associated with aging, it adopts the values and behaviors of the older generation. As generational effects occur, generations remain distinct over time. When life-cycle effects occur, the younger generation becomes more like the older generation as it ages.

A third kind of effect looks at changes affecting all generations. *Period effects* occur when the social and political context changes members of all generations. For example, intensive media coverage of drug problems during the late 1980s led Americans of all ages to express concern. In 1989, drugs were listed as the most serious problem facing the country among all age groups in many polls.

GENERATIONS AND ATTITUDES ABOUT WOMEN

There have clearly been some period effects in attitudes toward the role of women. For example, the public has become more supportive of working women over time. Although we take it for granted that women who do the same work as men ought to receive the same pay (even though they may in fact not), this view has not always been universally endorsed. And not all generations have responded similarly in how they view women's role.

Most studies have reported that age is a significant predictor of support for feminist programs and organizations. Studies in the 1970s and 1980s found that younger women were more supportive of egalitarian values, had higher levels of gender consciousness, and were more supportive of gender equality than were older women.

During the second half of the 1980s, however, controversy arose concerning the possibility of generational change in support for feminism. Bolotin reported the emergence of a postfeminist generation among young women—part of a general retreat from liberalism among the young.[1] Most of the scholarly research on this question has focused on the attitudes of college students. Studies have found that college women may support feminist ideals but reject the collective efforts of the women's movement,[2] that there is support for equal rights but not for feminism,[3] and that the term *feminist* evokes negative connotations even among students who support gender equality.[4]

Others have argued, however, that college students do not reject feminism per se, but want to redirect the movement to their own needs.[5] Research has suggested that college women become progressively more supportive of feminism during their academic years as they experience sex discrimination.[6]

All these studies limit their analysis to college students. Although there is good theoretical reason to focus attention on the attitudes of college women (college education is a strong predictor of support for feminism), it is important to examine changing support for feminism among all women. Moreover, most research has not been conscious of its assumptions: Some studies assume that support for feminism among the young is related to life cycle, but others assume lasting generational differences. This study, therefore, will examine the pattern of support among different generations of women over the period 1972–1984. The period covers the rise of feminism and the early Reagan era. The data come from the American National Election Studies of 1972, 1976, 1980, and 1984.[7]

POLITICIZED FEMINIST CONSCIOUSNESS

Scholars who focus on the women's movement have argued that feminist support is best understood in terms of group consciousness. One of the earliest activities of the feminist movement was consciousness raising—attempting to develop a politicized feminist consciousness among women.[8] Klein suggested that individuals who acquire a feminist consciousness must go through three steps.[9] First, women must recognize their membership in a group (women) and that they share interests with that group. Second, women must reject the societal rationale for the situation of the group; that is, they must blame society for the disadvantaged status of women. Finally, women must recognize the need for group solutions to problems.

Gurin, Miller, and Gurin adopt a similar strategy, arguing that group consciousness consists of social group identification, power discontent, system blaming, and a collectivist orientation.[10] In other research, feminist consciousness has been defined as follows: Nonfeminists are defined as those women who do not believe that women should have an equal role with men in society, potential feminists are classified as those who believe in an equal role for women but do not support the women's liberation movement, and those who believe in an equal role and who support the movement are defined as having a politicized feminist consciousness.[11]

Support for the women's liberation movement is measured by a feeling thermometer item, which asks respondents to place the women's liberation movement (along with other social and political groups) on an imaginary scale that ranges from 0° (representing extreme coolness) to 100° (representing extreme warmth). Because individuals differ in the patterns of their responses to these items, responses were adjusted to account for individual differences.[12]

Table 1 presents the frequency distributions of the measure across the period of this study. Actual feminist consciousness increases between 1972 and 1976, then remains relatively steady through 1984.

Table 1 also contains the Percentage Difference Index (PDI) for each of the four studies. The PDI is a summary measure created by subtracting the percentage of women who are nonfeminists from the percentage of women with a politicized feminist consciousness. It provides us with a single number to compare across years.

Table 1   Distribution of Feminist Consciousness

	1972	1976	1980	1984
Not feminist	61%	50%	50%	50%
Potential feminist	26	28	30	31
Feminist	13	21	22	19
(N)	(1,322)	(1,254)	(726)	(1,063)
PDI	−48	−29	−28	−31

POLITICIZED FEMINIST CONSCIOUSNESS AND GENERATIONS

Cohort, or generational, analysis allows us to compare women who came of age at different times across years. That is, instead of comparing samples of individuals of the same age group (which is forever in flux as individuals age into or out of the group), we can compare samples of a constant coming-of-age cohort. Cohort analysis allows us to start to sort out life-cycle (or maturation) effects from generational (or cohort) effects.

In order for cohort analysis to be meaningful, the cohorts need to be defined according to eras. That is, the boundaries of each cohort should to the greatest extent possible represent transitions in the relevant social context. Fortunately, the task of defining cohorts relevant to the women's movement has already been taken on.

Sapiro (1980) defined seven coming-of-age cohorts relevant to women's history:

> The eras or transitions are marked by either events of particular importance to women or by the type of broad characterizations we often use to mark off historical periods. Thus, the ratification of the Nineteenth Amendment serves as a time marker, and the twenties, characterized by a post-suffrage flurry of recognition of women, is distinguished from the Depression era. Of particular interest is the transition from World War II, the era of Rosie the Riveter and

Table 2   Coming-of-Age Cohorts*

Presuffrage	Pre 1920
Twenties	1921–1929
Depression	1930–1939
World War II	1940–1945
Mystique	1946–1959
Sixties	1960–1966
Women's Liberation	1967–1977
Complacent/Reagan	1978–1984

Note:

*The cohorts are defined according to periods in which the respondent turned 18.

national day care centers, to the thirteen-year period characterized by Betty Friedan as the time of the "Feminine Mystique," a "dark age" in women's history according to feminist observers. Although the entire post-1960 period saw the growth of social movements and policy-making aimed at equality, it is further divided by the birth of the Women's Liberation Movement.[13]

In addition to Sapiro's seven cohorts, an additional cohort is defined in the 1984 study, the Complacent or Reagan era cohort. Table 2 shows a breakdown of these cohorts. Whereas Sapiro defined cohorts according to when respondents turned 21, for this analysis, respondents are placed in cohorts according to the year they turned 18. Sapiro chose age 21 because it was for most of this century the legal age of majority, the age at which young people struck out on their own, and the average age of marriage for women. In this analysis, the younger age of 18 is used because individuals would seem to be more impressionable at this age—and will be making the choices in very early adulthood about education, careers, and forming their own families. These decisions will affect their life circumstances even three years into their futures when they turn 21.

COMING-OF-AGE COHORTS AND FEMINIST CONSCIOUSNESS

Table 3 shows politicized feminist consciousness by coming-of-age cohort. The oldest cohort, women who came of age before women won the right to vote, exhibited very low feminist consciousness in 1972 and did not increase its level of consciousness in 1976. By 1980 there were too few members of this cohort left to analyze (only 20 in the sample; the youngest members would have been 78 years old.) Women who came of age during the 1920s also exhibited very low levels of feminist consciousness in 1972 and, unlike women as a whole, did not increase their level of feminist consciousness in 1976. This cohort did increase its level of consciousness somewhat by 1980, but this declined in 1984. Overall, the cohort exhibited stability over time, with low levels of feminist consciousness.

The Depression cohort also remained fairly stable over time. Feminist consciousness was slightly higher among this cohort in 1976, but this effect was temporary. This cohort was still more conservative than women as a whole.

The World War II cohort, like the older cohorts, exhibited very low levels of feminist consciousness in 1972, when these women were aged 50 to 55. The level of feminist consciousness increased in 1976 but fell off slightly in 1980 and declined again in 1984.

The Mystique cohort, the mothers of the baby boom, in each year exhibit a higher level of feminist consciousness than the older cohorts. Despite the fact that this cohort bucked the demographic trends by marrying earlier and having more children than the older cohorts, in the 1972–1984 period it was more feminist than the older cohorts. Feminist consciousness among this cohort seesawed; it increased from 1972 to 1976, declined in 1980, and increased again in 1984.

Table 3 Coming-of-Age Cohorts and Feminist Consciousness

	1972	1976	1980	1984
Presuffrage				
Not	74%	74%	—	—
Potential	20	19	—	—
Feminist	6	7	—	—
PDI	[−68]	[−67]	—	—
(N)	(138)	(92)	—	—
Twenties				
Not	70%	72%	64%	75%
Potential	23	19	27	14
Feminist	7	9	9	12
PDI	[−63]	[−63]	[−55]	[−63]
(N)	(149)	(122)	(68)	(52)
Depression				
Not	66%	61%	66%	66%
Potential	21	26	22	24
Feminist	13	13	12	10
PDI	[−53]	[−48]	[−54]	[−56]
(N)	(194)	(184)	(93)	(124)
World War II				
Not	67%	49%	62%	68%
Potential	28	36	30	19
Feminist	5	14	8	13
PDI	[−62]	[−35]	[−54]	[−55]
(N)	(137)	(111)	(59)	(79)
Mystique				
Not	60%	49%	54%	47%
Potential	28	29	32	33
Feminist	12	22	14	20
PDI	[−48]	[−27]	[−40]	[−27]
(N)	(311)	(196)	(141)	(189)
Sixties				
Not	52%	36%	42%	41%
Potential	31	36	35	36
Feminist	16	28	23	22
PDI	[−36]	[−8]	[−19]	[−19]
(N)	(219)	(196)	(113)	(143)
Women's Liberation				
Not	44%*	39%	40%	41%
Potential	30	28	29	36
Feminist	25	32	30	23
PDI	[−19]	[−7]	[−10]	[−18]
(N)	(164)	(303)	(215)	(325)

(continued)	1972	1976	1980	1984
Complacent				
Not	—	—	—	44%
Potential	—	—	—	39
Feminist	—	—	—	18
PDI	—	—	—	[−26]
(N)	—	—	—	(119)

Note:

*Only part of the Women's Liberation cohort had turned 18 in 1972. The complete cohort did not come of age until 1977.

The Women's Liberation cohort displays a higher level of feminist consciousness than the Sixties cohort in 1972. In each year after 1972, however, these two cohorts exhibit similar levels of feminist consciousness. These two cohorts exhibit the highest levels of feminist consciousness in each year. Even for these two cohorts, however, the PDI is never positive; there are never more women at the highest level of consciousness than women at the lowest level.

By 1984 the Complacent cohort had come of age. Whereas the overall trend had been for each successive cohort to exhibit a higher level of feminist consciousness than older cohorts, this youngest cohort reversed the trend. The Complacent cohort's distribution on the politicized feminist consciousness measure closely resembles that of the Mystique cohort. Although these 18-to 24-year-old women are less feminist than women who came of age in the 1960–1977 period, they are more feminist than women as a whole in 1984.

It is interesting to note that the primary difference between women in the Complacent cohort and the Women's Liberation and Sixties cohorts is that fewer members of the younger cohort support the women's liberation movement. The majority of all three cohorts strongly support an equal role for women, but the "potential feminist consciousness" of the youngest cohort is less likely to be politicized; they are less likely to strongly support the women's liberation movement. One question this brings up is whether the term *women's liberation movement* was relevant to young women in 1984. In survey research, there is a tension between maintaining comparability of questions across time and keeping questions meaningful. It is possible that by 1984 the term *women's liberation movement* was an anachronism, especially to young women.

Does the lower level of feminist consciousness as measured here mean that women of the Complacent cohort are less supportive of feminist issue positions than women in the Women's Liberation and Sixties cohorts? We can compare the Complacent cohort to the Women's Liberation and Sixties cohort (combined) on feminist issues that were included in the 1984 study. These include measures of attitudes toward abortion, government efforts to improve the social and economic position of women, and male superiority.[14] Also included is a question of whether respondents feel close to feminists.

The Complacent cohort was somewhat less liberal on abortion than the Women's Liberation/Sixties cohort. On the issues of government efforts to improve the social and economic status of women and male superiority, no statistically significant differences emerged. Women of the Complacent cohort were slightly less likely to indicate they felt close to feminists, but the difference is not statistically significant. Overall, women of the Complacent cohort are only slightly less supportive on feminist issues than women of the Women's Liberation/Sixties cohort.

SUMMARY

A number of events occurred during the 1972–1984 time period that shaped attitudes: the mobilization of the women's movement, the passage by Congress of the Equal Rights Amendment (ERA) and its early successes, the formation and mobilization of the anti-ERA coalition, the strong antifeminist platform of the Republicans in 1980, and the Reagan presidency. Moreover, the tenor of news coverage of the movement changed markedly over the course of this period, from strongly negative to evenhanded.

In 1972 the women's movement did not have very much support. Only 13 percent of women in the study demonstrated a politicized feminist consciousness, and 61 percent did not even appear to have the potential for developing one. By 1976 one in five women exhibited a politicized feminist consciousness, and this level of support was maintained through 1984.

The biggest increase in feminist consciousness during this period (1972–1976) occurred among women who were in their thirties and forties in 1976 (the Sixties, Mystique, and World War II cohorts). Older women showed little or no increase, and younger women (the Women's Liberation cohort) had less room to move because they had started out with higher levels of support than any other cohort.

Cohort analysis revealed that generational turnover helped to increase the level of feminist consciousness from 1972 to 1976, as more feminist younger women replaced more traditional older women. The most feminist women were those who came of age during the period of social activism in the 1960s and the development of the women's movement in the 1970s. The youngest women, those who came of age in the late 1970s and early 1980s, were less feminist than the Sixties and Women's Liberation cohorts, but more feminist than women overall. There is some evidence for a postfeminist cohort here, but the level of decline in support was not precipitous. Furthermore, in 1984 these younger women were almost as supportive of feminist issue positions as women of the Sixties and Women's Liberation cohorts.

Although it is impossible to speak with certainty, there appear to have been both generational and period effects at work. Moreover, clear cohort differences persist over time, suggesting that generational effects are strong.

Whether the Complacent cohort will increase is not clear. A number of studies (Renzetti, 1987; Bayer, 1975; Komarovsky, 1985) have reported changing attitudes among this cohort as they are exposed to sex discrimination. Although sex discrimination was much more blatant in earlier eras, young women who grew up during a period of rapid role change and rising expectations for women are unlikely to be as tolerant of discrimination as those who grew up expecting it. It is difficult to be complacent in the face of discrimination.

NOTES

1. Susan Bolotin, "Views from the Post-Feminist Generation," *New York Times Magazine*, October 1982.

2. Mirra Komarovsky, *Women in College* (New York: Basic Books, 1985).

3. M. Jacobson, "You say Potato and I Say Potato: Attitudes toward Feminism as a Function of Its Subject-Selected Labels," *Sex Roles*, 7 (1981), pp. 349–354.

4. M. Jacobson and W. Koch, "Attributed Reasons for Support of the Feminist Movement as a Function of Attractiveness," *Sex Roles*, 4 (1978), pp. 169–174.

5. Betty Friedan, *The Second Stage* (New York: Summit Books, 1981).

6. Alan Bayer, "Sexist Students in American Colleges," *Journal of Marriage and the Family*, 37 (1975), pp. 391–397; Mirra Komarovsky, *Women in College*; C. Renzetti, "New Wave or Second Stage? Attitudes of College Women toward Feminism," *Sex Roles*, 16 (1987), pp. 265–277.

7. The data used in this article were made available by the Interuniversity Consortium for Political and Social Research. The data for the American National Election Studies were originally collected by the Center for Political Studies. Neither the collectors of the original data nor the Consortium bear any responsibility for the analyses or interpretations presented here.

8. C. Renzetti, "New Wave," pp. 265–277.

9. Ethel Klein, *Gender Politics* (Cambridge, MA: Harvard University Press, 1984).

10. Patricia Gurin, Arthur Miller, and Gerald Gurin, "Stratum Identification and Consciousness," *Social Psychology Quarterly*, 43 (1980), pp. 30–47.

11. Elizabeth Adell Cook, "Measuring Feminist Consciousness," *Women & Politics*, 9 (1989).

12. Support for the women's movement is based on the relative feeling thermometer for the women's liberation movement. This relative feeling thermometer is calculated as follows. First, a personal mean is calculated for each respondent across the twelve social groups common to the four surveys (blacks, conservatives, middle-class people, labor unions, poor people, whites, liberals, big business, black militants, civil rights leaders, and the military). This personal mean is subtracted from a respondent's rating of the women's liberation movement, and the remainder is divided by the personal mean [(score − mean)/mean]. The relative feeling thermometer thus represents percentage difference from the mean for the twelve groups. A score of 10 percent or more above their personal mean is defined here as support for the women's liberation movement.

13. Virginia Sapiro, "News from the Front: Intersex and Intergenerational Conflict Over the Status of Women," *Western Political Quarterly*, 33 (1980), p. 263.

14. This measures combines two questions that ask respondents to indicate their reaction (ranging from "strongly agree" to "strongly disagree") to two statements: "Men are just better cut out than women for important positions in society" and "Most men are better suited emotionally for politics than are most women."

FURTHER READING

BAYER, A. Sexist students in American colleges. *Journal of Marriage and the Family*, 37 (1975), pp. 391–397.

BOLOTIN, S. Views from the post-feminist generation. *New York Times Magazine*, October 1982.

CONOVER, P. The influence of group identifications on political perception and evaluation. *Journal of Politics*, 46 (1984), pp. 760–785.

CONOVER, P. Group identification and group sympathy: Their political implications. Paper presented at the annual meeting of the Midwest Political Science Association, April 1986.

COSTAIN, A. N. Representing women: The transition from social movement to interest group. *Western Political Quarterly*, 34 (1981), pp. 100–113.

FREEMAN, J. *The politics of women's liberation.* New York: David McKay, 1975

FRIEDAN, B. *The second stage* New York: Summit Books, 1981.

GURIN, P. Women's gender consciousness. *Public Opinion Quarterly*, 49 (1986), pp. 143–163.

GURIN, P. MILLER, A., and GURIN, G. Stratum identification and consciousness. *Social Psychology Quarterly*, 43 (1980), pp. 30–47.

JACOBSON, M. You say potato and I say potato: Attitudes toward feminism as a function of its subject-selected labels. *Sex Roles*, 7 (1981), pp. 349–354.

JENNINGS, K., and NIEMI, R. *Generations and politics* Princeton, NJ: Princeton University Press, 1981.

JENNINGS, K., and NIEMI, R. Continuity and change in political orientations: A longitudinal study of two generations. In E. Dreyer and W. Rosenbaum (Eds.), *Political opinion and behavior*, 3rd ed. North Scituate, Ma: Duxbury 1976.

KOMAROVSKY, M. *Women in college*. New York: Basic Books, 1985.

KLEIN, E. *Gender politics*. Cambridge, MA: Harvard University Press, 1984.

LAU, R. Reference group influence on political attitudes and behavior: The importance of the social, political, and psychological contexts." Paper presented at the annual meeting of the American Political Science Association, Chicago, September 1983.

MILLER, A., GURIN, P., and GURIN, G. Electoral implications of group identification and consciousness: The reintroduction of a concept. Paper presented at the annual meeting of the American Political Science Association, September 1978.

MILLER, A. H., HILDRETH, A. M., and SIMMONS, G. L. The political implications of gender group consciousness. Paper presented at the annual meeting of the Midwest Political Science Association, April 1986.

MILLER, A., SIMMONS, G. L., and HILDRETH, A. M. Group influences, solidarity, and electoral outcomes. Paper presented at the annual meeting of the American Political Science Association, September 1986.

RENZETTI, C. New wave or second stage? Attitudes of college women toward feminism. *Sex Roles*, 16 (1987), pp. 265–277.

SAPIRO, V. News from the front: Intersex and intergenerational conflict over the status of women. *Western Political Quarterly*, 33 (1980), pp. 260–277.

TAYLOR, V. The future of feminism in the 1980s. In L. Richardson and V. Taylor (Eds.), *Feminist frontiers*. Reading, MA: Addison-Wesley, 1983.

THORNTON, A., and FREEDMAN, D. Changes in sex role attitudes of women, 1962–1977. *American Sociological Review*, 44 (1979), pp. 831–842.

WILCOX, C. Popular support for the Moral Majority in 1980: A second look. *Social Science Quarterly*, 68 (1987), pp. 157–166.

WILCOX, C., SIGELMAN, L., and COOK, E. Some like it hot: Individual differences in responses to group feeling thermometers. *Public Opinion Quarterly*, 53 (1989), pp. 246–257.

Gender, Partisanship, and Background Explain Differences in Grass-Roots Party Activists' Political Attitudes

Anne E. Kelley

William E. Hulbary

Lewis Bowman

Several years ago Jeane Kirkpatrick pointed out that women had a long way to go to overcome various forms of domination in the political process of many societies. Describing the difficulties for women in political participation in the 1970s, she wrote:

> Few aspects of social life are more completely or universally male dominated than politics. . . . The advent of democracy and women's suffrage has given women a voice in important political decisions in some countries, but in the United States and elsewhere, universal suffrage has had limited impact on male dominance of power processes.[1]

Many current assessments are not so bleak. Why not? In recent years women have turned out to vote at rates equal to or greater than those for men. Although success has been slower than many expected, women increasingly have been seeking and winning public office.[2] And, once in office, women often have been more likely to give policy priorities to issues of particular concern to women.[3] Since 1980 women have begun separating themselves from men on a range of issues, on partisan attachment itself, and on support for candidates. During the 1980s many began referring to these gender differences as a "gender gap" in contemporary politics.[4] Irene Natividad, former head of the National Woman's Political Caucus, described this differentiation in terms of a gender gap "[which] is permanent, . . . keeps getting bigger, and . . . is going to change the national agenda in the future."[5]

Anne E. Kelley is an associate professor of government and international affairs at the University of South Florida; William E. Hulbary is an associate professor of government and international affairs at the University of South Florida; until recently, Lewis Bowman was a professor of government and international affairs at the University of South Florida; he is currently unaffiliated.

What can be said about this phenomenon among highly partisan political activists in a transitional party setting such as Florida? Women now constitute a majority of the electorate in Florida.[6] After 1935, legally, the political parties were required to fill precinct committee posts with equal numbers of men and women; this enabled women to participate at the same rate as men in grass-roots party activities. The questions we addressed included:

1. How do political ideology and issues differ by gender, partisanship, and social background among local party activists?
2. Is there a gender gap at the local grass-roots level among Florida's party precinct committeepersons?
3. Is there evidence that increased grass-roots party activism among women made any difference in the political attitudes they carried into the political process?
4. Would partisanship, state regional residence, or social background characteristics override the impact of gender on attitudes?
5. Would Florida's female party activists differ from male party activists *over all* in political attitudes?
6. Would female party activists differ in political attitudes from the male activists *within* each of Florida's two major political parties?[7]

HISTORICAL PERSPECTIVE

Histories of Florida barely mention the political activities of women in the early years.[8] Even after the struggle for suffrage granted by the Nineteenth Amendment (1920), for women in Florida and elsewhere in the United States, winning the privilege of voting did not lead to great changes in women's political behavior or their impact on politics.

Beginning in the 1930s, women's involvement was primarily at the local level, where a relatively large number of party posts and a few elective or appointive offices were available. But this did not lead to immediate success in winning public office. As Carver has reported, ". . . few women ran for office; fewer were elected."[9] Those elected to office tended to win elections through extraordinary force of personality or by the more usual widow's route.

In the 1960s and 1970s women's influence increased in Florida as demographic changes occurred. Women entered the state's work force, colleges, universities, and professions in record numbers. The dramatic influx of non-Southern residents in central and south Florida produced two cultures with differing views of the role of women. First, a traditional culture developed in the more rural, northern part of the state, with conservative views of women's roles. Second, a nontraditional culture developed in the more populous central and southern parts of the state, with liberal views of women's roles.[10]

During the same period, women's political participation patterns changed substantially. In the major counties, female voter registrants outnumbered men. More women were elected to public offices at the state and local levels. Many of these were born outside of Florida, were college graduates, and were active in party or community organizations.

Additional changes in party rules brought far greater representation of women, as well as blacks, youth, and other groups. The party organization had become a conduit for the advancement of women in politics.[11] More than is generally appreciated, political party organizations provided a point of entry for women who sought political activism. As recently noted,

> Women's efforts to organize, as well as the political parties' responsiveness to their demands for greater representation, aided women's efforts to play a greater role in politics. Involvement through various organized efforts played a key role in propelling women into party politics in Florida, as well as elsewhere.[12]

Although the success of women in politics has not been as great in the South as in other regions, party organizational activity has been a major contributor to the success of women in Southern politics.[13]

The nature of the party system, and indeed the game of politics itself, changed considerably during the same period. Accounts of electoral realignment and realignment politics often overlook the importance of party organizational changes.[14] In Florida, however, the growth of two-partyism has given party activists the opportunity to participate in a party more congruent with their political attitudes and ideologies. Over a period of time this produced substantial "party sorting" in which the grass-roots party activists switched parties to find a more comfortable ideological home.[15] This movement of activists from party to party produces greater ideological congruence within each party and wider ideological differences between the parties. If this is the case, then partisanship becomes more important in explaining ideological and issue differences, while gender and other variables become less important.

GENDER, PARTY, IDEOLOGY, AND ISSUES

Partisan differences in attitudes about political ideology and issues are sizable and well documented: Democrats tend to be more liberal, Republicans more conservative. Of course, the fit between ideology and partisanship is not perfect, but the correlation is strong and persistent. Party activism, in turn, amplifies the size of these ideological differences. The ideological split between Democrats and Republicans is larger among party activists than in the general electorate.[16]

The emergence of a gender gap in the 1980s also indicated increasing gender differences in political ideology and issue attitudes.[17] This gap was clear and persistent, but one should analyze and interpret it cautiously. The idea of a gender gap may overstate the differences between men and women. Gender differences on issues and ideology, though important, tended to be relatively small. When gender differences appeared, partisanship and party differences often were played down or ignored. When party differences were taken into account, as they usually are in studies of party activists, partisan differences were larger than gender differences. Furthermore, the gender gap that emerged in the 1980s included gender differences in candidate preference and party identification as well as issues and ideology. When party was held constant, men and women within the same party (whether party activists or rank-and-file voters) tended to be more similar in attitudes toward issues and ideology. Costantini and Bell found a slight and sometimes inconsistent pattern of ideological divergence associated with gender.[18] Studying California party activists, they found substantial interparty ideological differences regardless of gender. Partisan ideological differences, however, were generally greater among women than among men. Within each party women were less moderate than men—that is, more liberal among Democrats and more conservative among Republicans.

IDEOLOGY AND ISSUES AMONG FLORIDA'S PARTY ACTIVISTS

What were the attitudes of Florida's precinct party activists toward political ideology and issues? How did these attitudes differ by gender, party, or other relevant characteristics?

Political and Social Issues

We asked Florida's party activists to indicate their position on a wide range of issues concerning social welfare programs, social issues, domestic fiscal policy, government intervention, and foreign policy. A review of the issues appears in Table 1 and reveals a number of interesting results. As anticipated, large differences between the parties were evident on virtually every issue. Regardless of gender, Democrats were consistently more liberal than Republicans, usually by a margin of 20 to 30 percentage points. Moreover, the differences between Democratic and Republican women were at least as large as those between Democratic and Republican men.

Apart from these large interparty differences, there were some gender differences within each party. Though smaller than the interparty differences, these gender differences revealed some interesting and consistent patterns. First, consider the gender differences on social issues that are of direct and immediate relevance to women, such as affirmative action, a proposed antiabortion amendment and the Equal Rights Amendment. In both parties, women were consistently more liberal than men on these issues by about 7 or 8 percentage points.

Among the Democrats this difference was not limited to social issues but was evident on nearly every issue. Female Democrats also were more liberal than their male counterparts on social welfare policy, domestic budget issues, foreign policy, and government intervention. On issues such as "rapid development of nuclear power," an "increase in defense spending," and reducing "Florida's budget," gender differences were more than 10 percentage points. On other issues the gender gap was smaller, but it was nearly always in a liberal direction

Table 1 Liberal Attitudes on Political Issues by Party and Gender[a]

ISSUE ITEMS	DEMOCRATS		REPUBLICANS	
	Men	Women	Men	Women
Social welfare				
Cuts in domestic spending	57	64	16	15
Support national health insurance	72	82	27	33
Government aid to remedy unemployment	71	67	16	15
Government guaranteeing jobs	66	69	25	21
Federal aid to education	52	52	15	20
Government aid for low-cost health care	86	89	54	45
Social issues				
Affirmative action	79	86	39	53
Antiabortion amendment	65	73	50	58
Equal Rights Amendment	75	83	28	31
Domestic budget				
Amendment to balance national budget	35	38	14	15
Amendment to roll back Florida's budget	70	82	31	35
Foreign policy				
Increase in defense spending	62	76	20	21
Military intervention in Lebanon	87	85	71	58
Government intervention				
Rapid development of nuclear power	48	74	16	34
Leave electric power to private sector	56	57	21	22

Note:

[a] Table entries indicate the percentage of respondents giving a liberal response ("strongly favor," "favor," "oppose," or "strongly oppose") on each item. Whether "favor" or "oppose" responses were liberal responses depended on the wording of the item.

(women more liberal than men).[19] Thus, across a wide range of issues, female party activists were consistently more liberal than men in the Democratic party.

Among Republicans, no consistent ideological differences between men and women appeared other than those on social issues. On nearly all other issues, gender differences among Republicans were small and not consistently liberal or conservative. On the one or two issues where relatively large gender differences occurred, the differences were ideologically inconsistent.[20]

Political Ideology

To generalize our results beyond specific issues and to focus more broadly on political ideology, we constructed a single overall political issue scale. An overview of the results obtained with this issue scale appear in Table 2. The scale combined the fifteen issue items listed in Table 1 and yielded a single measure of "issue" ideology that allowed us to classify party activists as very liberal, liberal, moderate, conservative, or very conservative.[21]

Variation by party and gender on the political issue scale indicates the

Table 2 Political Ideology by Party and Gender [a]

POLITICAL IDEOLOGY– POLITICAL ISSUE SCALE [b]	DEMOCRATS		REPUBLICANS	
	Men	Women	Men	Women
Very liberal	20	31	1	—
Liberal	38	41	5	10
Moderate	30	21	32	26
Conservative	9	6	42	42
Very conservative	3	1	21	22
(N)	(168)	(150)	(155)	(125)

Note:

[a] Table entries are percentages of column totals entered in parentheses beneath each column.

[b] Political ideology is measured by political issue scale scores, which were computed by averaging each respondent's score on the fifteen issue items. On each item and on the overall scale, a score of "1" was the most liberal score and a score of "4" was the most conservative. Scale scores were then collapsed so that 1–1.79 were classed as "very liberal"; 1.80–2.25 were "liberal"; 2.26–2.74 were "moderate"; 2.75–3.20 were "conservative"; and 3.21–4.00 were "very conservative."

extent of interparty differences in ideology. Regardless of gender, Republicans were substantially more conservative than Democrats. Among Republicans, gender differences were negligible, with Republican women tending to be a little more liberal than men. Among Democrats, gender differences were larger but in the same direction, with women tending to be more liberal than men.

SELECTED CHARACTERISTICS AND IDEOLOGY

What helps account for these variations in men and women's political ideology? We expected the state's politicocultural regions as well as selected social characteristics of the party activists to provide considerable insight into these differences.

Regional Variations in Ideology

We examined regional differences in ideology in relation to party and gender. As shown in Table 3, in every region of the state Democrats were distinctly more liberal than the Republicans. North Florida party activists tended to be more conservative than those in central/southwest Florida, who in turn were slightly more conservative than those in southeast Florida. This was especially true among Republicans. In central/southwest Florida, however, the Democratic men were somewhat more conservative than expected and the Democratic women were somewhat more liberal than expected.

Among Republicans there were only minor gender differences in each of the three regions. Gender differences were small among north Florida Democrats as well. Only among central/southwest and southeast Florida Democrats were gender differences in political ideology fairly large. In these two regional

Table 3 Political Ideology and Gender by Party and Selected Social Background Variables [a]

SOCIAL BACKGROUND VARIABLES		POLITICAL IDEOLOGY	DEMOCRATS		REPUBLICANS	
			Men	Women	Men	Women
Region of Florida [b]	North	Liberal	58	60	—	8
		Moderate	29	26	16	12
		Conservative	14	15	84	80
	Central/ Southwest	Liberal	54	77	5	7
		Moderate	30	18	34	32
		Conservative	17	5	61	62
	Southeast	Liberal	64	79	10	19
		Moderate	33	19	40	26
		Conservative	2	2	50	56
Occupation [c]	Higher status	Liberal	55	79	5	11
		Moderate	34	15	35	25
		Conservative	11	6	60	64
	Lower status	Liberal	42	59	3	8
		Moderate	47	38	23	28
		Conservative	11	3	73	64
	Retired	Liberal	67	85	5	13
		Moderate	16	10	32	33
		Conservative	16	5	63	54
	Other (not in labor force)	Liberal	[d]	62	[d]	5
		Moderate	[d]	24	[d]	27
		Conservative	[d]	14	[d]	68
Education	Less than college	Liberal	57	69	5	10
		Moderate	33	24	35	30
		Conservative	10	6	60	61
	Four-year college degree	Liberal	52	71	4	9
		Moderate	31	21	23	23
		Conservative	17	8	72	69
	Advanced degree	Liberal	63	77	6	12
		Moderate	26	15	35	18
		Conservative	11	8	58	71
Family income	Less than $30,000	Liberal	66	81	7	13
		Moderate	27	15	33	28
		Conservative	7	4	60	58
	$30,000– $39,999	Liberal	64	61	3	13
		Moderate	19	27	37	20
		Conservative	17	12	60	67
	$40,000 or more	Liberal	36	62	6	—
		Moderate	49	27	20	26
		Conservative	15	11	74	74

(continued)

SOCIAL BACKGROUND VARIABLES		POLITICAL IDEOLOGY	DEMOCRATS		REPUBLICANS	
			Men	Women	Men	Women
Age (years)	Less than 40	Liberal	61	74	12	5
		Moderate	27	26	29	27
		Conservative	12	—	59	68
	40–54	Liberal	41	67	—	3
		Moderate	44	20	34	25
		Conservative	15	13	66	72
	55 or more	Liberal	65	77	5	12
		Moderate	25	18	31	29
		Conservative	10	5	64	59

Notes:

[a] Table entries are percentages of party/gender/social background subgroups that were liberal, moderate, or conservative. Political ideology is measured by the political issue scale. "Very liberal" and "liberal" are collapsed into the "liberal" category, and "very conservative" and "conservative" are collapsed into the "conservative" category.

[b] North Florida includes counties from Ocala, Florida, north. Southeast Florida includes the counties along the Atlantic coast south of Vero Beach and around to Key West. The rest of Florida's counties are included in the central/southwest category. See Suzanne L. Parker, "Are Party Loyalties Changing in Florida?" *Florida Public Opinion*, 1 (Winter 1985), pp. 16–20.

[c] Higher status jobs include professional/technical and managerial or administrative jobs. Lower status jobs include blue-collar, clerical, and sales jobs. "Other (not in the labor force)" consists primarily of homemakers but also includes some volunteer workers, students, and so forth.

[d] Too few cases for meaningful analysis.

areas female Democrats were more liberal than Democratic men by about 15 to 20 percentage points. The female Democrats of central/southwest and southeast Florida were the most liberal of all the groups defined by region, gender, and party.

Our data indicate that in each region, party and gender differences in political ideology were apparent in varying degrees. Additionally, our findings suggest that north Florida possesses a more traditional southern culture, which encourages political conservatism among both male and female partisans.[22] The more nontraditional culture in southern Florida, on the other hand, seems more conducive to greater liberalism among party activists there.

Social Background and Ideology

Apart from region, other social background factors also might help account for the observed gender and party differences in political ideology. To examine these possibilities we analyzed the association between political ideology and each of four social background variables. As indicated in Table 3, we began with (1) occupational status, followed by (2) education, (3) family income, and (4) age.

Occupational Status. Political ideology varied little by occupational status among Republicans. Among Republicans, men in lower status jobs and women in the "other" category (primarily homemakers) were slightly more conservative, while retired women were slightly less conservative. By contrast, among Democratic activists, women were consistently more liberal than men regardless of occupational status. The gender difference among Democrats was especially large in the higher status occupational group. High-status female Democrats and retired female Democrats were the most liberal groupings defined by party, gender, and occupation. In comparison, lower status men were the least liberal Democrats, although they were still more liberal than the Republicans by a large margin.

Educational Level. Gender-related educational differences were fairly small among Republicans. Republican women with advanced college degrees tended to be more conservative than male Republicans with advanced degrees. At lower levels of education male and female Republicans were quite similar in ideology. Those Republicans with less than a college education were less conservative than those with higher educational levels.

Among Democratic activists, women were consistently more liberal at all educational levels. The gap in ideology was greater at higher educational levels (four-year college degree or higher). Thus, the most educated Democratic women were more liberal than any other group, and the most educated Republican women were among the most conservative.

Family Income Level. In surveys of the mass public since the 1930s, family income and affluence were generally related to political ideology in a consistent, straightforward manner; the more affluent tended to be more conservative and the less affluent, more liberal. Often the correlation was not strong, but the direction of the relationship was fairly consistent. The data on family income among Florida party activists were consistent with this general trend. Furthermore, with only two exceptions, gender differences in ideology were fairly small at all income levels in both parties. The two exceptions are lower income Democrats (less than $30,000) and higher income Democrats ($40,000 or more). In these two groups, women were more liberal than men by a fairly large margin. Lower income Democratic women were distinctively more liberal than others in the Democratic party, and higher income Democratic men were distinctively less liberal.

Age. In Table 3 those who are "less than 40" were born after World War II. During their youth they experienced a period of rapid expansion in federal social programs and in civil rights and equal rights for women, a period when the traditional views of men's and women's roles were being redefined. Thus, we expected younger activists, especially younger female activists, to show more support for the liberalism of the period in which they reached maturity. However, our data about age and political ideology did not entirely support this thesis.

There was no linear decline in liberalism with increasing age. In each party, men and women less than 40 years old were among the most liberal, but they were slightly less liberal than those 55 or older. Those in the middle age category (40–54) were the least liberal age group, especially in the Democratic party. Among Republicans, women were actually slightly more conservative than men in the two youngest age groups (less than 55) and only slightly more liberal than men in the oldest age group. In contrast, Democratic women were consistently more liberal than men regardless of age, and the gender difference was greater among Democrats than Republicans at all age levels.

SUMMARY

We have addressed these questions:

1. How are gender and party associated with the distribution of political attitudes and ideologies among Florida's grass-roots political party activists? Is there a "gender gap?"
2. Are other social background variables like occupation, education, family income, and age associated with party and gender differences?

Our data show that partisanship explains a large portion of the variation in political ideology among Florida's party activists. Overriding all other considerations, the Democrats tended to be liberal and the Republicans tended to be conservative. Party realignment within party organizations is in progress because of these ideological differences, *and* the realignment process is reinforcing these differences in a complicated "party sorting" process.[23]

Gender provides considerable explanation for political liberalism in the Democratic party organization, but somewhat less explanation for political conservatism among Republican organizational activists. On virtually all issues Democratic women were as liberal as or more liberal than Democratic men. On social issues directly relevant to women (the ERA, abortion, and affirmative action), female party activists in each party were consistently more liberal than men. On other issues, however, the Republican men and women had similar views. Republican women reinforced the party's conservative stance in a number of issue areas.

State regional variations were related to political issues and ideological differences among the Democratic and Republican activist women. In each party, female political activists in north Florida were more conservative than their counterparts in south Florida. Male activists in each party exhibited similar regional differences. The political conservatism of north Florida did not diminish party and gender differences. Instead, it magnified the conservative orientation of men and women in both parties.

Occupational status, education, and family income also helped explain ideological and issue differences among Florida's party activists. Democratic women of higher occupational status, higher educational attainment, and lower income were more liberal than expected. In contrast, more educated and affluent Republican women tended to have more conservative views.

The gender differences in political attitudes seem to be a catalyst which is pushing the Democratic party organization in liberal directions. At the grassroots party activist level in Florida, as well as at other levels, the Democratic party and women have had a symbiotic relationship in which the party was attractive to women because it supported their political views. This is especially true for affluent, better educated women with higher status jobs. In turn, these Democratic women supported the organization. In this process the Democratic women helped push the Democratic party further along the road to liberalism. The Republican party got reinforcement in conservative directions from a selected stratum of its female party activists; but generally, among the grass-roots *Republican* activists, gender seemed to be less independently associated with political ideology.

NOTES

1. Jeane J. Kirkpatrick, *The Presidential Elite* (New York: Russell Sage Foundation, 1976), p. 397.

2. For a summary of the current situation, and data illustrating change in women in elective office in the United States from 1975 through 1989, see "Women in Elective Office 1989," a fact sheet of the Center for the American Woman and Politics, Eagleton Institute of Politics, Rutgers University, December 1989.

3. See the assessments of a 1988 national survey of female and male state representatives and senators about their policy priorities in Susan J. Carroll and Ella Taylor, "Gender Differences in Policy Priorities," *CAWP News & Notes*, 7 (Winter 1989), pp. 3–4.

4. Kathleen A. Frankovic, "Sex and Politics—New Alignments, Old Issues," *P.S.*, 15 (Summer 1982), pp. 439–448.

5. Cited in Paul Taylor, "The GOP Has a Woman Problem—George Bush's Gender Gap Is Showing Throughout the Party," *Washington Post National Weekly Edition*, July 4–10, 1988, p. 9.

6. Anne H. Shoemyen, ed., *1987 Florida Statistical Abstract* (Gainesville: University Presses of Florida, 1987).

7. The data utilized in our analysis of Florida party activists are derived from a mail survey of a random sample of Florida Democratic and Republican precinct committeepersons. The survey was conducted during 1984. The Democrats' response rate was 52 percent (321 usable questionnaires); for the Republicans the rate was 57 percent (291 usable questionnaires). Among the Democrats responding, 48 percent were women; among the Republicans, 45 percent were women.

8. This section utilizes material from Joan S. Carver, "Women," in Manning J. Dauer (Ed.), *Florida's Politics and Government*, 2nd ed. (Gainesville: University Presses of Florida, 1984), pp. 294–308.

9. Carver, "Women," in *Florida's Politics and Government*, p. 296. See also Albert K. Karnig and B. Oliver Walter, "Election of Women to City Councils," *Social Science Quarterly*, 56 (March 1976), pp. 605–613.

10. This follows Carver's interpretation; see her chapter, "Women," in *Florida's Politics and Government*, p. 299.

11. For example, from 1968 to 1984 the proportion of women among the delegates and alternates to the Democratic presidential nominating convention jumped from 13 percent to 50 percent; among the Republicans it jumped from 16 percent to 44 percent. See Frank J. Sorauf and Paul Allen Beck, *Party Politics in America*, 6th ed. (Glenview, IL: Scott, Foresman, 1988), Table 12.1.

12. See Nancy McGlen and Karen O'Conner, *Women's Rights: The Struggle for Equality in the Nineteenth and Twentieth Centuries* (New York: Praeger, 1983), pp. 105–106.

13. R. Darcy, Susan Welch, and Janet Clark, *Women, Elections, and Representation* (New York: Longman, 1987).

14. See the discussion of this omission in James L. Gibson, "The Role of Party Organizations in the

Mountain West: 1960–1980," in Peter F. Galderisi, Michael S. Lyons, Randy T. Simmons, and John G. Francis (Eds.), *The Politics of Realignment: Party Change in the Mountain West* (Boulder, CO: Westview Press, 1987), pp. 197–219.

15. Among the 1984 party precinct committeepersons in Florida 33 percent of the Republicans and 13 percent of the Democrats reported previous affiliation in the opposition party. See Lewis Bowman, William E. Hulbary, and Anne E. Kelley, "Party Sorting at the Grassroots: Stable Partisans and Party Changers among Florida's Precinct Officials," in Robert P. Steed, Laurence W. Moreland, and Tod A. Baker (Eds.), *The Disappearing South?* (Tuscaloosa: University of Alabama Press, 1990), p. 56.

16. John S. Jackson III, Barbara L. Brown, and David Bositis, "Herbert McClosky and Friends Revisited: 1980 Democratic and Republican Party Elites Compared to the Mass Public," *American Politics Quarterly*, 10 (1982), pp. 158–180; Warren E. Miller and M. Kent Jennings, *Parties in Transition* (New York: Russell Sage Foundation, 1986), pp. 189–219.

17. Frankovic, "Sex and Politics," pp. 439–448; Robert S. Erikson, Norman R. Luttbeg, and Kent L. Tedin, *American Public Opinion*, 3rd ed. (New York: Macmillan, 1988), pp. 199–203.

18. Edmond Costantini and Julie Davis Bell, "Women in Political Parties: Gender Differences in Motives among California Party Activists," in Janet A. Flammang (Ed.), *Political Women* (Beverly Hills, CA: Sage Publications, 1984), pp. 129–130.

19. The only exceptions were on "military intervention in Lebanon" and "government aid to remedy unemployment"; on these issues women were slightly less liberal than men, but the gender difference was quite small.

20. Relatively large differences occurred on only two issues—"rapid development of nuclear power," where Republican women were more liberal than Republican men, and "military intervention in Lebanon," where Republican women were more conservative.

21. Factor analysis indicates that the fifteen issue items constitute a single dimension of liberalism–conservatism. One factor accounts for more than 50 percent of the variance in the issue items. A separate measure of self-identified political ideology—a question that asked respondents how they perceived themselves in terms of the five ideological categories on the political issue scale—correlated very strongly with the political issue scale (Pearson's $R = .73$). This provides further evidence of the conceptual validity of the political issue scale. It indicates that the political issue scale scores correspond closely to the respondents' own perceptions of their political ideology.

22. Joan S. Carver, "Women in Florida," *Journal of Politics*, 41 (August 1979), pp. 941–955.

23. See Bowman, Hulbary, and Kelley, "Party Sorting at the Grassroots," pp. 56–70.

More than Pink and Blue:
Gender, Occupational Stratification,
and Political Attitudes

Gertrude A. Steuernagel

Thomas A. Yantek

There have been revolutionary changes in the lives of twentieth-century American women. Foremost among these changes are those related to women's employment outside the home. This is not to imply, of course, that prior to the 1900s women were not involved in paid employment. African-American women in particular have a history of combining family and work responsibilities. What is unprecedented about the current employment situation of American women, however, are the numbers of married women and women with preschool-aged children who are employed as wage earners in a part-time or full-time capacity. A few statistics are useful in understanding the depth and scope of this major social restructuring. In 1880 women constituted 14 percent of this nation's work force. One hundred years later this figure had increased to 42 percent.[1] During the same period, 1880 through 1980, the percentage of all women who were employed outside the home increased from 16 percent to 51 percent.[2] Equally dramatic changes occurred in the demographic profile of working women. In 1880, by far the largest segment of working women were single. Today, a majority of married women are numbered in the ranks of working women; and women with children are a significant part of the labor force.[3] As of 1986, over 50 percent of women with children age 3 and under were in the labor force.[4]

WOMEN AND OCCUPATIONAL SEGREGATION

An emphasis on these changes, however, obscures an important reality concerning American women's working lives. There is a significant characteristic of

Gertrude A. Steuernagel is an associate professor of political science and Thomas A. Yantek is an associate professor of political science at Kent State University.

women's employment that has not radically changed in recent times and is not likely to be altered in the near future. Most American women work in so-called pink-collar ghettos. An employed American woman today is more likely than not to find herself in an occupationally segregated profession. She will work with other women in jobs traditionally held by women—jobs that reflect what society sees as appropriate to women's roles as wives, mothers, and caregivers and that reflect women's supposed strengths as nurturers and helpmates. Women today, for example, account for 99 percent of all dental assistants, 97.4 percent of all child care workers, 91.1 percent of all data entry keyers, 85.2 percent of all elementary school teachers, 85.9 percent of all librarians, and 94.3 percent of all registered nurses.[5] In contrast, women account for only 4.4 percent of all dentists, 1.4 percent of all carpenters, 34 percent of all computer programmers, 36 percent of all college and university professors, 18.1 percent of all lawyers and judges, and 17.6 percent of all physicians.[6] Women, despite their race or ethnic group, are concentrated in low-paying and low-status jobs. Although the work force today is not as occupationally segregated as it was in the 1960s or the 1970s, occupational segregation by gender is greater even than occupational segregation by race.[7] Certain factors, such as changing attitudes concerning appropriate sex roles and legislation that has outlawed sex discrimination, have led to a small decline in the degree of occupational segregation by gender; but there is substantial reason to believe that it will continue to affect the lives of working women well into the next century.[8]

Some of the consequences for women of occupational segregation have been better documented than others. There is clear evidence that occupational segregation is involved in the wage gap. That is to say, it is one of the factors, possibly the most important, in explaining why women on the whole earn less than men.[9] The median annual income for all men age 15 and over who work year round in a full-time capacity is $25,894. The income for comparable women is $16,843.[10] Women aged 25 years and over constitute 30.5 percent of workers with earnings at or below the minimum wage. The comparable group of men make up 10.2 percent of such workers.[11]

In contrast, more information is needed on the impact of occupational segregation on women's conditions in the workplace. The area of workplace health hazards is a case in point. The risks to women in traditionally female occupations, for example, are less obvious than the risks to men in fields such as construction and welding.[12]

In particular, it is important to explore the effect of occupational segregation on women's political attitudes. Although there has been considerable research into the effect of work force involvement on women's political behavior, little has been done on the specific effects of occupational segregation. If we want to understand the political behavior of U.S. women, we need to understand the circumstances of their lives. Because there is considerable evidence that women's employment and their political behavior are related, we need to examine the relationship between the specific circumstances of that employment and their politics. Some research, for example, indicates that housewives and women employed in low-status, low-paying occupations (such as hairdresser and waitress) tend to show less support for feminism than do women in higher status, higher paying jobs such as teacher and accountant.[13] We have found evidence to suggest otherwise, at least in certain instances. This study, therefore, will address questions about the effects of occupational segregation on women's political attitudes, with special attention to the intersection of occupational segregation, class, and gender as they affect the political attitudes of women and men.

FINDINGS

Fortunately, there are available data that permit us to undertake a preliminary examination of the effects of occupational segregation on political attitudes. We utilize data from the 1984 University of Michigan National Election Study as well as statistics on occupational segregation and integration from the U.S. Bureau of the Census. To give just one example of the selection process, consider the case of identifying women in female-dominated occupations at the managerial/ professional (white-collar) level. Census Bureau tables reveal that the two professional occupations with the heaviest concentrations of women are registered nurse (95.8 percent) and librarian (87.3 percent). In the National Election Study (NES) a total of twenty-four respondents (all women, as it turns out) listed those occupations. Thus, those twenty-four women make up our subsample for examining the attitudes of professional women in female-segregated occupations. A similar pattern of identification was used for selecting the other subsamples.*

Table 1 presents responses to a question concerning fundamental attitudes about women's rights: the extent to which equal rights are seen as having been pushed too far. The very clear picture from Table 1 is that there are no real differences between male and female attitudes toward women's rights issues. Both men and women seem to be evenly split insofar as the overall thrust of the women's rights movement is concerned.

Such a broad generalization, however, may well be hiding attitudes that are actually affected by socioeconomic status and/or occupational segregation. To allow for such a possibility, Figure 1 examines the same question concerning women's rights, but now utilizing some of the subsamples discussed earlier.

Concentrating initially on the responses from the white-collar (professional-managerial) occupations, it can now be seen that there are indeed some noteworthy differences among groups. Men in traditionally male occupations (MALESEG) are the least supportive of the push for women's rights. Somewhat surprisingly, however, men in integrated jobs (MALEINT) are more supportive of the push for women's rights than either of the women's subgroups.

The picture becomes even more interesting when the blue-collar (work-

---

*In the case of several categories it was necessary to go beyond merely the two most segregated occupations in order to allow for an adequate subsample size.

Table 1   Support for Women's Rights

We have gone too far in pushing equal rights in this country.

	MALE	FEMALE
Agree	46%	44%
Neutral	12	12
Disagree	42	44

ing-class) respondents are considered. Here the two integrated-occupation categories are most strongly opposed to the equal rights movements (more so than any of the professional-level categories). Among working-class respondents the high degrees of opposition among both men and women in integrated jobs may be related to the competition for a declining number of industrial-sector jobs in the face of affirmative action initiatives. Men in these integrated occupations are likely to be the most threatened by such programs, and hence to oppose them. For their part, women who have already obtained such jobs themselves (FEM-INT) would be the most likely to feel the backlash from the disgruntled males just discussed. Having themselves already achieved the economic security they had been seeking, such women might very well turn "conservative" and oppose further pushes for equal rights, as a way of alleviating the pressures heaped upon them by their threatened male colleagues.

Figure 1-a   Support for Women's Rights (White-Collar Respondents)

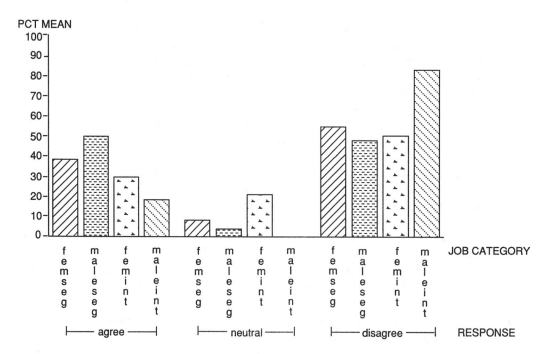

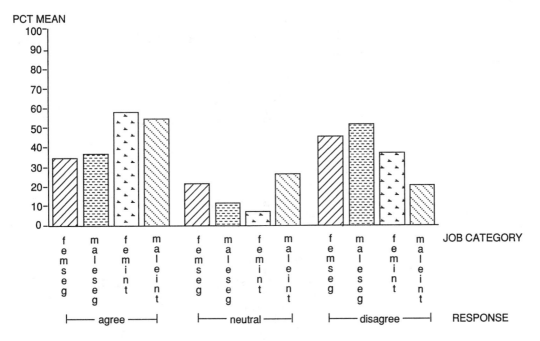

Figure 1-b Support for Women's Rights (Blue-Collar Respondents)

We might very well expect attitudes about equal rights from those in professional occupations, on the other hand, to be very different from the views expressed by the working classes, and in fact that proves to be the case. Among white-collar workers, the feminist-leaning attitudes of males in integrated occupations stand in marked contrast to the conservative views of men who work in male-segregated occupations.

One way of gaining some insight into those kinds of differences is to look at some basic demographic characteristics of the subsamples used. Table 2 paints an informative picture of our different groups of respondents. Let us concentrate first on the white-collar respondents (in the left half of the table). As one might expect, on the basis of their professed attitudes, men in traditionally male (segregated) jobs tend to be older, wealthier, more Republican, and more conservative than men in integrated professions. Even more interesting is the self-professed level of political interest for the two groups. Men in segregated occupations tend to be only somewhat interested in things political, whereas those men who work at integrated jobs are by and large very interested in politics. The most important distinction between the two groups, however, may well be their educational achievements. One-third of the segregated males are not even college graduates, and another quarter possess only the bachelor's degree. Among integrated males, on the other hand, roughly half are college graduates, and an equal proportion have gone to graduate school. Interestingly, almost identical patterns of educational attainment distinguish segregated and inte-

Table 2 A Demographic Portrait of the Occupation Subsamples

	WHITE-COLLAR				BLUE-COLLAR			
	Females in Segregated Occupation	Males in Segregated Occupation	Females in Integrated Occupation	Males in Integrated Occupation	Females in Segregated Occupation	Males in Segregated Occupation	Females in Integrated Occupation	Males in Integrated Occupation
Ideology								
Liberal 1	14%	7%	8%	18%	5%	16%	5%	3%
2	14	7	8	9	15	5	16	14
3	5	14	17	36	40	5	11	31
4	10	—	—	—	—	—	—	—
5	24	38	33	27	10	26	42	10
6	19	21	25	—	15	26	21	21
Conservative 7	14	14	8	9	15	21	5	21
Party Identification								
Strong Democrat 0	8	6	7	9	14	12	8	17
1	33	9	36	36	28	15	24	30
2	13	9	14	46	14	8	20	13
3	—	9	—	9	10	23	28	10
4	8	16	—	—	14	8	8	13
5	25	34	29	—	10	23	12	7
Strong Republican 6	13	16	14	—	10	12	—	10
Interest in Politics								
Very much	46	38	36	64	21	30	19	27
Somewhat	46	55	64	36	50	44	31	43
Not much	9	7	—	—	29	26	50	30

84

Education								
Not high school graduate	—	—	—	—	31	37	36	36
High school graduate	4	—	—	—	31	48	58	48
Graduate								
Some college	29	34	—	9	31	11	7	13
College grad	50	25	14	46	7	4	—	3
Graduate work	17	41	86	46	—	—	—	—
Age								
Under 30	29	16	7	18	38	30	32	36
30–39	46	45	50	46	17	29	26	25
40–49	25	23	22	9	28	26	29	26
50–59	—	24	21	27	14	11	10	13
60 & over	—	3	—	—	4	4	3	—
Income								
Average category	$15,000–17,000	$30,000–35,000	$15,000–17,000	$17,000–20,000	$5,000–7,000	$14,000–15,000	$10,000–11,000	$15,000–17,000
Range	$7,000–Over $5,000	Under $3,000–Over $75,000	$7,000–30,000	$12,000–35,000	Under $3,000–30,000	Under $3,000–40,000	Under $3,000–20,000	Under $3,000–40,000
Modal self-assigned social class	Average middle	Average middle	Average middle	Average middle	Average working	Average working	Average working	Average working

grated women in professional-level occupations. Although it is always difficult to prove causal relationships, there does seem to be a strong indication here that increased educational attainment and political awareness bring with them a greater tolerance for equal rights.

That conclusion is given further support when we consider the demographic breakdown of the working-class subsamples. Contrasts with their professional counterparts are most obvious in terms of income and perceived social class, as would be expected. More important for this study, though, is that the blue-collar subsamples exhibit considerably less political interest and decidedly lower levels of education, on average, than do the white-collar workers. These characteristics are particularly pronounced within the two "integrated" groups—which also happen to be the groups most opposed to the equal rights movement.

The conclusions that we justifiably can draw now emerge in much sharper detail. Studies of political attitudes and behaviors that look only for simple differences based on the sex of the respondent can be misleading. A better way of studying such questions is to allow for the effects of such important factors as childhood and adult socialization agents, such as family, education, and work. To examine further the effects of those kinds of influences, we now turn our attentions to some other issues that have exhibited a "gender gap."

Support for Social Spending

Moving beyond the question of an abstract level of support for women's rights, we want to look now at the extent of support for government spending on programs that are tied closely to the needs of women as an economic class. Table 3 presents the simple breakdown, by sex, of public opinion concerning funding levels for both Social Security and Medicare.

The two questions provoke nearly identical patterns of responses, with attitudes clearly affected by the sex of the respondent. Quite obviously, women

Table 3   Support for Social Spending

Should federal spending on Social Security be increased, decreased, or kept about the same?		
	MALE	*FEMALE*
Increased	45%	58%
Kept the same	50	40
Decreased	5	3

Should federal spending on Medicare be increased, decreased, or kept about the same?		
	MALE	*FEMALE*
Increased	43%	55%
Kept the same	51	41
Decreased	6	4

are far more supportive of increasing the levels of spending for such programs than are men.

As Figures 2 and 3 demonstrate, however, there is more to the attitudes represented in Table 3 than simple male versus female self-interest. In fact, upon this reexamination of the questions, the sex of the respondent, in and of itself, seems to have little to do with it. Rather, attitudes appear to be determined more by social class than by sex. In general, those in blue-collar occupations are more supportive of the so-called "middle-class entitlements" than are their professional-managerial counterparts (who probably receive similar kinds of benefits through their employment).

Beyond that general pattern it also can be seen that women in traditionally female-segregated jobs are by far the most supportive group—a phenomenon no doubt closely related to their ranking at the very bottom among all groups in terms of average income (see Table 2).

Perceptions of National Progress

A final set of political attitudes we wish to examine are those measuring perceptions of progress made by the United States in the economic and foreign relations spheres. Table 4 displays those views, while controlling for the effects of the sex of the respondent.

Quite clearly, men were more sympathetic to the Reagan-sponsored

Figure 2-a   Support for Social Security (White-Collar Respondents)

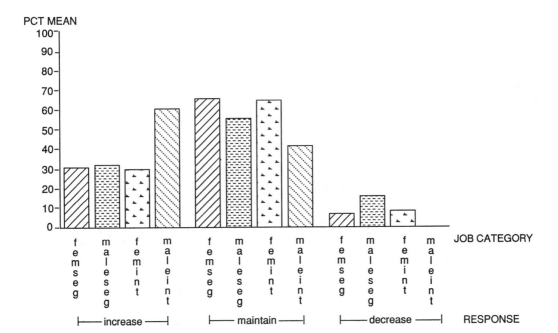

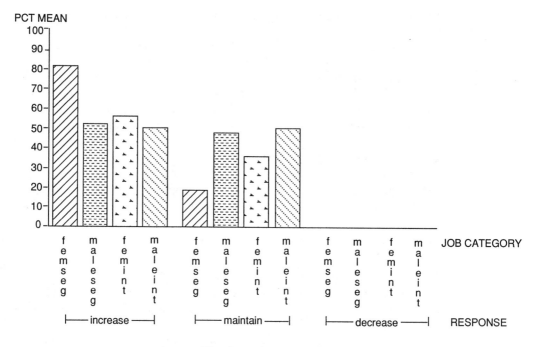

Figure 2-b   Support for Social Security (Blue-Collar Respondents)

Figure 3-a   Support for Medicare (White-Collar Respondents)

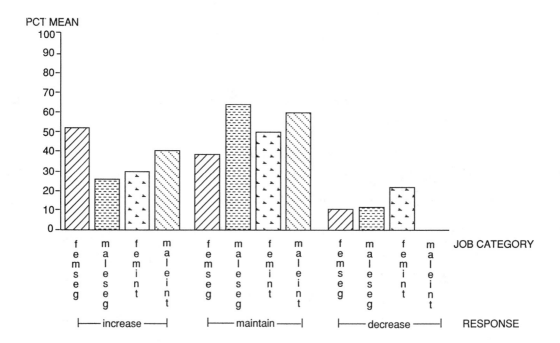

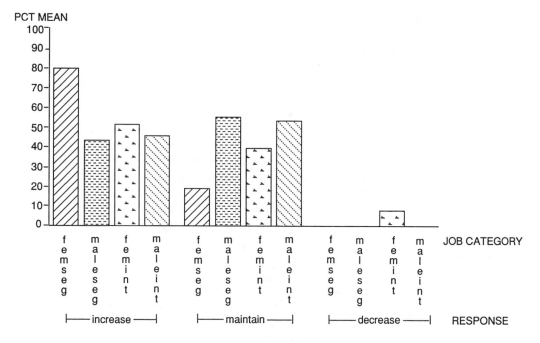

PCT MEAN

Figure 3-b Support for Medicare (Blue-Collar Respondents)

Table 4 Perceptions of National Progress

Would you say that over the past year the nation's
economy has gotten better, stayed the same, or gotten worse?

	MALE	FEMALE
Gotten better	51%	36%
Stayed the same	29	37
Gotten worse	20	27

During the past year, would you say that the
United States' position in the world has grown
weaker, stayed about the same, or gotten stronger?

	MALE	FEMALE
Gotten stronger	40%	28%
Stayed the same	35	43
Grown weaker	26	29

notion that the United States under his guidance was both better off economically and more influential internationally. A majority of all men sensed real economic progress under Reagan, and a plurality sensed the same kind of progress in the foreign policy arena. In contrast, pluralities of women on both questions were less "bullish on America," apparently feeling that if the United States had not necessarily gone backwards, neither had the country advanced. One might suspect immediately, however, that such opinions—particularly the economic question—would be influenced by factors such as occupation and social class. In Figures 4 and 5, then, we present the opinion on those same questions, but this time controlling for the effects of social class and occupational stratification.

Looking first at the question of economic progress, we see (not unexpectedly) that most of those in white-collar jobs exhibit satisfaction that real progress has been made. Only integrated males (recall their liberal, Democratic leanings) were not of that opinion, in general. On the other hand, among blue-collar respondents only men in traditionally male occupations expressed overall satisfaction with the direction of the economy. The strongly conservative, Republican leanings of this group (see Table 2) no doubt contribute mightily to this group's perception of economic progress under a conservative, Republican president.

Turning to the question of the United States' position in the global order, an interesting pattern of responses reveals itself. Each of the four categories of male respondents—both segregated and integrated components of both the

Figure 4-a Perception of National Economy (White-Collar Respondents)

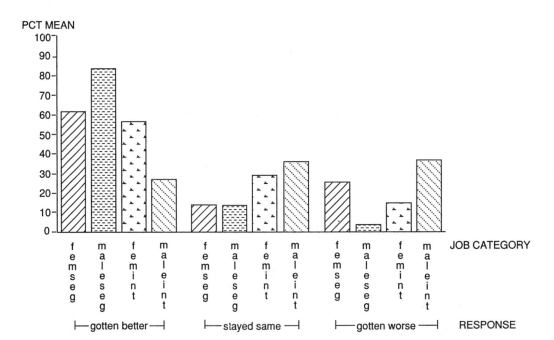

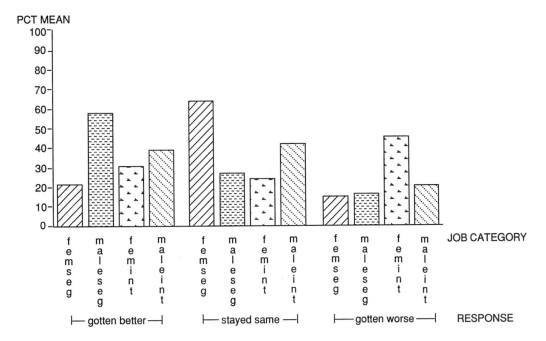

Figure 4-b   Perception of National Economy (Blue-Collar Respondents)

Figure 5-a   Perception of U.S. World Position (White-Collar Respondents)

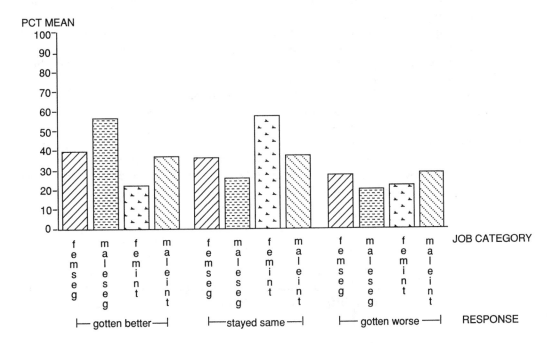

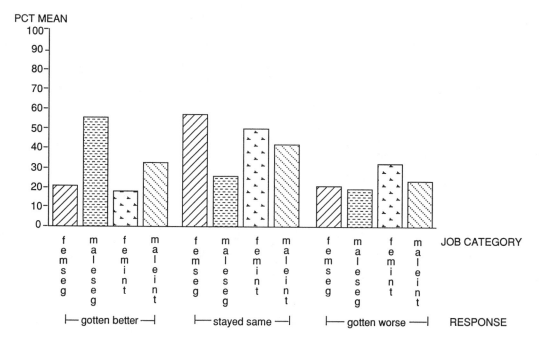

Figure 5-b   Perception of U.S. World Position (Blue-Collar Respondents)

white-collar and blue-collar subsamples—is noticeably more confident of the United States' place in the world's "pecking order" than is its respective female grouping. Significantly, no class-based pattern can be distinguished on this question, unlike the patterns for the questions previously studied. Rather, it appears in this instance that respondents in gender-segregated jobs—whether male or female, white-or blue-collar—perceived a stronger United States than did those in integrated occupations. In an issue area that has been identified in the past as one of the most clearly divided along male–female lines, it is easy to imagine that the moderation of attitudes among those in integrated occupations (in comparison with their work-segregated counterparts) is due to a sharing of views while on the job. That is to say, the more "hawkish" attitudes of men likely are tempered by the more "dovish" attitudes of women. (Similarly, the more peaceful attitudes of women can be thought of as being moderated somewhat by the more belligerent attitudes of men, in those integrated occupations.)

SUMMARY

The findings of this study are consistent with much of the current research in the field of gender and politics. Baxter and Lansing have indicated, for example, that women and men differ on certain "humanitarian" issues.[14] The women in our study did display a more consistent pattern of support for humanitarian positions than did their male counterparts. A majority of the women supported increases in federal spending for Social Security and Medicare, whereas a majority of the men believed that such spending should remain the same or be decreased.

More importantly, however, our study suggests the need to look beyond the sex of the respondents if we want to understand the significance of gender and its relationship to political behavior. Biological males and females become gendered males and females in the context of particular cultures and particular historical periods. It is useful to think of gender in terms of what it represents for individuals. Gender viewed in this way becomes for an individual a set of opportunity structures that a particular culture values. In the United States today, for example, gender is involved in the kinds of work experiences people choose or find themselves directed toward. As a result of sex-role socialization, life-cycle demands, and discrimination, women tend to cluster in what we have referred to as female-segregated jobs. The figures we have examined indicate that the experiences they have in these jobs affect their political attitudes. We can also speculate that since adult socialization appears to affect political attitudes, the longer women remain in those positions, the more their work experiences will affect their political attitudes. Unfortunately, the data currently available to us do not allow for a test of this time-related hypothesis. What the data do tell us is that gender and politics research must not confuse sex and gender. Although there are some clear differences between male and female political attitudes, factors such as class and occupational segregation-integration clearly shape and are shaped by gender.

This emphasis on gender in political research also calls into question traditional notions of class. The meaning of class for people and its effect on their political attitudes are colored by factors such as occupational segregation–integration and gender. Our analysis of support for women's rights, for example, suggests that we cannot examine either gender or class as an isolated factor. Likewise, our analysis of support for social spending suggests that intensity of attitude is also a function of gender, class, and occupational segregation–integration. Moreover, the issue of the United States' position in the global order suggests that in some instances the factor of occupational segregation–integration may be more influential than class.

We can use this study as a starting point to think about complex questions concerning gender and politics. The attitudes of the white-collar men in integrated professions, for example, are feminist. This may well have consequences for the emergence of a feminist voting bloc in U.S. politics. The attitudes of blue-collar men in integrated professions, in contrast, suggest we may yet witness the emergence of a backlash, antifeminist vote.

Clearly, as the workplace changes, so will U.S. political life. The hows and whys of these changes present a challenge to citizens and political scientists alike.

NOTES

1. Lynn Weiner, *From Working Girl to Working Mother: The Female Labor Force in the United States, 1820–1980* (Chapel Hill: University of North Carolina Press, 1985), p. 4.

2. Weiner, *From Working Girl*, p. 4.

3. Weiner, *From Working Girl*, p. 7.

4. Sara E. Rix, ed., *The American Woman 1988–89* (New York: W. W. Norton, 1988), p. 375.

5. Rix, *American Woman*, p. 382.

6. Rix, *American Woman*, p. 382.

7. Patricia A. Roos, *Gender and Work* (Albany: State University of New York Press, 1985), p. 39.

8. Andrea H. Beller, "Occupational Segregation and the Earnings Gap," in *Comparable Worth: Issue for the 80's*, Vol. 1 (Washington, DC: U.S. Commission on Civil Rights, 1984), p. 23.

9. Beller, "Occupational Segregation," p. 32.

10. Rix, *American Woman*, p. 393.

11. Rix, *American Woman*, p. 391.

12. *Women's Health: Report of the Public Health Service Task Force on Women's Health Issues*, Vol. II (Washington, DC: U.S. Department of Health and Human Services), p. 16.

13. Ethel Klein, *Gender Politics* (Cambridge, MA: Harvard University Press, 1984), p. 108.

14. Sandra Baxter and Marjorie Lansing, *Women and Politics: The Invisible Majority* (Ann Arbor: University of Michigan Press, 1983).

3

WOMEN AND ELECTIONS: THE UPHILL STRUGGLE

Many scholars considered the post–World War II era a quiescent time for white, middle-class American women. After a period of wartime involvement, women supposedly retreated into a more traditional lifestyle. Between 1946 and 1968, however, almost 100 women entered legislatures in the South, a particularly traditional region. Data indicate that they were predominantly women who were already involved in the public sphere in one or more ways. Even though many were serious legislators, the press emphasized their domesticity and femininity instead of their legislative achievements. Joanne V. Hawks and Carolyn Ellis Staton critique this period of transition—and reflect on the political environment for these Southern women.

We then move from the late 1960s to a study conducted in 1976, in which two scholars found that women were elected to fewer than 10 percent of the seats on U.S. city councils. Using data from still a decade later, Susan A. MacManus and Charles S. Bullock III, study the influence of governmental structure on female city council representation. That is, they determine whether single-member district election systems, council size, incumbency return rate, length of term, staggered terms, and majority vote requirements make it more difficult for women to win elections. Their research data are drawn in the spring of 1986 from the 211 cities with 1980 populations over 25,000 in eleven Southern states (Alabama, Arkansas, Florida, Georgia, Louisiana, Mississippi, North and South Carolina, Tennessee, Texas, and Virginia). Although the researchers occasionally observed variations across the structural variables they considered, the overwhelming thrust of their findings is that structural features are not strongly associated with whether women serve as council members. Just as in the 1970s, their research shows that structural features are no more than weak determinants of female representation on city councils. This holds true in spite of growing numbers of women on city councils. Thus, gender may still be somewhat of an impediment to representation—but electoral structures are not.

Despite the fact that political parties are not mentioned in the U.S. Constitution, we know that they form the nucleus of our system of government. The history of the parties roughly parallels the evolution of our political system. Congress is organized around the two-party system. We elect presidents who run on either the Democratic or Republican ticket, despite infrequent challenges from third-party candidates.

How, then, could we describe the influence of political parties on females who campaign for public office? Have the parties helped or hurt women? Have changes in party leadership benefited contemporary women? Or is the party philosophy still targeted more toward male candidates?

Barbara Burrell looks at the possible positive and negative effects of party decline and how this affects women. In tracing party leadership over the past couple of decades, she finds party leaders moving from opposition to encouragement of women candidates generally, although sexism still exists in the political party environment.

On the Eve of Transition: Women in Southern Legislatures, 1946–1968

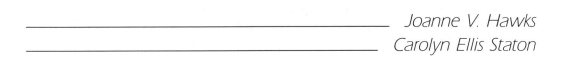

Joanne V. Hawks
Carolyn Ellis Staton

This study focuses on women who served in Southern legislatures in the period following World War II, beginning with the election of 1946 and culminating in 1968. During this period—especially in the earlier years—middle-class women received many signals that their proper sphere encompassed home, family, and related activities. The willingness of women to enter the legislature against society's traditional expectations of them may have been a mild form of rebellion, but it was nonetheless real. To some extent the women serving between 1946 and 1968 were transition figures, standing between an earlier group of legislative women whose mere presence made them important and a later group of more activist women. They set the stage for the political women of the 1970s and 1980s, the activist women who benefited directly or indirectly from the women's movement.

The postwar legislators followed a group of trailblazers, women who had emerged from the suffrage movement with new rights and imperatives. These earlier women had begun moving into Southern legislatures in a slow but steady stream in the decade of the 1920s.[1] Most were short-term legislators; few served more than one or two terms. For the most part, they could be characterized as Southern progressives, people who wanted to use state government as a means of ameliorating conditions in their communities.[2] Many of them were especially concerned with the needs of women, children, and persons with mental, physical, and moral handicaps. Even though much of their proposed legislation did not

Joanne V. Hawks is director of the Sarah Isom Center for Women's Studies and assistant professor of history at the University of Mississippi. Carolyn Ellis Staton is professor of law at the University of Mississippi Law Center.
Part of the research for this paper was supported by a Basic Research Grant from the National Endowment for the Humanities.

pass, they brought certain needs into focus as matters of public concern. Just as importantly, they established the right and ability of women to serve competently as state legislators.

In the Depression and World War II years, a slightly larger group of women were elected. By 1936 all eleven of the former Confederate states had female as well as male legislators.

After a period of wartime involvement in paid employment or volunteer services, many women in the late 1940s and early 1950s supposedly retreated into a more traditional lifestyle.[3] According to many historical and sociological treatises, the post–World War II era was a quiescent time for U.S. women, especially middle-class white women. Andrew Sinclair has called the postwar attitude New Victorianism because of its emphasis on sharp distinctions between male and female roles and proper behavior by women.[4] The prescription for the times called upon women to immerse themselves in private concerns surrounding their families and homes and to surrender activity in the public realm to the returning veterans.

In light of these generally observed patterns, it is interesting to consider the movement of women into Southern legislatures in the years following the war. In a region of the nation considered to be particularly traditional, where proper sex roles had been carefully defined and political participation had long been regarded as a white male preserve, women began entering Southern legislatures in increasing numbers. Although the incidence varied from a low of one person in Alabama to a high of nineteen in the neighboring state of Mississippi, a total of ninety-three women were seated in the legislatures of the eleven former Confederate states between 1946 and 1968.

HOW WOMEN ENTERED THE LEGISLATURE

One means by which women entered legislatures was what has been termed "the widow's route," a method whereby a wife succeeded to a seat formerly held by her deceased husband. During this period, twenty-four women from the eleven states in this study entered via succession. Twenty-one were widows elected or appointed to complete their husbands' legislative terms. Two were wives who ran when their husbands resigned before their terms were completed. One, Maud Isaacks, was a daughter who succeeded her father. Most were elected to office, although a few were appointed. Of the entire group of successors, only Maud Isaacks of Texas served for an extended period of time.[5] Most finished the husband's unexpired term and then retired from office. A few ran for reelection, but most of those who were reelected served only one additional term before retiring or being defeated. Their positions seemed to be regarded by many voters as a gesture of courtesy. For instance, when Governor Earl Long of Louisiana appointed Mrs. E. D. Gleason to complete her husband's term, he expressed doubt about his authority to make the appointment, but he assured his audience that she was a nice lady and had promised not to run again.[6]

Thus, approximately 25.5 percent of the total group of women serving between 1946 and 1968 were "fill-ins" for seats that were deemed to "belong" to their predecessors. But what of the remaining 74.5 percent? Who were they and what motivated them to seek office?

Data indicated that they were predominantly women who were already involved in the public sphere in one way or another, as professional or business women, local officeholders, political party workers, or active members of women's organizations. Fifty-four had a profession or business in which they were contemporaneously engaged or which they had previously practiced. By far the largest single group—twenty women—were teachers. Nine women were attorneys. Ten were owners or co-owners of businesses. Two were farmers, two journalists, two physicians, and two government workers. The remainder held various other positions in the business world.

At least six women had held local political office before running for the legislature, most of them as city or county council members. Even more had served on local and state executive committees of their party, worked with the women's division, or helped in the campaigns of others before seeking office themselves. Of the nine Republican women elected during this period, most had been heavily involved in Republican party politics and were committed to strengthening two-party politics in their states. Several of the women were from political families.

In addition to these two groups—professional and business women and those with political activity of one kind or another—most of the other women were involved significantly in one or more women's organizations. At least two women became interested in politics as a result of their participation in Parent–Teacher Associations (PTAs). Other women were involved in Federated Women's Clubs, Business and Professional Women, the League of Women Voters, the American Association of University Women, the Farm Bureau (or related Home Demonstration groups), garden clubs, and other groups. Through these organizations they became aware of issues and gained a sense of how to accomplish things through their club work. In many cases, their legislative interests mirrored the concerns of the organized groups in which they had worked or held leadership positions. Maxine Baker of Florida (1963–1973) said, "I wanted to serve in the Legislature to try to accomplish some of the things I had been working for during my years as member and President of the Florida League of Women Voters. . . ."[7] Others, like Carolyn Frederick of South Carolina (1964–1976), a member of the American Association of University Women, had lobbied legislators in behalf of interests supported by their organizations, only to find that legislators tended to be longer on promises than on favorable action. Kathryn Stone of Virginia (1954–1966), a national vice-president of the League of Women Voters, admonished women to join service and civic organizations to learn skills and to move on to the political arena from there.[8] She believed that women should not confine themselves to any one civic group but should become involved in party politics.[9]

Stone's comments were closely echoed by Grace Hamilton of Georgia:

If you are concerned about working in the legislative branch of government, you had better get some experience in working other than in the legislature on the matters that concern you. . . . If you look at people who have been effective legislators, they usually have been effective in something that was non-political, related to issues before them. I personally think that the League of Women Voters is a good training, very good training to have, but I think sometimes you need to graduate from the League.[10]

Some of the women worked primarily with one particular organization; many were active in several and held membership in many more. At least eighteen women appeared to be heavily involved in club work. A few of these could also be grouped with one or both of the categories previously discussed. In fact, women who had several connections with the public sphere seemed to be especially likely at some point to consider public office.

LEGISLATIVE ISSUES

A survey of the issues in which the female legislators expressed interest leads to rather predictable findings. Many issues came readily to their attention as mothers and community volunteers. Education was a key interest, with many in favor of strengthening the public schools, providing child care and kindergartens, and raising teachers' pay. Other concerns included health, mental health, aid to the handicapped, problems of children and youth, care of the aged, alcohol and drug abuse, consumer and environmental protection, and election reform. Rural legislators often focused on agricultural problems while those elected from urban districts concentrated their efforts on urban problems including the need for adequate representation in the legislature and better services in their areas.

A few of the women expressed concern for the so-called women's issues of the day. Jury service for women appeared to be the most generally supported proposal. A federal equal rights amendment was a more problematic issue. The few who were outspoken supporters of equal rights for women were balanced by a similar number who opposed the concept. Many women preferred to equivocate or to avoid the issue altogether.

Middle-class, mature women, long trained to be conciliatory persons—peacemakers—often seemed reluctant to take on highly controversial issues. In a period when civil rights, women's rights, youth protest, and antiwar and antiestablishment issues were eroding society's postwar complacency, most of the Southern legislative women avoided identification with any of these divisive movements. They concentrated instead on gradual elimination of community problems and provision of government services to segments of the society who had unmet needs.

Civil Rights Issues

Of all the contemporary issues, the civil rights issue struck nearest to home. Clearly, the easiest way to deal with the problems of the day was to ignore them, and it is amazing how many of the legislators during this period managed to do just that. But for others the issues had to be confronted, and women, like their male counterparts, lined up on both sides of the civil rights question.

In Virginia, in particular, women could not avoid the issue. In the aftermath of the United States Supreme Court's decision in *Brown v. Board of Education*, Virginia almost immediately sought to forestall school integration by a number of measures, some as extreme as closing whole school systems. One is struck by the courage of the moderates and liberals during this time in Virginia politics. Most of the women legislators favored compliance with the law and opposed massive resistance. The usually ultrachivalrous male-dominated assembly proved that it had its raw side; it could behave rudely toward them when they tried to keep the Virginia schools open.[11]

Although most of the Virginia women delegates supported compliance, such was not the case everywhere. In Mississippi, for instance, just the opposite situation prevailed. The segregation establishment reigned supreme. As Jack Bass and Walter DeVries have stated,

> these were not ordinary times. The executive director of the Citizens Council . . . had begun preparing [Governor] Barnett's speeches. Citizens Council members were named to the State Sovereignty Commission, the official state segregation committee and a propaganda arm of the Citizens Council. . . . The Citizens Council claimed 80,000 members in the state. . . .[12]

The female legislators seemed to oppose attempts to integrate the schools as stridently as most of the male delegates. At least two women were part of the segregation establishment, the White Citizens Council and the State Sovereignty Commission. Occasionally, a legislator who proclaimed that she was a segregationist would, however, champion the rights of others. A notable example occurred in Mississippi when Senator Orene Farese argued vehemently against passage of a bill that would have eliminated the property tax exemption for churches that used their facilities on an integrated basis.[13]

Because of these stands, Farese felt compelled in her next senatorial campaign to proclaim staunchly her segregationist views. In her campaign literature she maintained that her purpose in opposing the removal of tax exemptions for integrated churches was to keep segregation intact and preserve tax exemptions for churches.[14] Perhaps, like many other politicians of the day, Farese maintained a certain façade of segregation that did not always conform to other ideas that she held.

By 1967, the civil rights movement had begun to have a significant impact on portions of the South, legislative resistance notwithstanding. Because of the movement and *Baker v. Carr*, the United States Supreme Court decision that mandated "one man, one vote," legislative redistricting was required. One result of redistricting was to increase voting strength in urban areas—places where there might be a large population of blacks. It is not surprising then that in 1967 three black women in the South entered their state legislatures: Barbara Jordan of Texas, Dorothy Brown of Tennessee, and Grace Hamilton of Georgia. The civil rights movement, by changing both the social climate and the laws, gave them opportunities for political office that they had previously lacked.

PRESS IMAGES

The times were changing, but the public's image of women in politics was not changing at the same pace. This was best indicated by contemporary press coverage, which emphasized femininity. The renewed emphasis on femininity may have been a result of a covert campaign to force women out of the traditionally male jobs that many had held during the war years. It may also have been an effort to glamorize the homemaker so that she, as consumer, might aid in the improving economy. Moreover, as the country recovered from the difficult war period, some people longed to return to a less confused, less complicated world.

In the postwar period, press treatment of female legislators primarily covered personal rather than political aspects of their lives. Articles on these women tended to focus on specific female roles. A prevalent form of feature article was the portrait of the lady legislator as family member, either wife, mother, homemaker, or grandmother. Orene Farese, who served along with her husband in the Mississippi legislature during the 1950s, was consistently spotlighted in her domestic roles. The following excerpt from a feature story about her is characteristic of the coverage she received:

> Mrs. Farese, though public minded, is a very domestic and home loving person. . . .
>
> She is a capable housekeeper and a wonderful homemaker. With the help of a full time maid she cares for their four bedroom, two bathroom home. . . .[15]

Farese discussed her cooking, sewing, and home decorating abilities.[16] The article proceeded to describe her to the readers:

> When you see this lovely senator-elect . . . she will most likely be wearing a stunning tailored dress or suit in one of her favorite colors, the blues, aqua or yellow in medium tone.[17]

The newspaper account contained virtually no mention of Farese's legislative and political interests. She was treated primarily as a housewife who went to the legislature.

A somewhat more muted example of the lady legislator as homemaker occurred with Grace Rodenbough of North Carolina. Although Rodenbough, who served in the legislature from 1953 to 1966, was a woman of considerable stature, the press on several different occasions focused on her fondness for her antebellum home.[18] Rodenbough might play a significant role in the legislature, but she was still seen as the Southern aristocratic lady.

Rodenbough's fellow North Carolinian, Mary Faye Brumby, was subjected to similar treatment. When Brumby went to the legislature, she took her

11-year-old son along. Her child care arrangements were highlighted in the press.[19] By taking her son with her to the capital rather than leaving him at home, she avoided being seen as the abandoning mother who pursued her own interests.

Although some accounts were brief in their mention of the legislators' children, comment was usually made. For instance, Iris Blitch of Georgia, who later went to Congress, was simply described as devoted to her children.[20]

The epitome of the legislator-as-wife stories involves Lillian Neblett Scott of Tennessee. Scott, always referred to as Mrs. Scott, was being routinely interviewed by a reporter from the Nashville *Banner* when her husband entered the room. The spotlight of the article immediately became *Mr.* Scott and his stories of marital harmony: "Somebody asked me how I made out with Lillian so active in politics, I just tole 'em that I still have my hot biscuits 365 days a year."[21] Scott continued his antics: "as the couple exchanged a look of deep affection and long understanding, 'I've never had to spank her.' "[22] Throughout the article, Lillian Scott is seen not as the incredibly active woman she was, but as a wife who knew her place. As is true of all of these features, there is an implicit statement that these women legislators were all right because, first and foremost, their principal roles were as wives and mothers.

Domesticity, Femininity, and Beauty

When they were viewed primarily as domestic creatures, female legislators lost their "strangeness." The same principle applied if the emphasis was on their femininity rather than their domesticity. Moreover, by their being pigeonholed as either a domestic or a feminine type, these women, working in a nontraditional forum, threatened no one. For example, articles such as the following 1954 feature in the *Jackson Daily News* made the idea of female legislators more palatable to the public:

> The universal feminine preoccupation with weddings, babies, and bringing up children reaches strongly into the Mississippi legislature. . . .
>
> Far from being a sentimental interest, confined to cooing over the newlywedded or recently born, theirs is an informed concern aimed at changes in the laws. . . .[23]

The article went on to provide an apologia for these women:

> . . . it is, perhaps, to the state's advantage to number among its lawmakers those whose beliefs are conditioned by the previous primary experience of wife, mother, and frequently teacher.[24]

Since the days of Scarlett O'Hara, femininity and gracious beauty have been part of the mystique of Southern womanhood. The beauty queen has been a consistent Southern type, one with which Southern society felt comfortable. In many instances, by emphasizing pulchritude, Southern society was able to accept women on its own terms, and by doing so, could avoid accepting them as serious legislators. Ruth Williams of South Carolina was linked with "the rustle of silk and the faint scent of perfume" and managed "somehow, to cling to her femininity and still compete with men. . . ."[25]

Mary Shadow of Tennessee, like Williams, was young and single when she entered the legislature. Shadow, however, married during her legislative stint. News of the marriage was widely featured. Shadow, a college teacher, was quoted as saying that in her forthcoming marriage she wanted to cook, keep house, and raise a large family. One article was captioned "Miss Shadow Plans to Keep House, Raise Family."[26] Upon Shadow's marriage it was assumed that she would become a traditional housewife.

Because of the emphasis on femininity, there was a never-ending discussion of physical appearance. To some extent this focus suggested to the public that, after all, these female legislators were more female than legislator. Blitch was often described as "an attractive brunette"[27] with "a perfect size 12 figure."[28] Shadow was described as a "pretty, charming legislator";[29] and Betty Jane Long of Mississippi was depicted as "lovely."[30] Mississippi's Mary Lou Godbold and Orene Farese "add[ed] much to the lustre of [the legislature]. And the men [were] all in favor of the ladies."[31]

Kathryn Stone of Virginia, in particular, was the topic of much publicity about her physical appearance. The press found it noteworthy that one Virginia senator said to another upon seeing Stone presiding in the senate, " 'Have you ever seen a lovelier creature presiding from the chair of the president of the Senate?' whereupon the other senator then responded, 'I yield to the lovely creature. . . .' "[32] On another occasion, the press claimed that "Mrs. Stone . . . is the prettiest thing to hit the General Assembly since Sarong Siren Dorothy Lamour dropped in at the Capitol one day a few years ago. Besides looks . . . she has brains."[33] Another feature described her clothing and home decor.[34] No matter how significant these women were as legislators and politicians, their colleagues and the press trivialized them in many instances by focusing on irrelevant considerations.

As if to stereotype them even further, the press played up the emotional nature of these women. Blitch is depicted as on the verge of tears when an adverse amendment was added to her original bill.[35] When Orene Farese opposed taxing churches that did not practice segregation, she was choked with tearful emotion.[36] Although the situation may have warranted tears, no comment is made in the coverage of the heated senate debate about the emotions of her male colleagues.

How Women Legislators Were Treated

During this period when there was an emphasis on the female attributes of the women politicians, several of them were singled out for what was then considered a chivalrous tribute. When only one woman served in a legislative body, she might be entitled sweetheart of the senate or house or some honorific variation. Blitch was named queen of the Georgia General Assembly,[37] Collins was elected sweetheart of the Alabama house,[38] and Berta Lee White of Mississippi was designated sweetheart of the senate.[39] In Collins's case, this meant that the house members might on occasion be addressed as "Mister Speaker, gentlemen of the House and sweetheart of the House."[40] In some instances the chivalry was rather overdone. For example, in making seat assignments at the beginning of the session, the speaker of the Georgia house announced that "the Lady of the House [Blitch] and the physically handicapped will get their first choice of seats."[41] Sometimes the chivalry became quite time-consuming. When the speaker of the Virginia house instructed Kathryn Stone, the sole female legislator, to make a communiqué to the senate, Stone was accompanied by the entire Virginia house delegation to the senate chambers. The newspaper described the event as a "chivalry safari."[42]

When the female legislators occasionally acted out of character from the role in which the public had cast them, it was definitely noted. Thus, when the women were perceived as politicians rather than as ladies, they were likened to males. For instance, the newspaper remarked that "Mrs. Blitch had to fight like a man."[43] Perhaps it was her ability to fight like a man that won Blitch the sobriquet, "the wench from Clinch."[44] In Mississippi when three women were elected to the legislature in the same term, it was noted that they could fare well against strong male opposition.[45] The tenacity of Clara Collins was editorialized as "stubbornness, albeit justified."[46] It was with Martha Evans of North Carolina that the press had a field day. Practically every story about Evans mentioned that she was a redhead with a temper to match. For instance, in one article she was referred to as "a red-headed pepperpot."[47] Evans, who was held in a certain amount of esteem for her work, was excused by the press from stepping out of the traditional role of Southern womanhood:

> In Raleigh she'll stand on her own small feet. . . . That's because she's always felt she is the equal of the male politician. And she's "been around," as the saying goes among office seekers.[48]

The women were newsworthy. When they conformed to the stereotyped version of Southern womanhood, they were viewed as nonthreatening. When they did not conform to the standard image, the media nevertheless tried to force them into that mold. When they were not susceptible to being molded, they were excused, as was Evans, on the basis of being an "outsider." They were less novel than the women who preceded them in the earlier decades, but the public was still not quite comfortable with them and still regarded them as curiosities.

SUMMARY

Female legislators of the post–World War II era tried to live up to societal expectations of them as women while they practiced their political skills. For some, the substance of lawmaking was secondary to their role as lady legislator.

For most, the legislature was not a stepping stone to greater political heights, but it was a forum for public service. By their service these women set the stage for the more activist, more ambitious, and more political women who succeeded them.

NOTES

1. Anne Firor Scott, *The Southern Lady: From Pedestal to Politics, 1830–1930* (Chicago: University of Chicago Press, 1970), pp. 186–211.

2. Dewey W. Grantham, *Southern Progressivism: The Reconciliation of Progress and Tradition* (University of Tennessee Press, 1983), pp. 410–422.

3. William H. Chafe, *The American Woman, Her Changing Social, Economic, and Political Roles, 1920–1970* (Oxford University Press, 1972), pp. 176–178, 199–212. Chafe's bibliography includes many other treatises on the subject.

4. Andrew Sinclair, *The Emancipation of the American Woman* (New York: Harper & Row, 1965), pp. 354–367.

5. Mary Beth Rogers (Ed.), *Texas Women: A Celebration of History* (Texas Foundation for Women's Resources, 1981), p. 100.

6. Baton Rouge *State-Times*, August 5, 1959, Sec. A, p. 11.

7. Questionnaire completed by Maxine Baker, January 21, 1986, in possession of the authors.

8. Richmond *Times-Dispatch*, March 23, 1954.

9. Ibid.

10. Taped interview with Grace Hamilton, conducted by the authors, August 8, 1984, in possession of the authors.

11. See, e.g., Richmond *Times-Dispatch*, February 23, 1958.

12. Jack Bass and Walter DeVries, *The Transformation of Southern Politics: Social Change and Political Consequence since 1945* (New York: Basic Books, 1976), p. 196.

13. Unnamed, undated clipping in possession of the authors.

14. *The Southern Advocate*, July 23, 1959.

15. *Jackson Advertiser–TV News*, September 15, 1955, p. 6.

16. Ibid.

17. Ibid.

18. *The News and the Observer* (Raleigh), January 17, 1963, p. 8.

19. Unnamed clipping, February 14, 1965.

20. *Atlanta Constitution*, October 6, 1949, p. 26.

21. Nashville *Banner*, January 10, 1957, p. 8.

22. Ibid.

23. *Jackson Daily News*, January 24, 1954.

24. Ibid.

25. *The State* (Columbia), November 6, 1964, Sec. A, p. 1.

26. *The Nashville Tennessean*, November 19, 1950, Society Section, p. 1.

27. *Atlanta Constitution*, October 6, 1949, p. 27.

28. *Atlanta Constitution*, October 24, 1954.

29. *The Nashville Tennessean*, January 7, 1948, p. 8.

30. *Jackson Daily News*, August 29, 1955, p. 2.

31. Unnamed clipping, January 12, 1958.

32. Richmond *Times Dispatch*, March 15, 1954, p. 4.

33. Richmond *Times Dispatch*, January 13, 1954, p. 16.

34. Richmond *Times Dispatch*, November 11, 1953.

35. *Atlanta Constitution*, January 27, 1953, p. 1.

36. Jackson *Clarion-Ledger*, March 27, 1956, p. 1.

37. *Atlanta Constitution*, October 6, 1949, p. 26.

38. *Advertiser-Journal* (Montgomery), Alabama Sunday Magazine, August 16, 1965, p. 12.

39. Questionnaire completed by Berta Lee White, in possession of the authors.

40. *Advertiser-Journal* (Montgomery), Alabama Sunday Magazine, August 15, 1965, p. 12.

41. *Atlanta Constitution*, January 11, 1949, p. 1.

42. Richmond *News Leader*, March 9, 1954.

43. *Atlanta Constitution*, October 24, 1954.

44. *Atlanta Constitution*, December 28, 1970.

45. *Jackson Daily News*, August 29, 1955, p. 2.

46. *Montgomery Advertiser*, August 13, 1967.

47. *Durham Morning Herald*, November 18, 1962, Sec. C, p. 9.

48. Ibid.

Women on Southern City Councils: Does Structure Matter?

Susan A. MacManus
Charles S. Bullock III

In 1976, in the first empirical study of the extent to which women win seats on U.S. city councils, Karnig and Walter reported that women were elected to fewer than 10 percent of the municipal posts. The authors concluded that "in local politics, sex is even more critical than race in impeding equitable representation."[1]

In exploring why so few women serve on local, state, and national governing bodies, scholars have focused on three major categories of explanations. Extensive attention has been given to factors restricting the candidacy of female officeseekers. These factors include attitudinal barriers, generally sex-role stereotyping on the part of voters, party leaders, and the potential candidates themselves, the effect being to restrict female candidacies and successes.[2]

Another common approach to the study of the success rates of female candidates has been to focus on environmental determinants, such as community demographic, socioeconomic, and political-cultural characteristics.[3] For example, Karnig and Walter looked at the relationship between women's candidacy and election rates and city size, Southern location, and various income and education measures. But unlike the literature on the determinants of racial and ethnic minority candidate success, they found that these independent measures "have only feeble impact on female candidacy and elections levels."[4] No single variable accounted for as much as 5 percent of the variance in any of the women's votes. Subsequent studies by other scholars produced similar results.[5] Demographic and socioeconomic models have *consistently* been poor predictors of the degree to which women get elected to city councils throughout the United States. As

Susan A. MacManus is a professor of political science at the University of South Florida; Charles S. Bullock III is a professor of political science at the University of Georgia.

noted, this result differs from the findings in studies that examine the socioeconomic factors associated with racial and ethnic minority electoral success.[6]

A third approach to the study of the determinants of female city council representation has been to look at the relationship between various governmental structural arrangements, such as at-large elections, council size, term of office, and pay for office.[7] In general, governmental structural variables, like demographic and socioeconomic variables, have not been very powerful predictors of female electoral success.[8] For example, Karnig and Walter reported only a weak correlation (.12) between the percentage of candidates elected at large and the overall women's election rate; MacManus reported similarly weak coefficients.[9] Welch and Karnig found that even when socioeconomic and office prestige factors were held constant, "election type explained less than one percent of the variance in female representation."[10]

Interestingly, however, in light of their findings, Welch and Karnig predicted that "in the long run women might do better in district than in at-large races because of the greater name recognition and financial support necessary even to get the nomination in at-large contests."[11] The purpose of our research is to determine whether their prediction has, in fact, come true.

THE STUDY

Using data from a decade later (1986), we test whether Welch and Karnig's prediction has yet been realized with regard to greater female representation under single-member district election systems. We also examine the impact of other governmental structural variables on female city council representation. The factors we consider include council size, incumbency return rate, length of term, staggered terms, and majority vote requirements. There have been suggestions that each of these structures makes it more difficult for women to win elections.[12] We explore whether these structures have become more important determinants as larger numbers of women have gained political office,[13] gender-based stereotypes have eroded,[14] and the socioeconomic gap has narrowed somewhat.[15]

We also examine whether these structures have significantly different impacts on black females. Research on black women has often posited that politically they are doubly disadvantaged by race and gender.[16] Other research suggests this interaction between race and sex is not as powerful as previously suggested.[17] There has been little evidence that electoral structures significantly impede the election of black females.

Our data were gathered in the spring of 1986 from the 211 cities with 1980 populations over 25,000 in 11 Southern states (Alabama, Arkansas, Florida, Georgia, Louisiana, Mississippi, North Carolina, South Carolina, Tennessee, Texas, and Virginia). Some studies have suggested that the South is "the region most likely to manifest differences between males and females toward the role of women and politics."[18] One scholar has noted that "opportunities for women have been particularly limited in the South, where the myth of the southern lady has served as a golden cord binding women to traditional roles."[19] Earlier studies that used regional location as a predictor found that whereas female representation levels were slightly lower in the South, the bivariate relationship between Southern location and the percentage of women elected was statistically insignificant. Consequently, if we find no support for relationships between structural variables and female representation in the South, we would not expect these relationships to be significant in other regions.

GOVERNMENTAL STRUCTURES AND WOMEN

The previous review of the literature examining the relationship between various governmental structural arrangements and female representation in the 1970s reported only weak correlations. A decade later, we reexamine these relationships. We begin with a review of the hypothesized directions of impact.

Electoral Format: At-Large versus District Elections

Traditionally, scholars have found that at-large elections are more "women-friendly" than district-based election systems.[20] Weaver states that:

> Any type of multimember district is more hospitable to women than the single member district system. This includes at-large systems, semi-proportional systems, such as the single transferable vote (rank order), or party list/proportional representation. The single member district system, by contrast, favors males from the largest ethnic group in each district.[21]

Weaver and others hypothesize that voters "are more apt to give one of several votes to a woman when they are limited to only one vote."[22] Likewise, nominations are easier to come by in multiple-seat settings because party and organizational slating groups are more prone to see the advantages of "balanced tickets." Finally, women are more likely to capture council seats in an at-large setting because "Women as women are not especially advantaged in district elections because district boundaries do not increase their chances of being extraordinarily large majorities in the same way districts do for black . . . [males]."[23]

The advantage of at-large elections holds true for all women, regardless of race and ethnicity. In 1979, Karnig and Welch found that neither black nor Mexican-American females benefited from single-member districts or other political structural arrangements. The authors offered this explanation: "It is likely that black women possess fewer socioeconomic and other resources—including appropriate positions and complementary roles from which to enter black politics . . . than do black men. As a consequence, black men may not only dominate their ethnic group's representation—as white Anglo and Mexican-American men also do—but black males are also the only minority able to take advantage of district elections."[24] A more recent study by Herrick and Welch reconfirmed the advantage of at-large elections for black and white women.[25] Thus, we hypothesize that:

> H_1: At-large election systems will be characterized by higher percentages of female council members than district-based systems.
>
> H_{1a}: Purer at-large systems (non-district-based) such as pure at-large and at-large from posts will be characterized by higher percentages of female council members than at-large systems with geographical residency requirements or mixed systems (some at-large; some single-member district seats).
>
> H_2: At-large election systems will have the same positive effect on black female representation as on white female representation. At-large election systems will be characterized by higher percentages of black female council members than district-based systems.

Majority Vote Requirement (Runoffs)

This structural feature was alleged to have a discriminatory impact on female representation by the former president of the National Organization for Women (NOW), Eleanor Smeal (1984).[26] In making this claim, Smeal was joining the charge made by Jesse Jackson during his 1984 presidential quest. Jackson had prophesied that

> if Section 5 [of the Voting Rights Act] is enforced and registrars are accessible, and you end second primaries which keep black people, Hispanics, women and poor people from a securer justice, you'll get 12 to 20 black, Hispanic and female Congresspersons by next November.[27]

A staunch supporter of efforts to modify the North Carolina majority vote requirement also saw women as victims. According to Mickey Michaux, the chair of the state Legislative Black Caucus, when questioned about a proposal to reduce the share of the vote needed to nominate from 50 to 40 percent, "I think it [the change] will lead to at least the nomination, and the election of more blacks and women because they are the ones who have suffered from the 50 percent [rule] and this gives them the chance."[28]

The rationale behind allegations that runoffs hurt the electoral chances of blacks is straightforward. Jackson and Michaux reasoned that a black might win a plurality against a primary field with several whites. In head-to-head competition in the runoff, however, if the whites united behind the remaining white candidate and if white turnout exceeded black turnout, the black candidate would lose the runoff. The analogous situation for gender would have a female frontrunner from the primary defeated in the runoff by the male candidate who survived the initial winnowing.

Recent empirically based research has not found the speculations of Smeal and Jackson to be warranted. In an analysis of congressional and state nonjudicial primary runoffs between 1970 and 1983, Bullock and Johnson found that female party leaders fared better in runoffs than did the frontrunners in an all-male runoff.[29] Several studies of the impact of runoffs at the municipal level found "no systematic bias against minority and female front-runners forced into runoffs."[30] Therefore, we do not expect majority vote requirements to have differential impacts on the levels of white and black female council representation. We hypothesize that:

> H_3: Female representation levels on city councils in cities that have majority vote requirements will not differ significantly from levels in cities that have plurality systems.

> H_4: Black female city council representation levels in cities that have majority vote requirements will not differ significantly from levels in cities that have plurality systems.

Staggered Terms

Staggered terms have not been the focus of study with regard to their impact on females, but the effect on minorities has been examined. Davidson described a scenario in which staggered terms could have a discriminatory impact by limiting the impact of single-shot voting. Single-shot voting has, at times, been used by groups in pure at-large electoral systems where voters can express preferences for more than one councilmember, with the positions going to the top vote-getters. Through single-shotting, a group concentrates its influence by voting for its favorite but for none of the other candidates.

To illustrate, let us assume that each voter can register as many as five preferences, with the five most popular candidates being elected. By single-shotting, a group supports its favorite but gives no support to anyone else since all candidates are competing to finish in the top five. Davidson suggested that staggered terms could dilute a minority group's ability to single-shot by reducing the number of positions to be filled per election.[31] For example, if staggering the terms means that only three councilmembers are elected in some years and two are elected two years later, rather than all five being elected simultaneously, then a group's favorite would have to finish in the top two or three, depending on the year.

Despite the logic behind Davidson's claim, a large-scale empirical test of his hypothesis revealed no statistically significant difference between black representation levels in cities with staggered terms and those without.[32] Therefore, we hypothesize that:

> H_5: Female representation levels in cities with staggered terms will not differ significantly from levels in cities with simultaneous terms.

> H_6: Black female representation levels in cities with staggered terms will not differ significantly from levels in cities with simultaneous terms.

Size of Council

Welch and Karnig hypothesized that larger councils would yield greater levels of female representation.[33] Their hypothesis was based on Diamond's study of state legislatures. Diamond theorized that larger councils were indicative of an office being "less desirable and less important" which would enhance females' chances of winning it.[34] The results of Welch and Karnig's study did not confirm this hypothesis. The correlation coefficient between number of council seats and the female council proportion was a statistically insignificant .06.

Although there is not much evidence of council size having an impact on female representation, some data suggest that larger councils enhance minority representation.[35] In recent research, however, the size of the council appears to be a structural feature whose impact on minority representation is rather weak and conditional, first on the size of the minority population,[36] and second on geographical residential patterns.[37] We hypothesize that:

> H_7: Council size is not a significant predictor of female representation on city councils.

> H_8: Black female representation on city councils will not be enhanced by larger council size.

Length of Term

Longer terms of office are viewed as more attractive than shorter terms. Term length is another example of what Welch and Karnig consider to be an indicator of the desirability and importance of a political office.[38] Thus, they anticipated a negative relationship between length of term and female representation levels. However, they found no relationship between length of term and female representation. Therefore, we do not expect to find a relationship either.

> H_9: Length of term is not a significant predictor of female representation on city councils.

There is also very little evidence of longer terms disadvantaging blacks.[39] The argument in favor of longer terms is often related to election costs. Karnig and Welch actually found nonsignificant higher levels of black representation in cities with longer council terms. They attributed this to the attractiveness and prestige of the longer term. In a later study based on 1986 data, Bullock and MacManus found that length of term was not a significant predictor of black representation.[40] Therefore, we hypothesize that:

> H_{10}: Length of term is not a significant predictor of black female representation.

Incumbency

Most studies recognize incumbency as powerful in explaining municipal electoral outcomes, particularly in nonpartisan settings.[41] High incumbency return rates are still a deterrent to the entry of women and minorities into political office, especially where there are none at present.[42] But where women and blacks are represented, incumbency has no significant racial or gender-based differentials in its impact. For example, Bullock found that incumbency advantages both minorities and whites.[43] Black incumbents tend to get more white crossover votes than in their initial election, perhaps because white fears are eased by a successful performance.[44]

Incumbency works the same across gender groups according to Darcy, Welch, and Clark.[45] Female incumbents have just about the same advantage as male incumbents. Therefore, based on studies showing no racial or gender-based differentials in incumbency return rates (the measure we use in our study), we hypothesize that:

> H_{11}: Incumbency return rate is not a significant predictor of female city council representational level.
>
> H_{12}: Incumbency return rate is not a significant predictor of black female city council representational level.

In summary, we expect to find higher levels of female city council representation in the 1980s but little support for governmental structures as determinants of electoral success.

FINDINGS

Across the 211 cities in the 11 Southern states, there were 252 women on city councils in the spring of 1986. The average percentage of women on city councils was 17, up considerably from the figures reported in studies based on data from the 1970s (Karnig and Walter, mid-1975—9.7 percent; MacManus, 1976—10 percent; Welch and Karnig, 1978—13 percent), although those were national averages, not just from the South.[46] In the aggregate, only one-third of our cities had no female representation. In contrast, Welch and Karnig's study showed a much larger percentage of councils without any women (44 percent).[47] As the figures in Table 1 show, however, the percentage of cities with no women on their councils varies sharply across the 11 Southern states. Women have achieved representation on a larger number of councils in Virginia, North Carolina, and Florida. They have fared badly in Alabama and Arkansas.

In 11 of our cities, women constituted at least 50 percent of the council. The highest percentage of female councilmembers occurred in Orlando and North Miami, where women made up two-thirds of the councils. Table 1 shows that the share of council seats held by women varies across states. At the low end were Alabama, Arkansas, Tennessee, and Louisiana, where the average proportion of councilwomen was less than 12 percent. At the upper end were North Carolina, Florida, and Virginia. In each of these states women averaged more than one in five council seats, and in North Carolina the figure was closer to one in three.

The states where larger percentages of women serve on city councils are those characterized by higher population growth rates. Some scholars have found

Table 1 Incidence of Women on City Councils by State

| Southern State | Number of Cities | PERCENTAGE OF WOMEN ON COUNCILS | | | Percentage of Cities with No Females on Council |
		Minimum Percentage	Maximum Percentage	Mean Percentage	
Alabama	15	0%	44%	7%	73%
Arkansas	10	0	29	8	70
Florida	48	0	67	25	19
Georgia	12	0	33	17	25
Louisiana	12	0	43	11	50
Mississippi	9	0	33	13	44
North Carolina	17	0	63	31	18
South Carolina	8	0	33	14	25
Tennessee	13	0	23	10	31
Texas	52	0	50	13	38
Virginia	15	0	44	21	13

Source: Telephone survey of 211 cities with 1980 populations 25,000 or above in 11 Southern states, Spring 1986.

that the in-migration of persons from other regions has helped break down racial and gender stereotypes in the South.[48]

Electoral Districting Format

There is less range in the proportion female across the five types of electoral formats. Women were somewhat more likely to serve in cities in which elections were pure at large, from single-member districts, or in which some members were elected at large while others ran in single-member districts (a mixed format). Fewer women were chosen when elections were citywide but individuals ran for a specific post or were required to live in a residency district. As Table 2 demonstrates, however, the range is narrow, with the mean running from 13 to 19 percent.

Each type of system included some cities in which no woman served in 1986. The type of election system is still not a significant predictor of female city council representation. Welch and Karnig's predictions about single-member districts yielding greater representation has not yet come true, although the gap between pure at-large and single-member districts has narrowed. (Welch and Karnig's 1978 data showed an average of 10 percent elected under single-member district systems and 15 percent under pure at large;[49] our 1986 data show 17 percent for single-member districts and 19 percent for at large.)

Majority Vote Requirement (Runoffs)

More than 80 percent of the cities had a runoff provision. Despite former NOW President Eleanor Smeal's contention that runoffs are "no help to women,"[50]

Table 2 Incidence of Women on City Councils by Type of Electoral Districting

Type of Council Election System	Number of Cities	PERCENTAGE OF WOMEN ON COUNCILS		
		Minimum Percentage	Maximum Percentage	Mean Percentage
Pure at-large [1]	54	0	67%	19%
At-large by post [2]	32	0	40	13
At-large by residency [3]	23	0	43	13
Mixed [4]	54	0	55	18
Single-member districts [5]	48	0	67	17

Notes:

[1] In a pure at-large system, the candidates receiving the highest number of votes are elected.

[2] In an at-large by post system, candidates file for a specific seat or post (which has no geographical definition) and the candidate receiving the highest vote for each post or seat is elected.

[3] In an at-large by residency system, a candidate must run for the seat in the district in which he/she resides but is voted upon citywide. The candidate receiving the highest vote for each seat is elected.

[4] In a mixed system, some candidates run and are voted on at large citywide, and others run from single-member districts and are voted on only by those living in their districts.

[5] In a single-member district system, a candidate must live in the specific geographical district from which he or she runs as a candidate. Only residents of that district may vote for the candidates running from their district. The highest vote-getter in each district is elected.

Source: Telephone survey of 211 cities with 1980 population 25,000 or above in 11 Southern states, Spring 1986.

there is no evidence that having to poll a majority reduces the presence of women on the council. The mean for runoff and plurality cities is identical, confirming what Fleischman and Stein found in Texas cities.[51] While the means in Table 3 are identical, all of the cities with the largest percentages of women councilors employ a runoff. No plurality city was more than 50 percent female; seven runoff cities had a female majority.

Staggered Terms

The use of staggered terms, like a majority vote requirement, bears no consistent relationship to the size of the female component on a city council. Table 4 reports that the range in percentage female in cities that staggered terms and in those that elect all members simultaneously is almost identical, confirming our hypothesis. The difference in means for the two groups is less than 4 percentage points and is not statistically significant.

Size of Council

The size of the council bears no relationship to the incidence of women. The slope when percentage female is regressed on size of council is .0015, which is half as large as its standard error (.0032).

Table 3 Incidence of Women on City Councils by Share of Vote Needed for Election

Type of Vote Required to Win	Number of Cities	PERCENTAGE OF WOMEN ON COUNCILS		
		Minimum Percentage	Maximum Percentage	Mean Percentage
Plurality vote[1]	33	0%	50%	17%
Majority vote[2]	178	0	67	17

Notes:

[1] Under a plurality vote system, the candidate receiving the highest number of votes is elected, even if the candidate does not receive a majority (50% + 1). No runoff election is required.

[2] To win, a candidate must receive a majority of the votes cast (50% + 1). If a candidate does not receive a majority in the first round of balloting, a runoff election between the two candidates receiving the highest number of votes in the initial balloting is required.

Source: Telephone survey of 211 cities with 1980 population of 25,000 or above in 11 Southern states, Spring 1986.

Length of Term

The presence of female councilors is unaffected by the length of a city's council terms. Although there is a slight indication that women councilors are less frequent in cities in which terms are longer ($b = -.005$), the relationship is not statistically significant from zero (standard error = .012). The insignificant relationships between size of the council and length of council term suggest that the office-prestige theory as an explanation for female representation is not well supported, at least at the municipal level.

Incumbency

The rate at which incumbents were returned in the previous elections is not related to the percentage of women on the council. When percentage female is regressed on the proportion of incumbents reelected, the slope (.033) is some-

Table 4 Incidence of Women on City Councils by Whether Terms Are Staggered

Structure of Council Terms	Number of Cities	PERCENTAGE OF WOMEN ON COUNCILS		
		Minimum Percentage	Maximum Percentage	Mean Percentage
Simultaneous terms[1]	83	0%	63%	15%
Staggered terms[2]	128	0	67	18

Notes:

[1] In cities with simultaneous council terms, all city council seats are filled at the same election.

[2] In cities with staggered council terms, a limited number of council seats are filled in the same election year; the remainder are filled in another election year. Not all council seats are filled in the same year.

Source: Telephone survey of 211 cities with 1980 populations 25,000 or above in 11 Southern states, Spring 1986.

what smaller than its standard error (.042). This result confirms our hypothesis as well as the findings of other scholars.

Multivariate Analysis

The results of the bivariate analysis offer little reason to expect that the set of independent variables used here will be successful in predicting the incidence of female councilors. Our expectations were borne out. A number of combinations of predictors were tried, and the most successful one included three predictors: the dichotomous variables indicating the presence of staggered terms, election at large to posts, and election at large but with a residency requirement. This model explains only 3 percent of the variance, and none of the predictors has a coefficient twice as large as its standard error. The signs for the predictors indicate a weak tendency for women to serve in cities that have staggered terms and do not elect at large for specific posts or from residency districts.

Black Female Councilmembers

Of the 252 women serving on Southern city councils, 51 (20 percent) were black. Despite the small number of black women on councils, an exploration was launched to determine if their presence was systematically related to the three election-related variables considered in this paper. We hypothesized that they would not be. It is assumed that the primary factor in the election of black women is the percentage black of the city's population. This assumption is based on the large body of literature cited earlier that examines the determinants of black city council representation. Therefore, the percentage black in a city's population is interacted with dichotomous variables for each of several features relating to electoral formats. Because each interaction term includes percentage black, it is not possible to estimate a single equation as was done in the preceding section. (A model that includes percentage black with terms for electoral districting, majority vote, and use of staggered terms has serious collinearity problems.)

The model that incorporates measures of electoral format explains 10 percent of the variance (see Table 5). The coefficients for interaction terms created by multiplying percentage black and three of the electoral systems (at-large with residency requirements, pure at-large, and single-member district) were twice as large as their standard errors, with the first of these having the largest slope. No other terms in Table 5 were statistically significant. The impact of the interaction terms for at large with residency requirements (BLRESIDE) is reduced if we adjust for the negative values of the dummy variables associated with those terms (that is, RESIDE) although the small size of this term relative to its standard errors means that, in a statistical sense, it does not differ significantly from zero.

The interaction term for cities having single-member districts is statistically significant, which conforms with other research showing that blacks are more likely to be elected in cities using single-member districts.[52] An analysis of this data set in which black presence on city councils without regard for sex was

Table 5 Regression Model for Predicting the Percentage of Black Women on Southern City Councils Including Election System Interactive Predictor Variables

Percentage of black women = .019 + .123 BLPURE + .221 BLRESIDE + .066 BLMIXED
on Southern city councils   (.054)   (.103)   (.050)

                  + .162 BLSMD + .116 BLPOST + .003 PURE
                   (.056)   (.076)   (.022)

                  − .004 POST − .016 RESIDE + .030 MIXED
                   (.024)   (.026)   (.024)

                  + .002 SIZE − .006 LENGTH − .020 PCTINC
                   (.001)   (.005)   (.016)

           R^2 = .15   Adjusted R^2 = .10

Notes: Predictor (independent) variables included in the model are:

BLPURE   = Percentage black in population * pure at-large elections
BLRESIDE = Percentage black in population * at-large with residency requirement
BLMIXED = Percentage black in population * mixed systems
BLSMD   = Percentage black in population * single-member districts
BLPOST   = Percentage black in population * at-large, run for posts
PURE   = Dummy variable for at-large elections
POST   = Dummy variable for at-large elections in which candidates run for specific posts
RESIDE   = Dummy variable for at-large election systems that have residency requirements
MIXED   = Dummy variable for mixed election systems in which some candidates run at large and others for district seats
SIZE   = Number of council seats
LENGTH = Length of council terms
PCTINC   = Proportion of incumbents returned in most recent election

The R^2 (proportion of the variance explained by the predictor variables) is low (15%; adjusted R^2, 10%). This means the model is not very effective in explaining why black females get elected to southern city councils.

considered found single-member districts to be associated with a higher incidence of blacks in the South but not in other regions.[53] But this study, which does consider gender, finds that the rate at which percentage black in the population translates into black councilwomen in single-member district cities is less than in at-large cities that have a residency requirement. Our finding that black women do not fare better in single-member district cities is consistent with other research that analyzes both race and gender. As previously noted, this research shows that only black males are advantaged by single-member districts.[54]

    Table 6 reports a model that interacts percentage black with majority and plurality vote systems. Both interaction terms were statistically significant, and size of the council just missed being significant at the .05 level. The slope for plurality systems is larger than the slope for majority vote cities, but the low *R*-square signals that predictions based on this model will often be wide of the mark. The results, while showing a tendency for more black females to serve on

Table 6 Regression Model for Predicting the Percentage of Black Women on Southern City Councils Including Majority Vote Requirement Interactive Predictor Variables

Percentage of black women   = .010 + .117 BLMAJVOT + .204 BLPLUVOT   .
on Southern city councils   (.029)   (.078)

$$+ \; .011 \; \text{MAJVOTE} + \; .002 \; \text{SIZE} - \; .006 \; \text{LENGTH}$$
$$(.022) \qquad\qquad (.001) \qquad\quad (.005)$$

$$- \; .021 \; \text{PCTINC}$$
$$(.016)$$

$$R^2 = .14 \qquad\qquad \text{Adjusted } R^2 = .11$$

Notes: Predictor (independent) variables included in the model are:

BLMAJVOT = Percentage black * majority vote required

BLPLUVOT = Percentage black * plurality vote system

MAJVOTE   = Majority vote required for election

SIZE   = Number of council seats

LENGTH   = Length of council terms

PCTINC   = Proportion of incumbents returned in most recent election

The R^2 (proportion of the variance explained by the predictor variables) is low (14%; adjusted R^2, 9%). This means the model is not very effective in explaining why black females get elected to Southern city councils.

councils elected at large from residency districts and by plurality vote, are neither substantively nor statistically significant.

Other variables considered had only weak relationships with the percentage of black councilwomen. Interaction terms for staggered and nonstaggered terms were not statistically different from zero. As shown in Tables 5 and 6, black women were slightly more likely to serve on larger councils. There was essentially no relationship between the proportion of incumbents returned in the last election or the length of terms and the presence of black women on councils.

CONCLUSIONS

In this chapter the impact of several structural variables on the incidence of women on the city councils of the South has been explored to determine if structure has become more important. Although we occasionally observed variations across the categories considered, the overwhelming thrust of our findings is that structural features are not strongly associated with whether women serve as council members. The same conclusion is appropriate for the incidence of black female councilors.

In the South, women are not disadvantaged by majority vote requirements or the use of staggered terms, nor are they especially likely to serve on the councils of cities that elect some or all members from single-member districts. In some contexts, women and racial or ethnic minorities are lumped together as groups that are disadvantaged vis-à-vis white males. This study has shown the inappropriateness of this lumping together of minorities and women. We have confirmed what other scholars have also found, namely that black males are sometimes advantaged by structures that do not advantage black females, especially single-member districts.

Just as in the 1970s, our research shows that structural features are no more than weak determinants of female representation on city councils (also true for black female representation). This holds true in spite of growing numbers of women on councils. Gender may still be somewhat of an impediment to representation—but electoral structures are not.

NOTES

1. Albert K. Karnig and Oliver Walter, "Election of Women to City Councils," *Social Science Quarterly*, 56 (1976), p. 107.

2. See for example: Jeane Kirkpatrick, *Political Women* (New York: Basic Books, 1974) Marcia Manning Lee, "Why Few Women Hold Public Office: Democracy and Sexual Roles," *Political Science Quarterly*, 91 (Summer 1976), pp. 297–314; Sharyne Merritt, "Winners and Losers: Sex Differences in Municipal Elections," *American Journal of Political Science*, 21 (November 1977), pp. 731–744; Irene Diamond, *Sex Roles in the Statehouse* (New Haven: Yale University Press, 1977); Susan Welch, "Recruitment of Women to Political Office: A Discriminant Analysis," *Western Political Quarterly*, 31 (September 1978), pp. 372–380; Susan G. Mezey, "The Effects of Sex on Recruitment: Connecticut Local Offices," in Debra W. Stewart (Ed.), *Women in Local Politics* (Metuchen, NJ: Scarecrow Press, 1980), pp. 61–85; Diane L. Fowlkes, Jerry Perkins, and Sue Tolleson Rinehart, "Gender Roles and Party Roles," *American Political Science Review*, 73 (September 1979), pp. 772–780; Ronald D. Hedlund, Patricia K. Freeman, Keith E. Hamm, and Robert M. Stein, "The Electability of Women Candidates: The Effect of Sex Role Stereotypes," *Journal of Politics*, 41 (May 1979), pp. 513–524; Wilma Rule, "Why Women Don't Run: The Critical Contextual Factors in Women's Legislative Recruitment," *Western Political Quarterly*, 34 (March 1981), pp. 60–77; Laurie E. Ekstrand and William A. Eckert, "The Impact of Candidate's Sex on Voter Choice," *Western Political Quarterly*, 34 (March 1981), pp. 78–87; Susan Carroll and Wendy Strimling, *Women's Routes to Elective Office* (New Brunswick, NJ: Rutgers University, Center for the American Woman and Politics, 1983); Jerry Perkins, "Political Ambition among Black and White Women: An Intragender Test of the Socialization Model," *Women and Politics*, 6 (Spring 1986), pp.

27–40; Audrey Seiss Wells and Eleanor Catri Smeal, "Women's Attitudes towards Women in Politics: A Survey of Urban Registered Voters and Party Committeewomen," in Jane S. Jaquette (Ed.), *Women in Politics* (New York: Wiley, 1974), pp. 54–72; Trudy Haffron and Susan Gluck Mezey, "Support for Feminist Goals among Leaders of Women's Community Groups," *Signs*, 6 (1981), pp. 737–748; Keith T. Poole and L. Harmon Zeigler, *Women, Public Opinion, and Politics: The Changing Political Attitudes of American Women* (New York: Longman, 1985).

3. See Karnig and Walter, "Election of Women"; Susan A. MacManus, "Determinants of the Equitability of Female Representation on 243 City Councils," Paper presented at the annual meeting of the American Political Science Association, 1976; Welch, "Recruitment of Women"; Susan Welch and Albert K. Karnig, "Correlates of Female Office Holding in City Politics," *Journal of Politics*, 41 (1979), pp. 478–491. Albert K. Karnig and Susan Welch, "Sex and Ethnic Differences in Municipal Representation," *Social Science Quarterly*, 60 (1979), pp. 465–481; David B. Hill, "Political Culture and Female Representation," *Journal of Politics*, 43 (February 1981), pp. 151–168.

4. Karnig and Walter, "Election of Women," p. 610.

5. MacManus, "Determinants of Equitability"; Karnig and Welch, "Sex and Ethnic Differences."

6. See, for example, Leonard Cole, "Electing Blacks to Municipal Office: Structural and Social Determinants," *Urban Affairs Quarterly*, 10 (September 1974), pp. 17–39; Albert K. Karnig, "Black Representation on City Councils: The Impact of District Elections and Socioeconomic Factors," *Urban Affairs Quarterly*, 12 (December 1976), pp. 223–242; Susan A. MacManus, "City Council Election Procedures and Minority Representation: Are They Related?" *Social*

Science Quarterly, 59 (June 1978), pp. 153–161; Theodore Robinson and Thomas R. Dye, "Reformism and Black Representation on City Councils," *Social Science Quarterly*, 59 (June 1978), pp. 133–141; Delbert Taebel, "Minority Representation on City Councils," *Social Science Quarterly*, 59 (June 1978), pp. 142–152; Albert K. Karnig and Susan Welch, *Black Representation and Urban Policy*, (Chicago: University of Chicago Press, 1980); Richard L. Engstrom and Michael D. McDonald, "The Election of Blacks to City Councils: Clarifying the Impact of Electoral Arrangements on the Seats/Population Relationship," *American Political Science Review*, 75 (June 1981), pp. 344–354; Albert K. Karnig and Susan Welch, "Electoral Structure and Black Representation on City Councils," *Social Science Quarterly*, 63 (March 1982), pp. 99–114.

7. See Karnig and Walter, "Election of Women"; MacManus, "Determinants of Equitability"; Welch, "Recruitment of Women"; Welch and Karnig, "Correlates of Female Office Holding."

8. Karnig and Walter, "Election of Women."

9. MacManus, "Determinants of Equitability."

10. Welch and Karnig, "Correlates of Female Office-Holding," p. 490.

11. Ibid., p. 491.

12. See Karnig and Welch, "Sex and Ethnic Differences"; Welch and Karnig, "Correlates of Female Office Holding"; Eleanor Smeal, "Eleanor Smeal Report," *Eleanor Smeal Newsletter*, 2 (June 28, 1984), p. 1.

13. Center for the American Woman and Politics, *Women in Elective Office 1975–1980* (New Brunswick, NJ: Rutgers University, Center for the American Woman and Politics, 1981); Denise Antolini, "Women in Local Government: An Overview," in Janet Flammang (Ed.), *Political Women* (Beverly Hills, CA: Sage, 1984).

14. Susan Welch and Lee Sigelman, "Changes in Attitudes toward Women in Politics," *Social Science Quarterly*, 63 (June 1982), pp. 312–322; Lee Sigelman and Susan Welch, "Race, Gender, and Opinion toward Black and Female Candidates," *Public Opinion Quarterly*, 48 (Summer 1984), pp. 467–475.

15. Sara E. Rix (Ed.), *The American Women 1987–88: A Report in Depth* (New York: W. W. Norton, 1987).

16. See, for example, Shirley Chisholm, *Unbought and Unbossed* (Boston: Houghton Mifflin, 1970); Elizabeth M. Almquist, "Untangling the Effects of Race and Sex: The Disadvantaged Status of Black Women," *Social Science Quarterly*, 56 (June 1975), pp. 129–142; Mae C. King, "Oppression and Power: The Unique Status of the Black Woman in the American Political System," *Social Science Quarterly*, 56 (June 1975), pp. 116–128; Karnig and Welch, "Sex and Ethnic Differences"; Susan Welch and Philip Secret, "Sex, Race, and Political Participation," *Western Political Quarterly*,

34 (March 1981), pp. 5–16; Richard D. Shingles, "The Black Gender Gap: Double Jeopardy and Politicization." Paper presented at the annual meeting of the Midwest Political Science Association, 1986.

17. Sandra Baxter and Majorie Lansing, *Women and Politics: The Invisible Majority* (Ann Arbor: University of Michigan Press, 1981); Sigelman and Welch, "Changes in Attitudes"; Allen Wilhite and John Theilmann, "Gender Differences in Voting for Female Candidates: Evidence from the 1982 Election," *Public Opinion Quarterly*, 49 (Summer 1985), pp. 179–197.

18. See, for example, Joan S. Carver, "Women in Florida," *Journal of Politics*, 41 (August 1979), pp. 941–955; Eleanor C. Main, Gerald S. Gryski, and Beth Schapiro, "Different Perspectives: Southern State Legislators' Attitudes about Women in Politics," *Social Science Journal*, 21 (January 1984), pp. 21–28.

19. Carver, "Women in Florida," p. 941.

20. See Enid Lakeman, "Electoral Systems and Women in Parliament," *Parliamentarian*, 67 (July 1976), pp. 159–162; and R. Darcy, Susan Welch, and Janet Clark, *Women, Elections, and Representation* (New York: Longman, 1987).

21. Cited in Wilma Rule, "Does the Electoral System Discriminate Against Women?" *PS* (Fall 1986), p. 30.

22. Ibid.

23. Rebekah Herrick and Susan Welch, "The Impact of At-Large Elections on Representation of Black and White Women," *National Political Science Review* 3 (1992) pp. 62–67.

24. Karnig and Welch, "Sex and Ethnic Differences," p. 473.

25. Herrick and Welch, "The Impact of At-Large Elections on Representation."

26. Smeal, "Eleanor Smeal Report."

27. From an interview with Jesse Jackson, *New York Times*, December 28, 1983, p. 12.

28. Quoted in John Flesher, "Primary Vote Law Passed," *Greensboro News and Record*, July 1, 1989, pp. B1–B2.

29. Bullock and Johnson, "Sex and the Second Primary," *Social Science Quarterly*, 66 (December), pp. 933–944.

30. Arnold Fleischman and Lana Stein, "Minority and Female Success in Municipal Runoff Elections," *Social Science Quarterly*, 68 (June 1987), pp. 378–385; Charles S. Bullock III and Susan A. MacManus, "The Impact of Staggered Terms on Minority Representation," *Journal of Politics*, 49 (May 1987), pp. 543–552; Charles S. Bullock III and Susan A. MacManus, "Municipal Electoral Structure and the Election of Councilwomen," *Journal of Politics*, 53 (February 1991), pp. 75–89.

31. Chandler Davidson, "Minority Vote Dilution: An Overview," in Chandler Davidson (Ed.), *Minority*

Vote Dilution (Washington, DC: Howard University Press, 1984), pp. 1–23.

32. Bullock and MacManus, "The Impact of Staggered Terms."

33. Welch and Karnig, "Correlates of Female Office-Holding."

34. Diamond, "Sex Roles."

35. See, for example, Taebel, "Minority Representation"; Karnig and Welch, *Black Representation*; Robert J. Mundt and Peggy Heilig, "District Representation Demands and Effects in the Urban South," *Journal of Politics*, 44 (November 1982), pp. 1035–1048.

36. See Michael D. McDonald and Richard L. Engstrom, "Council Size and the Election of Blacks from Single-Member Districts: Classifying an Apparent Inconsistency between Theory and Data." Paper presented at the Thirteenth World Congress of the International Political Science Association, 1985; Bullock and MacManus, "The Impact of Staggered Terms."

37. See Taebel, "Minority Representation"; Arnold Vedlitz and Charles A. Johnson, "Community Racial Segregation, Electoral Structure, and Minority Representation," *Social Science Quarterly*, 63 (December 1982), pp 729–736.

38. Welch and Karnig, "Correlates of Female Office Holding."

39. John Kramer, "The Election of Blacks to City Councils: A 1970 Status Report and a Prolegomenon," *Journal of Black Studies*, 1 (June 1971), pp. 443–476; Karnig and Welch, *Black Representation*.

40. Charles S. Bullock III and Susan A. MacManus, "Structural Features of Municipal Elections and Black Representation," Paper presented at the annual meeting of the Southern Political Science Association, 1987.

41. Welch, "Recruitment of Women."

42. Darcy, Welch, and Clark, *Women, Elections, and Representation*, p. 150.

43. Charles S. Bullock III, "Racial Crossover Voting and the Election of Black Officials," *Journal of Politics*, 46 (February 1984), pp. 238–251.

44. William E. Nelson, Jr., and Philip J. Meranto, *Electing Black Mayors* (Columbus: Ohio State University Press, 1977).

45. Darcy, Welch, and Clark, *Women, Elections, and Representation*.

46. Karnig and Walter, "Election of Women"; MacManus, "Determinants of Equitability"; Welch and Karnig, "Correlates of Female Office Holding."

47. Welch and Karnig, "Correlates of Female Office Holding."

48. See, for example, Carver, "Women in Florida"; Albert K. Karnig and Paula D. McClain, "The New South and Black Economic and Political Development: Changes from 1970 to 1980," *Western Political Quarterly*, 38 (December 1985), pp. 539–550.

49. Welch and Karnig, "Correlates of Female Office-Holding."

50. Smeal, "Eleanor Smeal Report."

51. Fleischman and Stein, "Minority and Female Success."

52. See Engstrom and McDonald, "The Election of Blacks"; Chandler Davidson and George Korbel, "At-Large Elections and Minority Group Representation: A Reexamination of Historical and Contemporary Evidence," *Journal of Politics*, 43 (1981), pp. 932–1005.

53. Bullock and MacManus, "Structural Features of Municipal Elections and Black Representation."

54. Karnig and Welch, "Sex and Ethnic Differences"; Herrick and Welch, "The Impact of At-Large Elections on Representation."

John Bailey's Legacy: Political Parties and Women's Candidacies for Public Office

Barbara Burrell

Long-time Connecticut Democratic state party leader and Democratic National Committee chair John Bailey once declared in an infamous comment, "the only time to run a woman is when things look so bad that your only chance is to do something dramatic." John Bailey's actual behavior, however, suggests a contrary image of the relationship between party organizations and women candidates. He is credited with mentoring a number of women politicians, among them Ella Grasso, former governor of Connecticut, and his daughter, U.S. Representative Barbara Kenneally.[1] These contradictory images characterize the complicated relationship between political parties and aspiring female candidates—which is the subject of this essay. It focuses on the concept of parties as organizations, outlining their response to the idea of women running for public office in the contemporary feminist era.

A priority of the contemporary women's movement in this country has been to elect more women to public office. Women's rights activists have viewed party organizations as obstacles to the achievement of greater equality between the sexes in elective officeholding. Hostility, however, may no longer characterize party organizational attitudes and behavior toward female candidates. What is the impact of party organizations on women's quests for public office? Over the past two decades, have dramatic changes occurred in the response of party organizations to the idea of women running for elective office? Let us look at the movement of party leaders from hostility to advocacy regarding women's candidacies. National party organizations, especially in the 1980s, have responded much more favorably to women's candidacies than in previous years.

Barbara Burrell is an honorary fellow at the Women's Studies Research Center at the University of Wisconsin, at Madison.

A number of factors account for this transformation: political expediency, changes in party leadership personnel, and women's organizing. Examples of local party opposition to women's candidacies for top elective positions, however, still exist. This is evidenced by the experiences of Harriet Woods in 1982, when she announced her candidacy for the U.S. Senate from Missouri, and of Betty Tamposi, who in 1988 sought the Republican nomination for U.S. Congress in New Hampshire's second district. Woods has remarked that when she entered the Missouri Democratic primary, the state Democratic leaders rejected her because she "was too liberal, too urban, and even worse, a woman."[2] Tamposi was publicly scolded by her state's U.S. senator, Gordon Humphrey, who told her to stay home with her children. According to Senator Humphrey, "there is no way a mother of a two-year-old child can serve her constituents."[3] Betty Tamposi lost that primary. Yet parties have become much more permeable to female candidates, and these anecdotes hardly capture the totality of responses women have received from their parties in recent elections.

THE SCHOLARLY TRADITION

Many scholars have sought to explain "why there are so few women in public office."[4] Others have sought to explain variations in levels of female officeholding.[5] Certainly party would be a major factor in such considerations. The women and politics literature views party organizations as negative gatekeepers for women's candidacies.[6] The parties' literature generally presents a contrary picture of decline and transformation in the life of the parties. These changes, which have important implications for female candidates and their campaigns, need to be explored and incorporated into women and politics' research. As Baer has recently noted, "an entire area of political science *central* to the political influence of women—political parties—has been both ignored and misunderstood."[7] We need to test our images against empirical reality and assess changes over time in the party responses to women's quests for public office.

The declining status of parties in U.S. politics has been a dominant theme of the literature on contemporary parties. This pessimistic assessment of the parties' organizational life is most important for our focus on women's candidacies. Academics and journalists have described party organizations, especially at the local level, as either having disappeared or having become skeletal remains of once vibrant groups.[8] If, indeed, party organizations have become rather insignificant entities, then it would be a meaningless exercise to discuss their impact on women's candidacies. Male and female candidates would organize their own campaigns and depend on their own resources to win elections.

On the contrary, two factors regarding the life of the parties stimulate consideration of the relationship between parties and women's candidacies:

1. The party decline thesis has been challenged, especially concerning the organizational life of the parties.[9]

2. The negative impact of party organizations on women's candidacies continues to be a prominent theme of the literature on women candidates.[10] This suggests the presence of viable party organizations.

Women's rights activists, too, continue to emphasize party leadership opposition to women's candidacies in recent elections. For example, a Women's Campaign Fund spokesperson complained at the end of the 1986 election that women in statewide races were unable to enlist the full support of the party to the extent enjoyed by male candidates of equal caliber, and that "the old boys couldn't stand these women getting so close to the nominations for governorships."[11]

THE IMPACT OF PARTIES

Research on the impact of parties on the recruitment and nomination of female candidates and their campaigns should consider several possibilities:

1. Party organizations have declined and, therefore, because of their irrelevance no longer serve as barriers to women's candidacies.
2. Party decline has had a negative impact on women's candidacies.
3. Party leadership has become supportive of female candidates and now plays a positive role in their recruitment.

We also need to remember that the two major parties are not monolithic organizations and power structures. Thus, levels of support may vary. Regional variations in political culture also have influenced support for more women in political life.[12]

The Democratic and Republican parties have different political cultures. This difference has influenced their organizational response to demands for greater equality between the sexes in elective officeholding. Republicans, according to Jo Freeman, "have a unitary party in which great deference is paid to the leadership, activists are expected to be 'good soldiers,' and competing loyalties are frowned upon . . . power flows downward, separate and distinct groups are potentially dangerous."[13] The Democratic party, on the other hand, "is a coalitional, pluralistic party." Groups demand representation and have been officially recognized within the Democratic National Committee. In the Democratic party legitimacy is determined by whom you represent, and in the Republican party by whom you know and who you are. It is reasoned that women would be more likely to make it in the Republican party as individuals, not as group advocates, whereas many Democratic women have made it by challenging the leadership.

As early as 1974, the Democratic party sponsored a Campaign Conference for Democratic Women aimed at stimulating the election of more women to political office.[14] Similar conferences did not occur within the Republican party until a decade later, when political expediency took over. This is not to say, however, that the Republican party has necessarily been less receptive to female candidacies. Indeed, Eleanor Smeal, former chair of the National Organization for Women, has credited the Republican party with acting more affirmatively than the Democratic party in supporting women's candidacies.[15] But as an organized group within the Democratic party infrastructure, feminists could impose themselves on the leadership—in addition to having a sympathetic ear within the liberal wing of the party. The fact that nearly all the female members of the U.S. House of Representatives in the 1970s were Democrats reflects this organizational basis of representation within the party. Most of these women won their seats not because they were championed within their local party organizations, but because they challenged the local party structure and beat it.[16]

Further, research has found differences between the two major parties in their receptivity to women's candidacies. This pattern, however, is not consistent over time and across office levels. Rule's 1974 study, even while controlling for Southern states, singled out Democratic party dominance as a barrier to women's recruitment to state legislative office. In the same period, however, women's congressional ranks consisted almost exclusively of Democrats, as mentioned before.[17] Both patterns have changed in the past decade and a half. Nechemias reports that "by 1984 . . . outside of the South the Democratic party no longer operates as a constraint on women's access to state houses."[18]

The number of female major party nominees for the U.S. House of Representatives doubled between 1972 and 1984 (from 32 to 65). Since then it has leveled off (see Table 1). Increases in the numbers of female Republican nominees principally account for this rise. Female Republican nominees (and lawmakers) were scarce at the beginning of this time period. Over the course of these elections, however, Republicans gained parity with the Democrats, not only in the number of their female nominees, but also in the number of those elected to the House. Given the much smaller overall Republican representation in the

Table 1   Female Nominees and Winners, U.S. House of Representatives, 1972–1986, by Party

| | NOMINEES | | WINNERS | |
	Democrats	Republicans	Democrats	Republicans
1972	24	8	12	2
1974	30	15	14	4
1976	34	20	13	5
1978	26	18	11	5
1980	28	25	10	9
1982	28	27	11	9
1984	30	35	11	11
1986	30	34	12	11
1988	33	26	14	11

Note:

1989–1990 special elections brought the total number of female Democratic representatives to 15 and female Republicans to 13.

House, women are now a larger proportion of their membership than of the Democrats.

THE TRADITIONAL RELATIONSHIP BETWEEN PARTY
ORGANIZATIONS AND FEMALE POLITICIANS

The problem for would-be female elected officials has not so much been prejudice among the voters as hostility from the party apparatus and leadership. Women in former Mayor Richard Daley's Chicago organization "[had] no status, never had status and will not attain status," according to a 1974 description.[19] This statement captures the traditional attitude of male party leaders to the idea of sharing power with female politicians. The outdated attitudes of such organizational leaders were a major barrier to women achieving elective office. Susan and Martin Tolchin's *Clout* abounds with tales of horror regarding party opposition to women's candidacies in both major parties.[20] Gaining a party nomination is perceived to be harder than achieving a general election victory.

Scholars have also assessed the impact of parties on women's campaigns. In 1976, Darcy and Schramm examined voter response to female candidates in U.S House races for 1970 through 1974. They found the electorate indifferent to the sex of congressional candidates at the general election stage; that is, female candidates did as well as male candidates in similar situations. They concluded that the reason that so few women were serving in Congress was due to the recruitment and nomination process; it was noted that "the districts in which the nomination process manages to draw women are still the few, atypical, largely Democratic urban districts."[21] This was, however, only an assertion on the authors' part, not the result of any empirical analysis of the nomination process.

John Bailey's comment suggested that female candidates receive party backing disproportionately in districts dominated by the opposition party. Gertzog and Simard provide the most definitive piece of empirical evidence on this "hopeless candidacies" thesis as explaining why so few women serve in the U.S. Congress. Analyzing the nomination patterns for the U.S. House of Representatives between 1916 and 1978, they concluded that "women have been nominated for hopeless contests more often than men."[22] But they also speculated that with increasing numbers of women running for public office, the numbers in the hopeless category should decline. Such a trend, however, has run up against a shrinking opportunity structure for newcomers seeking a seat in the House. Incumbents have become increasingly advantaged, making more and more races hopeless for challengers, both male and female.

For example, "hopelessness" marked the candidacies of an incredible 91 percent of nonincumbent women nominated for the U.S. House in 1984. But 86 percent of the male nonincumbent candidates also faced incumbents.[23] Few political opportunities existed in that election for newcomers of either sex. More definitively, Darcy and others have presented data from the 1970–1984 period indicating no evidence that women candidates were being systematically recruited for hopeless races for Congress.[24] The problem for female candidates is that hopelessness characterizes most House races by nonincumbents, irrespective of the candidate's gender.

Several studies have employed candidates' or public officials' recall as a measure of the level of party recruitment activity on behalf of female candidates. Over one-half of the 50 female state legislators interviewed by Jeane Kirkpatrick in 1972 believed that "men in party organizations try to keep women out of leadership positions."[25] Susan Carroll surveyed major-party female candidates for state legislative, statewide, and congressional offices in primaries and/or general elections nationwide in 1976. She asked questions about the importance of others' encouragement in their decisions to run for office, whether they had talked with party leaders during the early stages of deciding to run, who initiated such talks, and the nature of party leaders' reactions to their proposed candidacies. Carroll concluded that a significant minority of women candidates had no contact whatsoever with party leaders regarding their candidacies. In those instances where party leaders had been involved in recruitment:

1. Party-initiated contact with female candidates was far less frequent, and the reactions of party leaders less positive, at statewide and congressional levels than at the state legislative level.
2. Party leaders often recruited women to run as sacrificial lambs in districts where the candidate of the opposition party was almost certain to win the general election.
3. The parties seem disproportionately to have recruited women to run in multimember rather than single-member districts.[26]

Unfortunately, we do not know whether these conclusions are a characteristic of women's campaigns. For example, a study of men's campaigns for public office might show the same findings. These conclusions attributed to gender may reflect general trends. That is, parties may exhibit little involvement in the recruitment of male as well as of female candidates except in adverse circumstances for the party.

Two studies have made the crucial male–female comparisons. Carroll and Strimling's survey of male and female local and state elected officials found few differences between the sexes regarding the role of parties in their recruitment. The differences that were present often benefited the female official. Large majorities of women and men who ran in partisan races for offices at all levels say that party leaders supported their initial bids for their present positions. Except for state representatives and local council members, female officeholders in partisan races more often reported being supported by party leaders in their bids for office than did their male counterparts. Similarly, except for state representatives and local council members, women more often than men were recruited to run for office by party leaders. The authors conclude that women may find it more difficult than men to run and win without the backing of their parties.[27] It should be noted that only winners were surveyed in this study.

Darcy and others conclude from an analysis of 1,000 male and female city council members that "political party leaders, traditionally thought to be important barriers to women seeking office, no longer appear to be so, at least at the local level."[28] Party encouragement was a factor equally affecting the decision of men and women to run for local office, and males and females reported equal levels of party support. These empirical studies show a trend toward a lessening of gender as a factor in party recruitment at the local level. It remains to be determined if such a trend characterizes the situation at higher levels of officeholding, and whether it is the result of party decline or party transformation.

THE NEGATIVE IMPACT OF PARTY DECLINE?

Even if one challenges the literature emphasizing party decline, certainly party organizations are less influential in nomination decisions today. How should we view the effect of this trend on female candidacies? If party organizations traditionally tended to pose an obstacle to women's recruitment, their lessened influence should have favorable consequences for female candidates. But a number of authors have suggested the possibility that the decline of parties has adversely affected women's political opportunities. From a cross-national perspective, Matthews has found that weak political parties, the entrepreneurial style of primary nominations, and candidate-oriented election campaigns seem "to discriminate against women politicians. . . . In countries with stronger parties, nominations controlled by established party leaders and proportional representation elections, women have a somewhat easier time of it."[29]

Raisa Deber has made a similar point in her study of female congressional candidates in Pennsylvania. The few women who had "won office were those who did receive organizational backing from a major party organization or from another strong faction." She concludes that "to the extent that party loyalty can elect candidates who are 'different,' 'reform' can act to remove the one force that has elevated outsiders."[30] Robert Bernstein has shown that a decline occurred in the percentage of women winning open-seat races for the U.S. House of Representatives in the 1970s compared with the 1960s. He argued that this decline was accounted for, at least in part, by the breakdown in party control, which has made it increasingly possible for ambitious candidates to compete for congressional nominations. Contests for open-seat nominations have pitted "young men in a hurry" against women without that kind of drive. Consequently, women have become less competitive in open-seat primaries.[31] Commenting on Bernstein's work, Darcy and others suggest that primaries "may actually work against behind-the-scenes party efforts to recruit women congressional candidates for desirable races."[32] Indeed, a review of national party activities in the 1980s suggests that if party organizations had more control over the nomination process, more women in the past decade would have received major-party nominations for high office.

NATIONAL PARTY ACTIVITIES AND WOMEN'S CANDIDACIES
IN THE 1980S

The 1980s represent a new era in national party approaches to the idea of women as elected public officials. It is a period characterized by positive steps to promote women's candidacies. Such promotion is limited by the parties' weakened ability to structure primary situations, although at least the Republican party has endorsed and provided resources to female candidates in some contested primaries.

One cause of this transformation is that women have increasingly become party leaders. Of course, they may be leaders of organizations with little life or influence in the electoral process, or they may be catalysts in the revival of the parties or whatever presence parties do make. The role of gender has not been explored in the transformational process of the parties. It may be that the "good old boys" are being replaced by women who are often feminists.

Feminists have obtained positions of leadership in the national party organizations at the same time that national party organizations have expanded their resources and role in federal and state-level campaigning. Ann Lewis, political director of the Democratic party in the early 1980s, is a major example. Mary Louise Smith, who served as chair of the Republican National Committee during the Ford administration, had been a founding member of the Iowa Women's Political Caucus. The presence of such individuals in party leadership positions provides opportunities to use the allocation of party resources for the recruitment of female candidates and for assistance in their campaigns.

Women have emerged as leaders at the state and local levels also. (In 1988, ten of the Democratic and six of the Republican state party chairs were women.) Massachusetts provides an example of the difference female presence makes at the state party leadership level. The Massachusetts Democratic Party's female executive director played an instrumental role in the establishment of the Women's Impact Network (WIN) in 1988. Realizing that the party organization could not favor female candidates, especially in primary contests (of crucial importance in this one-party dominated state), she developed this network dedicated to raising money for progressive Democratic women candidates outside the formal party structure.

Note, too, the response of Betsy Toole, New York State's Democratic party vice-chairwoman, when Barber Conable announced his retirement in 1984 as U.S. representative from the 30th congressional district. She said, "Women—that's what went through my mind when I first heard Conable's seat was vacant. The right woman could win in this district, you know."[33]

One can also find examples of local party bias *toward* female candidates. Such a situation occurred in at least one Massachusetts state legislative district in 1988. Here one party's town committees formed a recruitment caucus to search for a candidate. The perception is that the presence of feminist group activists in the caucus predisposed it to support a woman over several potential male candidates. Although facing primary opposition, the female candidate, endorsed by the caucus and the party's three town committees, won an easy victory. Also, one of the two female newcomers elected to the Massachusets House of Representatives in 1988 had previously served as chairperson of her Democratic town committee.

The transformation of party leadership from all male to a more sexually integrated group has contributed to the development of a more favorable party response toward female candidates. Promoting women's campaigns also became good politics in the 1980s. The "gender gap," which gained such prominence in the early part of the decade, made the parties, and especially the Republican party, cognizant of the positive advantages of promoting female candidates. Parties want above all else to win, and women candidates have come to be perceived as winners.

The political expediency of a party's being out in front in the promotion of women candidates is illustrated by a statement from the chair of the Republican Senatorial Campaign Committee (RSCC), Senator Richard Lugar, in 1983: "A concerted drive by the Republican Party to stamp itself as the party of the woman elected official would serve our nation as well as it served our own political interests. . . . The full political participation of women is a moral imperative for our society, and intelligent political goal for the Republican Party." Thus, he pledged to "commit the RSCC to the maximum legal funding and support for any Republican woman who is nominated next year, regardless of how Democratic the state or apparently formidable the Democratic candidate. I am prepared to consider direct assistance to women candidates even prior to their nomination, a sharp departure from our usual policy."[34]

This pledge, however, did not result in even the close election of any new Republican women to the U.S. Senate in 1984. However, the party did break precedent by giving female senatorial candidates $15,000 each to use in their primaries against other GOP contenders.[35] It is relatively easy for a party with a flush treasury, as the Republican party had in 1983, to make a big public relations splash by advocating women's candidacies in seemingly hopeless situations. The real test comes when the office is perceived as being winnable. Women need early support in open-seat primaries, but this is not likely to occur in either party because of the potential backlash from other candidates in such primaries. Thus, women will continue to make only the most modest of gains in their representation in national offices.

The Democrats have also adopted special strategies for female candidates for federal office. For example, former U.S. Representative Tony Coelho, in his tenure as chair of the Democratic Congressional Campaign Committee, established the Women's Congressional Council to raise money for female House candidates. According to Mr. Coelho, "Not only have we not done enough, but what the women candidates legitimately have said is that we don't give them enough help up front . . . it is important to 'invest' in women running for the House by aiding them early in their electoral efforts."[36] His goal in 1986 was to raise $200,000 for women running for the House of Representatives.

Research on the financing of U.S. House of Representatives' races shows no discrimination in party contributions to women nominees in recent elections (Table 2).

Table 2 Average Amount of Party Contributions to Male and Female Congressional Nominees, 1980–1984

	DEMOCRATS		REPUBLICANS	
	Men	Women	Men	Women
1980	$2,717	$2,056	$ 8,822	$10,369
1982	$2,820	$2,609	$12,140	$13,788
1984	$3,414	$3,474	$10,754	$11,651

In 1983 both parties sponsored national conferences for female party activists to

1. Inform them of party policies
2. Urge them to run for office
3. Provide training workshops in campaigning[37]

The national parties have also established units to aid women candidates. In 1982 the Democratic party created the Eleanor Roosevelt Fund, which provided support to women running for state and local office through 1986. It contributed more than $300,000 nationwide. In 1986, six candidates for statewide office received financial support from the fund. The fund also provided in-kind services, such as direct mailings, training sessions, and networking with political action committees. In keeping with the 1984 Democratic party platform, it also assisted progressive women candidates who were pro-choice on abortion. In addition, the fund has developed a women's recruitment project in four states to encourage the general involvement of women in party politics. The Democratic party continues to hold special sessions within its regional training workshops for new candidates.

For female GOP candidates, the National Federation of Republican Women (NFRW) is an autonomous, financially independent affiliate of the Republican National Committee. This grass-roots organization, which lists 160,000 dues-paying members, runs regional candidate seminars and campaign management schools for female activists. The NFRW expanded the focus of its programs as women's political interest evolved from volunteerism to campaign management and, in the late 1980s, into the recruitment and training of female candidates. In 1989 the NFRW sponsored five regional weekend campaign management schools for members, a program begun in 1979.[38] The federation has most recently established Project '90, a candidate recruitment program aimed at finding and training Republican women club members to run for state and local office. With the context of Project '90, the federation conducted a women's candidates' seminar in Washington. As Baer states, the NFRW "advances[s] the cause of women in the party".[39]

In 1988, for the first time, both national party platforms included statements endorsing "full and equal access of women and minorities to elective office and party endorsement" (Democrats) and "strong support for the efforts of women in seeking an equal role in government and [commitment] to the vigorous recruitment, training and campaign support for women candidates at all levels" (Republicans). These planks are indeed only symbolic statements, not substantive mandates to implement specific action. Their significance lies in the recognition by the parties of the problems of female candidates and the influence of women within the parties to make that recognition explicit and public.

CONCLUSION

Today, party roles in women's campaigns to seek nomination and run for public office are vastly different from those at the beginning of the contemporary feminist era. Sexism still exists, but the party environment generally is much more friendly toward female candidates. Women have become important leaders in these organizations. Local party groups no longer control recruitment and nomination of candidates; therefore, prejudiced attitudes of "old pols" are of less concern to aspiring female politicians. National party organizations have emerged from campaign irrelevancy to become a source of significant resources, technology and candidate assistance.[40] The national committees' philosophy toward women as nominees has passed through several stages—from indifference to special attention in the 1980s to mainstreaming in the 1990s. Party leaders now see female candidates as the rule as much as the exception. Women have access to the same resources and assistance as male candidates. Party organizations have become positive forces in women's candidacies.

Some women's rights activists, however, view the situation differently. They look at the end result and see a problem. Only 5 percent of the members of the U.S. House of Representatives are women, as are only 2 of the 100 U.S. Senators. Women represent about 17 percent of all state legislators. Women have made few gains in obtaining executive positions; in 1990 three women sought major contenders for governorships in three of our largest states (Massachusetts, Texas, and California), and one was victorious. It is now accepted that women have equal access to financial resources with male candidates once they obtain a major-party nomination, but access to early money is still believed to be more of a problem for female than for male candidates. Parties are not equipped to provide greater resources in preprimary, contested races. But that is exactly what women's rights activists would advocate.

NOTES

1. Kenneth Cooper, "Gender Gap Still Yawns Wide in Massachusetts Politics," *Boston Globe*, October 10, 1986, p. 1.

2. Bella Abzug, *Gender Gap* (Boston: Houghton Mifflin, 1984).

3. Laura Kiernan, "Humphrey: Motherhood Remarks 'Just Plain Stupid,' " *Boston Globe*, September 9, 1988, p. 1.

4. R. Darcy and Sarah Slavin Schramm, "When Women Run against Men," *Public Opinion Quarterly*,

41 (Spring 1977), pp. 1–12; Susan Carroll, *Women as Candidates in American Politics* (Bloomington: University of Indiana Press, 1985); Robert Bernstein, "Why Are There So Few Women in the House?" *Western Political Quarterly*, 39 (March 1986), pp. 155–163; R. Darcy, Susan Welch, and Janet Clark, *Women, Elections, and Representation* (New York: Longman, 1987).

5. Irene Diamond, *Sex Roles in the State House* (New Haven: Yale University Press, 1977); Wilma Rule, "Why Women Don't Run: The Critical Contextual Factors in Women's Legislative Recruitment," *Western Political Quarterly*, 34 (March 1981), pp. 60–77; Carol Nechemias, "Changes in the Election of Women to U.S. Legislative Seats," *Legislative Studies Quarterly*, 12 (February 1987), pp. 125–142.

6. See, for example, Denise Baer's review in "Political Parties: The Missing Variable in Women and Politics Research," Paper presented at the annual meeting of the Midwest Political Science Association, Chicago, April 1990.

7. Ibid.

8. Frank Sorauf, *Party Politics in America* (Boston: Little, Brown, 1980).

9. Cornelius Cotter, James Gibson, John Bibby, and Robert Huckshorn, *Party Organizations in American Politics* (New York: Praeger, 1984); Xandra Kayden and Eddie Mahe, *The Party Goes On* (New York: Basic Books, 1985); William Crotty, *Political Parties in Local Areas* (Knoxville: University of Tennessee Press, 1986).

10. Carroll, *Women as Candidates*; Denise Baer and David Bositis, "Political Coalitions and the Changing Character of Gender and Race in American Political Parties," Paper presented at the annual meeting of the Northeastern Political Science Association, November 1986; Thomas Volgy, James Schwarz, and Hildy Gottlief, "Female Representation and the Quest for Resources: Feminist Activism and Electoral Success," *Social Science Quarterly*, 67 (March 1986), pp. 156–168.

11. Lavinia Edmunds, "Women Who Won," *Ms.* (January 1987), pp. 29–33.

12. Nechemias, "Changes in the Election of Women"; Woodrow Jones and Albert Nelson, "Correlates of Women's Representation in Lower State Legislative Chambers," *Social Behavior and Personality*, 9 (1981), pp. 9–15.

13. Jo Freeman, "The Political Culture of the Democratic and Republican Parties," *Political Science Quarterly*, 101 (1986), pp. 327–356.

14. Austin Scott, "Democratic Women See Gains in 1974," *Washington Post*, March 31, 1974.

15. Jo Freeman, "Feminist Activities at the 1988 Republican Convention," *PS: Political Science and Politics*, 22 (1989), pp. 39–46.

16. Susan Tolchin and Martin Tolchin, *Clout—Womanpower and Politics* (New York: Capricorn Books, 1976).

17. Rule, "Why Women Don't Run: the Critical Contextual Factors in Women's Legislative Recruitment," *Western Political Quarterly*, (1981), pp. 60–77.

18. Nechemias, "Changes in the Election of Women."

19. Mary C. Porter and Ann B. Matasar, "The Role and Status of Women in the Daley Organization," in Jane Jaquette (Ed.), *Women in Politics* (New York: Wiley, 1974).

20. Tolchin and Tolchin, *Clout*.

21. Darcy and Schramm, "When Women Run," p. 10.

22. Irwin Gertzog and M. Michele Simard, "Women and 'Hopeless' Congressional Candidacies," *American Politics Quarterly*, 9 (October 1981), pp. 449–466.

23. Barbara Burrell, "The Political Opportunity Structure of Women Candidates of the U.S. House of Representatives in 1984," *Women & Politics* (Spring 1988).

24. Darcy et al., *Women, Elections, and Representation*, p. 83.

25. Jeane Kirkpatrick, *Political Woman* (New York: Basic Books, 1974), p. 100.

26. Carroll, *Women as Candidates*.

27. Susan Carroll and Wendy Strimling, *Women's Routes to Elective Office* (New Brunswick, NJ: Eagleton Institute of Politics, 1983).

28. Darcy et al., *Women, Elections, and Representation*, p. 38.

29. Donal Matthews, "Legislative Recruitment and Legislative Careers," *Legislative Studies Quarterly*, 9 (November 1984), pp. 547–585.

30. Raisa Deber, " 'The Fault, Dear Brutus': Women as Congressional Candidates in Pennsylvania," *Journal of Politics*, 44 (May 1982), pp. 463–479.

31. Bernstein, "So Few Women."

32. Darcy et al., *Women, Elections, and Representation*, p. 82.

33. Linda Fowler and Robert McClure, *Political Ambition* (New Haven: Yale University Press, 1989), p. 102.

34. Richard Lugar, "A Plan to Elect More GOP Women," *Washington Post*, August 21, 1983, p. C8.

35. Alison Muscatine, "Women in Uphill Struggles for Senate Seats," *Washington Post*, June 25, 1984, p. A4.

36. "Washington Talk," *New York Times*, May 26, 1986, p. B6.

37. Juan Williams, "Republicans Told Women on Slate a Help," *Washington Post*, June 4, 1984, p. A4.

38. Baer, "Political Parties."

39. Ibid.

40. Kayden and Mahe, *The Party Goes On*; Paul Herrnson, *Party Campaigning* (Cambridge, MA: Harvard University Press, 1988).

4

LEGISLATURES, WOMEN, AND POLICYMAKING

How have women fared in running for other elective offices? Marcia Lynn Whicker, Malcolm Jewell, and the editor find that there is an unequal representation of women in the Congress. These researchers find that, across the more than seventy years since women secured the right to participate politically with the passage of the Nineteenth Amendment, female representation in Congress has increased from a minuscule 0.2 percent of total membership in 1922 to only 5.2 percent in 1988. At that rate of increase, women will not achieve equality in representation until the year 2,582. This study also shows that women who do obtain congressional office do so at an older age than their male counterparts, serve significantly fewer terms, and are less likely to seek reelection. Thus, the gap between democratic rhetoric and representational reality for women is great, despite a significant narrowing in the experiential backgrounds of men and women who are elected to Congress.

On the other hand, we find that women's election to state assemblies and senates has increased 100 percent from 1974 to 1984. Further, analysis indicates two trends occurring simultaneously in the last decade. One includes building on previous gains in Republican-moralistic states' assemblies, with accompanying increases in women's election to their state senates. Another trend has been occurring in the "new wave" states. Whether Democrat-or Republican-dominated or competitive, and regardless of their political culture, large proportions of women are being elected to their state assemblies.

The most striking characteristic of the "new wave" states has been the positive impact of the women's movement within them. Other changes have included the beneficial effect of multimember legislative districts on women's recruitment. Yet, few modifications occurred in the South, where change was sporadic and uneven. Wilma Rule's essay looks at these trends in women's election to state assemblies and senates over the ten-year period from 1974 to 1984. By 1984, she finds that the lack of opportunity for women to move up from the legislature to Congress that was observed in the 1970s had disappeared in the 1980s.

When one contrasts Rule's findings with those of the MacManus and Bullock essay in Chapter 3, there is a puzzling contradiction: MacManus and Bullock find that multimember (at-large) districts and single primaries do not help women in city council races. Rule, on the other hand, finds that multimember (at-large) districts and single primaries do help female candidates in state legislative races.

Women in Congress

Marcia Lynn Whicker
Malcolm Jewell
Lois Lovelace Duke

EXPLANATIONS OF THE PARADOX OF FEMALE VOTING STRENGTH AND REPRESENTATIONAL WEAKNESS

At one level, a paradox surrounds women in politics. While constituting about 53 percent of the population, women have held only a fraction of elected offices at all levels of government.[1] As a political group, women exhibit considerable voting strength but, simultaneously, representational weakness, especially at the national level. In 1988, women held only 28 of the 535 total seats in Congress (5.2 percent). This small percentage of women as a proportion of total national representation contrasts with still small but nonetheless more than double percentages of female representation at subnational levels of government. Women held 46 of the total 330 statewide elected executive positions in state government in 1990 (13.9 percent); 1,272 of the total 7,461 state legislative seats (17.1 percent) in 1990; 8.9 percent or 1,653 out of 18,483 county governing board seats in 1988; and 14.3 percent or 14,672 out of 102,329 municipal elected offices (mayors and members of municipal governing boards) in 1985.[2]

Women who attempt to enter the political elite continue experiencing considerable difficulty.[3] One study of women in three Midwestern state legislatures found that they polled significantly fewer votes and won significantly fewer elections than men.[4] Further, women held fewer seats in professionally developed legislatures and city councils, in part due to stiffer male opposition in states

Marcia Lynn Whicker is professor of public administration, Rutgers University, Newark, New Jersey. Malcolm Jewell is professor of political science, University of Kentucky. Lois Lovelace Duke is associate professor of political Science, Clemson University.

"This article originally appeared in _Free Inquiry in Creative Sociology_, Vol. 19. No. 2, 1991, Reprinted with permission."

and communities where the compensation is higher, the tenure is longer, and the prestige of officeholding is greater.[5].

The weakened political position of women in elected politics has been tied to their weakened economic condition in the market place. Rossi anticipates that as female participation and success in the labor force increases, so will the electoral potency of women candidates.[6] Other factors offered to explain the discrepancy between female voting strength and elected legislative representation include personality differences,[7] situational factors,[8] and sex-role socialization.[9]

Situational Explanations of the Paradox

Situational factors include a lower socioeconomic status for many women, little free time, less occupational experience than men have, and lower educational status. These factors have contributed to the absence of women in state legislatures, which have frequently been "launching roles" for men elected to Congress. Yet these factors alone explain only part of the political paradox for women. According to one study using 1970s data, if women had attained the same occupational and educational status as men, they would have constituted about 25 percent of state legislatures, rather than the 5 percent of the upper houses and 8 percent of the lower houses they then constituted.[10]

Socialization Explanations of the Paradox

Socialization includes the development of stereotypical attitudes that only a restricted range of behaviors are appropriate for women, and that politics is typically a male domain.[11] "Female values" of nurturing and caretaking are viewed by both men and women as incompatible with the rough-and-tumble action and toughness that politics and effective leadership require.[12] Thus, women have not as readily perceived politics as a viable option for themselves.

Voter Stereotypes as Explanations of the Paradox

Women candidates have faced considerable hurdles in winning voter approval, since voters, as well as potential female candidates, have been influenced by sex-role stereotyping.[13] While men have been viewed by voters in terms of occupational roles, women have been perceived in terms of domestic roles.[14] Stereotypical bias is based on the gender of the candidate and not the voter, since men and women have shown little differences in their reported unwillingness to vote for a woman candidate.[15] In one study, women candidates were rated more intelligent and concerned about people, but men candidates were still perceived as more knowledgeable about politics and considered stronger.[16]

The disadvantage women experience in voter perceptions is stronger if they are in their childbearing years and are the mothers of small children.[17] Voter perceptions of candidate acceptability have affected the willingness of mothers of small children to become candidates. In another study, women with small children were found to be as politically active as women without small children except in running for public office. Politically active men with small children were equally as likely to be candidates as those without children.

Challenges to Voter Discrimination as the Explanation for the Political Paradox for Women

Various studies have questioned voter and contributor discrimination as an explanation of the political paradox for women, including challenges to the supposition that female candidate attractiveness can be negative, that voters and party leaders react negatively to female candidates, and that gender rather than incumbency is the primary handicap confronting women candidates.[18] Sigelman, Sigelman, and Fowler explored whether physical attractiveness contributes to voter stereotyping of female candidates.[19] They found complex and indirect effects of femininity and female candidate attractiveness on voters. While perceived attractiveness had no direct impact on voter willingness to support the female candidate, it was positively related to perceptions of dynamism and femininity, which in turn were positively related to voter willingness to vote for the woman candidate. Thus, voter stereotyping of women in domestic roles undercut their willingness to elect women, but perceptions of female candidates as dynamic and feminine enhanced their willingness to vote for women.

Other scholars have contradicted findings that women candidates are less successful than men candidates when confounding factors are controlled. In an analysis of five 1982 elections in which women ran as major-party candidates for high-level offices—governor in Vermont and Iowa, and U.S. Senator in Missouri, New York, and New Jersey—Zipp and Plutzer found that the sex of the candidate had little impact on voting.[20] Another study of voters' perceptions and attitudes using data from the 1982 American National Election Survey suggests that female candidates are not at a disadvantage when controls for incumbency are considered. When incumbency was controlled, voters were more likely to have contact with female candidates; were about as likely to recognize their name; made somewhat more favorable references to female candidates, and were just as likely to vote for women.[21]

Nor are women inferior fund raisers,[22] or forced by party leaders to run only in overwhelmingly "hopeless" races.[23] Women are more likely, however, to be challengers. The political opportunity structure for any political challenger tends to restrict the number of women elected to office, since incumbents tend to win reelection and most incumbents are men.[24]

INCREASING OPPORTUNITIES FOR WOMEN AT THE NATIONAL LEVEL?

1984 as a Watershed Symbol Only?

If challengers to the political paradox for women are correct, opportunities for and visibility of women at the national level should be increasing, especially in the recent past. In 1984, Democrat and former House member from New York

Geraldine Ferraro achieved the status of becoming the first woman vice-presidential candidate for either major political party. This historic event led some observers at the time to conclude that the elections in that year may represent a
watershed for women in obtaining national political visibility. In 1984, an unprecedented 65 women, 35 Republicans and 30 Democrats, also obtained a major-
party nomination for U.S. House races, an 18 percent increase over the 55
women who received major-party nominations for House races in 1982.[25]

With offers of assistance from the Women's Campaign Fund, the
Women's Trust, the National Women's Political Caucus, and the National Organization for Women, female candidate campaign organizations began to tap
additional sources for assistance and to increase in professionalism.[26] Concern
over a portending "gender gap," with popular reports circulating that women
were beginning to disproportionately favor Democratic candidates, led the Republican party to promise to fund women senatorial candidates at levels as high
as possible. Democrats responded to such pledges with their own promises of
support for national female candidates.

Yet despite increased potential for advances in national political power
for women, the general election outcomes in 1984 were disappointing to advocates of women as elected officials. Election results only preserved the status
quo in terms of number of women in the U.S. House. While all female House
incumbents who ran were victorious, two incumbents did not run, including
Ferraro, who ran for vice-president instead. These Democratic losses in the
number of women in the House were offset by Republican gains. Thus, only 22
women out of 435 members where elected to the 99th Congress, constituting
only 5 percent of House membership, a figure unchanged from the number and
percentage of women in the 94th Congress.

A Worldwide Political Paradox for Women?

Nor is the percentage of women in Congress substantially different from the
number of women in Parliament in Britain. In 1974, with women there as in
the United States constituting over 50 percent of the electorate, 96 percent of
all the members of the British Parliament were male. In 1976, the total number
of British MPs (Members of Parliament) who were women was 28, a number
roughly equivalent to the number in Congress. In the 1970s, the trend in British
politics for female candidates appeared to be an increasing number of female
candidates standing for election, but no significant gain in the number obtaining
office.[27]

A Decline in Stereotypical Assignments for Women
Members of Congress

Despite their small numbers within Congress, by the 98th Congress, women who
did succeed in getting elected were no longer linked along sex-stereotyped lines
to health, education, and children.[28] Only one of the 23 women in Congress at
that time held a committee assignment on the Education Committee, while 2 or
more women were on Armed Services, Appropriations, Science and Technology,

Commerce, Budget, Public Works, and Transportation. The only committee associated with traditional women's issues to which a proportionately large number of women were assigned (6 women) was the Special Committee on Aging.

Some stereotypes related to women still remain, founded somewhat in reality. In a study of women who served in the House between 1915 and 1976, Gehlen found that congruent with the stereotypical niceness and nurturing often associated with female roles, women members were more reluctant than their male colleagues to oppose programs that they did not support.[29]

A Shift to Solo Campaigning with Few Gains in Numbers

By the early 1980s, the nature of congressional campaigns for female candidates had changed. With one exception, women elected in the 98th Congress entered the electoral race on their own and fought vigorous campaigns to achieve office, a shift in the prevailing pattern until recent years of women succeeding their deceased fathers and husbands.[30]

This shift from spouse succession to solo campaigning, however, has not resulted in a rise in the number of women becoming national representatives. The number of women House members and senators in the 101st Congress did not increase appreciably over previous years. With only 28 of 435 House members female, women constituted 6.2 percent of the House. With 2 out of 100 senators female, women constituted a minuscule 2 percent of the U.S. Senate. Thus, of the total 535 national representatives, the 28 women serving were 5.2 percent. Of these 28 women, only one, a Democratic House member from Illinois, was a black female.

DIFFERENCES BETWEEN MALE AND FEMALE MEMBERS OF CONGRESS: ARE THEIR CONGRESSIONAL CAREERS CONVERGING?

This essay examines differences between male and female members of Congress for both background characteristics and measures of congressional "success." If those who do not believe discrimination is the primary explanation for the small number of women in national office are correct, then the political career paths of men and women should become more similar across time as women enter the labor force with greater frequency and assume a variety of jobs previously held by men only. If, however, voter stereotyping and other discriminatory factors are still important, then the political career paths and measures of success for male and female members of Congress should still be different, and little convergence will occur.

Data and Methodology

The data used here is a merged set drawn from the roster of U.S. congressional officeholders and biographical characteristics of the U.S. Congress, 1789–1989, covering the 1st to the 101st Congress. The dataset contains variables describing congressional service and background characteristics for each person who has served in the U.S. Congress from March 1789 through July 1989. A record exists for every Congress in which each individual has served, as well as for each chamber in which each individual has served, constituting 41,209 cases. Thus, statistics are reported here for both the total number of two-year congressional terms served by women, as well as for women as a percentage of the total number of individuals serving in Congress.

Prior to gaining the right to vote in the 19th Amendment to the U.S. Constitution in 1921, women did not participate actively as a group in politics. This analysis begins after the 67th Congress, and covers the 68th through the 101st Congress. Women are compared here to men serving in Congress at the same time.

Number of Women in Congress, by Year

Table 1 shows that the number of women in Congress has always been small. In the 68th Congress, immediately after the ratification of the 1921 amendment, only one lonely woman was a national representative. Between the 68th and 101st Congresses, the percentage of women in both houses rose steadily, if slowly and not consistently, from 0.2 percent to 5.2 percent—again increasing to only 5.0 percent of the total membership of Congress in 66 years. At that average rate of increase in the number of women per 66 years, women will not achieve 50 percent of the representation in Congress until the year 2,582—almost 600 years from now.

Table 1 also differentiates between Congresses when the White House was occupied by a Republican and those when the president was Democratic. Despite the image that Democrats are more supportive of women's rights, plus the greater frequency with which Democratic party platforms have adopted pro-women stances in recent years, the average number of women serving in Congress under Republican presidents (15.4, or 2.8 percent) is slightly higher than the average number of women serving under Democratic presidents (11.6, or 2.1 percent).

In part, this partisan differential reflects the increase in the number of women in recent years relative to the number in earlier years, and the fact that the presidency has been dominated by Republicans since 1968. Yet during the presidencies of Democrats Harry Truman, John Kennedy, and Jimmy Carter, the number and percentage of women in Congress fell, while during the presidencies of Republicans Eisenhower, Nixon, Reagan, and Bush, the number and percentage of women in Congress rose slightly. Perhaps, also, during the pro-women administrations of Democrats, pro-women voters become complacent about increasing representation, while during the less supportive administrations of Republican presidencies, pro-women voters become galvanized to work for and support women congressional candidates. Also, the number of women in Congress during the pro-family conservative years of the 1950s was slightly

Table 1 Number of Women in Congress, by Year

ELECTION	CONGRESS	PRESIDENT AND PARTY	NUMBER OF WOMEN IN CONGRESS	PERCENTAGE
1922	68	Warren G. Harding (R)	1	0.2
1924	69	Calvin Coolidge (R)	3	0.5
1926	70		5	0.9
1928	71	Herbert C. Hoover (R)	9	1.6
1930	72		8	1.5
1932	73	Franklin D. Roosevelt (D)	8	1.5
1934	74		8	1.5
1936	75	Franklin D. Roosevelt (D)	9	1.6
1938	76		9	1.6
1940	77	Franklin D. Roosevelt (D)	10	1.8
1942	78		9	1.6
1944	79	Franklin D. Roosevelt (D)	11	1.9
1946	80		8	1.4
1948	81	Harry S. Truman (D)	9	1.6
1950	82		9	1.6
1952	83	Dwight D. Eisenhower (R)	13	2.3
1954	84		16	3.0
1956	85	Dwight D. Eisenhower (R)	15	2.8
1958	86		19	3.4
1960	87	John F. Kennedy (D)	20	3.6
1962	88		14	2.5
1964	89	Lyndon B. Johnson (D)	13	2.4
1966	90		12	2.2
1968	91	Richard M. Nixon (R)	11	2.0
1970	92		15	2.7
1972	93	Richard M. Nixon (R)	16	2.9
1974	94		19	3.5
1976	95	Jimmy Carter (D)	19	3.5
1978	96		17	3.1
1980	97	Ronald Reagan (R)	24	4.4
1982	98		24	4.4
1984	99	Ronald Reagan (R)	25	4.6
1986	100		26	4.8
1988	101	George Bush (R)	28	5.2

SUMMARY BY PARTY OF PRESIDENT	REPUBLICAN	DEMOCRAT
Number of Terms	18	16
Average Number of Women per Congress	15.5	11.6
Percentage of Women per Term	2.8%	2.1%

higher than in the activist, more liberal decade of the 1960s, a decade that saw the launching of the second major women's movement in the United States in the twentieth century.

Making Individual-Based Comparisons

Table 2 examines the differences between men and women in terms of numbers serving and background characteristics, looking at individuals as the basis for comparison. Since 1921, 3,653 individuals have served in Congress—2,993 in the House and 660 in the Senate. Woman have made up only 3.3 percent of those individuals. Throughout two centuries of U.S. history, women have had little role in national lawmaking, since only 107 women have served in the House and 14 women in the U.S. Senate. Despite the small number of women in the Senate, proportionately the number of women who have served in the House is not statistically significantly greater (probability of chi-square = .08). Nor do women differ significantly from men in the regions from which they are elected (probability = .34). While 62.0 percent of all women who have served in Congress have been Democrats, political party is also not significantly related to gender of the representative (probability = .29).

If women in Congress do not differ from their male counterparts in region, chamber to which they are elected, and political party, do they differ in background characteristics? Men and women are both equally likely to have attended public secondary school prior to entering college, but do differ in college background (significance = .03). Women are more likely to have attended private colleges (53.7 percent) than are men (44.0 percent), but men are more likely to have attended Ivy League colleges (13.7 percent) than women (0.2 percent). A higher percentage of men (29.8 percent) attended state universities than women (25.6 percent), while a slightly higher percentage of women (14.9 percent) than men (12.5 percent) attended no college at all.

Women are now more likely to be elected to Congress on their own rather than as widows succeeding their deceased husbands. From 1916 to 1940, however, 56 percent of women elected to the House were widows of congressmen who had represented the same district. That proportion dropped to 40 percent in the 1941–1964 period and to 30 percent in the 1965–1974 period; it continued to decline to only 9 percent in the 1980 and 1982 elections.[31]

Despite the reduction in the number of women members of Congress replacing deceased fathers or husbands in recent years and the increase in the number of women engaging in solo campaigning, women differ significantly (probability of chi-square = .00) from men in having relatives in Congress. Among women, 33.9 percent had at least one relative who had served in Congress, but only 7.2 percent of men had at least one relative who had served in Congress.

Men and women also differed in prior service before entry into Congress (probability = .00). A much greater percentage of women (32.2 percent) than men (16.7 percent) had no prior government service. While similar proportions

Table 2 Number of Men and Women in Congress, 68th–101st Congress

	MEN		WOMEN		TOTAL		PROBABILITY OF CHI-SQUARE
	Number	Percentage	Number	Percentage	Number	Percentage	
Individuals serving:							
	3,532	96.7	121	3.3	3,653		
By chamber:							.08
House	2,886	81.7	107	88.4	2,993	81.9	
Senate	646	18.3	14	11.6	660	18.1	
By region: (1M)							.34
Northeast	928	26.3	32	26.4	960	26.3	
Midwest	1,071	30.3	29	24.0	1,100	30.1	
South	996	28.2	36	29.8	1,032	28.3	
West	536	15.2	24	19.8	560	15.3	
By Party: (1M)							.29
Democrat	1,898	53.7	75	62.0	1,973	54.0	
Republican	1,612	45.6	46	38.0	1,658	45.4	
Other	21	0.6	0	0.0	21	0.6	
By relatives in Congress: (1M)							.00**
None	3,278	92.8	80	66.1	3,358	91.9	
1 or more	253	7.2	41	33.9	294	8.1	
By secondary education: (6M)							.39
Unknown	137	3.9	7	5.8	144	3.9	
Public school	2,775	78.7	89	74.2	2,864	78.6	
Private school	614	17.4	24	20.0	638	17.5	
By college: (3M)							.03*
None	442	12.5	18	14.9	460	12.6	
State University	1,051	29.8	31	25.6	1,082	29.6	
Private College	1,552	44.0	65	53.7	1,617	44.3	
Ivy League	484	13.7	7	0.2	491	13.5	
By prior service: (3M)							.00**
None	590	16.7	39	32.2	629	17.2	
Local	1,639	46.4	56	46.3	1,695	46.4	
State	1,161	32.9	23	19.0	1,184	32.4	
Federal	139	3.9	3	2.5	142	3.9	

Notes:

* Significant at the .05 level. #M = number of male cases missing.

** Significant at the .01 level. #W = number of female cases missing.

Percentages are adjusted for missing cases.

of men (46.4 percent) and women (46.3 percent) had local government experience previously, men (32.9 percent) were more likely to have gained state government experience than women (19.0 percent). Few members of either gender had previous federal experience.

Making Comparisons on the Basis of Two-Year Congressional Terms

Table 3 explores similar questions using total number of two-year terms in Congress served since 1922 (18,737) as the universe, rather than total number of individuals who served. In contrast to the proportion of women who served

Table 3 Number of Two-Year Congressional Terms Served by Men and Women, 68th–101st Congress

	MEN		WOMEN		TOTAL		PROBABILITY OF CHI-SQUARE
	Number	Percentage	Number	Percentage	Number	Percentage	
Terms served by men and women:							
	18,275	97.5	462	2.5	18,737		
By chamber:							.00**
House	14,754	80.7	420	90.9	15,174	81.0	
Senate	3,521	19.3	42	9.1	3,563	19.0	
By region: (3M)							.00**
Northeast	4,561	25.0	159	34.4	4,720	25.2	
Midwest	5,214	28.5	116	25.1	5,330	28.5	
South	5,703	31.2	98	21.2	5,801	31.0	
West	2,794	15.3	89	19.3	2,883	15.4	
By Party: (1M)							.62
Democrat	10,490	57.4	265	57.4	10,755	57.4	
Republican	7,716	42.2	197	42.6	7,913	42.2	
Other	68	0.4	0	0.0	68	0.4	
By relatives in Congress: (2M)							.00**
None	16,942	92.7	321	69.5	17,263	92.1	
1 or more	1,331	7.3	141	30.5	1,472	7.9	
By secondary education: (16M, 1W)							.01**
Unknown	543	3.0	25	5.4	568	3.0	
Public school	14,607	80.0	353	76.6	14,960	79.9	
Private school	3,109	17.0	83	18.0	3,192	17.1	
By college: (5M, 1W)							.00**
None	1,989	10.9	66	14.3	2,055	11.0	
State University	5,720	31.3	113	24.5	5,833	31.1	
Private College	8,105	44.4	247	53.6	8,353	44.6	
Ivy League	2,456	13.4	35	7.6	2,491	13.3	
By prior service: (9M, 1W)							.00**
None	2,799	15.3	110	23.9	2,909	15.5	
Local	8,596	47.1	237	51.4	8,833	47.2	
State	6,057	33.2	93	20.2	6,150	32.8	
Federal	814	4.5	21	4.6	835	4.5	

Notes:

* Significant at the .05 level. #M = number of male cases missing.

** Significant at the .01 level. #W = number of female cases missing.

Percentages are adjusted for missing cases.

(3.3 percent) as a percentage of the total number of individuals in Congress during that study time span, the number of total terms served by women falls to 2.5 percent, indicating that those few women who are elected to Congress on average are serving fewer terms than their male counterparts.

When total number of terms rather than total individuals form the universe from which men and women in Congress are compared, both chamber and region are significantly related to gender at the .00 level. The number of terms women served in the House (90.9 percent) as a percentage of total terms served by women in both houses is significantly greater than the terms served by men in the House (80.7 percent) as a percentage of the total terms served by men in both houses. This contrasts with political party affiliation, where of the total terms served by men, the percentage served by men who are Democrats (57.4 percent) is virtually identical to terms served by Democratic women as a percentage of the total number of terms served by women (57.4 percent).

Women have fared considerably better in the Northeast and considerably worse in the South than have men in obtaining congressional office, relative to the performance of each gender in other regions. Women have fared marginally better in the West and marginally worse in the Midwest than men. The percentage of terms served by women who are elected from the Northeast (34.4 percent) is significantly greater than the percentage of terms served by men elected from the Northeast (25.0 percent). The percentage of terms served by women elected from the South (21.2 percent) is significantly less than the percentage of terms men served from the South (31.2 percent). Women were somewhat more likely to be from the West (19.3 percent) than men (15.3 percent), and somewhat less likely to be from the Midwest (25.1 percent) than men (28.5 percent).

Using terms served as the unit of analysis, similar patterns emerge for male–female differences in relatives in Congress, college attended, and prior government service to those that appeared when individuals served was the unit of analysis. Each of these variables continues to be significantly related to gender of the member of Congress. Women are more likely to have had at least one relative in Congress and to have attended private colleges, and are less likely to have served at the state level prior to entering Congress. Additionally, secondary education is significantly related to gender, with women slightly less likely (76.4 percent) than men (80.0 percent) to have attended public schools.

Measures of Congressional Success

Table 4 examines measures of congressional success for individuals by gender. The age at which the member first entered Congress, the total years served in Congress, and the member's reason for leaving Congress are all significantly related at the .00 level to the gender of the member. In each instance, women are less successful than men. Service after leaving Congress is not related to gender.

On average, women are older (49.3 years old) than men (45.4 years of age) when they first enter Congress. Women serve an average of 6.6 years, 4.2 years less than the average years (10.8) served by men. The most common reason women leave Congress is a decision to not seek reelection (40.0 percent) while only 20.2 percent of men leave Congress because they do not seek reelection. Men (11.9 percent) are far more likely than women (2.5 percent) to have died in office. Women (6.7 percent) are slightly less likely than men (10.4 percent) to have been defeated in a general election.

Table 4 One-Way ANOVA and Contingency Table Results for Congressional Success, by Sex

CONGRESSIONAL SUCCESS	MALE		FEMALE		TOTAL		PROBABILITY
	Mean		Mean		Mean		of F
ANOVA: Age first in Congress	45.4		49.3		45.5		.00**
Total years served	10.8		6.6		10.7		.00**
Frequencies, percentages:	Number	Percentage	Number	Percentage	Number	Percentage	of Chi-Square
Reason left Congress (2M, 1W)							.00**
Unknown, N.A.	992	28.1	18	15.0	1,010	27.7	
General election defeat	367	10.4	8	6.7	375	10.3	
Died in office	419	11.9	3	2.5	422	11.6	
Did not seek reelection	713	20.2	48	40.0	761	20.8	
Sought other elective office	249	7.1	12	10.0	261	7.2	
Accepted federal office	75	2.1	0	0.0	75	2.1	
Elected to other House	115	3.3	1	0.8	116	3.2	
Resigned, withdrew, expelled	92	2.6	2	1.7	94	2.6	
Still serving	508	14.4	28	23.3	536	14.7	
Number of levels after Congress (553M, 28W)							.84
None	2,207	74.1	70	75.3	2,277	74.1	
One	655	22.0	21	22.6	676	22.0	
Two	110	3.7	2	2.2	112	3.6	
Three	7	0.2	0	0.0	7	0.2	

Notes:

* Significant at the .05 level.

** Significant at the .01 level.

#M = Number of male cases missing or dead.

#W = Number of female cases missing or dead.

Percentages are adjusted for missing and dead cases.

Comparing Congressional Careers across Time by Decade

Table 5 examines trends in national representation by gender across time. When terms served is the unit of analysis, the proportion of women holding congressional office has increased from 0.8 percent of total congressional membership in the 1920s to 4.7 percent in the 1980s. Female representation in the House went from 1.0 percent in the 1920s to 5.3 percent in the 1980s, while Senate membership rose from 0 to 2.0 percent across the same time span.

   While some aspects of qualifications had previously divided men and women—whether or not the individual had a relative who had served in Congress and the type of precongressional service held—men and women are becoming more similar. In the 1920s, 88.7 percent of all men serving in Congress did not have a relative who had served in the same institution, but only 22.2 percent of all women in Congress had no relative who had served there. This reflects the fact that many women were widows of members who died in office. By the 1980s,

Table 5 Men and Women, by Two-Year Term, by Decade

	MEN		WOMEN	
	Number	Percentage	Number	Percentage
Terms served by men and women:				
1920s	2206	99.2	18	0.8
1930s	2739	98.5	42	1.5
1940s	2747	98.3	47	1.7
1950s	2675	97.4	72	2.6
1960s	2685	97.5	70	2.5
1970s	2637	96.8	86	3.2
1980s	2586	95.3	127	4.7
By chamber:				
House				
1920s	1782	99.0	18	1.0
1930s	2219	98.5	34	1.5
1940s	2209	98.1	43	1.9
1950s	2157	97.1	64	2.9
1960s	2167	97.2	62	2.8
1970s	2129	96.3	82	3.7
1980s	2091	94.7	117	5.3
Senate:				
1920s	424	100.0	0	0.0
1930s	520	98.5	8	1.5
1940s	538	99.3	4	0.7
1950s	518	98.5	8	1.5
1960s	518	98.5	8	1.5
1970s	508	99.2	4	0.8
1980s	495	98.0	10	2.0
By relatives in Congress:				
None:				
1920s	1957	88.7	4	22.2
1930s	2464	90.0	20	47.6
1940s	2522	91.8	23	48.9
1950s	2498	93.4	36	50.0
1960s	2530	94.2	44	62.9
1970s	2499	94.8	79	91.9
1980s	2472	95.6	115	90.6
By prior service:				
None:				
1920s	387	17.5	11	61.1
1930s	532	19.4	22	52.4
1940s	564	20.5	14	29.8
1950s	510	19.1	23	31.9
1960s	303	11.3	12	17.1
1970s	174	6.6	5	5.8
1980s	329	12.8	23	18.3
Local:				
1920s	1067	48.4	7	38.9
1930s	1346	49.1	17	40.5

Table 5   (continued)

	MEN		WOMEN	
	Number	Percentage	Number	Percentage
1940s	1340	48.8	25	53.2
1950s	1268	47.4	40	55.6
1960s	1198	44.6	46	65.7
1970s	1072	40.7	40	46.5
1980s	1305	50.6	62	49.2
State:				
1920s	677	30.7	0	0.0
1930s	750	27.4	3	7.1
1940s	742	27.0	8	17.0
1950s	792	29.6	3	4.2
1960s	1015	37.8	7	10.0
1970s	1214	46.0	36	41.9
1980s	867	33.6	36	28.6

however, 95.6 percent of all men in Congress had no relative there, while 90.6 percent of all women also had no relative who had served in Congress. Plainly, women had reached almost the same percentage as men on this characteristic, and were being elected in their own right, rather than on the name recognition and contacts of deceased husbands.

A similar picture emerges when the precongressional service for both genders is examined. In the 1920s, 61.1 percent of women in Congress, contrasted with only 17.5 percent of men there, had no prior government or political experience. By the 1980s, these two percentages had almost converged, so that only 12.8 percent of men and 18.3 percent of women in Congress had no prior government experience. In the 1980s, half of men and half of women in Congress had local experience before entering Congress. A slightly higher percentage of men (33.6 percent) than women (28.6 percent) had previous state-level experience. Despite this difference, however, the gaps between the experiential backgrounds of men and women in Congress have narrowed significantly across the sixty-six-year time span studied.

CONCLUSION

Much has been written about the inroads women have made in politics in gaining elected office in recent years, especially at the state and local levels. Greater political participation by women has been viewed as beneficial.[32] Women are said to have unique contributions to make based on their differential role socialization, their greater concern with group harmony, and their emphasis on caring for future generations. The full participation of women, as well as all disadvantaged groups, would implement democracy in its highest and purest form, producing regime legitimacy, and would expand the talent pool from which national leaders are selected.

Despite such rhetoric and a significant narrowing in the experiential backgrounds of men and women who serve in Congress, the reality is that women have played virtually no role in shaping the nation's laws. Women could not vote in most states prior to 1921, and since then have succeeded in achieving only token representation in Congress. Not only do women almost never obtain congressional office, but once elected, by every measure examined here, they are less successful. The gap between Democratic rhetoric and representational reality for women is great.

NOTES

1. Ronald D. Hedlund, Patricia K. Freeman, Keith E. Hamm, and Robert M. Stein, "The Electability of Women Candidates: The Effects of Sex Role Stereotypes," *Journal of Politics*, 41 (1–2) (1979), pp. 513–524; and Carol Nechemias, "Changes in the Election of Women to U.S. State Legislative Seats," *Legislative Studies Quarterly*, 12 (February 1987), pp. 125–142.

2. Center for the American Woman and Politics. Eagleton Institute of Politics (New Brunswick, NJ: 1990).

3. Irene Diamond, *Sex Roles in the State House* (New Haven: Yale University Press, 1977); Susan Welch, "Recruitment of Women to Public Office," *Western Political Quarterly*, 31 (September 1978), pp. 372–380; Susan Gluck Mezey, "The Effects of Sex on Recruitment: Local Connecticut Offices," in Debra Stewart, (Ed.), *Women in Local Politics* (Metuchen, NJ: Scarecrow Press, 1980); Ruth Mandel, "The Image Campaign," in James David Barber and Barbara Kellerman, (Eds.), *Women Leaders in American Politics* (Englewood Cliffs, NJ: Prentice-Hall, 1986), pp. 261–271; and Robert Darcy, Susan Welch, and Janet Clark, *Women, Elections, and Representation* (New York: Longman, 1987).

4. Margery M. Ambrosius and Susan Welch, "Women and Politics at the Grassroots: Women Candidates for Office in Three States," Paper presented at the annual meeting of the Western Social Science Association, April 1981.

5. Diamond, *Sex Roles*; David B. Hill, "Political Culture and Female Political Representation," *Journal of Politics*, 43 (1–2) (1981), pp. 159–168.

6. Alice S. Rossi, "Beyond the Gender Gap: Women's Bid for Political Power," *Social Science Quarterly*, 64 (1983), pp. 718–733.

7. Hedlund et al., "Electability of Women Candidates."

8. Ruth Schwartz Cowan, "The Industrial Revolution in the Home: Household Technology and Social Change in the Twentieth Century," *Technology and Culture*, 17 (1976), pp. 1–23.

9. Marcia Manning Lee, "Why Few Women Hold Public Office: Democracy and Sex Roles," *Political Science Quarterly*, 91 (1–2) (1976), pp. 297–314; and Marcia Lynn Whicker and Jennie J. Kronenfeld, *Sex Roles: Technology, Politics, and Policy* (New York: Praeger, 1986).

10. Darcy et al., *Women, Elections, and Representation*.

11. B. E. Forisha, *Sex Roles and Personal Awareness* (Morristown, NJ: General Learning Press, 1978); R. D. Hess and J. V. Torney, *The Development of Political Attitudes in Children* (Chicago: Aldine, 1967); J. Boles and H. Duriot, "Stereotyping of Males and Females in Elected Office: The Implications of an Attitudinal Study," Paper presented at the annual meeting of the Midwest Political Science Association, April 1980; J. Boles and H. Duriot, "Political Woman and Superwoman: Sex Stereotyping of Females in Elected Office," Paper presented at the annual meeting of the Midwest Political Science Association meeting, April 1981; R. B. Deber, "The Fault Dear Brutus: Women as Congressional Candidates in Pennsylvania," *The Journal of Politics*, 44 (1982), pp. 463–479; L. Ekstrand and W. Eckert, "The Impact of Candidate's Sex on Voter Choice," *Western Political Quarterly*, 34 (1981), pp. 78–87; Hedlund et al., "Electability of Women Candidates"; Virginia Sapiro, "If U.S. Senator Baker Were a Woman: An Experimental Study of Candidates' Images," *Political Psychology*, 3 (1–2) (1981–1982), pp. 61–83; Lee Sigelman and Susan Welch, "Race, Gender, and Opinion toward Black and Female Presidential Candidates," *Public Opinion Quarterly*, 48 (1984), pp. 462–475.

12. F. L. Gehlen, "Women Members of Congress: A Distinctive Role," in M. Githens and J. L. Prestage

(Eds.), *A Portrait of Marginality: The Political Behavior of American Women* (New York: Longman, 1977), pp. 304–319.

13. Elizabeth Holtzman and Shirley Williams, "Women in the Political World: Observations," *Daedalus*, 116 (1987), pp. 25–33.

14. Marcia Lynn Whicker and Todd Areson, "The Maleness of the American Presidency," *Journal of Political Science*, 17 (Spring 1989), pp. 63–73; and Mandel, "The Image Campaign."

15. Susan Welch and Lee Sigelman, "Changes in Public Attitudes toward Women in Politics," *Social Science Quarterly*, 62 (June 1982), pp. 312–322.

16. Margaret Mericle, S. Lenart, and K. Heilig, "Women Candidates: Even If All Things Are Equal, Will They Get Elected?" Paper presented at the annual meeting of the Midwest Political Science Association, April 1989.

17. Hedlund et al., "Electability of Women Candidates."

18. A. Karnig and B. O. Walter, "Election of Women to City Councils," *Social Science Quarterly*, 56 (1976), pp. 605–613; Ekstrand and Eckert, "The Impact of Candidate's Sex"; Robert Darcy and S. Schramm, "When Women Run against Men," *Public Opinion Quarterly*, 41 (1977), pp. 1–12; and R. Bernstein, "Why Are There So Few Women in the House?" *Western Political Quarterly*, 39 (1986), pp. 155–163.

19. Lee Sigelman, Carol K. Sigelman, and Christopher Fowler, "A Bird of a Different Feather? An Experimental Investigation of Physical Attractiveness and the Electability of Female Candidates," *Social Psychology Quarterly*, 50 (1) (1987) pp. 32–43.

20. John F. Zipp and Eric Plutzer, "Gender Differences in Voting for Female Candidates: Evidence from the 1982 Election," *Public Opinion Quarterly*, 49 (1985), pp. 179–197.

21. Darcy, Welch, and Clark, "Women, Elections, and Representation," pp. 73–81.

22. Barbara C. Burrell, "Women's and Men's Campaigns for the U.S. House of Representatives, 1972–1982: A Finance Gap?" *American Politics Quarterly*, 13 (1985), pp. 251–272; and Robert M. Darcy, M. Brewer, and C. Clay, "Women in the Oklahoma Political System: State Legislative Elections," *The Social Science Journal*, 21 (January 1985), pp. 67–78.

23. I. Gertzog and M. M. Simard, "Women and 'Hopeless' Congressional Candidacies: Nomination Frequencies, 1916–1978," *American Politics Quarterly*, 9 (1981), pp. 449–466; and Janet Clark, Robert Darcy, Susan Welch, and M. Ambrosius, "Women as Legislative Candidates in Six States," in J. A. Flammang (Ed.), *Political Women: Current Roles in State and Local Government* (Beverly Hills, CA: Sage, 1985).

24. Robert Darcy and James R. Choike, "A Formal Analysis of Legislative Turnover: Women Candidates and Legislative Representation," *American Journal of Political Science*, 30 (1) (1986), pp. 237–255.

25. Barbara C. Burrell, "The Political Opportunity of Women Candidates for the U.S. House of Representatives in 1984," *Women and Politics*, 8 (1988), pp. 51–68.

26. Susan Carroll, *Women as Candidates in American Politics* (Bloomington: Indiana University Press, 1985).

27. Elizabeth Vallance, *Women in the House: A Study of Women Members of Parliament* (Atlantic Highlands, NJ: Athlone Press, 1979).

28. Rossi, "Beyond the Gender Gap."

29. Gehlen, "Women Members of Congress."

30. Irwin Gertzog, "Changing Patterns of Female Recruitment to the U.S. House of Representatives," *Legislative Studies Quarterly*, 4 (1979), pp. 429–445.

31. Darcy, Welch, and Clark, *Women, Elections, and Representation*.

32. Ibid.

Why Are More Women
State Legislators?

Wilma Rule

During the Vietnam years and the civil rights struggles of the 1960s, a new movement was born.[1] Young women had been told to "shut up and make sandwiches" by the men who were planning antiwar and antisegregation protests. The women asked themselves, "Why are we kept in the kitchen while the men make the decisions?" Meanwhile, older women in Washington were speaking out against the gender inequality in the law and the workaday world. With the growing questioning of these inequities, the women's movement came into being. In the 1960s there were few women in the halls of political state power: only 4 percent of state legislators were women. By 1974, of those in state assemblies and senates, 6 percent were women. By 1984, the numbers had doubled to 12 percent, and by 1988 they constituted 16 percent.[2] Although 84 percent of state legislators are male, women's political strength in state houses and senates is beginning to reach a critical mass. As women's numbers grow, legal gains can be made not only for women and children, but also for protecting and promoting the state's environment, health, and a peacetime prosperity.[3]

This article asks:

1. What are the reasons women's election to the fifty state assemblies and senates increased 100 percent in the decade 1974–1984? (see Table 1).
2. What are the factors that are more favorable in the 1980s than in the 1970s?

Wilma Rule is adjunct professor of political science at the University of Nevada, Reno.

Original article appeared in the *Western Political Quarterly*, vol. 43 (June 1990). This version, revised by the author, is reprinted with permission by the author and the University of Utah, copyright holder.

In order to arrive at an explanation of women's growing power in 1984, past research is replicated and then other variables are added in an effort to understand the changes that have occurred since the 1970s. We examine whether women are still likely to be elected in states with small populations and large legislatures, as was true in the 1960s and 1970s.[4] Also we ask whether one can predict women's increases in the 1980s from the proportions in individual states in the 1970s.[5] We expect that states favorable in past decades will continue to be so, while at the same time others are now providing new opportunities for women's election to legislatures.

We also examine the relationship of Democratic or Republican party dominance and women's recruitment to state assemblies and senates.[6] Are Republican party–dominated states (i.e., those with 60 percent or more Republican members in the legislature) still favorable grounds for women's election, as in the 1960s and 1970s? And are Democratic party states still unfavorable? We expect that the legislative barriers to women in the Democratic party, particularly in the Northern states, came down in the 1980s. But we also anticipate that the Republican party states remained favorable grounds for women's election in that decade.

Competitive states—those that are not dominated by one party or another—had no relationship to women's election in the 1970s. We expect that trend to continue. This is because those states varied in the money that was spent for social welfare in the 1970s. Low-social-welfare states usually are not favorable for women's election to state legislatures, while those that spend more for this purpose are.[7]

Several scholars have observed that women are likely to be recruited in states that have a "moral" political culture, and are unlikely to be elected in "traditional" and "individualistic" states.[8] In moral states—such as those in most of New England as well as Arizona, Oregon, and Washington—politics is everybody's business. Elected officials are expected to be selfless and committed to promoting the public's interest. In the "traditional" state politics of the Southern states, by contrast, government is of, by, and for a privileged few, usually white males. And in the "individualistic" states of Illinois, Massachusetts, and New York, government is viewed as if it were a business serving various competing interests for the state officeholders whose career is politics. This study anticipates that states with moral cultures will continue to be favorable and that women's recruitment in traditional and individualistic states will increase over a decade earlier.

Recently attention has turned to a new question: Does it make a difference in women's recruitment if legislators are elected under different election procedures? Yes, several scholars found, it does make a considerable difference.[9] They discovered that when voters could choose two or more representatives for the legislature instead of one from each district, many more women got elected to their state houses.

We expect that the importance of multimember districts for women's

Table 1 Women in U.S. State Legislatures, 1974 and 1984

STATE	STATE SENATE Number of Senators	STATE SENATE Number of Women 1974	STATE SENATE Number of Women 1984	STATE HOUSE Number of Members	STATE HOUSE Number of Women 1974	STATE HOUSE Number of Women 1984	Percentage of Women in Both Houses* 1974	Percentage of Women in Both Houses* 1984
Alabama	35	0	1	105	1	5	1%	4%
Alaska	20	1	2	40	6	4	12	10
Arizona	30	3	4	60	10	12	14	18
Arkansas	35	1	0	100	2	7	2	5
California	40	1	2	80	2	12	3	12
Colorado	35	3	6	65	5	19	8	25
Connecticut	36	3	8	151	17	33	10	21
Delaware	21	1	3	41	6	7	11	16
Florida	40	1	1	120	6	18	4	16
Georgia	56	0	2	180	2	17	1	8
Hawaii	25	1	3	51	3	12	5	20
Idaho	35	1	3	70	6	12	7	14
Illinois	59	3	8	118	8	18	5	11
Indiana	50	3	4	100	6	14	6	12
Iowa	50	4	1	100	7	13	7	9
Kansas	40	1	2	125	3	21	2	13
Kentucky	38	2	2	100	3	8	4	7
Louisiana	39	1	0	105	2	5	2	3
Maine	33	1	6	151	16	35	9	22
Maryland	47	4	2	141	8	33	6	19
Massachusetts	40	2	7	160	7	19	3	9
Michigan	38	0	1	110	6	12	4	9
Minnesota	67	0	8	134	6	18	3	13
Mississippi	52	1	0	122	5	3	3	2
Missouri	34	1	1	163	10	18	6	10
Montana	50	2	2	100	7	12	6	6
Nebraska**	49	1	7				2	14
Nevada	21	1	2	42	4	3	8	8
New Hampshire	24	2	5	400	83	111		27
New Jersey	40	3	2	80	6	8	8	8
New Mexico	42	2	1	70	0	6	2	6
New York	61	3	5	150	4	15	3	10
North Carolina	50	1	6	120	8	20	5	15
North Dakota	53	3	3	106	10	12	8	10
Ohio	33	3	0	99	5	12	6	9
Oklahoma	48	0	1	101	2	10	1	7
Oregon	30	2	6	60	9	13	12	21
Pennsylvania	50	1	1	203	6	8	3	4
Rhode Island	50	1	5	100	3	13	3	12
South Carolina	46	0	2	124	5	10	3	7
South Dakota	35	1	4	70	5	10	6	13
Tennessee	33	0	1	99	4	9	3	8
Texas	31	1	0	150	5	11	3	6
Utah	29	0	1	75	6	6	6	7
Vermont	30	3	4	150	17	29	11	18

Table 1   (continued)

STATE	STATE SENATE			STATE HOUSE			Percentage of Women in Both Houses*	
	Number of Senators	Number of Women		Number of Members	Number of Women			
		1974	1984		1974	1984	1974	1984
Virginia	40	0	2	100	6	11	4	9
Washington	49	1	8	98	12	19	9	18
West Virginia	34	1	2	100	9	12	7	10
Wisconsin	33	0	2	99	6	24	5	20
Wyoming	30	1	2	62	4	16	5	20
Average							5.7	
Percentage		3.8	8.1		7.1	13.7		12.1

Notes:

* Percentages are computed on the basis of numbers of state senate and house members in 1974 and 1984. The numbers of senate and house members in this table are for 1984.

**Nebraska is unicameral.

Source: "Women State Legislators as of January, 1974" (New Brunswick, NJ: Center for the American Women in Politics, Eagleton Institute of Politics, Rutgers, 1974) and Council of State Governments, *State Elective Officials and the Legislatures, 1983–1984* (Lexington, KY: Council of State Governments).

election to state legislatures will be upheld in this study. Also, we expect that the single primary (in which the candidate with the most votes wins the nomination) will be favorable to women. The double or runoff primary in some Southern states requires that a candidate achieve an absolute majority vote before she or he runs in the final election.[10] A majority of votes is more difficult to achieve for a woman legislative candidate than it is for a male contestant. In consequence, the author expects that fewer women will be elected to legislatures in double-primary states.

This essay also examines whether the legislature is still a dead end for women legislators, as it was in the 1970s when few were elected to Congress. Where large proportions of women were elected to legislatures in low-population states (such as New Hampshire), few were elected to Congress; also, where a small proportion was recruited to the legislatures in high-population states (such as California), only a small number also went on to Congress.[11] We hypothesize that this situation has changed in the 1980s, with more opportunity for women legislators to move up to Congress and to statewide offices such as governor and secretary of state.

Of considerable interest is whether the women's movement has played a significant role in this period of great change in women's legislative representation. We expect that with the growth of the women's movement, there has developed a reciprocal relationship among women at various levels of government that had not been present before. Specific women's organizations, such as the National Organization for Women, are also expected to have aided women's recruitment in the 1980s.[12] In turn, an important base of women's organizations has been women in the work force and professional women. It is expected that these changes in women's work outside the home have had a favorable impact on women's legislative recruitment in the 1980s as in the 1970s.

The factors promoting or hindering women's recruitment to state senates have been given scarce research attention, perhaps because few women were elected to them. However, the percentage of women in state senates has doubled in the last decade and in 1984 reached 8 percent. Women's recruitment to state senates may be of interest not only because it will broaden the representativeness of those chambers but also because it will provide a future pool of experienced and credible women candidates for the U.S. House of Representatives, which in 1990 was about 94 percent male.

We suggest that women's recruitment to state senates has a time-lagged, two-tiered pattern. We expect that those states where women were first elected in large numbers to state assemblies in the 1960s and 1970s, such as many in New England, will now have the largest percentages of women state senators. This is likely because women who have served some terms in the assembly and who have become well known should have greater chances for state senate election than those without a legislative background.[13]

METHODOLOGY

Our analysis required the gathering of some 80—sometimes overlapping—political and socioeconomic contextual variables. For example, we collected data on the extent of party dominance in each house of the fifty legislatures for 1974 and 1984, as well as the strength of parties at the local and state levels. The data were collected primarily from standard sources (see Box 1).

Numerous and different statistical tests on various sets and subsets were conducted. These included Pearsonian correlations, factor analysis, and stepwise

---

SOURCES FOR VARIABLES

Council for State Governments. *The book of the states*, 1972–1973, 1974–1975, 1983–1984, and 1985.

National Center for Educational Statistics. *Earned degrees conferred*, 1972–1973, 1973–1974, and 1979–1980.

National Organization for Women.

Official Catholic Directory. Wilmette, IL: National Register Publishing Company, 1983.

U.S. Bureau of the Census. *Characteristics of the Population, 1980; General Social and Economic Characteristics, 1980; Statistical Abstract of the United States, 1981, 1984, 1985, 1986, 1988, 1989* (Washington, DC: U.S. Government Printing Office, 1986).

multiple regressions. The bivariate correlational analysis included separate and combined sets of the percentages of women in the assemblies and senates for the 1974 and 1984 periods in all fifty states, and in forty non-Confederate states. From this analysis, the direct relationship between women's election to state legislatures and political and socioeconomic variables was determined. The results are presented in Table 2.

Then, a rotated orthogonal factor analysis using all the variables was undertaken. One objective was to verify the interpretation of the correlational analysis by employing another test using the same data; another was to provide a basis for reducing the data set. The factor analysis resulted in nine factors with closely interrelated variables clustered in each factor. Factor 1, for example, contained these statistically significant variables: three measures of state Republican party strength, a moral culture scale, and higher levels of education. From this analysis the dataset was winnowed to 39 significant variables (see Box 2).

The next step involved multiple regression analyses with the reduced data set. Stepwise multiple regression was used to determine which were the most predictive nonoverlapping variables for women's legislative recruitment in 1984. Six regressions were run. Three used the decade's percentage increases in

Table 2 Continuity and Change in Women's Recruitment to State Assemblies and Senates, 1974–1984 (Based on Pearsonian Correlations)

I. CONTINUING FAVORABLE FACTORS, 1974–1984
Republican party dominance of legislatures***
Moral state political culture***
Higher AFDC payments**
No second primary**

II. CONTINUING UNFAVORABLE FACTORS, 1974–1984
Democratic dominance of legislatures, especially in former Confederacy states***
Traditional Southern culture***

III. FACTORS NO LONGER UNFAVORABLE, 1984
Small assemblies in high-population states‡
Low-income states‡

IV. NEW CONTEXTUAL CONDITIONS AIDING WOMEN'S RECRUITMENT, 1984
Individualistic state culture***
Multimember assembly districts*
Women in U.S. Congress**
Women in labor force***
Professional women**
National Organization for Women***

Notes:

***Significant at the .001 level.

**Significant at the .01 level.

*Significant at the .02 level.

‡Not statistically significant.

Sources: Refer to Box 1.

VARIABLES USED FOR REGRESSION ANALYSES

Percentage women in assemblies and senates, 1984, and in both chambers
Increase in percentage women in assemblies and senates, 1974–1984, and in both chambers
States with multimember districts in assemblies and/or senates
States with primary runoffs
Women with professional degrees
Per-pupil educational expenditures
Aid to Dependent Children
Ranney Index of party dominance
Assembly and state competitiveness
Democratic dominance of state assemblies and senates
Average strength of local Democratic and Republican parties
Average strength of state Democratic and Republican parties
Percentage of women in state's congressional delegation, 1973–1983
Average percentage women in congressional delegation, 1973–1983
Percentage women state executive officers, 1983
Average percentage women state executive officers, 1973–1983
Percentage women in U.S. House delegation, 1973–1983
Johnson's individualistic and traditional state ratings
Sharkansky's cultural scale
Ratio of state population to assembly and senate seats
Ratio of state population to chapters of the National Organization for Women

women's election to the state assemblies, the senates, and both chambers as dependent variables—that is, the ones for which we wish to find "causes." The result of these analyses is presented below in the section entitled "The New Wave: States with the Most Increases, 1974–1984." In the remaining three analyses the dependent variables were the 1984 percentage of women in state assemblies, senates, and both chambers. The latter regression was selected for presentation as Table 3. It represents a parsimonious yet comprehensive summary of the most significant variables for explaining women's legislative election in 1984.

FINDINGS

Continuity and Change in All Fifty States, 1974–1984

The contextual variables related to women's political recruitment in the last decade are summarized in Table 2. They are based on simple bivariate correlations. In section I of Table 2, the continuing favorable contextual factors from the 1970s are presented. These are descriptive of Republican-dominated New England states. In section II are listed two continuing negative factors for women's recruitment—Democratic party dominance of the assemblies and state senates and traditional culture. Although the negative correlation with Democratic party dominance has declined in the last decade, it is still significant in the following ten former confederate states: Alabama, Arkansas, Florida, Georgia, Louisiana, Mississippi, North Carolina, South Carolina, Texas, and Virginia.

In section III, the previously unfavorable relationship of small assemblies in high-population states no longer is a negative contextual factor as, for example, in the California of 1984. Nor are states that have a low per capita income. In the following section, there are six new variables that have emerged as significant for women's recruitment during the ten-year period. These include individualistic state cultures, such as those in the Midwest, and states with multimember assembly districts.

The remaining four favorable variables relate in various ways to the growth of the women's movement. The first shows a relationship between the election of women in Congress to greater representation of women in the same state's legislatures. Women's labor force participation and the presence of a large proportion of women professionals are also significant. Finally, women's associations (as represented in our data set by ratios of chapters of the National Organization for Women to state population) are shown to be highly correlated with greater percentages of women in state legislatures.

The New Wave: States with the Most Increases, 1974–1984

To further understand why it is easier to elect women to the state legislatures in 1984 as compared to a decade earlier, we analyzed the characteristics of states that had the greatest percentage increases in women's recruitment in the decade. Nineteen "new wave" states—almost 40 percent of the states—had increases above 100 percent in either their state assembly or senate, or in both. The proportion of women legislators in Connecticut, Maine, and North Carolina at least doubled in both houses.

Six states averaged about 300 percent increases in women in their assemblies: California, Florida, Hawaii, Kansas, Maryland, and Rhode Island. All represented completely new ground for greater representation of women in state assemblies. Other high growth lower houses included those in Colorado, Connecticut, Maine, North Carolina, Wisconsin, and Wyoming.

The "new wave" senates included these five new grounds for large increases in female senators: Massachusetts, Maine, Minnesota, North Carolina, and Washington. Others that showed at least 100 percent gains in female senators included these previously above-average state senates: Connecticut, New Hampshire, North Carolina, and Oregon.

Women recruits in these states make up an avant garde who are precursors to the future direction of women's state recruitment. This avant garde was generally neither hindered nor helped by either Republican or Democratic party dominance or by a competitive party system. For election to the assembly, women were recruited in every political culture, whether traditional, individualistic, or moralistic. But women's recruitment in the state senates that had the highest increases was limited primarily to the moralistic states, with the traditional culture still a negative factor. Generally, the fast-growing senates were in states that had the highest women's increases in assemblies in 1974. Therefore, new ground is broken first in the assemblies and then in the senates, usually within a decade.

The most striking characteristics of these "new wave" states are the favorable contextual conditions for women's recruitment at several levels of government. These include high proportions of women in the work force and in the professions, along with more chapters per population of the National Organization for Women. In these large-and small-population "new wave" states, there is greater opportunity for women to be elected not only to the state legislature but to statewide office and Congress, as well.

Most Powerful Predictors of Recruitment in 1984

Our final analysis ascertains the most powerful predictors of women's assembly and senate recruitment as of 1984. In the stepwise multiple regression in Table 3, each variable may be regarded as a separate dimension. Highly intercorrelated clusters of variables have been removed through the computer routine in order to provide a parsimonious list and to avoid complicating the results with multicolinearity. The percentage that each variable explains is given in the last column of the table, and the total explained by the nine variables is 76 percent.

Table 3 contains contextual factors that relate to the two 1984 trends the data have previously shown. The first trend is the continuance of the 1974 favorable contextual pattern for assemblies and senates, as in independent variables 1 (percentage women in 1974 assemblies), 5 and 6 (higher educational and Aid to Families with Dependent Children [AFDC] expenditures), and 7 (the single primary). These four variables explain 45 percent of the variance. The second trend is that of the "new wave" states now favorable to women's election to state legislatures. These new wave variables are 2 (percentage women in Congressional delegation), 3 (more professional women), 4 (percentage women statewide officials), 8 (more NOW chapters per population), and 9 (multimember state senate districts). These five variables explain 31 percent of the variance in women's 1984 legislative recruitment.

SUMMARY

This analysis shows that women's recruitment to state legislatures has doubled because of two trends occurring simultaneously in the last decade. As expected, there was a building on the gains in the Republican-moralistic states most favorable to women in the 1960s and 1970s. Growth in their assemblies has been followed a decade later by substantial increases in their state senates as well. At

Table 3 Most Powerful Predictors of Greater Women's Recruitment to State Assemblies and Senates, 1984 (Multiple Stepwise Regression)
(N = 50)

INDEPENDENT VARIABLES*	MULTIPLE CORRELATION COEFFICIENT (R)	CUMULATIVE PERCENTAGE OF VARIANCE EXPLAINED (R^2)	PERCENTAGE VARIANCE EXPLAINED BY EACH VARIABLE
1. Percentage women in 1974 state assemblies	.61	37	37
2. Percentage women in state congressional delegation, 1974–1984	.72	52	15
3. Percentage women professionals	.76	58	6
4. Percentage women statewide officials	.80	64	6
5. State educational expenditures	.82	67	3
6. State AFDC expenditures	.83	69	2
7. Single primary	.85	72	3
8. National Organization for Women	.86	75	3
9. Multimember senate districts	.87	76	1

Note:

*The F ratio when each of the variables was entered into the equation was significant at less than the .001 level.

Sources: refer to Box 1.

the same time, women's dramatic legislative increases in the "new wave" states indicate that Democratic party dominance is no longer a barrier in these states. Nor is the individualistic culture of "new wave" states an obstacle that could adversely affect women's eligibility, nomination, and election.

Although the traditional culture of the South and Democratic party dominance remain generally negative for women's recruitment, even here there are modifications. In 1984, Florida had 16 percent women in the legislature, and North Carolina 15 percent, both considerably above the national norm. Both are among the "new wave states" since they augmented the representation of women over 200 percent in the last decade. The remaining nine former Confederate states—Alabama, Arkansas, Georgia, Louisiana, Mississippi, South Carolina, Tennessee, Texas, and Virginia—were still below the national norm. Change is going on in the former Confederate states, but it is sporadic and uneven. Thus, our anticipation about the barriers in the Democratic party states coming down is only partially confirmed.

Turning to structural arrangements, both multimember district states and those with single plurality primaries were favorable to women's legislative recruitment in 1984. Contrary to expectations, states with multimember districts—of which there were 22 in both state assemblies and senates—began to be significant for women's election to legislatures in this decade, rather than earlier. Among the new wave states with multimember districts were Maryland, North Carolina, Washington, and Wyoming. Florida and Hawaii, which changed from multimember districts to single member as late as 1982, were also among the new wave. In both 1974 and 1984, the single primary was favorable. These electoral system arrangements should be viewed as political resources that, when used, can boost women's recruitment considerably when other contextual factors are favorable.

Yet multimember districts and single primaries are not a cure-all for women's low representation in U.S. state legislatures. It appears that no electoral arrangement can ensure women's legislative growth without a pluralistic nominating system of parties or other significant political groups.[14] Nevertheless, states with multimember districts usually provide much greater political opportunity for all women—Anglo and minority—than single-member district states do.[15]

The data presented in Tables 2 and 3 further substantiate the observations by other writers, including Mandel[16] and Carroll, that the women's movement has made a considerable impact in women's election to political office. We interpret the significant relationship of women in the state congressional delegation and statewide offices to legislative recruitment as follows: They serve at a minimum as models for women's eligibility and nomination, and most likely as helpful with party influentials in recruiting and supporting women candidates. In turn, women professionals and organizations such as NOW have provided womanpower to assist in making women's candidacies succeed at the polls.

The lack of opportunity for women to move up from the legislature to Congress that was observed in the 1970s has disappeared in the 1980s. Previously, women in low-population states with large legislatures were ordinarily not recruited to Congress, nor were women in high-population states with small legislatures. Now both types of states have turned around. In states where legislative service was previously a dead end, women now have political opportunities for election to statewide office as well as to the U.S. Congress. This significant change bodes well for modest increases of women in the House of Representatives as more women gain legislative, and particularly state senate experience from which to launch their campaigns for the U.S. House.

In conclusion, it is getting easier to recruit women to state legislatures because, spurred on by the women's movement, previous legislative gains have been augmented and new ground has been broken, providing expanded opportunities for women's eligibility, nomination, and election.

NOTES

1. J. Freeman, *The Politics of Women's Liberation* (David McKay, 1975); S. Baxter and M. Lansing, *Women and Politics.* (Ann Arbor: University of Michigan Press, 1980); E. Peterson, "The Kennedy Commission," in I. Tinker (Ed.), *Women in Washington* (Beverly Hills, CA: Sage, 1983).

2. *Statistical Abstract of the United States, 1989.* For the women's percentage in legislatures, 1951 to 1967, see C. Nechemias, "Changes in the Election of Women to U.S. State Legislative Seats," *Legislative Studies Quarterly,* 12 (1) (February 1987), p. 126.

3. S. Welch, "The Impact of Women in State Legislative Office," Paper presented at the World Congress of the International Sociological Association, July 9–15, 1990, Madrid, Spain.

4. E. Werner, "Women in the State Legislatures," *Western Political Quarterly,* 19 (1968), pp. 40–50; I. Diamond, *Sex Roles in the State House.* (New Haven: Yale University Press, 1977).

5. Diamond, *Sex Roles.*

6. W. Rule, "Why Women Don't Run: The Critical Contextual Factors in Women's Legislative Recruitment," *Western Political Quarterly,* 34 (March 1981), pp. 60–77.

7. Ibid.

8. See Diamond, *Sex roles*; D. Hill, "Political Culture and Female Political Representation," *Journal of Politics,* 43 (1981), pp. 159–168; C. Nechemias, "Women's Success in Capturing State Legislative Seats," Paper presented at the meeting of the Midwest Political Science Association, 1985.

9. J. Clark et al., "Women as Legislative Candidates in Six States," in J. A. Flammang (Ed.), *Political Women* (Beverly Hills, CA: Sage, 1984) pp. 141–155. See also R. Darcy, S. Welch, and J. Clark, *Women, Elections, and Representation,* rev. ed. (New York: Longman, 1992) and S. J. Carroll, *Women as Candidates in American Politics* (Bloomington: University of Indiana, 1985). See also W. Rule, "Multi-member Districts, Minority and Anglo Women's and Men's Recruitment Opportunity," and subsequent chapters on Maryland and Arizona in W. Rule and J. Zimmerman (Eds.), *U.S. Electoral Systems: Their Impact on Women and Minorities.* (Westport, CT: Greenwood, 1992).

10. A. P. Lamis, "The Runoff Primary Controversy: Implications for Southern Politics." *PS,* 7 (1984), pp. 782–787. See also C. S. Bullock and L. K. Johnson, "Sex and the Second Primary," *Social Science Quarterly,* 66 (1985), pp. 933–944.

11. See Rule, "Why Women Don't Run."

12. T. J. Volgy, J. E. Schwartz, and H. Gottlieb, "Female Representation and the Quest for Resources: Feminist Activism and Electoral Success," *Social Science Quarterly,* 66 (1986), pp. 156–168.

13. G. Jacobson, G. Kernell, and S. Kernell, *Strategy and Choice in Congressional Elections.* (New Haven: Yale University Press, 1981).

14. W. Rule and I. Krauss, "Aquino's Rise to the Presidency: Testing a Model of Women's Recruitment," Paper presented at the Third Interdisciplinary Congress on Women, Dublin, July 1987.

15. W. Rule, "Multi-member Legislative Districts, Minority and Anglo Women's."

16. R. Mandel, *In the Running: The New Woman Candidate* (New York: Ticknor & Fields, 1981).

5

THE EXECUTIVE BRANCH: WOMEN AND LEADERSHIP

A growing list of nations in this century have selected female heads. These have included Great Britain, the Philippines, Argentina, Israel, Iceland, and India. However, the United States has not yet succeeded in electing a woman as our chief executive. The U.S. presidency has remained a bastion of maleness. Marcia Lynn Whicker and Todd W. Areson research the reasons for this and find four factors that account for the unlevel presidential "playing field" that women candidates face: (1) the presidential system of direct, popular election; (2) the paucity of women with experience in the three presidential "launching roles"; (3) the difficulty women face in securing campaign funding for national and subnational races; and (4) long-standing public images of a conflict for women—and not for men—between familial and political roles. Let us next look at the results of their study.

The Maleness of the American Presidency

Marcia Lynn Whicker
Todd W. Areson

INTRODUCTION

The U.S. presidency has been a bastion of maleness. Aside from being First Lady, the closest a woman has come to presidential power was the 1984 Democratic vice-presidential nomination of Geraldine Ferraro. The earlier 1972 presidential candidacy of Democrat Shirley Chisholm, a black woman from New York, was discounted by both the press and the public on sexual and racial grounds. In the 1988 primaries, Democratic U.S. Representative Pat Schroeder from Colorado briefly considered running for president but was unable to raise the necessary funds.

Yet women in more socially conservative societies, where fewer advances for women might be expected, have served as the chief executives of their countries. Throughout the decade of the 1980s, Conservative party leader Margaret Thatcher was prime minister of Britain. In 1990, Mary Robinson became president of Ireland, which is governed through a parliamentary system. Indira Gandhi was prime minister of India from 1966 until her assassination in 1984 by religiously motivated Sikh extremists. Golda Meir, a former schoolteacher from Milwaukee, served as the prime minister of Israel during the late 1960s and early 1970s.

Isabel Peron, the second wife of Argentine leader General Juan Peron, was elected president of that country in 1974, becoming the first woman head of state in the Western Hemisphere. In 1962, Sirimavo Bandaranaike was elected prime minister of her native Sri Lanka, following the 1959 assassination of the

Marcia Lynn Whicker is a professor of public administration at Rutgers University, Newark, New Jersey. Todd W. Areson is a local government consultant in Richmond, Virginia.

former prime minister, her husband. And, with the fall of Ferdinand Marcos in the Philippines in 1986, Corazon Aquino was elected president there in a bitter and contentious campaign.

Why are women becoming chief executives in countries more socially traditional than the United States while still being excluded from the White House in all but secondary roles? The purpose of this essay is to explore this crucial political—and no longer merely academic—question.

THE PARLIAMENTARY SYSTEM VERSUS THE U.S. PRESIDENTIAL SYSTEM

One indisputable fact concerning the female leaders cited here is that—with the exceptions of Peron and Aquino, who succeeded to leadership roles after the deaths of politically prominent husbands—they achieved their power in parliamentary systems. Prime ministers are not elected directly by the people but are chosen by their fellow party members, since the prime minister is the leader of the dominant party in parliament.[1] Party members and long-term colleagues likely have less traditional bias against women as political leaders than does the general electorate.[2]

In aspiring to leadership of a political party, parliamentary members start with an equally recognized legitimacy: All have been elected from their districts or in national elections, depending on whether single-member districts or proportional representation is the electoral basis. Party members seem to operate on a rough merit system, which provides rewards of power and leadership based on political and legislative performances.[3] Both male and female party members, once elected, have similar opportunities to excel in the tasks of creating national agenda, developing legislation, and shepherding proposals around or over legislative hurdles. In this arena, paying one's professional dues is important, recognized, and generally rewarded.

Only since 1980 have women come to be elected national chief executives in popular elections. In June 1980 Vigdis Finnbogadottir became the world's first popularly elected head of state in Iceland. In April 1990 Violetta Barrios de Chamorro was elected president of Nicaragua. (Michel Rocard, who became prime minister of the French Republic in June 1988, was appointed to that office by President Mitterand rather than elected.)

In the United States as well as in the various parliamentary systems, women active in party politics have become more similar to the men who are active. Between 1964 and 1976, the differences between male and female political elites in terms of social background, political status, political careers, and perceptions of the political process—all factors affecting one's potential for leadership—were decreasing. During that period, issue orientations were predominantly a matter of party agenda rather than of gender, with the exception of issues dealing directly with gender roles.[4] A 1990 study also confirms the narrowing of the gap between men and women in "political ambition," the pursuit of public office for personal self-enhancement.[5] Across a twenty-two-year period (1964–1986), women exhibited a marked increase in political ambition not matched by similar increases for men.

The United States differs from countries with parliamentary systems in that the national political leader (the president) is elected by the people through the electoral college system. Despite concern over the biases this system causes,[6] the electoral college rarely fails to confirm the popular vote.[7] In practice, U.S. presidential outcomes may be based less on political and legislative merit than on effective media exposure and communications, levels of campaign funding, and the personal appeal of the candidate.[8]

Although party identification does affect outcomes in U.S. elections, the role and influence of U.S. political parties have diminished steadily in recent decades as candidates have opted to build their own campaign organizations.[9] In parliamentary systems, by contrast, party discipline has remained crucial to national political leadership: parties control the nominating process and, through the selection of leaders, reward individuals who have provided loyal party service.

Women, while becoming leaders in political systems based more directly on merit, have fared less well in arenas where public opinion dominates.[10] In the United States, antidiscrimination legislation has been a relatively recent occurrence, dating to the 1960s. Usually changes in legislation, whether antidiscriminatory or otherwise, are influenced and supported by the pace of change in public opinion. Thus, women only achieved the right to vote in 1920, with state ratification of the Nineteenth Amendment to the Constitution.[11]

In other areas, especially in employment, where advancement for women was previously predicated on changes in public opinion, social legislation has been necessary for female gains. The Equal Pay Act of 1963, requiring equal pay for equal work by men and women, was the first federal law against sex discrimination in employment. In 1972 and again in 1974, two major expansions of that act extended coverage to executive, administrative, and professional employees and to most federal, state, and local government employees.[12]

It was the 1964 Civil Rights Act (Title VII) that safeguarded equal opportunity for women in employment in both hiring and advancement. Originally intended to protect blacks and other racial minorities, the 1964 act included equal opportunity for women as an amendment—a political miscalculation by opponents of the act. Intending to kill the act by including coverage of women, opponents were surprised when the amended act passed. Title VII also covers sexual harassment on the job.[13] The Pregnancy Disability Act of 1978, an amendment to Title VII, provides pregnancy protections for female employees.[14]

Social legislation has also been necessary to protect women from discrimination in nonemployment areas. Federal legislation has prohibited discrimination by institutions receiving federal funds. In marriage and divorce, it has taken a combination of both court suits and legislation to diverge from the English common-law assumption that husband and wife are one, with reciprocal and unequal rights.[15] Only in 1974, with the passage of the Equal Credit Opportunity Act, was sex discrimination in credit approval banned.[16]

Popular biases against women, partially overcome through social legislation, still exist in politics and can be expressed more directly in U.S. presidential electoral politics than in parliamentary selection of prime ministers. As Madison feared, majority rather than elite rule—a founding principle of the nation and one to which most citizens readily adhere—can sometimes be used as an instrument of bias and prejudice.

AN ABSENCE OF APPROPRIATE POLITICAL EXPERIENCE

A survey of the previous political experience of presidents and party nominees for president since 1960 indicates that three backgrounds emerge as the dominant training grounds for those who would be president—the offices of vice-president, U.S. senator, and governor.

John F. Kennedy, the first president born and elected in this century, was a Democratic U.S. senator from Massachusetts when he ran for the presidency in 1960. Democrat Lyndon Johnson, his successor, wielded great power for years as U.S. Senate majority leader before accepting the vice-presidency in 1960 after a failed presidential bid. Had he not become president as a result of Kennedy's assassination, Johnson likely would have run again for the White House.

The necessity of first being tested in these presidential proving grounds has not been limited to Democrats, of course. Republican Richard Nixon served in the U.S. Senate and as vice-president prior to his unsuccessful 1960 presidential bid against Senator John Kennedy and his successful 1968 bid against Vice-President Hubert Humphrey.

The pattern holds even with the one "accidental" president in recent years, Republican Gerald Ford. Ford was catapulted to the vice-presidency through the resignation of Nixon's corrupt vice-president, Spiro Agnew. Within a few months, Nixon's own resignation, brought about by impeachable charges of obstruction of justice in the Watergate affair, propelled Ford into the presidency in August 1974.

In recent presidential history—1976, 1980, and 1984—candidates with gubernatorial experience have captured the presidency. Democrat Jimmy Carter, elected in 1976, served as governor of Georgia before making his surprising successful bid for the White House as a Washington outsider. In both 1980 and 1984, former Republican California Governor Ronald Reagan easily defeated his Democratic opponent.

Even unsuccessful presidential nominees have acquired their political experience in the U.S. Senate, the vice-presidency, and the presidency. Former Vice-President Nixon, who opposed Senator Kennedy in 1960, fits this pattern. In 1964, Republican Senator Barry Goldwater ran unsuccessfully against Vice-President Johnson. Former Democratic Senator from Minnesota and incumbent Vice-President Hubert Humphrey was defeated by former Vice-President Nixon in 1968. In 1972, President Nixon defeated South Dakota Democratic Senator George McGovern.

In 1976, former Governor Jimmy Carter defeated incumbent President Gerald Ford and, in turn, former Governor Ronald Reagan defeated incumbent President Jimmy Carter in 1980. In 1984, President Reagan's unsuccessful Democratic opponent, Walter Mondale, had been both a Democratic senator from Minnesota and Carter's vice-president.

This pattern of formative political experience in the U.S. Senate, a governorship, or the vice-presidency continued to hold in 1988. All but one of the presidential and vice-presidential candidates fit the pattern, the exception being Jesse Jackson, a black Democratic candidate for president. Although Jackson ran in 1984 and again in 1988 before his candidacy was taken seriously, he did not attain his party's nomination for president or vice-president.

On the Republican side, the major contenders early in the 1988 race were Vice-President George Bush and U.S. Senate Majority Leader Robert Dole. Eventually, Bush gained the nomination and appointed Indiana Senator Daniel Quayle as his vice-presidential running mate. All fit the pattern.

Early in the 1988 presidential primaries, the Democratic picture was more chaotic. By the date of the so-called Super Tuesday primaries in March, the three major contenders were Massachusetts Governor Michael Dukakis, the Reverend Jesse Jackson, and Tennessee Senator Albert Gore. Only Jackson, the first black to contend seriously for the White House, deviates from the norm.

Traditionally, blacks in the United States have been excluded from the highest echelons of elected office and political leadership. The sole exceptions have been former U.S. Senator Edward Brooke of Massachusetts and current Governor Douglas Wilder of Virginia. Jesse Jackson compensated for this exclusion by pursuing those avenues of political power open to him, including leadership in the black church and in the civil rights movement.

Before the close of the 1988 primaries, Governor Dukakis had secured enough votes to gain the Democratic nomination, and appointed an established political insider, Texas Senator Lloyd Bentsen, as his running mate (see Table 1).

Candidates with other political backgrounds, including experience as a U.S. representative, traditionally have been unsuccessful in capturing their party's presidential nomination. Democratic Representative Morris Udall from Arizona in 1976 and Republican Representative John Anderson from Illinois in 1980 were unsuccessful presidential candidates. In 1988, the campaigns of both Democratic Representative Richard Gephardt from Missouri and Republican Representative Jack Kemp from New York faltered.

Paradoxically, five recent presidents have served in the U.S. House of Representatives—Kennedy, Johnson, Nixon, Ford, and Bush. Yet their service in the House has been coupled, *in each case*, with later experience in the Senate or the vice-presidency, two of the presidential "launching roles." Although five of the last seven presidents started in the House of Representatives, House experience in itself has not been sufficient to support a successful presidential nomination. The presidential candidacies of Morris Udall (Democrat), John Anderson (Independent), Jack Kemp (Republican), and Richard Gephardt (Democrat), all of whom had held no public office higher than the House, failed.

Table 1 Political Backgrounds of Recent Presidential Contenders

YEAR	WINNER	BACKGROUND	LOSER	BACKGROUND
1960	Kennedy	Senator	Nixon	Senator Vice-president
1964	Johnson	Senator Vice-president President	Goldwater	Senator
1968	Nixon	Senator Vice-president	Humphrey	Senator Vice-president
1972	Nixon	Senator Vice-president President	McGovern	Senator
1976	Carter	Governor	Ford	Vice-president President
1980	Reagan	Governor	Carter	Governor President
1984	Reagan	Governor President	Mondale	Senator Vice-president
1988	Bush	Vice-president	Dukakis	Governor

Nor can it be stated that the three traditional political backgrounds are irrelevant to or an improper proving ground for the presidency. Each provides an opportunity to develop the qualities and skills that presidents need. The first of these characteristics is high political visibility, combined with tempered experience in the exercise of power. The second is broad legislative experience; senators, vice-presidents, and governors all must sell their policies and programs to national and state legislatures as well as to the public at large.

Third, all three backgrounds require a working knowledge of national political issues and of the intricate intergovernmental balance between federal and state governments in achieving national domestic policy goals. One final advantage these backgrounds provide is rigorous practice in analyzing, staking out, communicating, and defending positions in a visible, public, and adversarial arena—not unlike what the presidential campaign trail requires.

Because few women have served in these presidential launching roles, the selection pool for female presidential candidates has been minimal. For example, in 1990, only 2 out of 100 U.S. senators and 3 out of 50 governors were women. No women have been elected vice-president. Only 6 percent of the seats in the House were held by women. With such a disproportionately small pool of women presidential candidates, the odds of women achieving the presidency in the near term are statistically negligible. History shows that aspirants to the presidency usually enter politics at subnational levels through either state or local elective office. But entering politics at any level presents barriers to groups that have been excluded, including the major barrier of fund raising.

CAMPAIGN FUNDING AND PAC POWER

Elections drive home the basic principle of politics: Money buys access to power. Political action committees (PACs), long guided by this principle, have grown in clout and number in recent years. Yet, women trying to enter politics at all levels have had difficulty raising money, especially from PACs. This is in part because they are more typically nonincumbents and in part simply because they are women.[17]

In politics as elsewhere, nothing succeeds like success. This produces a political catch-22 for would-be female candidates: PACs are more likely to support proven winners—that is, incumbents. As for nonincumbents, PACs give more freely to those perceived as more likely to win, typically white males. With lower budgets for their campaigns resulting from difficulties in fund raising, women often cannot take full advantage of modern campaign techniques, including use of the mass media, especially television, and of political pollsters. These handicaps reduce the likelihood of female challengers being elected.

Given their difficulty in fund raising from interest groups and especially from PACs, female candidates would benefit disproportionately from reforms in campaign financing. Public financing for presidential general elections has existed since the adoption of the Revenue Act of 1971, which provided the first-time income tax checkoff as a federal subsidy.[18] Although presidential candidates receiving public financing are limited in their total expenditures, their expenditures may be supplemented by independent spending—by PACs, for example. The Federal Election Campaign Act of 1971 established procedures for the public disclosure of contributions and expenditures of $200 or more. This law also set ceilings on the amount of contributions that presidential and vice-presidential candidates and their families could contribute as well as on the amount spent for media advertising.[19]

Because women have been considerably less successful historically in reaching the traditional presidential launching roles, they have benefited less from public financing for the presidency. Further, public financing has not been adopted for other national and subnational offices, including the U.S. Congress and major state offices, where women might compete both more readily and more successfully. Some members of Congress fear that public subsidies would encourage opponents by equalizing the resources available to incumbents and nonincumbents. Others believe, however, that the ceilings on total campaign spending that would necessarily accompany such additional public financing would further bias elections toward incumbents, who already have a proven track record and greater name recognition.

Despite such criticisms, proponents argue that the nation as a whole, not just female candidates, would benefit from the enactment of public financing legislation for Congress and other levels of government. These reforms would not only allow greater diversity in the pool of candidates for elective offices but also reduce the pressure on officials, once elected, to conform to special interests at the expense of national and constituents' interests.

THE IMAGE OF FEMALE CANDIDATES

Women have experienced additional handicaps to election to higher political office, in part because of the public image of women as candidates. Women are still viewed societally in terms of domestic roles, whereas men are viewed in terms of occupational roles. Female politicians are viewed as interlopers in the political arena who should function behind the scenes rather than out front as candidates.[20]

Female candidates, then, must convince the electorate that their home responsibilities are not too demanding to permit them to make the commitment required by political officeholding. Former Princeton, New Jersey, mayor Barbara Boggs Sigmund has referred to this as "the bind of your feminity."[21] A 1978 study of men's and women's campaigns found that women were asked more often how they would manage their family responsibilities if elected and whether their husbands and children approved of their political activity.[22] Men were not asked whether their wives and children approved of their political activity. Rather, familial approval of male political participation was assumed. In one poignant example of this double standard from the mid-1970s, U.S. Representative Martha Keys of Kansas married fellow Representative Andrew Jacobs of Indiana. They had met while serving on the House Ways and Means Committee. When each sought reelection in their districts, the political marriage became a campaign issue for Keys but not for Jacobs.[23]

Because of the political liability regarding family responsibilities that people associate with women, many female politicians are either single or widowed, or do not become active in politics until after their children are adults.[24] For example, Kathryn Whitmire, mayor of Houston, was a widow when she sought and was elected to political office. Barbara Jordan, former U.S. Representative from Texas and spokesperson for the Democratic party, never married. Nor did Elizabeth Holtzman, a Harvard lawyer and former U.S. representative from New York, who played a highly visible role in the Watergate hearings in the early 1970s. Geraldine Ferraro, the Democratic vice-presidential nominee in 1984, had older children by the time she gained national attention.

The public perception that married female candidates in their childbearing years will neglect their familial duties if they run for and hold elective office affects the likelihood of women achieving the presidency in two ways. First, it reduces the pool of available female candidates acceptable to the public. Second, it delays the entry into elective politics of those women who choose to marry and have children. Many female candidates never recoup this lost ground. During the period when women are bearing and raising children, their male counterparts who aspire to the presidency are gaining formative experience at the subnational and national levels. Men gain access to the requisite presidential launching roles on a schedule compatible with career advancement, whereas women face a substantially telescoped time frame, among other handicaps, for their advancement.

The negative image of women as candidates, especially those still in their childbearing years, continues to present a significant handicap. Election to political office requires the overt approval of over 50 percent of the electorate, in most cases. There is still a proportion of voters who will not support female candidates simply because they *are* women.[25] In highly competitive races and in races where an incumbent is being challenged—the typical races that women face—a successful candidate cannot afford to lose even a small fraction of that electorate automatically. Although the proportion of the electorate opposed to women on gender alone has been diminishing, this diminution is a slow process. Further, equality of opportunity in politics cannot be regulated or mandated given that it depends instead on shifts in public opinion. Some of the changes in political opportunities and electoral success for women, then, depend to a large extent on the pace of social change.

Birth control has played a helpful role in increasing the number of women in politics by allowing women to control the number and timing of their offspring. This control is crucial for those who contemplate a political career, especially while public perceptions continue to make it difficult for women with small children to engage in high-level elective politics.

CONCLUSION

We have discussed four factors that, traditionally, have diminished the opportunity for women to compete for the presidency:

1. The presidential system itself, which relies more closely on direct, popular election than does the parliamentary system, which elects its prime minister from among fellow party members
2. The paucity of women gaining experience in the presidential "launching roles" of the vice-presidency, the U.S. Senate, and governorships—roles that men have traditionally attained before competing, successfully or unsuccessfully, for the presidency
3. The difficulty women have experienced in securing PAC and other campaign funding for national and subnational races
4. Long-standing public perceptions that the traditional childbearing and child-rearing roles of women conflict with simultaneous participation in high-level elective politics.

Equality of opportunity has not been legislated in presidential politics or, for that matter, in elective politics at any level. Reforms that encourage female participation at subnational levels, such as public financing and other campaign reforms, will certainly contribute to the available pool of female presidential candidates. Ultimately, shifts in public opinion must also occur—including a recognition that political roles no more conflict with familial roles for women than they do for men—in order to level the "playing field" of U.S. presidential politics for women.

Although legislation has not been used in the United States in the past to increase female presence in high elective office, legislation to make equal representation a major goal has a recent precedent. The actions of the European Parliament can serve as an example of how the role of women in national politics may be enhanced and sustained. In the fall of 1988, the European Parliament, which represents the twelve countries in the Common Market, passed a resolution endorsing a quota and affirmative action system calling for equal numbers of men and women in the elected bodies of its member countries. Not only did this resolution pass the European Parliament, but also at least ten of the twelve member countries have adopted rules on quotas as well as timetables for increasing female representation in their national parliaments. Similar resolve to place women in the United States in equal numbers in presidential launching roles, as well as in appropriate subnational political roles in state legislatures and local governments, could well be legislated.

NOTES

1. Jean Blondel, *Government Ministers in the Contemporary World* (Beverly Hills, CA: Sage Publications, 1985).

2. Marcia Lynn Whicker and Jennie Jacobs Kronenfeld, *Sex Role Changes: Technology, Politics, and Policy* (New York: Praeger, 1986).

3. Richard Rose, "Government against Sub-Governments: A European Perspective on Washington," in Richard Rose and Ezra N. Suleiman (Eds.), *Presidents and Prime Ministers* (Washington, DC: American Enterprise Institute, 1980), pp. 284–347.

4. M. Kent Jennings and Barbara G. Farah, "Social Roles and Political Resources: An Overtime Study of Men and Women in Party Elites," *American Journal of Political Science*, 25, 1981, pp. 462–482.

5. Edmond Costantini, "Political Women and Political Ambition: Closing the Gender Gap," *American Journal of Political Science*, 34 (3) (August 1990), pp. 741–770.

6. John H. Yunker and Lawrence D. Longley, "The Biases of the Electoral College: Who Is Really Advantaged?" in Donald R. Matthews (Ed.), *Perspectives on Presidential Selection* (Washington, DC: Brookings Institution, 1973), pp. 172–203. Also see Nelson W. Polsby and Aaron Wildavsky, *Presidential Elections: Strategies of American Electoral Politics*, 6th ed. (New York: Charles Scribner's Sons, 1984).

7. Max S. Power, "Logic and Legitimacy: On Understanding the Electoral College Controversy," in Donald R. Matthews (Ed.), *Perspectives on Presidential Selection*, (Washington, DC: Brookings Institution, 1973), pp. 204–238.

8. Stephen Hess, *The Presidential Campaign*, 3rd ed. (Washington, DC: Brookings Institution, 1988). Also see Stephen J. Wayne, *The Road to the White House: The Politics of Presidential Elections*, 3rd ed. (New York: St. Martin's Press, 1988).

9. Frank J. Sorauf, *Party Politics in America*, 5th ed. (Boston: Little, Brown, 1984), pp. 425–429.

10. Ronna Romney and Beppie Harrison, *Momentum: Women in American Politics Now* (New York: Crown, 1988).

11. William Henry Clark, "What Votes Can Win?" in James David Barber and Barbara Kellerman (Eds.), *Women Leaders in American Politics* (Englewood Cliffs, NJ: Prentice-Hall, 1986), pp. 218–234.

12. J. E. Buckley, "Equal Pay in America," in Barrie O. Pettman (Ed.), *Equal Pay for Women: Progress and Problems in Seven Countries* (West Yorkshire, England: MCB Books, 1975).

13. U.S. Department of Labor, Bureau of Labor Statistics, *1981 Weekly Earnings of Men and Women Compared in 100 Occupations* (Washington, DC: U.S. Government Printing Office, 1982).

14. Sheila B. Kamerman, Alfred J. Kahn, and Paul Kingston, *Maternity Politics and Working Women* (New York: Columbia University Press, 1983).

15. Susan Deller Ross and Ann Barcher, *The Rights of Women: The Basic ACLU Guide to a Woman's Rights*, rev. ed. (New York: Bantam, 1983).

16. Joyce Gelb and Marian Lief Palley, *Women and Public Policies* (Princeton, NJ: Princeton University Press, 1982).

17. Whicker and Kronenfeld, *Sex Role Changes*, pp. 162–163.

18. Stephen J. Wayne, *The Road to the White House: The Politics of Presidential Elections*, 3rd ed. (New York: St. Martin's Press, 1988), pp. 36–41.

19. Ibid.

20. Ruth Mandel, "The Image Campaign," in James David Barber and Barbara Kellerman (Eds.), *Women Leaders in American Politics* (Englewood Cliffs, NJ: Prentice-Hall, 1986), pp. 261–271.

21. Lisa W. Foderaro, "Women Winning Locally, but Higher Office Is Elusive," *New York Times*, April 1, 1989, pp. 29, 32.

22. Susan Gluck Mezy, "Does Sex Make a Difference? A Case Study of Women in Politics," *Western Political Quarterly*, 31 (1978), pp. 492–501.

23. Virginia Sapiro, *Women: Political Action and Political Participation* (Washington, DC: American Political Science Association, 1983).

24. Cynthia Fuchs Epstein, "Women and Power: The Role of Women in Politics in the United States," in Cynthia Fuchs Epstein and Rose Laub Coser (Eds.), *Access to Power: Cross-National Studies of Women and Elites* (London: George Allen and Unwin, 1981).

25. Whicker and Kronenfeld, *Sex Role Changes*, p. 165.

6

THE COURTS: WOMEN AND DECISIONS

Does gender make a difference when it comes to the judicial branch? For example, if we had more female judges, could we expect to see more judicial decisions favorable to women? Elaine Martin investigates gender roles and judicial roles. She compares the views of male and female judges—even investigating the division of household labor for judges of both sexes.

Victor F. D'Lugin then researches the issue of whether U.S. courts discriminate against women in interpreting the laws. D'Lugin traces the treatment of women in the law and concludes that lack of credibility is used as a means to deny women equal justice within the court system. He finds that judges, juries, and attorneys use sexist assumptions to practice differential treatment in awarding credibility to men as compared with women.

Views from the State Bench:
Gender Roles and Judicial Roles

Elaine Martin

It is no news that women are underrepresented in public office in the United States, or that they are far better represented in local office than in state and federal office. Yet, it may be news to some that women are far less well represented in state judicial office than in state legislative office. In 1985, nearly 15 percent of state legislative seats, nationwide, were held by women; nine state legislatures had 20 percent or more female members.[1] In comparison, in 1987, fewer than 8 percent of state general jurisdiction trial court judgeships were held by women; about 9 percent of the intermediate appellate court judges and 6 percent of supreme court justices were women.[2] In 1987, twenty states had never had a female supreme court justice; five states had no woman judge on their major trial courts; and 15 more states had only two women.

These figures, dismal as they are, represent significant gains made in only one decade. In 1977, Beverly Blair Cook found only 145 women major trial court judges in the 50 states.[3] By 1987 this number had more than tripled, to 492 women.

Eligible Pool for Women Judges

The eligible pool from which female judges are drawn is also growing steadily. In 1970 only 5.4 percent of law students and 4.7 percent of lawyers were women.[4] By 1990, women made up over 40 percent of the nation's law students and 17 percent of lawyers.[5] In 1990 approximately 650 women served on limited-jurisdiction trial courts, mostly municipal and traffic courts, up from about 300 in 1980.[6] These lower court judges are part of the eligible pool for general-

Elaine Martin is an associate professor of political science at Eastern Michigan University.

jurisdiction and appellate courts at both state and federal levels. Thus, although the number of major trial court and appellate court women judges is not commensurate with the number of female lawyers or lower court judges, the continuing increase in the pool of eligibles suggests that an increase in higher court women judges will continue in the foreseeable future.

Unique Contribution of Women Judges

Given the current rate of increase and the likelihood of continued increase, it seems appropriate to ask if women judges have something unique to contribute to the operation of our system of justice. Research on other women in public office consistently suggests that women are more liberal and more sensitive to women's rights issues.[7] Very little comparable research has been done on women judges.

Such data as exist are sparse and contradictory. There is some evidence to suggest that women judges may have more liberal attitudes on women's issues than do men, but studies comparing decisional behavior of male and female judges generally conclude that women do not differ much from men, although there are apparently some circumstances in which judicial gender may influence decisions.[8] Unfortunately, with the exceptions of Cook's studies using simulated cases,[9] most studies of gender-linked judicial decisions are seriously flawed by the unavoidably small numbers of women and/or cases analyzed.

There is mounting evidence that our present court system operates far too often with "judges ready to translate racial and sexist views into law."[10] Thus, it is important to know if the presence of women judges may help to counterbalance what amounts to a "climate of condescension, indifference and hostility" toward female litigants and lawyers."[11]

DATA AND RESEARCH QUESTIONS

This study is a first attempt to try to establish some dimensions to the different gender-based perspectives male and female judges might bring to the bench. The overall purpose is to see if men and women judges themselves think women judges behave any differently, to determine if women are more likely than men to see the presence of gender bias in the court system, and to determine if women may be more willing to take judicial action to counterbalance any perceived gender bias.

In order to accomplish this purpose, three sets of questions were administered to a sample of men and women judges. The questions addressed: (1) respondents' perceptions of the role of women judges, (2) respondents' perceptions of gender bias in the courts, and (3) respondents' decisions on five hypothetical cases raising women's rights issues. A major underlying question is whether gender or feminist ideology is a more important influence on judicial attitudes. Therefore, all three sets of questions are examined by respondents' gender and commitment to feminist ideas.

All local and state, trial and appellate, women judges in attendance at the 1986 annual convention of the National Association of Women Judges (NAWJ) were surveyed (federal, administrative law, and retired judge members were excluded to obtain a total N of 125). The largest group of respondents was obtained at the convention itself by including the survey instrument in official registration packets. A follow-up by mail after the convention brought the response rate to an exceptional 87 percent ($n = 109$), assuring representativeness of the conference attendees.

Conference attendees, however, are probably not representative of the general body of female judges on the attitudinal variables tested. Although the NAWJ has a broad-based membership, including both Democrats and Republicans (Justice Sandra Day O'Connor is a founding member), and includes almost half of the women judges in the United States, it is in some respects a feminist-oriented organization. For example, it has as one of its major goals to increase the number of women judges, and its foundation wing (the Women Judges' Fund for Justice) actively seeks to educate judges to the problems of gender bias in the courts. One may reasonably expect, then, that members who attend the conventions would tend to hold stronger feminist positions than might the general membership; members might also reasonably be expected to be somewhat more feminist than nonmembers. Thus, this sample of women judges is very probably more feminist in its attitudes than the general run of female judges. There is reason to believe that the male sample may also represent a feminist bias. Men judges in the study were selected randomly from among those men sitting on the same courts as female respondents. In those very few cases where women judges had no male colleagues, men who sat on courts at the same level, in the same geographical location were queried.

The male response rates, however, were significantly lower than those of females. There is no way of knowing how representative the male respondents may be of the total sample in their attitudes, but the low response rate of 34 percent strongly suggests the possibility of bias.

In a sense, however, the present sample of men and women judges presents a best-case scenario, at least from a feminist point of view. That is, it provides an opportunity for asking whether, if the bench were composed of feminists of both sexes, gender would still have a significant impact on judicial attitudes.

Construction of Feminism Scale

The first step in the analysis was to determine which judge respondents were feminists and which were not. Judges were asked to agree or disagree, on a five-point scale, with the following four statements:

1. Women are already equal to men legally; it is up to the individual woman to take advantage of her opportunities.
2. Equality before the law is simply a first step to achieving women's rights; full equality will require major changes in the workplace and the family.

3. If they are to achieve full equality, women must organize and act politically to represent their own interests.

4. Current liberal feminism, as represented by such groups as NOW, really doesn't go far enough in its demands for change.

An arithmetic average of responses was calculated. Judges above the average were labeled feminists; those below, nonfeminists. This procedure created four categories of judge respondents: women feminists, men feminists, women nonfeminists, and men nonfeminists. Response to all other attitude questions were then analyzed, using these four subgroups.

RESULTS

Perceptions about the Role of Women Judges

Representation of Women.   Three questions examined judges' views about the potential benefits of increasing the representation of women on the bench. As might be expected, feminist women and nonfeminist men showed the greatest divergence in their attitudes about this issue. The pattern was less clear for nonfeminist women and feminist men.

Almost all women feminists (98.8 percent) agreed that "More women judges are needed because the bench without women does not reflect the total fabric of society." Women nonfeminists (87 percent) and men feminists (85 percent) ran a close second, and men nonfeminists were last, with fewer than 72 percent agreeing.

Feminists, both men and women, were more convinced than nonfeminists that "Men's view of women is affected positively by the presence of women judges." One hundred percent of men feminists and 97.6 percent of women feminists agreed with this optimistic view, compared to 86.4 percent of women nonfeminists and only 65 percent of men nonfeminists.

Both groups of women, feminists (85.4 percent) and nonfeminists (91.3 percent), felt strongly that "Women have certain unique perspectives and life experiences different from those of men that ought to be represented on the bench by women judges." Men were much less likely to agree, although feminists (73.7 percent) were more likely than nonfeminists (60.7 percent) to agree.

Behavior of Women Judges.   Three statements examined judges' views of how women judges behave on the job. Gender, overall, was a more important influence than feminist ideology in determining points of view. That is, women were more likely to agree with each other, and men were more likely to agree with each other, than with their feminist/nonfeminist counterparts of the opposite gender. Women judges were consistently more likely than men to feel that women judges behave differently from men, that women judges have an ability to bring people together that men do not have, and that women judges face special problems in the judicial system. However, men and women also differed by ideology.

Women feminists were more likely than women nonfeminists to agree strongly with the view that the role of women judges is unique and men feminists were more likely than men nonfeminists to express agreement. Judges were most likely to agree that women judges face special problems (over three-quarters of women and men feminists), and least likely to feel that women have special abilities to bring people together (less than one-third of all groups).

Perception of Gender Bias in the Courts

One question asked judges to agree or disagree with the statement: "Judges sometimes treat women attorneys, witnesses, or litigants in demeaning, condescending, or unprofessional ways." Outside evidence from a survey of gender bias in the New Jersey state courts indicates that in New Jersey, at least, this statement is accurate.[12]

The notion of gender bias in the courts is a particularly important and current issue. By 1990 over half the states in the United States had formed task forces to investigate the presence of gender bias in the courts. Extensive gender bias was found in all states with published reports as of 1990. In many of these states a woman justice on the state supreme court, or a woman judge from a lower state court, was instrumental in creating the task force. Clearly, this is an area of judicial behavior in which the presence of women seems to have particular significance.

Responses to the survey statement about gender bias indicate that feminism is as important as gender in influencing judges to see gender bias. Women feminists led all four groups of judges in the strength of their feeling that gender bias exists in the courts (96.4 percent), but women nonfeminists (95.5 percent) and men feminists (90 percent) were close behind. Men nonfeminists rank at the bottom, as usual, with only 62 percent accepting the idea that gender bias exists.

Perceptions of Hypothetical Women's Rights Cases

Five hypothetical cases raising controversial issues in women's rights were developed from published accounts of actual cases. The five cases raised issues of property rights for divorcing homemakers, abortion rights for minors, maternity leave, protection from sexual harassment, and rights for battered women. Respondents were asked to choose in favor of one party: the women litigants or their opponents. A description of the cases and the judges' hypothetical votes follows. Table 1 summarizes the judges' votes in each case, using the four groups, and their average voting score for all five cases.

Property Rights for Divorcing Homemakers. A 55-year-old woman is sued for divorce after 37 years of marriage to a successful businessman. Her four children are grown. She is willing to accept a 50/50 split on community property, requests no alimony, but demands 50 percent of her spouse's substantial retirement income at age 65. She did not work outside the home during her marriage but now has a job as a salesclerk. The job pays enough for her immedi-

Table 1 Hypothetical Cases

CASE:	WOMEN		MEN	
	Feminists	*Nonfeminists*	*Feminists*	*Nonfeminists*
Divorce	97.4%	93.3%	84.2%	83.6%
Abortion	96.2	73.3	78.9	75.0
Leave	92.3	82.4	94.7	92.6
Harassment	93.3	79.0	94.7	81.1
Battered	76.6	66.7	63.2	37.0
Summary	4.38	3.92	4.16	3.73
Score	(*n* = 360)	(*n* = 60)	(*n* = 95)	(*n* = 245)

ate needs but has no pension plan. Her husband is willing to pay her a portion of the face value of his annuities, but he refuses to share his income.

The woman litigant in this case got her greatest amount of support from women, both feminist (97.4 percent) and nonfeminist (93.3 percent). Men were less likely to award the woman her request for half of her ex-spouse's retirement income, although 84.2 percent of feminist men and 83.6 percent of nonfeminist men would have done so.

Abortion Rights for Minors.   A woman's boyfriend impregnates her 11-year-old daughter. Evidence indicates he has also sexually abused her 9-year-old daughter. The two girls are removed from the home by the Department of Social Services, which requests a court-ordered abortion for the older girl. The girl says she wants the abortion, but her mother protests that abortion is against her personal beliefs.

The case engendered its strongest pro-choice support from women feminists and its least support from women nonfeminists. Although 96.2 percent of women feminists would have granted the abortion, only 73.3 percent of women nonfeminists would do so. Both groups of men were more likely to grant the abortion than nonfeminist women. It appears that, as in the nation at large, the question of abortion rights for minors is a major divisive issue among women judges.

Maternity Leave.   A state law requires companies to give women four months' maternity leave and to reinstate them in the same or similar job. No provision is made for paternity leave. A woman sues because she is told no position is available when she attempts to return to work after taking her maternity leave. The company claims the law illegally discriminates against men and nonpregnant women and is too costly.

Men judges were slightly more generous than women judges in awarding this woman litigant maternity leave. Ninety-four percent of men feminists, 92.3 percent of women feminists, 92.6 percent of men nonfeminists, and 82.4 percent of women nonfeminists "voted" in favor of the woman's claim. It may be that women judges were fearful of "protective" legislation that might make it more difficult for women of childbearing age to get jobs. Before the women's movement, such protective legislation was often used as an excuse for employment discrimination against women. It remains a controversial issue.

Protection from Sexual Harassment. Two women are hired in a traditionally male-dominated occupation after a private company is ordered to end its sexually discriminatory hiring practices. Within six months one woman resigns, refusing to discuss her reasons for doing so; the other woman files suit against the company for sexual harassment. She claims that her male co-workers created a climate of intimidation through sexually suggestive remarks, jokes, anonymous notes and cartoons, and boisterous requests for sexual favors. Despite her complaints to management, no action was taken. The company claims she is overreacting to normal male camaraderie, needs to develop a sense of humor, and is trying to cover up for her own inability to adjust to a new work environment. They would like to replace her. She wants money damages and wants to continue in her job with company protection from harassment.

Feminists, both men and women, were more likely than nonfeminists, both men and women, to favor the woman litigant in this case. About 94 percent of feminists and about 80 percent of nonfeminists took a "pro-woman" stance.

Battered Women's Rights. A class action suit is filed against a metropolitan police department by a group of battered women claiming a lack of law enforcement for crimes of domestic violence. They request that the court impose new rules of intervention to replace the individual discretion of police officers and to require officer training in the new methods. The police chief objects to the possible erosion of officer discretion and the increased likelihood of suits for false arrest.

The battered women in this case got far less support in their claim than women litigants in any of the other four cases. The most dramatic drop was in the support from nonfeminist men—only 37 percent "voted" for the battered women. Feminist men, 63.2 percent, showed less support than nonfeminist women, at 66.7 percent. Although feminist women showed the most support, 76.6 percent, they also dropped dramatically from their usual over-90-percent support rate in the other cases. This case is different because support of the women litigants requires active judicial intervention in the established procedures of a law enforcement agency. It is on the cutting edge of *new* law, and creates *new* rights.

All Five Cases. Judicial respondents could have voted for women a total of five times. Each judge was given a voting score based on how many times he or she voted for the women litigants. Each group of judges was then given a summary score. These scores may be found on the bottom line of Table 1. The pro-woman score goes in the following order: feminist women (4.38), feminist men (4.16), nonfeminist women (3.92), and nonfeminist men (3.73). Thus, overall, neither feminism alone nor gender alone would enable us to predict how judges might vote. *Within* ideological types, however, women are more likely to cast pro-woman votes.

SUMMARY

This research began by asking if men and women judges bring different gender-based perspectives to the state bench. The answer appears to be qualified "yes." Men and women do have different perspectives, but the degree of difference has much to do with whether the judge is a feminist or not.

Item by item, feminist women judges consistently demonstrated the strongest pro-women stance on the attitudes tested in the questionnaire, and nonfeminist men consistently demonstrated the weakest agreement. However, differences between feminist men judges and nonfeminist women judges were often very small, and feminist men were sometimes more pro-woman than nonfeminist women.

Despite some variation on individual hypothetical cases, women feminist judges were the most likely to cast their votes for the women litigants; nonfeminist men were the least likely; and men feminists and women nonfeminists were in between. This pattern of voting in the hypothetical cases is similar to the pattern found among the four groups of judges on the gender attitude questions. Thus, it appears that, within ideological types, women are more likely than men to hold pro-woman attitudes and behave in a pro-woman manner when voting. However, differences between the groups were sometimes relatively small, with the most sizable and consistent differences being those between feminist women and nonfeminist men.

This study was conducted with an admittedly small number of judges who probably are more feminist than most judges. Future research should test the present findings with a larger and more representative sample. Other possibilities for future research include a focus on more direct connections between judicial attitudes and actual, rather than simulated, judicial behavior.

NOTES

1. R. Darcy, S. Welch, and J. Clark., *Women, Elections and Representation* (New York: Longman, 1987).

2. E. Martin, "State Court Political Opportunity Structures: Implications for the Representation of Women," Paper presented at the Annual American Political Science Association, August 1988.

3. B. Cook. "Women Judges: The End of Tokenism." in W. L. Hepperle and L. Crites (Eds.), *Women in Courts.* (Williamsburg, Va: National Center for State Courts, 1978).

4. B. Cook, K. O'Connor, and S. Talarico, *Women in the Judicial Process* (Washington, DC: American Political Science Association, 1983).

5. Darcy et al., *Women, Elections, and Representation*, p. 133.

6. National Center for State Courts, mailing list, 1987.

7. Darcy et al., *Women, Elections and Representation*.

8. H. Kritzer and T. Vhlman, "Sisterhood in the Courtroom: Sex of Judge and Defendant in Criminal Case Disposition," *Social Science Journal* 14 (1977), pp. 77–88; J. Gruhl, C. Spohn, and S. Welch, "Women as Policy-makers: The Case of Trial Judges," *American Journal of Political Science*, 25 (1981), pp. 308–322.

9. B. Cook, "Will Women Judges Make a Difference in Women's Legal Rights?" in Margherita Rendel (Ed.), *Women, Power and Political Systems* (Metuchen, NJ: Scarecrow Press, 1981).

10. J. Resnik, "On the Bias: Feminist Reconsideration of the Aspirations of Our Judges," *Southern California Law Review*, 61 (6) (1988), p. 1904.

11. *Report of the New York Task Force on Women in the Courts—1986* in *Fordham Urban Law Journal*, 15 (1986–1987), p. 17.

12. "The First Year Report of the New Jersey Supreme Court Task Force on Women in the Courts," *Women's Rights Law Reporter*, 9 (2) (1986), pp. 129–179.

On Credibility: Differential Treatment of Women and Men in the Law

Victor F. D'Lugin

Research on the impact of law and the legal system on women has a long history in the United States. Research studies have been produced that serve to inform and often mobilize women as to the sexist assumptions in the promulgation and implementation of law. One could argue that the law's continuing significance to feminists does not necessarily stem from the primary position of law in determining people's actual behavior but, rather, from the law's unique position as the assumed arbitrator of justice and its self-declared goal of objectivity and impartiality. If law can sanction, it can and often does sanctify sex discrimination. When law declares differential treatment, we have an imprimatur of significant weight.

It is therefore not surprising to read Grimke in the nineteenth century argue that "There are few things which present greater obstacles to the improvement and elevation of women to her appropriate sphere of usefulness and duty than the laws which have been enacted to destroy her independence." Law robs a woman of her "essential right" except to be counted "like the slaves of the South, to swell the number of law-makers."[1] In the nineteenth century the law gave legitimacy to an existence of women defined in terms of the roles they played and thereby denied both equality and personhood to women. Contemporary legal views concerning women seem to be a product of this history. Whether as daughters, wives, mothers, or homemakers, women have been defined in roles that the law accepts, and this acceptance demands compliance.

One key variable in understanding the treatment of women is the differential awarding of credibility to women and men. The principal hypothesis is that whereas men, regardless of role or rule, are assumed to *possess* credibility,

Victor F. D'Lugin is an Assistant Professor of Politics and Government at the University of Hartford.

women must *earn* credibility. It is suggested that the authority of juries, judges, and attorneys is used to the detriment of women and that a common link is that men's testimony and/or performance is assumed to be trustworthy and competent, credible, until and unless shown to be otherwise, whereas women are denied credibility until and unless they prove they possess it by some specific action.

TREATMENT OF WOMEN IN THE LAW

It may be useful here to review Blackstone's understanding of the legal position of a married woman, which is often quoted in works on the treatment of women in the law.

> By marriage the husband and wife are one person in law: that is, the very being or legal existence of the woman is suspended during marriage, or at least is incorporated into that of her husband; under whose wing, protection and cover, she performs everything and is therefore called by French law a *femme-covert* . . . under the protection and influence of her husband, her baron or lord.[2]

The points made by Blackstone reflect the attitude and practice found in much of the history of Anglo-American jurisprudence. The law as to coventure, "winged protection," was not reversed until *U.S. v. Dege* in 1960. For Blackstone, marriage results in the coming together of two entities to form one legal being. Even allowing for a romantic understanding of marriage, the problems raised by Blackstone are evident. The denial of rights associated with marriage is complete and total. It is not certain rights or privileges that are denied but, rather, the very "being or legal existence" of two people is now surrendered to one legal existence. Both legal being and standing are lost, for in the act of marriage the essential quality of individual personhood is denied. It is clear from Blackstone that it is women, not men, who give up any right of personhood. To create the unity of marriage, the "being and legal existence of woman is suspended." Unity can be accomplished in numerous ways, not the least of which is to create a single entity constituted of equal entities sharing authority. For Blackstone, women in marriage are "incorporated" into their husbands. Men retain all rights of personhood, including political and legal standing and dignity. If this denial of women's existence is in any doubt, Blackstone reminds us that women "perform everything" under the protective wing of the husband.

In the past twenty years a significant body of literature has emerged that attempts to analyze systematically the areas of law affected by such sexist biases. Substantial evidence now exists to show that in marriage qualifications, property rights, criminal law, voting rights, jury duty, tort law, employment law, and constitutional law, women are regarded not as persons but as embodiments of specified roles.[3] Discriminatory labor laws usually have been of two types: (1) laws that prohibited women from engaging in certain occupations and (2) laws that required that women be treated less favorably than men. Work was defined as a secondary consideration for women, or, more importantly, work should be only a secondary consideration. Therefore, the rewards or rights of women were declared not to equal those provided to men. Under the guise of "winged protection," courts upheld laws circumscribing activities outside the home for women. Even when individuals acted in a manner determined by courts to be "lacking in virtue," such as gambling or public drinking, courts upheld the right of men to act in these ways but not of women. Justice Felix Frankfurter was determined to uphold sex discrimination even when women "now indulge in the vices that men have long practiced." Just because men engage in "virtue lacking" activity does not mean, for Frankfurter, that states are obligated to permit women to engage in the same practices.[4]

SEX-ROLE ASSUMPTIONS AND THE LAW

Discrimination in law can also be noted in the areas of pornography, prostitution, sexual harassment, and rape. In each of these areas we see a long history of law favoring the actions of men at the expense of women. Much of the concern for these sexually related activities has been to embody "Western culture's celebration of the 'good' women and its condemnation of the 'bad' women."[5] Again the element of control is focused on the woman despite the need in each case for male collaboration. Taub and Schneider argue that discrimination in the law mandated the explicit exclusion of women from the public sphere of action. Women's activity was placed within the private sphere, where protection was either limited or nonexistent. The marriage contract was the principal means to accomplish this removal from public protection, and the same law precluded females from using contract law as a basis of litigation.[6]

In recent years judicial behavior has also come under review. One scholar reviewed decisions made by the Supreme Court during the early to mid-1970s. Interested in the degree to which each of the justices appeared to rely on principles of law or on a traditional sexist role expectation, Cook analyzed the Burger Court's decisions and determined a tendency for the Court to rely on traditional sex-role assumptions.[7] Crites, reviewing the attitudes of male judges in Alabama, showed that they uniformly assumed a "female personality construct" including such characteristics as emotion, sympathy, poor leadership skills, and passivity. These judges also showed a reliance on traditional female role expectations—wife, mother, homemaker—to explain the behavior of women.[8]

All of the research on the relationship between sex and the law can lead to only one conclusion. Our legal system operates with a set of sex-related assumptions concerning women and men. Although these assumptions are not uniform in all areas of law and although many are contradictory, one pattern does emerge. The differential treatment of women and men in the law overwhelmingly favors men at the expense of women. Women can receive equitable treatment only if they follow traditionally defined female role expectations. In a 1977 review of the treatment of women and men by the court, Johnston and Knapp summarize their findings:

Sexism, the making of unjustified assumptions about individual capabilities, interests, goals and social roles solely on the basis of sex differences, is as discernible in contemporary judicial opinions as racism ever was.[9]

A number of explanations have been offered in attempts to understand the continued reliance on sex-based stereotypes in the law. Each appears fruitful, although some are mutually exclusive. Perhaps the most basic and parsimonious is offered by Wikler.

> Though sexism *per se* is rarely mentioned as a potential source of biases by members of the judiciary, recognition of the very nature of the society in which judges have been socialized suggests that it could hardly be otherwise. Until recent challenges from the movements for women's rights, American society rigidly defined sex roles and held women in subservient and inferior status. And most adults in the United States, judges included, learned traditional sex stereotypes and misconceptions through the social institutions which still reflect and reenforce them.[10]

Other researchers have offered additional explanations. Some argue that the primary reason for gender differences is the superior–subordinate role relation between men and women. Subordinates suffer differential and disadvantageous treatment in general. Because women are most frequently forced into subordinate roles, they suffer the disadvantages of subordinates. The primary factor in gender discrimination is differential interpersonal power relations.[11] Klein and Kress argue that sexism is a function of the economic social stratification required in capitalist society and is just one reflection of the numerous inequities that the economic system demands.[12]

Therefore, one key variable for understanding the treatment of women in the practice of law is the differential awarding of credibility to women and men. The principal hypothesis is that regardless of the rule of law, men are assumed to possess credibility, whereas women must earn credibility. The hypothesis presented is not intended to replace the other arguments cited earlier. Rather, it is argued that credibility can be seen to supplement these arguments in such a way as to assist in both our understanding of differential treatment and possible remedies.

Within the formal legal procedures of an adversary court process, credibility plays a pivotal role. Although it is the responsibility of judges and juries to determine the relevant facts and law of a particular case, the testimony of witnesses and the behavior of all the parties involved is assumed to be trustworthy and competent unless specific evidence is introduced to raise doubt about the truthfulness of any information. If such doubt is raised, it still becomes necessary to assess conflicting claims with a sense of reasonableness. In the criminal law this is especially true where "every witness is presumed to be a person of capacity to deserve credit." The presentation of information in a court requires that the "presumption of credibility follows all unimpeached witnesses" (*Neace v. Commonwealth*, 26 S. W. [2d] 489, KY [1930]). Credibility can, of course, be challenged, but until such specific doubt is raised, all participants in a litigation are given credit for reporting what they understand to be actual fact.

DEFINING CREDIBILITY

Attempts to define credibility have been somewhat less successful than its application. Credibility calls for a judge, jury, and attorney to view each other and testimony as if they are "entitled to credit" (*Smith v. Jones*, 34 A. 424, 68 UT 132). The information provided is to be viewed as having substance or weight that should be considered as part of the court's decision-making process. Similarly, credibility includes a sense that the individuals involved, in any role, in a litigation have a "worthiness of belief" (*State v. Green*, 122 S. E. 178, 187 N. C. 466). We are not to assume that individuals are telling stories but, instead, are to recognize that they are presenting information concerning actual events or occurrences about which they are responding with confidence and trust (*Norland v. McCracken*, 18 N. C. 594, 596). Individuals speaking in a court are therefore granted a sense of truthfulness that is not necessarily awarded in informal interpersonal relations.

Contemporary U.S. law when directly addressing credibility as it relates to female witnesses is strong in its declaration of equality of credibility in a formal proceeding. In a divorce action, a male requested an appeal on the grounds that the original court gave too great a degree of credibility to the testimony of a female. The plaintiff's (male) attorney presented to the appeals court an elaborate argument citing philosophers and theologians who asserted that because of women's greater reliance on emotion over reason and sympathy over objectivity, their testimony was not of equal weight with that of a male. This 1912 case seemed to resolve the issue legally when the court ruled as follows:

> . . . plaintiff's attorney asserts that women, as a class, are untrustworthy and untruthful. We disapprove and reject the statement. Witnesses, whether male or female, differ in degree of prejudice, in the sway of self-interest, and in the lack of proper moral perceptions. But those influences against the truth, affecting either sex, are to be left to the court and jury (*Bliss v. Bliss*, 142 S. W. 1081, 1082. 161 MO. A, 70 [1912]).

The court's decision affirms the equal credibility of witnesses regardless of sex. The law as it stands, since at least 1912, is that credibility is to be assured regardless of sex, race, ethnicity, and religion. The only question as to the basic legal concept's applicability to groups within the population concerns its credibility as awarded to minors.

PROBLEMS SURROUNDING CREDIBILITY

Credibility, though poorly defined, would appear to be clear in its intent. Individuals involved in legal actions are assumed to be trustworthy until and unless they are impeached. Credibility requires that we grant trustworthiness and veracity to those we encounter in the court or as part of a legal investigation. This assumption of honesty of intent is to be upheld regardless of any group identification of the adult involved.

There are, however, at least three major problems associated with credibility as defined by law. Each of these problems is intrinsic to the operating definition and can in fact serve to circumscribe the intent of the law's use of credibility.

The first problem is the distinction between *credibility* and *competency*. It is assumed that credibility is not the same as the belief that an individual is competent or informed (*State v. Beal et al.*, 154 S. E. 167, 456 196 N. C. 278 [1930]). On first view, this would appear obvious. Individuals can be providing an honest and sincere presentation of what they know, but the situation may be one in which they are not truly in a position to know facts that are precisely relevant to the matter at hand. The distinction between *trustworthy* and *informed* is an important one. When we look further, however, we discover evidence that the two concepts are often confused in case law. To cite but one example:

> The credibility of a witness is a matter peculiarly for the jury, and depends not only upon his [*sic*] desire to tell the truth, but also and sometimes even to a greater extent upon his [*sic*] insensible bias, intelligence, means of knowing and powers of observation. (Cogdell U. R. R. 40 S. E. 202, 204, 129 N. C. 398, 40.)

Although we can agree that the presence of bias would affect credibility, "means of knowing" and "powers of observation" would appear to represent questions of competency rather than questions of credibility. As we will see in the discussion that follows, possible confusion between questions of credibility and those of competency can seriously diminish the assumed credibility of any individual.

A second problem surrounding credibility goes to the application of the term in legal procedure. As has previously been pointed out, credibility is an assumed characteristic awarded to each party involved in a legal action. Just because credibility is assumed, however, it cannot be argued that this trust is immune from challenge. The formal adversary model of the court is intended to provide the opportunity for an independent jury and judge to discern, if not the truth, then at least the truth in law. Cross-examination by attorneys is the principal means used to support the "combat" or "debate" function of the trial. By means of cross-examination it would be possible to discover relationships between the witness and the parties to the case, if any, and, if these are present, the degree to which they may call into question the witness's credibility. A witness's interests, motivation, inclinations, and prejudices, again if any, could be presented. This information is presented to the jury "to the end that an opportunity may be afforded for observing his [*sic*] demeanor and determining the weight and value" of the testimony (*State v. Beal*).

The question then becomes what areas of questioning are available to attorneys or judges to access the assumed credibility of individuals. Again in *State v. Beal* the answer is that ordinarily a witness may be asked any question that would lead to impeaching the testimony. If that is not broad enough, the court went on to state the following:

> It is not an interference with the constitutional rights and liberties of a witness to require him [*sic*] to disclose, on cross-examination, his [*sic*] present situation, employment, and associates, as, for example, in what locality he [*sic*] resides, what occupation he [*sic*] pursues, and whether or not he [*sic*] is intimately acquainted and conversant with certain persons; for, however these may disparage him [*sic*] in the eyes of the jury, they are of his [*sic*] own selection and constitute proper matters of inquiry. (*State v. Beal*, 167)

The court went on to state that any question is appropriate to determine the "character" of the witness. This open-ended pursuit is reinforced, somewhat forcibly, in another case. It is stated that "there is no such thing as legal equality of credibility between witnesses . . . the testimony of each is to be weighed." The question for judge and jury is the character, demeanor, and probability that what is said is true (*Brethauer v. Schorer et al.*, 70 A. R. 592, 81 Conn 143 [1908]).

There appears to be a reversal of the original burden of credibility. From a state of assumed credibility, we now see that credibility is a question in any court appearance. Any aspect of an individual life is available for review to attest to the general character of a witness. All this information is collected to present to a jury in order to "disparage" the overall character of the witness so as to deny credibility.

A third problem concerning credibility is suggested by the foregoing analysis. The determiner of credibility is the jury. Juries are empowered to answer the question of whether a particular witness, victim, or, for that matter, attorney deserves credibility. Part of the jury's responsibility is the assessment of the value or weight to be given testimony (*Waters v. Gurle*, 234 F. 532, 148 C. C. A. 298). We can see two implications when placing the responsibility for assessing the credibility of witnesses in the hands of the jury. First, credibility becomes another fact to be judged at a trial, not an assumed condition. Second (with even greater implications concerning the treatment of women), attorneys are now free to use whatever tactics are available to sway a jury, not as to the facts of a case, but as to the character of a witness, victim, or attorney. This leaves open the significant probability of a call to sex-based biases as a means to discredit women in the courts.

CREDIBILITY LIMITS EQUAL TREATMENT

It is here that credibility and its associated problems create specific limitations on the equal treatment of women and men in the courts. The very grounds for credibility (character assessment, worthiness of belief, and overall "acceptability" of any individual) leave women vulnerable to sexism and unequal power in the court. Let us review a few areas of law to suggest this connection. The intent is to show where further research is needed to explore the potential of credibility as an explanatory tool.

Most women enter the legal system as victims of crimes or as litigants. The decision to prosecute a particular criminal case rests with the prosecuting attorney, whom many regard as the single most powerful individual within the criminal justice system. Prosecutors determine whether to seek indictments, establish the charges to be brought, and decide whether to agree to any plea agreement. In a study of prosecutorial discretion, Stanko reports that most female victims of crime report a "secondary victimization." The victims with whom Stanko spoke indicate that police and prosecutors make them feel as if they contributed to their own victimization and, therefore, deserved what happened to them as a result of their own actions. In analyzing responses from prosecuting attorneys and observing preliminary interviews between prosecutors or police and victims, Stanko indicates that a decision to proceed with a case will, to a significant degree, be made if the victim possesses "stand-up qualities." The criteria for evaluating the qualities of a "stand-up victim" include prior relations between the victim and the accused and the victim's character. It is this last criterion that is more significant here. Prosecuting attorneys, according to Stanko, are looking for a woman who presents a neat appearance, is consistent in her testimony, and is articulate. For most prosecutors, these traits must be shown because the prosecutor assumes women are "passive, impulsive, hysterical, and sexually unmanageable."[13] As one attorney reported, there is a need for a victim to be a "proper moral woman." Just being able to report on the facts of one's victimization to police or the prosecuting attorney is a necessary but not a sufficient condition for the prosecutor to act on the crime.

Randall and Rose, in an attempt to explain this double standard, argue that women as victims must establish not just the legality of their claim but their legitimacy as both victims and "females" as well.[14] In their study of rape victims, Randall and Rose report that victims needed to establish by persuasion that they were deserving of the status of victim. The prevailing assumption by police and prosecutors was that unless this "proof" was provided, the victim's report of the facts was not, in itself, sufficient to proceed. The legitimacy of claim was based not on the behavior, circumstance, or intent of the accused in relation to the victim, but on the *qualities* or *character* of the victim.

In reviewing these studies, one notes how the issues of credibility, competency, and character analysis are used to the detriment of women. According to Stanko, women are viewed by prosecutors as lacking competency and therefore credibility. Similarly, Randall and Rose report that women must affirm their competency by proving that they can stand challenge in any area of their lives.

CREDIBILITY AND WOMEN ACCUSED OF CRIME

Kruttschnitt provides a similar analysis when reviewing the treatment of women accused of crimes.[15] In a study of the discretionary authority of judges in sentencing and prosecuting attorneys' plea-bargaining agreements with women accused of crimes, she notes a "respectable women" variable: "Regardless of the offense, the lower a woman's respectability, the greater the likelihood that she will receive a more severe sentence." Sentencing decisions include traditional concerns for prior record and perhaps for substance abuse. Women will be more seriously judged according to concern for "peer deviance," the respectability of their friends and associates, and a character rating from employers. Respectability is assumed to be a "feminine" determined characteristic. Although it is common to include such considerations when making decisions concerning sentencing of men convicted of crimes, Kruttschnitt suggests that this becomes primary for women accused of crimes. Women will be assessed on the basis of the degree of "feminine" qualities they possess and have exhibited in choosing their friends and their work. Credibility is challenged not on the basis of the facts of a case, but on the basis of the woman's lifestyle.

WOMEN, CREDIBILITY, AND RAPE

When analyzing the prosecutorial decision to proceed with a rape case, and in reviewing rape trials, Berger notes a movement in the burden of evidence. From a detached review of statutes defining rape, one could rightly determine that the proper cause of action in preparing for trial would be to determine the subjective state of mind of the victim and the objective behavior of the defendant. Rape cases would need to revolve around the question of whether the victim consented to the act of intercourse. The victim, as reported by her—and only by her—can indicate if she did or did not consent. Some form of corroboration might then be required to increase the probability of successful prosecution. The basic requirement, however, is the subjective condition of the victim. The other requirement is the actual behavior of the accused. Did he have sexual intercourse with the victim or not? Berger indicates that for prosecutors, judges, defense attorneys, and juries, the issue becomes one of the victim's objective behavior. The victim must have engaged in specific overt behavior of a consistent and persistent manner to prove her lack of consent. "The significance of the law of rape stems mainly from a deep distrust of the female accuser." The word, under oath, of the victim is not just insufficient but, other than the required formality of the charge, totally inadequate to proceed with a prosecution. Both credibility and competency will be questioned, and the female accuser is assumed to lack the "character" necessary to provide trustworthy testimony.

The issue thus is not the assumed credibility of the accuser but, rather, her assumed lack of credibility and the assumed reliability of the accused. To further amplify this point, Berger points out that the principal criterion in judging the prosecutorial possibility for rape cases is the "character for chastity pertinent." A victim who was not chaste at the time of the rape suffers an added "secondary victimization." It is accepted by the key figures (mostly male) in the legal system that "promiscuity imparts dishonesty." Juries become known as a group who "punish unchaste women by refusing to credit their accusation even in clearly meritorious cases involving no hint of precipitating conduct." If credibility is to be awarded to a woman who is the victim of a crime, she must be a (1) "stand-up," (2) "respectable," (3) "chaste," and (4) "morally proper" female—not person.[16]

Most jurisdictions have succeeded in eliminating the defense attorney's right to question the prior sexual history of rape victims. In trial practice, however, there are still present indications that a woman's character, not action or thought, will be the basis of legal judgment. Prior sexual conduct between the victim and the accused is still admissible—and the question therefore still revolves around the character of the victim, not the accused. Additionally, spousal rape is still an exclusion to the rape law of most states.

A final example should be cited to show the relative merit given to the credibility of male and female testimony. The California judicial instruction code recommends that the following be read to all juries in rape cases:

> It is a defense to a charge of forcible rape that the defendant entertained a reasonable and good faith belief that the female person voluntarily consented to engage in sexual intercourse. If from all of the evidence you have a reasonable doubt whether the defendant reasonably and in good faith believed she voluntarily consented to engage in sexual intercourse, you must give the defendant the benefit of the doubt and acquit him of said charge. (CALJIC 10.23)

Ultimately it becomes not a question of whether the victim consented or not, but only a question of whether the accused "entertained" a good-faith belief as to her consent. The woman's word or even her action is not to be of equal weight to the possible thought entertained in the mind of a man.

THE STATEMENTS OF WOMEN IN CRIMINAL CASES

In criminal prosecution, statements of women are given less worth or weight than those of men. This is principally discovered in the judicial and prosecutorial effort to restrict the credibility of victims or accused by relying on sexist assumptions about "proper behavior" for women or what constitutes a "feminine personality." Either consciously or subconsciously, male judges and male attorneys rely on a belief that the emotionality of women will undermine their credibility, and these stereotypes are used to influence juries and other court personnel. Although the "emotional condition" of any witness may serve as grounds for questioning competency of the testimony, it is, first, not a question of credibility and, second, a criterion that should be equally applicable to women and men.

One attempt to diminish the credibility of women in the courts is the dynamics of interpersonal interaction within the courtroom. This has been addressed only recently in the literature. The treatment accorded the personnel within the court—judges, attorneys, expert witnesses, and clerks—has been shown to have an impact on court decisions.[17] During the past decade, investigations have shown that the pervasive sexism of these interpersonal relations has been directed toward diminishing the credibility of female attorneys and judges.

The New Jersey Supreme Court Task Force on Women in the Courts reported on a survey of female and male attorneys and found what appeared to be "inequality of treatment of men and women in the legal and judicial environment." In the area of damage claims, the task force noted that a "dual valuation" system existed. Claims for damages by women were awarded lower cash assessments than similar damages to men. Would not the only interpretation be that women, as a class, are perceived as being of less worth then men? This feeling was reinforced when age was analyzed. It was shown that the likelihood of successful litigation for a female plaintiff decreased drastically with age, whereas a similarly situated male plaintiff experienced an increased chance of success. On the basis of the sexist belief as to the "proper" role of woman as wife and mother, the value of women is assumed to diminish with age.

CREDIBILITY OF FEMALE ATTORNEYS

Nearly two-thirds of the female attorneys in the New Jersey study observed incidents where women were treated in a disadvantageous manner by a judge; 80 percent of the female attorneys and 50 percent of the male attorneys reported such behavior by male counsel. The treatment of female attorneys was similar to the treatment of female witnesses. One-third of the male attorneys and three-quarters of the female attorneys reported observing judges treating female attorneys disadvantageously. Over 60 percent of the female attorneys reported such behavior by court personnel, and 86 percent of the female attorneys in this study reported that male counsel treated female counsel in a manner intended to have a negative effect on their credibility. This was done by the use of sexist jokes, sexual references, or sexist stereotypes.

One of the issues concerning the application of credibility in the courtroom was the fact that juries are empowered to assess both credibility and competence. The interpersonal treatment of women in court serves to diminish their credibility in the eyes of the jury. Juries receive these subtle and not so subtle messages. Hodgson and Pryor's study reported that individuals perceive female attorneys as less credible than male attorneys.[18] Women rated female attorneys as less intelligent, capable, expert, and experienced. If offered a choice, the women interviewed expressed a strong preference for male attorneys. This judgment is based on an accurate understanding of how the legal system treats women. The New York State Task Force found that (1) judges, male attorneys, and court personnel tended to award less credibility to female attorneys, witnesses, and litigants, and (2) that a woman's character, not her competency, could directly determine the outcome of a court proceeding.

A final observation concerning the credibility of women in courts can be found in trial practice manuals, which provide assistance to attorneys in developing the skills to handle a trial. One such manual, reported as representative, states: "Women, like children, are prone to exaggeration; they generally have poor memories."[19] Women, like children, are seen as possessing a lower level of seriousness, competency, and ability to report accurately on what has occurred than men. It is important to note that these statements go even further than a "sympathy" or "compassion" argument about women. This interpretation is that women are less likely than men to tell the truth not because they are more understanding or considerate. Rather, they are seen as unable to do so. The linking of women and children in the foregoing quote is a reminder of Blackstone. Women are perceived in law to be not "persons." Women, like children, do not possess the one necessary prerequisite for "personhood," which is adulthood.

SUMMARY

One key variable in understanding the inequitable treatment of women is credibility. By law, credibility is to be assumed and, therefore, awarded for all participants in a court action. In practice, however, the challenge to credibility has permitted and still permits judges, juries, and attorneys to use and manipulate sexist assumptions concerning females. This is done to the detriment of female victims, accused, and professional workers in the court.

To a significant degree, any redress of this situation would rely on a larger alteration of social and personal perceptions. As women gain greater access to positions of authority and influence in the social, economic, and political spheres, we would expect a diminishing of many sexist stereotypes. Realizing that the courts are more the responders to social reality than the creators, in time—but only in time—we may see a movement within the court to eliminate sex-based justice. It would appear that judges must be made to feel significant pressure to alter the dynamics of the courtroom. The judge, as chief administrator of a court, must set a tone and legal environment in which credibility is not used as a means to deny women access to equal justice.[20]

NOTES

1. Sarah Grimke, "Legal Disabilities of Women," in Wendy McElroy (Ed.), *Freedom, Feminism and the State* (Washington, DC: Cato Institute, 1982), p. 121.

2. William Blackstone, *Commentaries on the Law of England* (Washington, DC: Washington Law Book Company, 1941), p. 189.

3. L. Kanowitz, *Women and the Law: The Unfinished Revolution* (Albuquerque: University of New Mexico Press, 1969).

4. As quoted in ibid., p. 34.

5. Rosemarie Tong, *Women, Sex and the Law* (Totowa, NJ: Rowman and Allanhead, 1984), p. 193.

6. Nadine Taub and Elizabeth M. Schneider, "Perspectives on Women's Subordination and the Role of Law," in David Kairys (Ed.), *The Politics of Law:*

A Progressive Critique (New York: Pantheon, 1982), pp. 117–139.

7. Beverly Blair Cook, "The Burger Court and Women's Rights 1971–1977," in Winifred L. Hepperle and Laura Crites (Eds.), *Women in the Courts* (Williamsburg, VA: National Center for State Courts, 1978).

8. Laura Crites, "Women in the Criminal Courts," in Hepperle and Crites, *Women in the Courts.*

9. John D. Johnston, Jr., and Charles L. Knapp, "Sex Discrimination by Law: A Study in Judicial Perspective," *New York University Law Review,* 46 (October 1971), p. 676.

10. Norma Juliet Wikler, "On the Judicial Agenda for the 80's: Equal Treatment for Men and Women in the Courts," *Judicature,* 64 (5) (1980), pp. 13–14.

11. William M. O'Barr and Bowman K. Atkins, " 'Women's Language' or 'Powerless Language'?," in Sally McConnell-Ginet, Ruth Borker, and Nelly Furman (Eds.), *Women and Language in Literature and Society* (New York: Praeger, 1980).

12. Dorie Klein and June Kress, "Any Woman's Blues: A Critical Overview of Women, Crime and the Criminal Justice System," *Crime and Social Justice* (Spring/Summer 1976), pp. 34–49.

13. Elizabeth Anne Stanko, "Would You Believe This Woman? Prosecutorial Screening for 'Credible' Witnesses and a Problem of Justice," in Elizabeth Anne Stanko (Ed.), *Judge, Victim, Thief* (Evanston, IL: Northwestern University Press, 1986), pp. 64–70.

14. Susan C. Randall and Vicki M. Rose, "Barriers to Becoming a 'Successful' Rape Victim," in Lee H. Bowker (Ed.), *Women and Crime in America* (New York: Macmillan, 1981), pp. 336–353.

15. Candace Kruttschnitt, "Respectable Women and the Law," *The Sociological Quarterly*, 23 (Spring 1982), pp. 221–224.

16. Vivina Berger, "Man's Trial, Woman's Tribulation: Rape Cases in the Court Room," *Columbia Law Review*, 77 (January 1977), pp. 43, 45, 48.

17. Peter David Blanck, Robert Rosenthal, and LaDoris Hazzard, "The Appearance of Justice: Judges' Verbal and Nonverbal Behavior in Criminal Jury Trials," *Stamford Law Review* (1985), pp. 89–164.

18. Shri Hodgson and Bert Pryor, "Sex Discrimination in the Courtroom: Attorney's Gender and Credibility," *Psychological Reports*, 55 (1984), pp. 483–486.

19. As quoted in O'Barr and Atkins, " 'Women's Language,' " p. 95.

20. The original research for this work was initiated at the National Judicial Education Project of the NOW Legal Defense and Education Fund. The author expresses his thanks to Norma J. Wikler, Ph.D., and Carol L. Schlein, J.D., for assistance in preparing this research.

PUBLIC POLICY: THE FEMINIST PERSPECTIVE

7

Public policy in this country significantly influences the lives of American women. Diane D. Blair's article deals with the politics of reproduction and the implications for women as policymakers determine what is personal and what is political for women. Blair compares Margaret Atwood's *The Handmaid's Tale* (1986) and Ben Wattenberg's *The Birth Dearth* (1987). Both works deal with the politics of reproduction, but from completely different perspectives. Atwood, writing from a feminist perspective, describes an imaginary future of total misery and wretchedness for women, one in which women have been reduced to the function of breeders. On the other hand, Wattenberg, writing from what Blair describes as a "nationalistic perspective," deplores the current American "birth dearth," blaming it primarily on "working women" and proposing a variety of pro-natalist remedies. Both books use a simple style to convey a complex message. Blair argues that among the significant implications of these two books, especially when they are read in tandem, are:

1. That pro-natalism, justified by the United States's relatively low fertility rate, has climbed high on many conservative agendas
2. That this movement seriously jeopardizes many of the gains achieved by feminists in recent years
3. That the contemporary pro-natalist drive has long and powerful historical precedents.

Joan Hulse Thompson maintains that male exclusion has been a policy of the women's liberation movement for ideological, symbolic, and pragmatic reasons. She analyzes the transformation of the Congresswomen's Caucus into the Congressional Caucus for Women's Issues and raises questions about the viability of any political organization founded on gender and what this means with respect to future strategy for the women's movement. For example, is not the Family and Medical Leave Act just as important for men as it is for women? Thompson's case study of this act provides insight into legislation before Congress—the benefits and challenges that come from forging coalitions and compromises.

We next move from birth control as an issue of politics and the intricacies of the Family and Medical Leave Act to the role of the Supreme Court in shaping public policy. Despite the numerous laws prohibiting sex discrimination in a variety of public policy areas, Ruth Bamberger finds the insurance industry has retained the practice of discriminating by gender in determining coverage and premium rates. The industry argues its position on cost-efficiency and actuarial grounds. Civil rights and feminist groups have criticized such discrimination on grounds of fairness and prevailing social policy. Although they have pursued their cause through multiple channels of government, the Supreme Court is perceived to be the primary agent of policy change. Bamberger finds that, even though the Court has signaled that sex may be "suspect" as a classification, the Supreme Court's role as shaper of policy on this issue has been incremental at best.

Finally, in this chapter, we examine affirmative action and the program designed to correct past inequities in treatment of women and other minorities. Roberta Ann Johnson offers a generic definition of affirmative action and then does three things. First, she traces the development of the federal affirmative action policy from the issuing of Executive Orders by Presidents Roosevelt, Kennedy, and Johnson to its full implementation in the Department of Labor. Second, she summarizes and evaluates all the affirmative action cases decided by the Supreme Court, starting with the Bakke decision. Finally, using Census Bureau and Department of Labor statistics and secondary sources, she considers the ways affirmative action increases opportunities for women. Throughout her essay, the author recognizes affirmative action for its redistributive thrust.

Affirmative action and the women's movement have resulted in the removal of many obstacles for females—obstacles that crossed political, economic, social, cultural, and legal boundaries. One significant change, and one that brings forth emotional arguments on both sides, extends to the role of women in the military. Specifically, this debate centers around the question of whether the military should permit women in combat. With the intervention of U.S. forces in the activities of other countries, this issue has become even more salient to the U.S. public. Richard D. Hooker, Jr., reviews the current policy of the U.S. Army with respect to the role of women, examines court cases brought about as a result of this issue, and evaluates the arguments for those who would favor full participation of women in all aspects of military life versus those who take a more traditional approach toward the role of female soldiers.

The Handmaid's Tale
and The Birth Dearth:
Prophecy, Prescription, and Public
Policy

Six children [are] the minimum number for people of 'normal' stock; those of better stock should have more.

THEODORE ROOSEVELT, 1907

As that great author and scientist, Mr. Brisbane, has pointed out, what every woman ought to do is have six children.

SINCLAIR LEWIS, 1935

There is nothing to compare to the joy of having six children. If every American family did that, we'd certainly have the greatest nation in the world.

PHYLLIS SCHLAFLY, 1987[1]

This article looks at two recent works on the politics of reproduction: *The Handmaid's Tale*, by Margaret Atwood, and *The Birth Dearth*, by Ben Wattenberg.[2] Since the former is an imaginative work by a popular novelist and the latter is a research report by a Senior Fellow at the American Enterprise Institute, one might assume that they would have little in common. In fact, however, these two books provide some direct, and often disturbing, points of comparison.

Both, for example, open with a selection from the Book of Genesis. Wattenberg's choice is from Book 1, Chapter 28: "Be fruitful and multiply, and replenish the earth. . . ." Wattenberg does not dwell upon this specific scriptural imperative, but human reproduction, and the need for much more of it in the contemporary United States, is the theme of his book. *The Birth Dearth* consists of three major parts, all laden with demographic and other data. In the first

Diane D. Blair is a professor of political science at the University of Arkansas.

part, Wattenberg documents (and deplores) what he calls the United States's "fertility free-fall," a recent sharp decline in the total fertility rate (TFR) to below the population replacement rate of 2.1 children per woman. In the second part, Wattenberg offers his explanations for this "birth dearth" and outlines what he considers to be its most alarming economic, geopolitical, and personal consequences. Finally, Wattenberg suggests a long list of possible pro-natalist remedies for this present-day problem and impending crisis.

Atwood's scriptural epigram is both longer and more specifically woven into her novel. Indeed, the following biblical episode becomes both *raison d'être* and central ritual in the twenty-first-century political system she posits:

> And when Rachel saw that she bare Jacob no children, Rachel envied her sister; and said unto Jacob, Give me children or else I die. And Jacob's anger was kindled against Rachel; and he said, Am I in God's stead, who hath withheld from thee the fruit of the womb? And she said, Behold my maid Bilhah, go in unto her; and she shall bear upon my knees, that I may also have children by her. (Genesis 30: 1–3)

As the novel opens, fundamentalists, justifying their coup primarily on the grounds of an acute birth dearth, have seized power and established the Republic (actually the monotheocracy) of Gilead. The governing patriarchy, known as Commanders, has forced all women into rigidly stratified, socially useful functions. There are Wives, physically sterile but socially prominent women, who serve their Commander husbands as hostesses and household managers; Marthas, who do the cooking and cleaning; and Aunts, who run the Rachel and Leah Reeducation Centers in which women who have viable ovaries (that is, those who have given birth previously) and are "available" (divorced women, those married to divorced men, widows, and those deliberately widowed by the state) are trained to become proper Handmaids.

Handmaids, like the novel's narrator Offred (literally "of Fred," the name of the Commander to whom she is assigned) have only one function: to reproduce. As Offred wryly notes, she and her sister Handmaids are women of "reduced circumstances" (p. 8)—reduced, that is, to being nothing more than "two-legged wombs" (p. 136). Because their fecundity is so vital to natural survival, the Handmaids are well fed, relieved of all arduous work, and protected from physical danger. They are also, however, "protected" from many other ordinary activities which Offred, too late, realizes had been central to her previous happiness: reading, paid work, discussions of current events, privacy (as opposed to solitude), friendship (as opposed to a sterile "sisterhood"), and love (as opposed to enforced breeding).

During a Handmaid's period of maximum fertility, she is "serviced" by her Commander while lying between the spread legs of the Commander's Wife, a peculiar but strangely nonsexual arrangement. If sperm meets seed, there is an elaborate birthing ceremony nine months later in which the Handmaid delivers upon the Wife's welcoming knees. If repeated attempts at conception are unsuccessful, or if the resulting children are repeatedly born dead or deformed, the Handmaid is eventually exiled to a Third World colony to clean up toxic waste. In Gilead, a literal interpretation has been given to Rachel's, "Give me children, or else I die."

THE SIMILARITY OF THE TWO WORKS

Other than their genesis in Genesis, their central premise of a population short-fall, and their popularity (*The Handmaid's Tale* ran thirty-six weeks on the *New York Times* best-seller list, and a shortened and serialized version of *The Birth Dearth* was syndicated in many U.S. Newspapers), what do these two works have in common? First, both books are didactic; that is, they were designed to be instructive. Wattenberg acknowledges at the outset that his book is both "a specu-lation and a provocation" (p. 1). It is his genuine fear about the consequences of the birth dearth that has propelled him, a self-described optimist, into writing this "alarmist tract" (p. 10). According to Wattenberg, the very survival of Western civilization is at stake, and he chastises both liberals and conservatives for their failure to come right out and say what Wattenberg thinks urgently needs to be said: American women should be having more babies.

Atwood is somewhat more reticent in acknowledging the instrumentality of her intentions. "This book won't tell you who to vote for," she has said. "I do not have a political agenda of that kind."[3] Atwood, however, has long used her fiction for social criticism, and with specific reference to *The Handmaid's Tale* has observed: "Speculative fiction is a logical extension of where we are now. I think this particular genre is a walking along of a potential road, and the reader as well as the writer can then decide if that is the road they wish to go on. Whether we go that way or not is going to be up to us."[4]

This leads to the second point of clear comparability between the two works. Both are projectionist: They are grounded in present events and trends that are at least suggestive of a possible future. Wattenberg's projections are based on data and interpretations of data gathered from an impressive array of sources. Wherever he looks he finds evidence that in the "modern, industrial, free" nations (the United States, Canada, the nations of Western Europe, Japan, Australia, and Israel), the TFR is well below replacement rates. In contrast, the population of the "Soviet bloc" (the Soviet Union and Eastern Europe) will be increasing. Most alarming to Wattenberg, despite a "heartening" decline in Third World fertility, is that we are now

> awash in the fruit of those TFR's in the six-plus range from a generation ago. Today there are 1.1 billion women of child-bearing age in the less-developed world! Even if those women reduce their fertility as the U.N. projects, there will be a flood of Third World babies, a real flood. Third World population, which is now 3.7 *billion* persons, is slated to rise to over 8 *billion* people in the middle of the next century! (p. 44)

What concerns Wattenberg most deeply is that, if present reproductive trends continue, by 2025 the Westernized nations will constitute only 9 percent of the world's population, down from 22 percent in 1950 and 15 percent in the 1990s; and that 9 percent will not be enough to spread democratic values, technological advances, and economic benefits. Wattenberg ruefully notes, " 'Manifest destiny' was not the cry of a no-growth continent of old people" (p. 71).

Atwood's novel contains no charts and graphs. It is obvious, however, that she, like Wattenberg, is a very close follower of current events, from which she has gleaned a number of happenings and ideas, which she has woven into a grim dystopia. In the contemporary United States, for example, abortion clinics have frequently been bombed and burned. In Romania, doctors performing abortions until recently were subject to twenty-five years' imprisonment or even death.[5] In Atwood's imagined Gilead, abortionists are executed and their bodies hung from hooks on "The Wall," as a deterrent, or else they are dismembered in gruesome "particicution" ceremonies. In the United States, homosexuals are often subject to legal and social penalties; in Gilead, "gender treachery," being nonproductive, is a capital offense. In the last few years, courts in at least eleven U.S. states have ordered women, against their wishes, to submit to Caesarean section surgery when doctors decided that conventional childbirth could harm the fetus, and there have been increasing instances of litigation by the state in behalf of "fetus patients" against the bearing mothers; in Gilead, Handmaids are nothing but fetus-bearing vessels and must sacrifice all personal choice and pleasure in the fetus's behalf.[6] As in Gilead, so in the United States today, many major companies bar women under 45 from certain jobs that might diminish their fertility or damage a fetus; toxic wastes are increasingly being shipped to Third World nations; "pro-life" forces have frequently held symbolic "funerals" for fetuses; and at least one state legislature has now required "dignified" burial or disposal of fetal remains.[7]

As Atwood has emphasized, although her novel is futuristic, it is not utterly fantastic. "There are no spaceships, no Martians, nothing like that," she has pointed out. In fact, when asked if Gilead could possibly happen here, she responds that some of it "is happening now," and that, "There is nothing in *The Handmaid's Tale*, with the exception of one scene, that has not happened at some point in history."[8]

Obviously, both Wattenberg and Atwood have looked closely at certain contemporary events and circumstances, have extrapolated these events into a highly undesirable future, and have written their books to alert readers to the dangers the authors see ahead. Since in some ways the "solutions" Wattenberg advocates are related to the dangers Atwood warns against, it is somewhat surprising to find as much agreement as there is between the two regarding the major factors that have depressed present birth rates.

FACTORS PRODUCING THE BIRTH DEARTH

Both Wattenberg, with long lists and charts, and Atwood, by indirection throughout the novel and in a "scholarly" appendix at the novel's end, suggest that among the factors producing the "baby bust" have been better contraceptive techniques, more education and higher income for females, delayed marriage, more frequent divorce, more abortions due to legalization, increased infertility, and more open homosexuality. Most interesting, however, is that both writers—Wattenberg centrally, Atwood peripherally—implicate the women's liberation movement as possibly pushing us into undesirable futures.

For Wattenberg, the cause-and-effect relationship is very clear and entirely adverse. According to his analysis, "One clear root thought of the original [women's liberation] movement was this: Marriage, raising a family, or a large family, was no longer necessarily considered to be the single most important thing in a woman's life" (p. 127). As he has written elsewhere,

> About twenty years ago, corresponding almost exactly with the Birth Dearth—many women began to forge a new economic contract for themselves. They exchanged what anthropologists tell us was the original female contract—trading childbearing capabilities for economic sustenance in the home—for a version of the male practice—trading physical and mental labor for economic sustenance in the market.[9]

Hence, women's liberation led to women's presence in the work force; and "working women," according to Wattenberg, are "probably the single most important factor" causing the birth dearth.[10]

Such generalizations may disturb at least some of Wattenberg's readers, and certainly his feminist ones. Especially when the policy implications of Wattenberg's philosophy are being considered, however, it is good that he has made his central premises so plain. Wattenberg insists, for example, that he wants pro-natalist policies that will expand rather than limit women's choices, and he suggests scores of possibilities. If "working women" are the "single greatest cause" of the birth dearth, however, it seems obvious that all solutions will be partial until women leave the work force and resume their "original contracts."

For Atwood, the line between contemporary women's liberation and future Gileadean oppression is much more circuitous. In the "old times" (which, of course, are our times), Offred was sufficiently "liberated" to have had a college degree, a job, and a lover who eventually became her husband. Although she chose to have a child, many of her friends—working women who did not want the economic and other burdens of children, or who feared the fragility of the environment or the inevitability of nuclear catastrophe—did not. Others, because of the fertility-depressing and abortifacient effects of environmental pollutants, nuclear radiation, and toxic wastes, could not conceive or bear a healthy child. Furthermore, the sexual freedom and excesses of the "old times" produced not only fertility-impeding sexually transmitted diseases, but also an escalating atmosphere of contempt for and violence against women. Hence, among the chief demands of women's liberationists were increased respect for women and improved physical protection. Offred's own mother, she recalls, marched in demonstrations to "take back the night," enthusiastically participated in pornographic-book burnings, and often mouthed antimale slogans such as "A man is just a woman's strategy for making other women."

Society was "dying of too much choice," Offred recalls (p. 25):

Women were not protected then. . . . Now we walk along the same street, in red pairs, and no man shouts obscenities at us, speaks to us, desires us. . . . There is more than one kind of freedom, said Aunt Lydia. Freedom to and freedom from. In the days of anarchy it was freedom to. Now you are being given freedom from. Don't underrate it. (p. 24)

Following an emotional birthing ceremony from which all males, all doctors, and all anesthetics have been excluded, Offred utters one of the book's most poignant lines: "Mother, I think: Wherever you may be. Can you hear me? You wanted a woman's culture. Well, now there is one. It isn't what you meant, but it exists" (p. 127).

Atwood is a feminist, and the oppressions she describes can be much more clearly traced to the religious right than to the feminist left. Atwood's warning signals, however, are flashed at radical feminism as well as religious fundamentalism. Please remember, she seems to be saying, that the "protection" of women has always been the major justification for their oppression, and sometimes, however unfortunately, one must choose between freedom *from* and freedom *to*. Or, as Offred's Commander reminds her, "Better never means better for everyone. It always means worse for some" (p. 211).

As should be obvious by now, these two authors have written "message" books in order to convey diametrically different messages. Before further discussing those differences, however, one final similarity should be noted: Both authors employ a very simple style to clothe a highly complex message.

For many readers and book reviewers, it is the prosaic, unemotional tone with which Offred relates the most degrading and horrifying arrangements that makes the book so deeply disturbing. Leaving a particicution ceremony, where the Handmaids have been emotionally stampeded into tearing an accused rapist apart with their bare hands, they wish each other the conventional, "You have a nice day" (p. 281). Thoughts can quickly turn from death to dinner, from bodies hanging on The Wall to sundresses and ice cream cones.

Oddly, while the novelist is presenting her grim forecast with restrained but imaginative force, it is the research fellow who hammers the reader with tones of breathless, desperate urgency. As the material already quoted indicates, Wattenberg's voice is shrill, overwrought, semihysterical. His favorite punctuation mark is the exclamation point. And in his determination to persuade the widest possible audience, his words and sentences often go beyond the simple to the simplistic. In outlining possible economic incentives to produce additional offspring, for example, Wattenberg holds out the promise of "a nice green check" (p. 154), "a green federal check" (p. 157), "a green Social Security check" (p. 157), and "real green cash money" (p. 158). "In a nonfree country," he lectures his apparently unsophisticated readers, "the ruler, or rulers, can sit down around a big table and make policy" (p. 143). One of his pieces of pictorial persuasion is a python (the United States) swallowing a pig (the post–World War II baby boom). Should the pictures not be sufficiently clear, Wattenberg supplies the sound effects: "Gobble, gobble, suck, suck" (p. 34).

DIFFERENCES BETWEEN THE TWO WORKS

The following short excerpts, the first from Atwood, the second from Wattenberg, illustrate not only the unadorned style employed by each author, but also the profoundly different assumptions and values they bring to their work. In *The Handmaid's Tale*, Offred has been taken by her Commander to an illegal nightclub where the women are dressed in everything from chorus girls' shifts to old cheerleading costumes. Offred is dumbfounded, amused, and wildly curious, but any display of emotions could be fatal. Hence, she warns herself, "All you have to do, I tell myself, is keep your mouth shut and look stupid. It shouldn't be that hard" (p. 236). In the penultimate paragraph of *The Birth Dearth*, Wattenberg summarizes his solution to the impending crisis as follows: "After all, it's not such a big deal. All it involves is having another baby" (p. 169).

The reader quickly realizes that Atwood's "all" reverberates with the irony of centuries. In two simple lines, the author has captured the conventional wisdom passed down to women, and keeping them down, through the ages: Feign ignorance; don't ask questions; accept your lot; suffer in silence; what you don't know can't hurt you. In contrast, Wattenberg seems oblivious to the irony, and revolutionary implications, of his "all." Because women not only bear children, but generally have had the major responsibility for nurturing and raising them to adulthood, the ability to control one's reproductive choices is the sine qua non of woman's ability to live in relative freedom. Almost all the advances of recent decades have recognized the centrality of reproductive freedom to any other meaningful kind of economic, political, or personal freedom for women. Yet Wattenberg, with offhand ease, is apparently ready to jettison these hard-won achievements, and to do so with no apparent recognition of the magnitude of what he is advocating.

To be fair, Wattenberg rejects any overtly coercive solutions to the birth dearth. He opposes outlawing either contraception or abortion, and suggests that enthusiastically pro-natalist public education (using three-children-each Jeane Kirkpatrick and Sandra Day O'Connor as prominent role models, for example), could be effective when coupled with some lucrative economic incentives. Among the many possibilities he suggests are much more extensive and less expensive day care, very profitable tax incentives, forgiveness of college loans to child-producing couples, and reorganizing Social Security in recognition of the fact that people who have no children or even one child are "cheating": They are "free riders" who "end up drawing full pensions paid for by children who were raised and reared—at a large expense—by children of other people" (p. 154). Wattenberg suggests everything from personal ads in the *New York Times* (to destigmatize these possible paths to marriage and children) to kibbutz-style collectives in the suburbs, without ever advocating anything even approaching the Gileadean model of society.

His perspective, however, is a nationalistic one. His goal, he says, is to preserve and promote precious political and economic freedoms that can only survive if the "free world" remains stronger than the Communist world and than the less developed nations, which are only beginning to absorb the values and benefits of the Western model. If some individuals must sacrifice a little bit of liberty to secure the future of freedom, so be it.

Atwood is also centrally concerned with freedom; how easily it is under-valued (Offred wistfully remembers going to a laundromat with her own dirty garments and her own money in her own jeans pocket, or checking into a hotel room); how quickly it can be taken away (shortly after the coup, all Compucounts (credit cards) coded female are canceled, rendering all women economically dependent in a noncash economy); and above all, how important it is to watch, as Offred regrets she has not, as Atwood hopes her readers will, for signs of its endangerment.

Here especially *The Handmaid's Tale* brilliantly demonstrates the rele-vance of good social science fiction to politics. By taking a few parts of contempo-rary reality, exaggerating them, and extrapolating them into a possible future, Atwood makes her readers see the present more clearly, and recognize the possible dangers in what may otherwise appear beneficent, or at least benign.

IMPLICATIONS OF THE TWO WORKS

Read by itself, *The Handmaid's Tale* provides a fresh and interesting, sometimes alarming and sometimes amusing perspective on contemporary events and poli-cies. When it is read in tandem with *The Birth Dearth*, three implications seem especially noteworthy.

First, the mere fact that the "birth dearth" has climbed high on at least some conservative agendas is important for all political observers and policymak-ers to recognize. Pat Robertson's attempt in the October 1987 televised Republi-can presidential debate to propose a prohibition on abortion as the best way to "ensure the fiscal stability of the Social Security system" was widely dismissed as an isolated bit of idiocy; but references, following Wattenberg, to child-free families as "freeloaders" on Social Security are becoming increasingly common. As further examples of the rising popularity of strategic demography, Jack Kemp has been warning that "no nation can long remain a world power when its most precious resource (i.e. its population) is a shrinking resource"; Gary Bauer, when serving as President Reagan's domestic policy adviser, noted "a lot of very worrying evidence on the population decline"; Allan Carlson of the Rockford Institute has taken up the cause of pro-natalism; and Phyllis Schlafly, as quoted at the outset, is proselytizing the need for and joys of much larger families.[11]

Thus far, these seem to be only sentiments, but could the increased popularity of strategic demography help to explain the explosive sudden popu-larity of day care?[12] Does it not seem surprising that federal child care legislation, vetoed so vehemently by President Nixon in 1971 for its family-weakening impli-cations, denounced so thoroughly over the decades by the political right for its communal overtones, had emerged by 1988 as Senator Orrin Hatch's "number one policy issue"?[13] In *The Birth Dearth*, published in 1987, Wattenberg pointed out the strategic value of an issue like day care with the potential for uniting feminists and pro-natalists. Even earlier, in a 1986 interview on the meanings in *The Handmaid's Tale*, Atwood pointed out that:

> Any power structure will co-opt the views of its opponents, to sugarcoat the pill. The regime gives women some of the things the women's movement says they want—control over birth, no pornography—but there is a price. . . . Anyone who wants power will try to manipulate you by appealing to your desires and fears, and sometimes your best instincts. Women have to be a little cautious about that kind of appeal to them. What are we being asked to give up?[14]

Presumably, nothing must be "given up" to get good day care legislation. If it is easier for women to work and to have children, women can work more comfortably, possibly at better jobs, and also have more children. Still, does it make a difference that at least some recent converts to day care advocacy may be less concerned with the welfare of working women than with the number of their progeny? Should a beneficial public policy be rejected simply because the motives of at least some of its advocates may be distasteful? Probably not—but certainly one should be aware of these purposes and be alert to attempts to advance them.

Especially after reading *The Handmaid's Tale*, reading Wattenberg can seem a bit like being parachuted behind enemy lines—an infuriating experience, but also highly instructive. Senator Orrin Hatch's proposed day care bill, much like Wattenberg's suggested scheme, has no income test and emphasizes the free enterprise and corporate sector. It does not authorize even greater federal funding for women who stay home and have three or four or more children as Wattenberg suggests would be even more expeditious (since even working women with day care will probably stop at one or two children). Others on the right, however, are beginning to suggest that this would be not only the most equitable but also the most progeny-producing policy.[15] How will feminists respond to those who say that *they* are pro-woman and only want to provide equal treatment for those who choose the "traditional" female functions? If feminists want greater economic opportunities for women, can economic opportunities be denied to those who want to be Wives, or even Handmaids?

The debate over surrogate motherhood has just begun, and has already sharply divided feminists.[16] At least some, however, would argue for the legality of an arrangement under which a woman who desperately wanted her husband's child could freely contract with a willing surrogate, who might find surrogacy much more pleasant and profitable than her other employment options. However, what if surrogacy, and in vitro fertilization, gained legal status primarily as part of a national pro-natal policy? If it is acceptable to countenance using a woman's womb to produce children for potential parents who want them, is it more or less acceptable to use modern technology to increase a nation's population count?

Wattenberg frets that fewer children will mean fewer housing starts, fewer consumers, fewer soldiers, and a weaker national defense: "At an estimated cost of approximately $300 billion, it [he is referring to the Strategic Defense Initiative] could be put together only by amortizing it over a large population."[17] Are housing starts and aircraft carriers less or more valid reasons for surrogate motherhood than personal satisfaction? And if women want their unique reproductive function recognized and subsidized by a grateful nation, does the public good have more or fewer claims on private reproductive choices? With the Wattenberg thesis fresh in mind, it is somewhat alarming to note economist Sylvia Hewlett approvingly quoting Charles de Gaulle to the effect that "having a child for a woman is a little like doing military service for a man. Both are essential for the welfare of the nation, and we should support both activities with public monies."[18]

This leads to a second important implication of these two works: The line between what is personal and what is political is a very fragile one, which must be constantly patrolled. With the contemporary Supreme Court edging ever closer to what had come to be considered clear constitutional zones of privacy, this is surely a timely reminder, and one that feminists in particular may wish to ponder.

One of the earliest and most formidable obstacles that contemporary feminism encountered was a definition of politics so narrow as to exclude many of the issues and concerns of most importance to many women. There was a political sphere, which involved such matters as the gross national product and international spheres of influence and partisan realignment, and there was a personal sphere, which included such items as childbirth and child care. Policymakers, the media, even political scientists, did not "do" the politics of the family, or of rape, or of pornography, or of reproduction. Feminists have worked hard, and successfully, to get certain subjects into the public domain. It is largely because of their efforts that presidential candidates must now seriously address a whole range of "family" issues, that members of the U.S. Congress now regularly debate everything from teenage pregnancy to premenstrual syndrome, and that political scientists now schedule panels and sections on gender politics. What these two books suggest, however, is that once "women's" issues are in the public domain, they can become fair game for those who are not sympathetic to feminist aspirations. Feminists may see as obvious the legitimacy of demands for state entry into family affairs to prohibit and punish spouse abuse versus the nonlegitimacy of state regulation of maternal treatment of the fetus. Nonfeminists, however, may not recognize such a distinction.

Finally, these two predictive works, while focusing on the future, strongly suggest the advisability of remembering the past. There is absolutely nothing new about the concept of pro-natalism. Most of the world's cultures are now, and have always been, pro-natalist, and this specifically includes the United States. As the epigrams at the outset were selected to suggest, American women have periodically attempted to reduce and limit the size of their families only to be rebuked for their shameful lack of maternal and patriotic sentiments. The shame-sayers in the past were also nativist, jingoist, and ethnocentric. And, as in the past, white middle-class women are the favored scapegoats.

In the late nineteenth and early twentieth centuries, the political establishment, which of course was white and male, alarmed over the large families of recent immigrants as compared to the smaller families of earlier settlers, warned of "race suicide." Socialists countercharged that the call for large families was merely cloaking the capitalists' desire to fill their factories and armies.[19] Charlotte Perkins Gilman stormed at male hypocrisy:

> All this for and against babies is by men. One would think the men bore the babies, nursed the babies, reared the babies. . . . The women bear and rear the children. The men kill them. Then they say: We are running short of children—make some more. . . .[20]

Despite these and other protests, however, proponents of large families succeeded, temporarily at least, in idealizing them—and they could succeed again. As often as women have watched the hard-earned gains of periodic feminism swept back in succeeding waves of familialism, it is still easy to become time-bound, easy to assume that the contemporary women's movement is some kind of irreversible culmination of long centuries of progress. But the pro-natalist observations of strategic demographers have become a regular feature of the influential *Atlantic Monthly*.[21] And there is no small irony in the fact that one of the last issues of *Ms.* Magazine styled itself a "Special Mother's Issue"; featured on the front a classic, cover-girl mother and serene child; and, in an article on "Careers and Kids," highlighted three-child Justice Sandra Day O'Connor and five-child Judge Patricia Wald, both of whom temporarily dropped out of the labor force when their children were small. The pro-natal message is everywhere.[22]

Wattenberg himself seems genuinely insistent that coercive solutions to the birth dearth are unacceptable. Never, however, does he explicitly acknowledge what he tacitly assumes: the coercive potential of public opinion. Nor, of course, can he guarantee that those whom he persuades of the birth dearth's dire nature will be as observant of privacy and choice as he would prefer them to be.

It is often assumed that the biggest barrier to smaller families in years past, and still around the world today, has been the lack of efficient contraceptive methods. In fact, however, "Birth control has always been primarily an issue of politics, not of technology."[23] As demographers have documented at length, contraceptive methods are, and always have been, less significant than attitudes in shaping women's reproductive choices.[24] It is these attitudes that Wattenberg very much hopes to change, and that Atwood warns may be very, very malleable.

NOTES

1. Theodore Roosevelt, quoted in Linda Gordon, *Women's Body, Women's Right* (New York: Grossman, 1976), p. 141. Sinclair Lewis quote from *It Can't Happen Here* (New American Library, 1970), p. 19. Phyllis Schlafly's remarks from address to the Arkansas Governor's School for the Gifted and Talented, quoted in *Arkansas Democrat*, June 24, 1987.

2. Margaret Atwood, *The Handmaid's Tale* (Bos-

ton: Houghton Mifflin, 1986); Ben J. Wattenberg, *The Birth Dearth*, (New York: Pharos Books, 1987).

3. Quoted in Caryn James, "The Lady Was Not for Hanging," *New York Times Book Review*, February 9, 1986, p. 35.

4. Cathy N. Davidson, "A Feminist 1984," *Ms.* (February 1986); pp. 24–26, esp. p. 26.

5. For an analysis of thirty reported abortion clinic bombings between May 1982 and January 1985, see David C. Nice, "Abortion Clinic Bombings as Political Violence," *American Journal of Political Science*, 32 (February 1988), pp. 178–195. Romanian pro-natal policies are described in Dirk J. van de Kaa, "Europe's Second Demographic Transition," *Population Bulletin*, 42 (1987), pp. 3–57, esp. p. 30.

6. See Janet Gallagher, "Fetal Personhood and Women's Policy," in Virginia Sapiro (Ed.), *Women, Biology and Public Policy*, (Beverly Hills, CA: Sage, 1985), pp. 91–116; Lisa M. Krieger, "Fetus Definitions Create Medical, Legal Inconsistencies," *Arkansas Democrat*, January 27, 1988, p. 7A; and Eve W. Paul, "Amicus Brief in Forced Caesarean Case," *Insider*, February 1988, p. 2.

7. On workplace restrictions, see Cynthia Ganney, "The Fine Line between Fetal Protection and Female Discrimination," *Washington Post National Weekly Edition*, August 24, 1987, p. 11. On toxic wastes, see "Toxic Shipments to Third World Likely to Increase," *Springdale (Arkansas) News*, April 26, 1987. On Minnesota act requiring burial of fetal remains, see "Judge Blocks Forced Fetal Burial," *Arkansas Democrat*, August 22, 1987.

8. Quoted in Davidson, "A Feminist 1984," p. 24.

9. Ben J. Wattenberg and Karl Zinsmeister, "The Birth Dearth: The Geopolitical Consequences," *Public Opinion*, 8 (December–January 1986), pp. 7–13, esp. p. 13.

10. Wattenberg, *The Birth Dearth*, p. 120.

11. Pat Robertson's formula is as follows: "By the year 2000 we will have aborted 40 million children in this country. Their work product by the year 2020 will amount to $1.4 trillion, the taxes from them would amount to $330 billion and they could ensure the fiscal stability of the Social Security System." Quoted and criticized by Charles Krauthammer, "Win, Place, Show Ridiculous in Politics," *Arkansas Democrat*, February 21, 1988. "The child-free families of today are the freeloaders on social security tomorrow," according to George Gilder, "Children and Politics," *Public Opinion*, 10 (March–April 1988), pp. 10–11,

esp. p. 11. Jack Kemp and Gary Bauer, quoted in Allan L. Otten, "Birth Dearth," *Wall Street Journal*, June 18, 1987. Allan Carlson's views in "High-Tech Societies Don't Have High Enough Birthrates," *Washington Post National Weekly Edition*, April 28, 1986, pp. 23–24, and "What to Do, Part I," *Public Opinion*, 10 (March–April 1988), pp. 4–6. On Schlafly, see n. 1.

12. On the recent popularity of day care, see Barbara Kantrowitz with Pat Wingert, "The Clamor to Save the Family," *Newsweek*, February 29, 1988, pp. 60–61; and Cindy Skrzycki and Frank Swoboda, "Congress Has Discovered a New Problem: Child Care," *Washington Post National Weekly Edition*, February 29–March 6, 1988, p. 33.

13. On President Nixon's veto and past conservative opposition to day care legislation, see Jill Norgren, "In Search of a National Child-Care Policy: Background and Prospects," in Ellen Boneparth (Ed.), *Women, Power and Policy* (Elmsford, NY: Pergamon Press, 1982), pp. 124–139. Senator Orrin Hatch statement made on "The McNeil-Lehrer News Hour," January 7, 1988.

14. Quoted in James, "The Lady Was Not for Hanging," p. 35.

15. Carlson, "What to Do, Part I," p. 5. Mrs. Pat Robertson quoted to this effect in *Arkansas Democrat*, March 2, 1988.

16. See Robyn Rowland, "Technology and Motherhood: Reproductive Choice Reconsidered," *Signs*, 12 (Spring 1987), pp. 512–528.

17. Wattenberg and Zinsmeister, "The Birth Dearth," pp. 9–10.

18. Sylvia Hewlett, "What to Do, Part II," *Public Opinion*, 10 (March–April 1988), p. 7.

19. Gordon, *Women's Body, Women's Right*, pp. 140–145.

20. Quoted in Gordon, *Women's Body, Women's Right*, p. 145.

21. See R. J. Hernstein, "IQ and Falling Birth Rates," *Atlantic Monthly* (May 1989), pp. 73–79, and Jonathan Rauch, "Kids as Capital," *Atlantic Monthly* (August 1989), pp. 56–61.

22. See Edith Fierst, "Careers and Kids," *Ms.*, 16 (May 1988), pp. 62–64.

23. Gordon, p. xii.

24. Richard L. Clinton, "Population, Politics and Political Science," in Richard L. Clinton (Ed.), *Population and Politics* (Lexington, MA: Lexington Books, 1973), pp. 51–71, esp. pp. 54–55.

The Family and Medical Leave Act: A Policy for Families

Joan Hulse Thompson

> My name is Liberia Johnson. In 1978, I was employed by a retail store in Charleston, South Carolina. . . . I became pregnant. . . . I tried to work because the income was so important to my family. My doctor told me that I was hypertensive and I had a thyroid problem. . . . If I did not stop working I would have a miscarriage. . . . The store manager . . . told me my job would be there after my baby was born. . . . I left at three months pregnant. I had a difficult pregnancy. I was in the hospital three times because I almost lost my baby. When I had my baby, I went and got my six weeks checkup and the same day I went back to the store and asked for my job. . . . There was a new manager and he told me "I don't have a job."[1]

On October 17, 1985, Ms. Johnson, married and the mother of five children, told her story to a joint oversight hearing on Disability and Parental Leave chaired by Congresswoman Patricia Schroeder (D-CO). Congresswoman Mary Rose Oakar (D-OH) and nine congressmen, six Democrats and three Republicans, attended part of the three-hour hearing, which featured medical and academic experts, corporate and union representatives, and a local government official as well as another public witness, a single mother with an adopted daughter.

An oversight hearing is designed to attract attention from members of Congress, the press, and the public to an issue in hopes of gathering support for government action. Public witnesses like Liberia Johnson can play a brief but significant role. According to a veteran committee staff member, anecdotes are "the only thing that move people. A good public witness draws the rapt attention of the members."[2] They convince members of Congress in a very personal way

Joan Hulse Thompson is an assistant professor of political science at Beaver College in Glenside, Pennsylvania.

212

that legislation is needed to remedy an injustice. The more heart-wrenching their stories, the better.

How did a black woman, who formerly worked a cash register and became a baker at a small hospital, get to tell her story to Congress? Public witnesses are usually found by interest groups or by subcommittee staff, but in this case the Congressional Caucus for Women's Issues was responsible. Several caucus members, the caucus staff, and a few interested attorneys had been working on parental leave since early 1984. This issue illustrates the role of congresswomen and their caucus in developing and promoting a policy proposal to respond to the economic needs of women.

In 1989, House and Senate committees approved similar versions of the Family and Medical Leave Act (FMLA) (H.R. 770/S. 345) and in May 1990 the House approved an amended H.R. 770. In mid-June the Senate approved the House version of the FMLA by voice vote, but President Bush vetoed the legislation on June 29. On July 25, the override vote in the House fell short of the necessary two-thirds, and the president's veto was sustained (Table 1).

WOMEN IN CONGRESS AND THEIR CAUCUS

Since the first woman entered the House of Representatives in 1917, congresswomen have been outsiders. None ever belonged to either party's powerful yet informal social and political groups, such as Speaker Rayburn's Board of

---

Table 1 Provisions of the Family and Medical Leave Act (H.R. 770), Passed by the House May 1990 and by the Senate June 1990, Vetoed by President Bush

---

1. *Family Leave:* Employees may take up to 12 weeks of unpaid leave per year for the care of a newborn or newly adopted child, or for the care of a seriously ill child, parent, or spouse.

2. *Medical Leave:* Employees may take up to 12 weeks of unpaid leave per year for their own recovery from a serious medical condition.

3. *Conditions:* Health insurance, if it is provided by the employer, must be continued during the period of the leave. Employees are not entitled to more than 12 weeks leave in one year even if they have more than one of the reasons above. For a new child, only one parent may take leave at a time. Employers may require that a doctor certify a serious health condition in order to qualify for leave.

4. *Coverage:* Some part-time workers are covered. Employees must have worked at least 1,000 hours for one year to be eligible for leave. Highly paid workers in a firm may be denied reinstatement, under certain conditions. Other workers are entitled to the same or equivalent positions upon their return.

5. *Exemption:* Employers with fewer than 50 employees are exempt. Approximately 90 percent of all employers would be exempt and fewer than half of all employees would be covered.

6. *Enforcement:* Administrative and civil procedures will be available for enforcement. Violators will be liable for lost wages, benefits, and other compensation and up to three times that amount in damages.

7. *Federal Employees:* Federal government workers will be entitled to 18 weeks of family leave every two years and 26 weeks of medical leave per year.

8. *Congressional Employees:* Employees of the House of Representatives will have 12 weeks of leave, the same as private employees. Previous employee rights bills have usually exempted congressional employees.

Education or the Republican Chowder and Marching Society founded by Richard Nixon and Gerald Ford, among others.[3] As female politicians, they were isolated from the social network of male politicians and also from that of more traditional women outside of politics.

The congresswomen needed a support group. Congressmen have them, usually centered on the gymnasium or the golf course. One congresswoman explained the significance of such social groups as follows:

> Members who don't or can't participate in them are like the kid in college who has no one to study with; no one to exchange ideas with to get a broader idea of what's going on in the class; no one to work with to get the right kind of "vibes" about the course and the teacher. It takes longer for that kid to understand what is going on and often that student is never as good as he or she could be.[4]

The Congresswomen's Caucus, founded in 1977 by Elizabeth Holtzman (D-NY), Margaret Heckler (R-MA), and Shirley Chisholm (D-NY), had both social and policy goals. All the members were committed to the Equal Rights Amendment (ERA) and to increasing the number of women in public office. Frequent meetings provided an opportunity for "conviviality, affection, and good feelings."[5] Bipartisanship strengthened the organization's claim to speak for women nationally.

The Congresswomen's Caucus was not the first such organization, although its focus on member, rather than constituency, characteristics was unusual. Responding to the narrow circles of power in the prereform Congress and paralleling the growth of special-interest groups in the larger society, caucuses have flourished in the House. The Democratic Study Group was first in 1959. There were ten caucuses in 1974 and ninety by 1987.[6] Officially known as legislative service organizations, caucuses are voluntary associations of House members formed to help fulfill goals of representation, personal power, policy promotion, and reelection. Members from constituencies dependent upon the maritime industry have formed the Port Caucus, those with steel mills have joined the Steel Caucus, and so forth. Caucuses gather and distribute information, seek to influence congressional agendas, and attempt to build policy coalitions.

Whether or not congresswomen initially felt that they should represent women nationally, most soon realized that if they did not speak for women, no one else would.[7] However, not all congresswomen believed that the problems of women could best be addressed at the national level. Because they favored state, local, or private initiatives, most Republican congresswomen and some Democrats were out of step with the underlying liberal perspective of the Congresswomen's Caucus. Steps taken to convince all the women to join inhibited the caucus from taking positions on issues important to its most active members. But requiring greater policy agreement threatened to make the caucus a tiny, exclusively Democratic group with little hope of fulfilling its policy goals, especially in the conservative atmosphere of the early 1980s.

A NEW NAME FOR A COED CAUCUS

Recurrent financial problems, a House rules change, the conservative national tide, and a desire to be more effective on women's issues combined to lead the members of the Congresswomen's Caucus to invite congressmen to join their organization late in 1981. The following year the organization took on a new name, the Congressional Caucus for Women's Issues, and established an executive committee of congresswomen to set policy. The group has grown from a membership of 10 to well over 100, mostly men. Although some congresswomen do not belong,[8] co-chairs Pat Schroeder and Olympia Snowe (R-ME) are in a far better position now to pursue policy change in an institution where men hold the power positions, and to command the attention of the media and the public.

Another group that focuses on member characteristics and seeks to represent a national constituency is the Congressional Black Caucus. At its founding in 1969 it had nine members, three of them freshmen, and no blacks had ever served on the three most powerful House committees. By the mid-1980s, the Black Caucus had twenty members who among them chaired five standing committees, including Budget, two select committees, and 16 subcommittees including two on Ways and Means. By the end of the decade, Representative Bill Gray (D-PA) had advanced from chairman of the Budget Committee to Democratic Whip, the third highest position in the majority party leadership.

The congresswomen's group took longer to get organized, has never achieved equivalent unity and commitment, and was not making significant gains in power until it expanded to include sympathetic men. Although women do sit on the most powerful committees, no woman chairs a committee and those subcommittees they do chair are not among the most powerful. Women have been part of the leadership structure in both parties, but not yet as high as the party whip. The concerns of other caucuses have won greater recognition as caucus members gained positions within the formal power structure. But as a consequence of electoral defeat, retirements, ill health, and attempts for higher office, that path has not worked very well for women.

Expanding the women's caucus to include supportive congressmen proved to be a shortcut. By 1985 the male members of the caucus included the Speaker, the Majority Whip, nine committee chairs including Rules and three select committee chairmen. Although only about a dozen Republicans belonged to the caucus, they included ranking members of four committees. In 1990, having men in the caucus had the effect of multiplying fivefold its representation on the five committees that form an oligarchy of power in Congress.[9] When Family and Medical Leave passed the House, the caucus membership included the Speaker, the Majority Leader, the Majority Whip, and the chairman of the Rules Committee. Although neither party leaders nor committee chairs can assure congressional passage, it does help that women's issues now have publicly committed supporters in high places.

POLICY DEVELOPMENT BY THE CAUCUS

Attempts by the Congresswomen's Caucus to build coalitions or "to fashion and implement legislative strategies were . . . infrequent and superficial."[10] The expanded caucus could do more. The same year the caucus invited men to join, it also became the House coordinator for the Economic Equity Act, a package of bills initiated by Senator David Durenberger (R-MN) in response to the fate of the Equal Rights Amendment. The 98th Congress (1983–1984) was a very productive one for the caucus, largely because of the much publicized gender gap. Public opinion polls showed President Reagan to be much less popular with women than with men. Republican congressmen feared the women's vote, and Democrats in Congress were anxious to exploit their potential advantage. Child support enforcement and pension reform legislation, both included in the Economic Equity Act, were enacted before the 1984 election.[11]

After President Reagan's landslide victory over Walter Mondale and caucus leader Geraldine Ferrraro (D-NY), a caucus staff member reflected that "feminists are just poison"[12] now on the Hill. In a caucus-sponsored report, then–Caucus Director Anne Radigan explained:

> On Capitol Hill, legislators reacted negatively to the failure of the Democratic presidential ticket and its feminist adherents. Where only a few weeks earlier politicians had beaten a path to their doors, now feminist women's groups found themselves and their agenda held at a cool and measured distance.[13]

If women's economic issues were to make any progress in the 99th Congress, a new strategy would have to be found to replace the gender gap approach. For example, instead of describing legislation as for women, liberals could describe it as "pro-family," seizing that politically popular label from conservatives and the religious right. Perhaps the politically divisive abortion issue could even be bridged with legislation that would make it more economically feasible for women to choose to have children. Parental leave was the first initiative put forth under this new strategy, and the initial hearing described at the beginning of this article was crucial as the first test of this new appeal. Child care legislation would follow.

By the 1988 presidential election, both parties were talking about family policy proposals, including both parental leave and child care. In July 1989, Caucus Director Lesley Primmer explained that the recent Supreme Court decision on abortion had put that issue at the front of the congressional agenda. However, she added, "child care has been on the front burner this entire session and family and medical leave has a prominent place just short of child care" on Capitol Hill.[14]

PROS AND CONS OF GENDER NEUTRALITY

According to Anne Radigan, the caucus has long been committed to supporting gender-neutral legislation. Therefore, a bill for parental, not maternity, leave was introduced. Protective laws, such as weight-lifting restrictions, have been used to keep women out of higher paying, nontraditional jobs. Mandatory maternity leave, by treating pregnancy as a special condition, could well lead to further workplace discrimination against women, such as a reluctance to hire or promote a woman who might become pregnant.

The Pregnancy Discrimination Act (PDA), an amendment to Title VII of the Civil Rights Act of 1964, was enacted in 1978 in response to a U.S. Supreme Court decision, *Gilbert v. General Electric*, permitting employers to treat pregnancy differently from other medical conditions with respect to health insurance and leave policies. Under the PDA, women unable to work because of pregnancy or childbirth would have to be treated the same as other employees unable to work for other medical reasons. The law was gender-neutral, but it left millions of women unprotected because their employers provided no health insurance or disability benefits.

Also in 1978, the California legislature enacted a mandatory maternity leave program covering all employers in the state. In 1983, however, the law was challenged by a private employer who claimed that the state law constituted reverse discrimination against males and violated the federal mandate for gender neutrality. In 1984 this argument was successful in the federal trial court, although an appellate court later reversed the decision.

Representative Howard Berman (D-CA), who had sponsored the state law while in the legislature, and other California representatives decided to sponsor a bill at the national level that would mandate maternity and some paternity leave. They had the support of many California feminists who believed that "since women alone bear children they are at an indisputable disadvantage compared to working men and require an edge to help them remain competitive in the workplace."[15]

Also in 1984, a small drafting group of lawyers who had fought for the PDA and a caucus staff attorney began to look for a way to respond to the court decision: a manner in which to fill the coverage gap without abandoning the principle of gender neutrality. Their solution was to frame a broad policy mandating parental leave for both parents and medical disability leave for all workers.

A more narrowly drawn bill for pregnant women with a small paternity leave, to encourage a greater role for fathers in the care of newborns, would have had an easier time gaining support. Making parental leave optional for either parent enabled opponents to score points with such remarks as, "This is ludicrous in the extreme. I don't need eighteen weeks off if my wife has a baby."[16] Including all those temporarily medically disabled also greatly increased the cost of the bill to employers and, therefore, their resolve to oppose it.

CHARGES OF ELITISM AND DAMAGING REGULATION

Choosing to make the mandated leave unpaid kept the cost down and made the policy self-policing to some extent, but at the price of raising difficult issues of social class. Women's groups, like most interest groups, are composed primarily of women from the middle class and above. They are potentially vulnerable to charges of insensitivity to the real problems of working-class women in battles by their organizations for abstract principles of equality. That was why both the public witnesses at the October 1985 oversight hearing were black. One of Pat Schroeder's concluding remarks expressed her pleasure that, while "The bill looks like it is for 'Yuppies,' " the hearing had demonstrated that "It's for everyone." Demonstrating universality was clearly one of the goals of the congresswomen, the caucus staff, and the women's groups when they planned the initial hearing.

Nevertheless, opponents described the women's groups as "powerful special-interest groups" seeking to dictate policy against the best interests of both employers and the very employees whose interests they claim to represent. Testimony from the U.S. Chamber of Commerce at subsequent legislative hearings included references to the fact that, "All employees . . . will be subject to a uniform parental leave law, . . . whether they can afford to take advantage of it or not."[17] Furthermore, the business community argues that "any mandated benefit is likely to replace other, sometimes more preferable, employee benefits . . . [such as] flextime, child-care, dental or liberalized leave benefits."[18] In 1989 a Texas Republican expressed the view that only the upper classes would be able to take the leaves, while all workers would share the costs. He described the bill as " 'Yuppie' welfare—a perverse redistribution of income."[19]

The mandatory nature of the legislation is critical for both sides and cannot be compromised. Supporters proclaim that the proposal "breaks new ground in labor law,"[20] and, of course, business groups oppose it for exactly that reason. Proponents could and did compromise on the number of weeks of leave and the number of employees a company must have to be covered, but eliminating the mandatory nature of the regulation would leave nothing of substance. For business interests and their supporters in Congress, "Such legislation results in a loss of freedom of choice—the hallmark of our economic system."[21]

Government already regulates wages and working conditions. Further intrusions must be fought, according to the U.S. Chamber of Commerce, for the sake of maintaining the nation's international competitiveness and high rate of economic growth. Figures for employee benefit costs as a percentage of the payroll for Korea, Japan, and Taiwan are cited and shown to put U.S. industry at a disadvantage. European nations that grant paid family leaves are praised by supporters but criticized by the Chamber of Commerce for rates of job creation below that of the United States. The Chamber argued that the costs of mandated family leave would devastate small businesses. The law might even lead to discrimination in hiring, making it difficult for women of childbearing age to find employment.

To opponents, family leave is another well-intentioned but misguided intervention in the employer–employee relationship. They argue that it will not serve the interests of the nation or even those of working women. To proponents, family leave is the next step toward a more humane society, just as child labor and minimum-wage laws were fifty years ago. In response to complaints about cost, prime sponsor Senator Christopher Dodd (D-CT), declared, "It's mortifying that we can't offer a benefit like this that is a minimum standard of human decency."[22]

BUILDING SUPPORT FOR THE FMLA

According to then–Caucus Director Anne Radigan, the legislative strategy on the Family and Medical Leave Act (FMLA) assumed compromise would be necessary for success. She described the plan in 1985 as follows: "At first, try to be as all encompassing as possible, then go for as much as you can [realistically hope for], and finally get what you can."[23] Members of Congress tend to be pragmatic because they want tangible accomplishments to claim credit for back home.

Because public support is needed to win congressional support, the initial hearing and every subsequent hearing were planned with the media in mind. The first hearing had a star witness, Dr. T. Berry Brazelton, who has the charisma of a cable television star and the authority of a noted pediatrician and author. His testimony gave the bill the advantage of backing in the medical community. As hoped, he drew a feature story in the *Washington Post*. Subsequent hearings heard from a retail manager who recovered from cancer but was unemployed for two years, and a daughter who lost her job when she was absent caring for her father during the last weeks of his life.

After the first hearing the caucus staff monitored the media coverage and was both encouraged and discouraged. Both the AP and UPI wire services carried the story, but both talked about maternity leave. "What did we do wrong?" lamented Anne Radigan. "How was that connection, the language . . . misunderstood? We are talking so very clearly about parents, mothers *and fathers*." On the other hand, there was good coverage and an opportunity to build support before the opposition surfaced. Reflecting on media strategy three years later, Anne Radigan recalled that "most reporters covering the issue gave the bill a favorable spin."[24]

By 1989, *Congressional Quarterly* was referring to the FMLA as "a key item on the agenda . . . of organized labor."[25] At the first hearing in 1985, this point was made by a coal miner who prefaced his remarks with the question, "What's an official of a macho male coal miners union doing in a place like this?" He then described the parental leave proposal that the coal companies refused to accept in national contract talks in 1984, the growing number of women in coal mining, the changing family patterns in mining communities, and the special hardships facing rural families when their children are seriously ill. Medical treatment for cancer, for instance, is only available in major cities, requiring time off from work for travel to hospitals as far as two hundred miles away.

Although his stories were emotionally compelling, the United Mine Workers spokesman made it clear that he was coming to Congress because the union had been unable to get parental leave through in contract negotiations. In a sense, he was asking Congress to circumvent the collective bargaining process.

Unions want mandatory benefits so that their bargaining can focus on other demands.

Representative William Clay (D-MO), a black congressman and union ally, has called the FMLA "preventive medicine, [because it] . . . goes to the heart of what is causing families to struggle."[26] As a co-sponsor, Clay, the chairman of the Labor Management Subcommittee of the House Education and Labor Committee, proved valuable. However, his advocacy may also have strengthened the resolve of the business community. Clay is known for angry rhetoric, but not for legislative effectiveness.

Furthermore, Education and Labor is perceived as a partisan, ideological committee where liberals can win bills that will not pass in the more moderate House chamber or in the Senate. Opponents are more interested in compromise when they fear that without it they may suffer total defeat than they are when they can realistically anticipate eventual victory. Union support, though necessary for committee approval, was less important for enactment than the media coverage that would build support within the general public and therefore in the full chamber.

HOPES AND FEARS OF MANDATORY BENEFITS

While the caucus saw the FMLA as a first step in a new and desirable direction, opposition groups recognized that further encroachment was likely if this bill succeeded in any form. Academic specialists, comparing the United States with other Western democracies in Europe and with Canada, point out that in those countries payments are available to compensate for lost wages after childbirth. In the realization that such a proposal could not pass at this time, successive versions of the FMLA have provided for a study commission. This group would recommend means to provide salary replacement for employees taking parental and medical leaves. Those who wanted paid leaves were thus satisfied. A study commission would improve prospects for a future program of leaves paid for by employers, Social Security, or some other means.

Even more ominous from the perspective of the business community is the prospect that once one benefit is made mandatory, others will follow. Employers could be required to offer not only paid parental and medical leaves, but also health insurance to all employees and their families. Early in 1990 a congressional commission recommended such a mandatory benefits program for employers of over 100 persons, covering hospital and surgical services, prenatal care, and also mental health care.[27] In an era of tight federal budgets, the tendency is to shift social welfare costs, borne by the national government in many countries, to private business in order to avoid calling for higher tax revenues.

The implications of enacting Family and Medical Leave, then, go beyond the narrow domain of women's issues. Opting for a gender-neutral policy meant that passage, if accomplished, would be a major precedent for both governmental regulation of business and passing costs of social welfare programs on to private enterprise. Although this made passage more difficult, it also helped supporters attract a broader coalition than would have been likely for a narrowly drawn maternity leave bill.

EXPANDING THE FMLA COALITION

Back in 1985, Schroeder's original bill provided for disability leaves, defining *disability* as "a total inability to perform a job, a notion of disability that the disabled rights advocates had been struggling for years to overcome."[28] Substituting "medical leave" resolved the objections of the disabled and gained the support of five organizations, including the Disability Rights Education and Defense Fund.

At the suggestion of Congresswoman Roukema (R-NJ), ranking minority member of Clay's subcommittee, the proposal was expanded in 1986 from parental to family leave by including leave to care for seriously ill, elderly parents. This inclusion brought the politically powerful American Association of Retired Persons and another group into the coalition.

Public testimony made it clear that women with difficult pregnancies and those who could not afford to risk losing their jobs might choose to have an abortion for financial reasons. Mary Rose Oakar, a Roman Catholic and pro-life member, said at the initial hearing that "nothing is more sacred than children in their formative weeks," making parental leave "a real, positive, minimum response." She also pledged, in her role as chair of the subcommittee responsible for federal employee benefits, that the federal government would be a model employer. Dale Kildee (D-MI), also a devout Roman Catholic, added that the bill promised to be "a real vehicle for making this government pro-family." Other pro-life members and the U.S. Catholic Conference have supported the bill. However, antiabortion forces are not going to make a maximum effort for anything less than a prohibition of abortion.

Despite this diverse coalition of proponents, gaining congressional passage would require some business support. After questioning ten major companies about their leave provisions, a caucus staff member invited General Foods Corporation to testify at the first hearing in 1985. The company has a policy of *paid* disability and child care leaves as part of its plan to "meet contemporary and future needs of employees," explained its representative. Male employees had been reluctant to ask for leave, she continued, but recently a "very highly placed executive" had taken parental leave to be with his new baby and "he's being looked at as the domino." Such a company had an incentive to support the FMLA. The governmental mandate would require its competitors to pay the cost of a minimal benefit, while its benefit package would remain attractive to prospective employees. At a subsequent hearing, Southern New England Telephone testified that parental leave enabled them to retain trained employees.

While the U.S. Chamber of Commerce, the National Federation of Independent Business, and the American Society for Personnel Administration testified against the bill, congressional staff found other small business representatives to argue for the bill. These included the National Federation of Business and Professional Women's Clubs and the National Association of Women Business Owners. Pat Schroeder said that from small-business owners in her district she heard that "parental leave policies save employers the cost of hiring and training new employees. Most of all these policies help attract the best and the brightest, and retain a valued and trusted work force."[29]

With the cosponsorship of the four subcommittee chairs with jurisdiction, that stage in the legislative process caused no problems. The bill passed the full Post Office and Civil Service Committee without dissent, but it emerged from the Education and Labor Committee only after revisions to accommodate opposition concerns and garner Republican support. The primary focus was the cost for business, especially small business, to continue health insurance coverage of workers on leave and to hire replacements.

Actually, the first compromise made in 1986 was insufficient. A second, in 1987, increased the number of employees a company must have to be covered under the bill, exempted a few highly paid employees, shortened the number of weeks of leave, and raised the number of weeks worked to be eligible. The bill still covered part-time as well as full-time workers and mandated continued health benefits and job guarantees for family and medical leaves—but it would cover only 43 percent of employees and 10 percent of all employers.

Released in early 1987, the original cost estimate from the Chamber of Commerce for family leave alone was $16 billion; but this figure was based on the faulty assumptions that all workers would be replaced and that replacements would be paid more than regular workers. Under pressure, the Chamber reduced the estimated cost to $2.6 billion. After the compromises, the nonpartisan Government Accounting Office (GAO) estimated that the bill would cost $188 million annually.[30] On the basis of these figures, supporters estimated that the FMLA would cost employers only $6.50 per year per eligible worker. A report produced by the caucus research arm and the Women's Legal Defense Fund found that unemployment resulting from the absence of parental leave costs U.S. families at least $607 million a year—and costs taxpayers about $108 million a year for government assistance programs.[31]

CONGRESSIONAL PASSAGE AND PRESIDENTIAL VETO

With its strong public appeal, Family and Medical Leave has been viewed as a potentially powerful political issue throughout its consideration. In 1988 Democratic senators brought minimum wage increases, parental leave, and child care to the floor "in an openly partisan fashion," according to *Congressional Quarterly Almanac*. "While the Senate waited for conference reports on fiscal 1989 appropriations bills, Democrats used their power as the majority party to put on the floor all the labor and social legislation they wanted to highlight in the closing weeks before the November 8 elections."[32] A minimum-wage increase, a bill that was a higher priority than FMLA in the Education and Labor Committee and for the Democratic leadership, was enacted late in 1989. Since two-thirds of minimum-wage workers are women, it was also an important issue for the caucus.

Child care legislation, another major initiative of the caucus, passed the Senate in June 1989 and the House in March 1990. It is more expensive than the FMLA, but it helps more families and the money comes from the government—not private business. The debate on child care was more about how the government should structure its program than whether it should get involved. In the final hours of the session, with only a week left before the 1990 election, the Congress passed a compromise version acceptable to the president.

In May 1990, as the supporters of the FMLA celebrated its passage in the House, opponents declared it dead. A lobbyist for the National Association of Wholesaler-Distributors, Mary Tavenner, reported that, "I had John Sununu [White House Chief of Staff] look me straight in the eye and say that the president would veto it."[33] Opponents, who will not accept any form of mandatory leave provisions, won the battle with the backing of the president.

The substitute, negotiated just prior to House floor consideration, eliminated the possibility that the same worker would be eligible for both family and medical leave, totaling twenty-five weeks, in one year. The cap would be twelve weeks for either or both. Such changes made the law less burdensome and therefore this version picked up support. This revised version, which for the first time included care of a seriously ill spouse, was supported by 198 Democrats and 39 Republicans, while 54 Democrats and 133 Republicans opposed it. Three planned amendments were actually withdrawn by Republicans at the request of the White House, because their passage might have made the bill more attractive and made a veto more difficult to sustain.

Opponents had threatened a filibuster in the Senate, which would have required support from sixty senators to end debate and force a vote. Senator Dodd, the prime Senate sponsor, admitted that, "The Senate is a little more skittish about these family issues than the House is."[34] Republican Senator Durenberger, usually a dependable ally on women's issues, saw the costs of FMLA as unpredictable because temporary medical leaves and leaves for the care of sick family members are "virtually untested in the private sector."[35]

One-third of the Senators faced reelection in 1990, and those who opposed the FMLA were not anxious to participate in a filibuster or even have a recorded vote. Senate Majority Leader George Mitchell, a Democrat, worked out a deal with Senator Robert Dole, the Republican leader, to permit the FMLA to pass on a voice vote on the condition that Mitchell would schedule a vote on a constitutional amendment to make flag desecration a crime. Thus, each party was able to advance an issue it hoped would work to its advantage in the coming election.

There is no question that party politics and media strategies were decisive on the FMLA. In 1989 Schroeder said, "the worst rumor we hear up here is that the administration will ask us to schedule the bill [for floor action] around Mother's Day and then take men out of the bill."[36] Instead, the Speaker arranged for the FMLA to pass the House, with its gender neutrality and governmental mandate intact, just in time for Mother's Day 1990. After refusing to meet with Republican supporters of the bill, President Bush vetoed it on the Friday afternoon shortly before the July 4 holiday.

Although the veto killed the bill for the session, the issue remained for the fall campaign, the next Congress, and the 1992 election. In a national public opinion survey taken in June 1990, 74 percent favored a law guaranteeing up to twelve weeks of unpaid parental leave.[37] One columnist has predicted that the veto of FMLA, veto number 13 for Bush, will turn out to be unlucky for the President.[38]

CONCLUSION

Despite the failure of the veto override, the concept has entered the agenda of the national and state governments. Eighteen states, Puerto Rico, and the District of Columbia have some form of job protection for workers who need family leave, and many more states are considering such legislation. A few of these measures are more generous than the vetoed national version; the others are the same or less comprehensive. Laws in ten states provide only maternity leave, but newer statutes tend to be gender-neutral.[39] Experience with family and medical leave laws at the state level is beginning to provide information on actual costs and benefits that can used to argue for the national approach. As more states enact laws, corporations with work sites in more than one state will have a greater incentive to seek a federal standard and avoid conflicting state laws.

Early in 1991, the FMLA was reintroduced in Congress and, by November, both chambers had again approved similar versions. President Bush remains opposed and only in the Senate does a veto override seem possible. Whatever the fate of the FMLA, it has illustrated the role of the Caucus for Women's Issues in developing legislation, building a coalition across committee jurisdictions and coordinating the efforts of outside advocacy groups. Committee and personal staffs gradually took over staff responsibilities once the bill was launched. The caucus presence was continued through its information services and represented by its members, especially the congresswomen and their legislative assistants for women's issues. The current director, Lesley Primmer, once a legislative assistant to Olympia Snowe, observes that "moving legislation is done by personal and committee staff primarily, with the Caucus serving in an intermediate role."[40]

The caucus symbolizes what has been called the "second stage" of the women's movement because it is a partnership of congresswomen and congress-men.[41] Anne Radigan once explained their goal as follows:

> To get across to the public at large, that women's issues are everybody's issues. Women don't live in a vacuum, they don't exist alone, and they certainly don't exist in a "we against them" adversary relationship. Women are wives who are dependent, women are wives who are working, women are daughters who are going to school, women are elderly parents who are vulnerable. . . . This is a family sort of prerogative. . . . Women's issues affect everyone.[42]

NOTES

1. Liberia Johnson, Joint Hearing on Disability and Parental Leave, 2261 Rayburn House Office Building, October 17, 1985, tape-recorded by the author. Subsequent quotations from testimony at the same hearing will not be footnoted.

2. Anonymous staff interview with the author for a case study of pension reform legislation, Washington, D.C., July 19, 1984.

3. Irwin N. Gertzog, *Congressional Women: Their Recruitment, Treatment, and Behavior* (New York: Praeger, 1984), pp. 80–87.

4. Ibid., p. 89.

5. Ibid., p. 197.

6. Susan Webb Hammond, "Congressional Caucuses in the Policy Process," in Lawrence C. Dodd and Bruce I. Oppenheimer (Eds.), *Congress Reconsidered*, 4th ed. (Washington, DC: Congressional Quarterly Press, 1989), p. 355.

7. Joan Hulse Thompson, "Role Perceptions of Women in the Ninety-fourth Congress," *Political Science Quarterly*, 95 (Spring 1980), p. 73.

8. Marge Roukema (R-NJ), a supporter of the FMLA since 1987, does not belong to the caucus. There were 30 women in the 101st Congress, 28 in the House and 2 in the Senate. Of these, both senators belonged to the caucus, along with 19 House members. Of the 21 members of the caucus Executive Committee, 14 were Democrats and 7 were Republicans.

9. Lawrence C. Dodd and Bruce I. Oppenheimer, "Consolidating Power in the House: The Rise of a New Oligarchy," in *Congress Reconsidered*, pp. 48–50.

10. Gertzog, *Congressional Women*, p. 202.

11. Joan Hulse Thompson, "The Women's Rights Lobby in the Gender Gap Congress, 1983–84," *Commonwealth*, 2 (1988), pp. 19–35.

12. Anonymous staff interview with the author, October 1985.

13. Anne L. Radigan, *Concept and Compromise: The Evolution of Family Leave Legislation in the U.S. Congress* (Washingtion, DC: Women's Research and Education Institute, 1988), p. 12.

14. Lesley Primmer, executive director, Congressional Caucus for Women's Issues, personal interview with the author, Washington, D.C., July 28, 1989.

15. Radigan, *Concept and Compromise*, p. 8.

16. Macon Morehouse, "Parental, Medical Leave Bill Gets Markup in Senate," *Congressional Quarterly Weekly Report*, 47 (April 22, 1989), p. 892.

17. Christine A. Russell, director of the Small Business Center, U.S. Chamber of Commerce, "America's Small Businesses Cannot Afford Mandated Leave," public information release, no date, pp. 1–2 (obtained from its author, January 1990).

18. Ibid.

19. Brian Nutting, "Parental-Leave Bill Passed by Panel," *Congressional Quarterly*, 47 (March 11, 1989), p. 519.

20. Radigan, *Concept and Compromise*, p. 2.

21. Russell, "America's Small Businesses," p. 2. One precedent does exist. The Veterans' Reemployment Rights Act (1940) mandates up to four years of leave with job security for workers called to active military duty.

22. Morehouse, "Markup in Senate," p. 892.

23. Anne Radigan, executive director, Congressional Caucus for Women's Issues, personal interview with the author, Washington, D.C., October 18, 1985.

24. Radigan, *Concept and Compromise*, p. 15. Indeed, Ms. Radigan notes that some of the reporters had a special interest in the story because they were dissatisfied with the parental leave policies of their own employers.

25. Nutting, "Passed by Panel," p. 519.

26. "Family and Medical Leave Act of 1987 Introduced," *Update*, February 27, 1987, p. 13.

27. *Philadelphia Inquirer*, March 3, 1990, sec. A, p. 5.

28. Radigan, *Concept and Compromise*, p. 16.

29. "Family and Medical Leave Hearings in D.C. and on West Coast," *Update*, August 7, 1987, n.p.

30. "Capitol Boxscore," *Congressional Quarterly*, 47 (February 4, 1989), p. 243.

31. Roberta Spalter, Heidi Hartmann, and Sheila Gibbs, *Unnecessary Losses: Costs to Workers in the States of the Lack of Family and Medical Leave* (Washington, DC: Institute for Women's Policy Research, 1989), p. 3.

32. "Democrats Stymied on Parental-Leave Bill," *Congressional Quarterly Almanac* (1988), p. 263.

33. Alyson Pytte, "House Passes Parental Leave; White House Promises Veto," *Congressional Quarterly*, 48 (May 12, 1990), p. 1471.

34. *New York Times*, May 11, 1990, sec. B, p. 6.

35. Morehouse, "Mark-up in Senate," p. 892.

36. "Parental-Leave Bill Moves Forward," *Congressional Quarterly*, 47 (April 15, 1989), p. 815.

37. A Louis Harris Associates poll of 1,254 persons with a margin of error of plus or minus 3 percent. The other results were: opposed to such a law, 24 percent, and unsure, 2 percent. Cited in *New York Times*, July 26, 1990.

38. Ellen Goodman, "Ambushing Bush On Family Leave," *Philadelphia Inquirer*, August 1, 1990, sec. A, p. 9.

39. Donna Lenhoff and Sharon Stoneback, "Review of State Legislation Guaranteeing Jobs for Family or Medical Leaves," Women's Legal Defense Fund, August 1989, pp. 5–6; *New York Times*, July 27, 1990,

sec. A, p. 8; and "Family and Medical Leave Legislation in the States," Women's Legal Defense Fund, June 1991.

40. Primmer interview, July 28, 1989.

41. Betty Friedan, *The Second Stage* (New York: Summit, 1981), pp. 250–255.

42. Radigan interview, October 18, 1985.

Sex at Risk in Insurance Classifications? The Supreme Court as Shaper of Public Policy

Ruth Bamberger

Since the onset of the women's movement in the late 1960s, the private insurance industry has been confronted by civil rights groups, particularly feminist organizations, and government agencies over the treatment of insurance consumers whose risk potential is determined in part by gender classification. Numerous studies by congressional committees, state insurance commissions, and feminist ad hoc groups revealed practices whereby women in the same occupation, age, and health categories as men, were subjected to demeaning underwriting criteria, denied equal access to coverage and benefits, particularly in health and disability insurance, and charged higher premium rates. Men, too, were found to be victimized by gender classification, especially in auto insurance, where companies charge young males up to 50 percent more than women of the same age.

As a result of pressures on the insurance industry, almost half of the fifty states have adopted insurance regulations prohibiting differential treatment in coverage and benefits of males and females.[1] But gender is still widely used as a classification in setting premium rates for individual health, life, disability, auto, and retirement insurance. Only one state, Montana, prohibits by law the use of the gender classification for any purpose, including rate setting.[2] Two other states, Massachusetts and Pennsylvania, have banned differential rates through issuance of insurance department regulations, although the insurance industry has challenged this procedure.[3]

The insurance industry is the last holdout in the movement to eliminate sex discrimination from society. The industry's reluctance to change is a direct consequence of the nature of the product it markets. Its modus operandi is discriminatory; people who buy insurance are classified according to a number

Ruth Bamberger is a professor of political science at Drury College.

of factors supposedly related to their risk potential. Because gender is a cost-efficient classification (it is easily identifiable), and the industry has demonstrated through actuarial data that women and men have different morbidity and mortality experiences, insurers are most averse to giving up a classification system that to them is empirically sound. This means that women will continue to pay higher rates than men for health and disability insurance, while men will pay higher rates for life insurance, and young men higher rates for auto insurance.

THE INSURANCE INDUSTRY AND GENDER CLASSIFICATION

Criticisms of the insurance industry's use of the gender classification are numerous. The most basic is its acceptance of gender as an a priori differential. Simply stated, gender is used to justify using gender. What actuarial data tell us, then, is something about the average woman or man, but application of these averages to individuals grossly distorts reality, with unequal treatment as the result.[4] Stated another way, overreliance on the gender classification distorts the risk potential, as other meaningful risk factors are overlooked.

Critics also argue that continued use of the gender classification perpetuates traditional stereotypes of men and women. For example, underwriting manuals well into the 1970s labeled women as "malingerers, marginal employees working mainly for convenience, and delicately balanced machines eagerly awaiting a breakdown. . . . If a woman has disability coverage, the temptation exists to replace her earnings with an insurance income once work loses its attractiveness."[5]

Finally, insurers should not use a classification scheme over which the insured have no control. Sex, like race, is an immutable characteristic and therefore should not be used as a basis for determining costs and coverage of insurance policies. Critics document insurance practices prior to the civil rights movement whereby race was casually employed as a classification. This practice was eliminated because it was not acceptable social policy, even though blacks and whites had different morbidity and mortality rates. The same social policy should apply to the sex classification.[6]

FEDERAL COURTS AND SEX DISCRIMINATION IN INSURANCE

Even though the campaign to eliminate sex discrimination in insurance has been waged largely at the state level, where the insurance industry is regulated, a major vehicle for challenging industry practice has been the federal courts via Title VII of the Civil Rights Act of 1964. The law states that it is an unlawful employment practice for an employer "to fail or refuse to hire or to discharge any individual, or otherwise to discriminate against any individual with respect to compensation, terms, conditions, or privileges of employment, because of such individual's race, color, religion, sex, or national origin. . . ."[7] The Equal

Employment Opportunity Act of 1972 broadened Title VII to include in the definition of *employer* government agencies at the state and local levels.

Because many companies and government agencies provide compensation by way of insurance benefits to their employees, sex-based insurance plans became a viable target for calling into question the common practice of classification by sex. Civil rights and feminist groups surmised that if the federal courts would strike down sex-based employer plans that affected large numbers of people, this would have a spillover effect on the insurance industry. A careful examination of Supreme Court opinions in key cases provides clues about the direction of public policy in the controversy over the sex classification in insurance.

SEX CLASSIFICATION IN DISABILITY
AND RETIREMENT INSURANCE

Beginning with the 1970s, the Supreme Court decided several cases that have played a major role in defining the parameters of sex classification schemes in disability and retirement insurance. The disability cases, *Geduldig v. Aiello* (1974) and *General Electric v. Gilbert* (1976), raised the question of whether employer-sponsored disability plans that excluded pregnancy constituted unfair sex discrimination.[8] In both cases, the majority of the Court upheld the plans, arguing that the pregnancy exclusion was not a sex-based classification but a classification of "pregnant . . . and non-pregnant persons."[9]

Geduldig and *Gilbert* demonstrated the unwillingness of the Court to undo established insurance practice. The insurance industry has never considered normal pregnancy a disability; moreover, it argued in *Gilbert* that if pregnancy were included in an employee group plan, it would significantly drive up premium rates.[10] Public reaction after the *Gilbert* decision was so great that in 1978 Congress passed the Pregnancy Disability Act as an amendment to Title VII, requiring employers with disability plans to include pregnancy benefits.[11]

In 1978 the Supreme Court considered for the first time the validity of a sex differential in an employee retirement plan in *Los Angeles Department of Water and Power v. Manhart*.[12] The case involved a pension program of the Los Angeles Department whereby females made larger contributions from their salaries to the pension fund than males, on the basis that women as a class live longer than men. The department had calculated, from a study of mortality tables and its own employee experience, that women should contribute 14.84 percent more per monthly paycheck than men because they would draw more monthly payments from the fund over their average life span. The Court struck down the plan on a 6–2 vote. The central argument of the majority opinion, written by Justice Stevens, was that Title VII specifically prohibits discrimination against any *individual* on the basis of sex, and therefore it is illegal to treat one gender group differently from the other.

Although it appears that Stevens was attacking the common insurance practice of classifying by gender, he tempered the majority opinion by stating that Title VII was not intended to revolutionize the insurance industry: All that is at issue today is a requirement that men and women make unequal contributions to an employer-sponsored pension fund. Nothing in our holding implies that it would be unlawful for an employer to set aside equal retirement contributions for each employee and let each retiree purchase the largest benefit that his or her accumulated contributions could command in the open market. Nor does it call into question the insurance industry practice of considering the composition of an employer's work force in determining the probable cost of a retirement or death benefit plan.[13]

In 1983 the Supreme Court reaffirmed *Manhart* in *Arizona Governing Committee v. Norris*, though by a narrower margin, 5–4.[14] The state of Arizona's retirement plan differed from the Los Angeles plan in that employee contributions were not determined by sex; upon retirement, however, women's monthly payments were lower because of their longer life expectancy. The plan provided employees three options at retirement—a lump sum benefit, a fixed monthly payment over a fixed number of years, or a lifetime annuity. Women's benefits under the first two options were the same as men's, but the lifetime annuity option gave women a smaller monthly payment than men. The litigant in the case, Natalie Norris, in opting for the lifetime annuity, would be paid $320 per month at age 65, whereas a man in an identical situation would collect $354 a month.

Justice Marshall, who wrote the majority opinion, reaffirmed the Court's position in *Manhart*: "We have no hesitation in holding, . . . that the classification of employees on the basis of sex is no more permissible at the payout stage of a retirement plan than at the pay-in stage."[15]

In defending the retirement plan, the state of Arizona contended that Title VII was not applicable in their case, since retirement options were being offered through a third party (an insurance company) whose policies were comparable to what was available in the open market. The Court rebutted this argument by noting that when the state entered into such an agreement, it was the responsible agent for employee pension plans, and hence subject to Title VII requirements.

It should be noted that Justice Powell, who voted with the majority in *Manhart*, was on the minority side in *Norris*, precisely because the Arizona plan was provided by a third-party insurer. He believed that striking down such a plan, where the insurer used actuarially sound sex-based mortality tables, amounted to revolutionizing the insurance and pension industries, which *Manhart* went out of its way to avoid.[16]

THE NORRIS AND MANHART DECISIONS AND EMPLOYERS

The *Norris* decision had a wide-ranging impact on employer-sponsored pension plans. The Teachers Insurance and Annuity Association-College Retirement Equities Fund retirement plan for college teachers is a case in point. The system of unequal payments to male and female retirees had been in the federal court pipeline for several years prior to *Norris*. On the same day the Supreme Court handed down its decision in *Norris*, it remanded to the appellate courts two cases challenging the TIAA-CREF plan.[17] As a result, all TIAA-CREF participants now receive sex-neutral benefits on annuity income payments made after May 1, 1980.[18]

Another thorny problem faced by the Court in *Manhart* and *Norris* was the question of retroactivity. Should female employees in the Los Angeles Water and Power Department be entitled to back pay for their higher contributions to the pension plan, and should past annuity payments by female employees in the Arizona plan yield an equal monthly benefit to that of males upon retirement?

In *Manhart*, seven justices argued against retroactive pay. Stevens, speaking for the majority, alluded to a precedent in *Albemarle Paper Co. v. Moody*, where the Court established generous guidelines for awarding back pay for violations of Title VII, but that it was not to be given automatically in every case.[19] Granting retroactivity in a case like *Manhart* would not be practical, according to Stevens, as pension funds could be jeopardized by drastic changes in the rules.[20] It was enough of a blow for employers to adapt to the Court's decision requiring equal contributions from males and females.

In *Norris*, the number of justices arguing against retroactive payments was reduced to five, while four supported some kind of retroactive relief. Justice O'Connor, whose vote was crucial in the 5–4 vote striking down the Arizona plan, did not go along with the four justices who thought that relief should apply to all benefit payments made after the federal district court's judgment in *Norris*. O'Connor maintained, as did Stevens in *Manhart*, that the magnitude of a decision awarding retroactive relief would have the effect of disrupting current pension plans.[21]

THE SUPREME COURT AND GENDER CLASSIFICATION

A careful reading of the Supreme Court opinions relating to the validity of the sex classification in insurance reveals the limited scope of the justices' decisions. The Court has gone to great lengths in assuring the insurance industry that it has no intention of changing the way it does business. At the same time, however, it has conveyed the message that the sex classification in insurance is not acceptable in a Title VII context. Both *Manhart* and *Norris* sanctioned a principle of equality that prohibits treating men and women differently even if empirical evidence proves that as groups they do have different morbidity and mortality rates. The Court has made very clear that Title VII prohibits discrimination to *individuals* on the basis of sex.

The *Manhart* and *Norris* decisions have provided an impetus to civil rights and feminist groups to challenge the insurance industry's common use of the gender classification. One immediate consequence was a push in Congress in the late 1970s to pass legislation that would prohibit insurance companies nationwide from using the sex classification in determining coverage, benefits, and premium rates. Known as the Non-Discrimination in Insurance Act in the House and the Fair Insurance Practices Act in the Senate,[22] the bills were introduced under Congress's prerogative in the McCarran-Ferguson Act[23] and its authority to regulate interstate commerce and to legislate in matters of civil rights. Although the legislation received wide support from women's groups and organizations such as the American Association of University Professors, the American Association of Retired Persons, and the Leadership Conference on Civil Rights, the insurance industry waged an expensive lobby campaign that succeeded in killing the legislation.[24]

A SHIFT OF FOCUS TO THE STATES

Because of the bleak prospects for legislating change nationwide in insurance practices, and the reluctance of the federal courts to overrule the insurance industry's practice of gender classification, advocates for eliminating sex discrimination, led by the National Organization for Women, have shifted their focus to the states. Pennsylvania, a large insurance consumer state, has been a fertile ground for insurance litigation under the state's Equal Rights Amendment. In 1984 the state Supreme Court struck down an insurance company's sex-based rates, noting that the insurance commissioner was correct in looking to the state's ERA in determining if sex-distinct rates were contrary to state law and public policy. However, the decision did not prohibit the state legislature from enacting specific gender-based insurance laws if it deemed such action appropriate.[25] In 1986 the legislature passed a law that allowed insurance companies to use gender to determine auto policy premiums, but a 1988 Commonwealth Court decision voided the law. In 1989 the state supreme court upheld the lower court's ruling. The state insurance department broadly interpreted the state courts' opinions to include other gender based insurance products, and has issued regulations prohibiting companies from selling life and health insurance with different premium rates for women and men.[26]

Pennsylvania's move toward unisex insurance rates has not been without problems for supporters of the elimination of the gender classification in insurance. The National Organization for Women sharply criticizes the State Insurance Department for not requiring insurers to utilize other risk factors associated with accidents, life, and health when the gender classification is eliminated. For example, the merger of young women's and men's premium rates in auto insurance has resulted in an average increase in premium rates of 33 percent for approximately 600,000 women in Pennsylvania. According to NOW, such big increases are unwarranted, since young women drive fewer miles than young men. When mileage is not used to ascertain risk, women are overcharged. The non-use of mileage driven also affects the traditional unisex-rated adult class of women (the sex distinction is eliminated by most insurers in the insureds' mid-twenties), and NOW has estimated that *all* women in Pennsylvania are overcharged as a group by $100 million a year.[27] Just as the insurance industry has gone to court over the unisex rating issue, NOW has gone to court over the sex discriminatory effects of unisex ratings when state authorities do not require insurance companies to revamp their pricing schemes to reflect more accurately the meaningful risk factors.

NOW AND MUTUAL OF OMAHA

In 1984, the National Organization for Women (NOW) and the NOW Legal Defense Fund filed a $2 million lawsuit against Mutual of Omaha in the District of Columbia, charging that sex discrimination in Mutual's pricing of health and disability insurance violated the public accommodation law of the District's Human Rights Act.[28] Since twenty-six states have similar laws, NOW recognized that a favorable ruling would have wide repercussions. In 1987 a three-judge panel of the D.C. Court of Appeals dismissed the lawsuit on grounds that the Human Rights Act did not cover insurance companies' actuarial pricing practices. NOW lost a similar suit against Metropolitan Life in a New York State appeals court in 1987 on virtually the same grounds.[29]

At this time, the results of state litigation have been mixed, but organizations like NOW, encouraged by the equality principle laid down in *Manhart* and *Norris*, appear determined to continue their efforts to eliminate the sex classification in insurance. Their most potent weapon appears to be state equal rights amendments rather than more general human rights laws.

THE SUPREME COURT IN PUBLIC POLICY

It would be an overstatement to say that the Supreme Court has been the primary mover and shaker in shaping public policy on sex discrimination in the insurance industry. But one could cogently argue that in the American constellation of political decision makers, it has been a strategic actor. In *Manhart* and *Norris*, the Court declared a principle of equality contrary to common practice in a major U.S. industry. But its application was narrowly construed, meaning that it was hesitant to move too far away from the status quo. Moreover, the Court's rulings in *Geduldig* and *Gilbert* demonstrated its unwillingness to tamper with established insurance practice or to remedy any past discrimination that would place a financial burden on the insurer. In summary, the Court has served notice that the gender classification in insurance is at risk, but its role in eliminating the classification will be shared by state governments, which are at present the primary regulators of the insurance industry.

NOTES

1. Primary regulation of the insurance industry rests with the fifty states. This arrangement dates back to the mid-nineteenth century, when individual states legislated regulatory agencies to oversee the growing business of insurance. The McCarran-Ferguson Act, passed by Congress in 1945, reaffirmed state regula-

tion, though not exclusively. Congress reserved for itself the authority to enact insurance legislation under the following clause in McCarran: "No Act of Congress shall be construed to invalidate, impair, or supersede any law enacted by any State for the purpose of regulating the business of insurance . . . unless such Act specifically relates to the business of insurance." 15 U.S.C. 1012(b) (1982).

2. Montana Code Ann. 49-2-309 (1983).

3. *Kansas City Times*, August 25, 1987, p. 11D; *National Underwriter* (Life and Health-Financial Services Edition), February 26, 1990, p. 5.

4. An excellent example is the sex differential used in dental and vision care insurance. No medical explanations are available to verify differences between men and women. Yet the insurance industry uses the sex classification anyway, and indeed has established such a differential, with the result that women pay higher rates. Robert Randall, "Risk Classification and Actuarial Tables as They Affect Insurance Pricing for Women and Minorities," in *Discrimination against Minorities and Women in Pensions and Health, Life, and Disability Insurance*, Vol. I, U.S. Commission on Civil Rights, 1978, pp. 568, 576. To illustrate further, studies of mortality differences by sex show a considerable overlap between men and women with respect to the age at which death occurs. For over 80 percent of males, one can find a matching female who died at approximately the same time. Sex is not a reliable predictor of mortality, so that it would be misleading even to talk about an average man or average woman. For references to the debate over overlapping death rates of men and women, see Spencer Kimball, "Reverse Sex Discrimination: *Manhart*," 83 *American Bar Foundation Research Journal* 120–23 (1979), and Lea Brilmayer and others, "Sex Discrimination in Employer-Sponsored Insurance Plans: A Legal and Demographic Analysis," 47 *University of Chicago Law Review* 530–31 (1980).

5. Quoted in Suzanne Stoiber, "Insured: Except in Case of War, Suicide, and Organs Peculiar to Females," *Ms.* (June 1973), p. 114.

6. Anne C. Cicero, "Strategies for the Elimination of Sex Discrimination in Insurance," 20 *Harvard Civil Rights–Civil Liberties Law Review* 211 (1985); Brilmayer and others, "Sex Discrimination," 526–529.

7. 42 U.S.C. 2000e-2(a)(1).

8. *Geduldig v. Aiello*, 417 U.S. 484(1974). This case, challenging a California state disability plan, was argued on Fourteenth Amendment equal protection grounds. Other federal court cases referred to in this paper were argued on Title VII grounds. *General Electric v. Gilbert*, 429 U.S. 125 (1976).

9. 417 U.S. at 496–97 n. 20.

10. 429 U.S. at 131.

11. Pregnancy Discrimination Act as codified at 42 U.S.C. 2000e (k) (1982).

12. *Los Angeles Department of Water and Power v. Manhart*, 435 U.S. 702 (1978).

13. Ibid., at 717–18.

14. *Arizona Governing Committee v. Norris*, 463 U.S. 1073 (1983).

15. Ibid., at 1081.

16. Ibid., at 1099.

17. *Teachers Insurance and Annuity Association v. Spirt* and *Long Island University v. Spirt*, 691 F. 2d 1054, 463 U.S. 1223 (1983); *Peters v. Wayne State University*, 691 F. 2d 235, 463 U.S. 1223 (1983).

18. For a complete summary of TIAA-CREF action after *Norris*, see *News from TIAA-CREF*, October 9, 1984.

19. *Albermarle Paper Co. v. Moody*, 422 U.S. 405 (1975).

20. 435 U.S. at 718–23.

21. 463 U.S. at 1109–11. Five years after *Norris*, the Supreme Court ruled that the state of Florida did not have to pay $43.6 million in retroactive payments to male state employees whose spouses shared in their pension plans prior to *Norris*. At dispute in this case was a plan whereby male employees with spouses were paid less than female employees with spouses, on the basis that female spouses lived longer than the male spouses of female employees. *Florida v. Hughlan Long*, 56 *U.S. Law Week*, 4718–25 (1988).

22. For the House version of this legislation, see *Nondiscrimination in Insurance Act of 1983: Hearings on H.R. 100 before the Subcommittee on Commerce, Transportation, and Tourism of the Committee on Energy and Commerce*, 98th Congress, 1st Session 1–15 (1983). H.R. 100 was significantly weakened through the adoption of an amendment that would exempt sex discrimination in individual private insurance contracts. For the Senate version of this legislation, see *Fair Insurance Practices Act: Hearings on S. 372 before the Committee on Commerce, Science, and Transportation*, 98th Congress, 1st Session, 2–16 (1983).

23. Supra, 1.

24. The campaign cost the industry almost $2 million. A group called the Committee for Fair Insurance Rates was financed by thirty-three companies for the express purpose of "educating" the public about the adverse consequences of H.R. 100 and S. 372. Common Cause *NEWS*, September 21, 1983; *National Underwriter* (Life and Health Edition), October 1, 1983, p. 2.

25. Cicero, "Strategies," 232–234.

26. "Pennsylvanians Insured of Non-Sexist Policies," *Ms.* (August 1988), p. 84; *National Underwriter*, February 26, 1990, p. 5.

27. *NOW Times* (October–November–December 1988), p. 7, and *NOW Times* (February–March 1989), p. 11. For a complete explanation of NOW's allegations, see Patrick Butler and others, "Sex-Divided

Mileage, Accident, and Insurance Cost Data Show That Auto Insurers Overcharge Most Women," 6 *Journal of Insurance Regulation* 243–284 (Part I) and 373–423 (Part II) (1988).

28. *National NOW Times* (September–October, 1984), p. 5.

29. *New York Times*, August 16, 1987, p. 26E; *National NOW Times* (September–October–November 1987), p. 10.

Affirmative Action As
a Woman's Issue

 *Roberta Ann Johnson*

Debate about affirmative action is often heated and emotionally charged. It generates discussions about "merit";[1] it buries academics in Department of Labor statistics;[2] it absorbs lawyers and historians in interpretation of congressional intent;[3] and it bogs down the public policy experts with narrow implementation matters.[4] All this often misses the essential point about affirmative action, which is that its goal is redistribution.[5]

In what ways does a policy of affirmative action assist women to become fully integrated into schools, training programs, and jobs? We will (1) define affirmative action, (2) detail the development of federal affirmative action guidelines, (3) describe Supreme Court decisions relating to affirmative action, and (4) consider in what ways affirmative action is a woman's issue.

AFFIRMATIVE ACTION DEFINED

Affirmative action is a generic term for programs that take some kind of initiative, either voluntarily or under the compulsion of law, to increase, maintain, or rearrange the number or status of certain group members, usually defined by race or gender, within a larger group. When these programs are characterized by race or gender preference, "especially when coupled with rigorously pursued 'goals,' [they] are highly controversial because race and gender are generally

Roberta Ann Johnson is a professor of politics at the University of San Francisco.

"This is a revised version of an article that appeared in the *Journal of Political Science*, vol. 17, Nos. 1 and 2 (Spring 1989). Reprinted with permission."

The author would like to acknowledge Megan Andesha, a student at the University of San Francisco, who assisted in the research of the most recent Supreme Court cases.

thought to be 'irrelevant' to employment and admissions decisions" and "immutable characteristics over which individuals lack control."[6]

AFFIRMATIVE ACTION AND FEDERAL GUIDELINES

Significant moves to prohibit discrimination in the public sector began in the late 1930s and early 1940s, according to David Rosenbloom, who describes a series of Executive Orders, starting with the Roosevelt administration, that called for a policy of nondiscrimination in employment.[7] However, it is President John F. Kennedy's Executive Order issued March 16, 1981 that is usually seen as representing the real roots of present-day affirmative action policy.[8] Executive Order 10,925 required government contractors to take affirmative action, and established specific sanctions for noncompliance.[9] Nevertheless, even the Order's principal draftsperson admitted that the enforcement process led to a great deal of complainant frustration.[10]

Before another Executive Order would be issued, civil rights exploded onto the public agenda. A march on Washington held on August 28, 1963, brought 200,000 black and white supporters of civil rights to the Capitol. In response to this and other demonstrations, and as a result of shifting public sentiment. President Kennedy sent a civil rights bill to Congress and it was passed in 1964, after his assassination. The Civil Rights Act of 1964 included in its provisions Title VI, which prohibited discrimination on the basis of race, color, or national origin by all recipients of federal funds, including schools, and Title VII, which made it unlawful for any employer or labor union to discriminate in employment on the basis of race, color, religion, sex, or national origin. Title VII also created the Equal Employment Opportunity Commission (EEOC) for enforcement in the private sector.

The following year, 1965, President Lyndon B. Johnson issued Executive Order 11,246 barring discrimination on the basis of race, color, religion, or national origin by federal contractors and subcontractors.[11] On October 13, 1967, it was amended by Executive Order 11,375 to expand its coverage to women. One major innovation of the Order was to shift enforcement to the secretary of labor by creating an Office of Federal Contract Compliance (OFCC). Starting in 1968, the government established the enforceability of the Executive Order with legal action[12] and, for the first time, issued notices of proposed debarment (contract cancellation) using their administrative process.[13]

Prodded to be more specific about its standards, the OFCC began to spell out exactly what affirmative action meant in the context of the construction industry, and that became a model for all affirmative action programs.[14] During this period, President Richard Nixon played the role of champion of affirmative action, saving LBJ's Executive Order.

In 1968 OFCC focused on blacks in the construction industry. The result was the Philadelphia Plan, which was developed in three stages. First, OFCC required preaward affirmative action plans from low bidders in some labor market areas, like Philadelphia. But because there were no guidelines for acceptability, the industry pressured Congress, which stimulated an opinion from the comptroller general, who recommended that OFCC provide minimum requirements and standards by which programs would be judged. The second or revised Philadelphia Plan was then developed. It required that contractors submit a statement of "goals" of minority employment together with their bids which took into account the minority participation and availability in the trade, as well as the need for training programs. On September 23, 1969, the Labor Department issued its third and final set of guidelines for the Philadelphia Plan after having determined the degree to which there was discrimination in construction crafts. This final plan established ranges within which the contractor's goals had to fall and recommended filling vacancies and new jobs approximately on the basis of one minority craftsman for each nonminority craftsman.

The comptroller general found the revised plan illegal on the ground that it set up quotas. But the attorney general issued an opinion declaring the plan to be legal and advised the secretary of labor to ignore the comptroller general's opinion. The comptroller general then urged the Senate Subcommittee on Deficiencies and Supplementals to attach a rider onto their appropriations bill prohibiting the use of funds to pay for efforts to achieve specific minority employment goals. The Nixon administration lobbied hard in the House and succeeded in eliminating the rider. On reconsideration, the Senate also defeated the rider, and the Philadelphia Plan was saved.

In 1971 the Department of Labor issued general guidelines that had the same features as the Philadelphia Plan, making it clear that "goals and timetables" were meant to "increase materially the utilization of minorities and women," with underutilization being spelled out as "having fewer minorities or women in a particular job classification than would reasonably be expected by their availability. . . ."[15] The 1971 Department of Labor Guidelines were called Revised Order #4, and they were to govern employment practices by government contractors and subcontractors in industry and higher education.

Hole and Levine, in *Rebirth of Feminism*, document the initial exclusion of women from the guidelines. In 1970 Secretary of Labor Hodgson even publicly remarked that he had "no intention of applying literally exactly the same approach for women" as was applied to eliminate discrimination against minorities.[16] However, because of publicity and pressure by women's groups, by April 1973 women were finally included as full beneficiaries in the Revised Order #4.

What is important about the Philadelphia Plan and the Department of Labor guidelines is that they established not only the principle but also the guidelines for the practice of affirmative action that other civil rights enforcement agencies and even the courts would follow.

During the 1970s, administrative changes strengthened affirmative action. The Office of Management and Budget enlarged and refined the definition of *minority group* and, under President Carter, affirmative action efforts were consolidated. By Executive Order on October 5, 1978, OFCC went from overview responsibility, whereby each department had responsibility for the compliance of their own contractors (with uneven results), to consolidated contract compliance, whereby OFCC was given enforcement responsibility over all contractors;[17] overnight, 1,600 people who had been working for other departments were now working for Labor. The expanded program now was called the Office of Federal Contract Compliance Programs (OFCCP).

During the 1980s, there were attempts to weaken affirmative action. The Reagan administration publicly and continually criticized goals and timetables, calling them quotas.[18] By 1982 the OFCCP's budget and number of workers were significantly reduced. By 1983, while President Reagan used attitudes toward affirmative action as a litmus test to successfully reorganize the U.S. Commission on Civil Rights, his attempt to rescind or revise Executive Order 11,246 by specifically prohibiting numerical hiring goals was successfully stopped by opposition from within his own administration.[19] Nevertheless, during these years, the administration whittled away at the policy. In 1983 they instituted changes within OFCCP that affected the agency's case determinations and remedies, although by January 1987 some of these changes were rescinded. On January 21, 1987, Joseph N. Cooper, director of OFCCP, quit his job in protest. In an interview, he spoke candidly about the "number of officials in the Labor Department and elsewhere in the Administration who were intent on destroying the contract compliance program."[20]

THE BAKKE DECISION AND OTHER COURT DECISIONS

Affirmative action policy for student admissions has a very different history. Its source is Title VI of the Civil Rights Act of 1964 and Title IX of the Educational Amendments of 1972, not Executive Order 11,246. Title VI *requires* affirmative action steps to be taken in admissions *only as a remedy* for past discrimination. However, most minority affirmative action admission programs were self-imposed.[21] Title IX (subpart B, section 106.17) of the Educational Amendments of 1972, which prohibits *sex* discrimination, also calls for affirmative steps to be taken to remedy "past exclusion." A case having to do with minority affirmative action in admissions became the most well known and celebrated test of the principle of affirmative action.

Justice Lewis Powell announced the *Bakke v. University of California* Supreme Court decision to a hushed courtroom on the morning of June 28, 1978. He said, "We speak today with notable lack of unanimity." In fact, the 154 pages of judicial text presented *six* separate opinions and *two* separate majorities.[22]

Allan Bakke wanted to be a medical doctor. In 1973, at age 33, while employed as a full-time engineer, he applied to a dozen medical schools, one of which was the University of California—Davis, and was turned down by all of them. The next year, after a second rejection from the twelve medical schools, Bakke sued the University of California in the California Court system claiming that Davis's use of racial quotas was what had excluded him from medical school.

The *Bakke* case was not a strong one for those who supported affirmative action. On trial was an admissions program that reserved 16 of its 100 places for minority students (blacks, Hispanics, and Asians), which looked like an admissions "quota" system. Furthermore, the Davis Medical School was founded in 1968, so the school could not claim that affirmative action was a remedy for past years of discrimination.

In this case, fifty-eight amicus curiae briefs were filed and "The Court seemed less a judicial sanctum than a tug of war among contesting lobbyists."[23] When the dust cleared, the Court found a way both to admit Allan Bakke, now age 38, to the Davis Medical School and to defend the practice of Affirmative Action. By a 5–4 margin, the Court rejected the Davis program with a fixed number of seats for minorities; but also, by a different 5–4 margin, the Court accepted race-conscious admissions as being consistent with the Constitution and with Title VI.[24]

OTHER COURT DECISIONS AFTER BAKKE

Two cases that followed *Bakke, Weber* in 1979 and *Fullilove* in 1980, helped clarify the legal picture on affirmative action. In a 5–2 decision in *Weber* (two Supreme Court members did not participate) it was ruled permissible under Title VII for the private sector voluntarily to apply a compensatory racial preference for employment.

Brian Weber was an unskilled laboratory employee at the Gramercy, Louisiana, plant of the Kaiser Aluminum and Chemical Corporation. In 1974, while blacks made up 39 percent of Gramercy's general labor force, at the Kaiser plant, only 2 percent of the 273 skilled craft workers were black. Kaiser instituted a training program for their unskilled workers earmarking half the trainee openings for blacks until the percentage of black craftspeople corresponded to their proportion in the labor force. Weber had more seniority than some of the blacks chosen for the program. The Court, however, argued that Kaiser's affirmative action program was a reasonable response to the need to break down old patterns of segregation.

The following year, in *Fullilove*, the Supreme Court decided, 6–3, that a congressional affirmative action program, a 10 percent set-aside of federal funds for minority business people, provided in the Public Works Employment Act of 1977, was also permissible under the Constitution.

Fullilove v. Klutznick was decided during the summer of 1980.[25] Chief Justice Burger wrote the majority opinion, which found the "limited use of racial and ethnic criteria" constitutionally permissible when its purpose was to remedy the present effects of past racial discrimination. With this case, Father Mooney suggests that, with certain qualifications, the Supreme Court legitimized affirmative action as a policy for U.S. society.[26] But not so when it came to layoffs.

In 1984, when layoffs were concerned, the Court shifted from its permissive view on classwide "race conscious remedies." On June 12, 1984, the Supreme Court issued its decision in *Firefighters Local Union No. 1784 v. Stotts*, which focused on the extent to which seniority systems may be overridden as part of court-ordered relief to remedy discrimination in employment. It was a 6–3 decision.

Carl Stotts was a black firefighter in the Memphis, Tennessee, Fire Department. He brought a class action lawsuit into federal district court in 1977 alleging discriminatory hiring and promotion practices in the department. This resulted in a consent decree in 1980 requiring that the percentage of black employees in each job classification be increased to the proportion of blacks in the local labor force.

The next year, because of budget problems, the city began to make plans to lay off firefighters on a seniority basis (last hired, first fired). "Black firefighters asked the court to prohibit the layoff of black employees. The court ordered the city not to apply its seniority policy in a manner that would reduce the percentage of blacks in the department. The case was appealed to the Supreme Court."[27]

The Supreme Court said that the seniority system could not be disregarded in laying people off and that although there was protection for actual victims of discrimination, "mere membership in the disadvantaged class was an insufficient basis for judicial relief."[28] In other words, a seniority system could be used to lay people off even though many blacks would be the first to go. The same was true in *Wygant v. Jackson Board of Education*, which was decided May 19, 1986.

In *Wygant*, nonminority teachers in Jackson, Michigan, challenged their terminations under a collective bargaining agreement requiring layoffs in reverse order of seniority unless it resulted in more minority layoffs than the current percentage employed. This layoff provision was adopted by the Jackson Board of Education in 1972 because of racial tension in the community that extended to its schools. In a 5–4 decision, the court said that this system of layoffs violated the rights of the nonminority teachers even though (unlike the case of *Stotts*) it was a part of their collective bargaining agreement. Powell, writing for the Court, argued that he could not find enough to justify the use of racial classifications.[29] Affirmative action was not as important as seniority when it came to layoffs.

Nevertheless, the "principle" of affirmative action actually survived in the majority's opinion in *Wygant*. The Court again affirmed that under certain circumstances policies using race-based classifications were justified. It was just that for the majority, these were not the right circumstances. Marshall's words written in his dissenting opinion ring true. "Despite the Court's inability to agree on a route, we have reached a common destination in sustaining affirmative action against constitutional attack."[30] His assessment was to be proved correct in the February 25, 1987, case, *US v. Paradise*, and in the March 25, 1987, case, *Johnson v. Transportation Agency, Santa Clara County*.

In a 5–4 decision, in the *Paradise* case, the Court upheld a federal district court judge's order requiring Alabama to promote one black state police trooper for each white trooper from a pool of qualified candidates. Justice Brennan wrote the plurality opinion justifying the affirmative action program because of the "egregious" nature of previous bias against blacks. Justice Powell, in a concurring opinion, emphasized that the "quota" did not disrupt seriously the lives of innocent individuals; Justice Stevens's concurring opinion emphasized that the Court-imposed plans fell within the bounds of reasonableness, whereas the dissenters emphasized the undue burden the plan placed on the white troopers.

In the *Johnson* case, six of the nine Supreme Court Justices approved of Santa Clara county's affirmative action program. In 1978 Santa Clara's transit district's board of supervisors adopted a goal of a work force whose proportion of women, minorities, and the disabled equaled the percentage of the county's labor force at all job levels. Women constituted 36.4 percent of the relevant labor market, and although women made up 22.4 percent of the district workers, they were mostly in clerical positions with none in the 238 skilled jobs. In 1979 Diane Joyce and Paul Johnson competed, along with five others who were all deemed "well qualified," for the job of dispatcher, a skilled position. They had all scored over 70, the passing grade, in an oral examination conducted by a two-person panel. Johnson tied for second with a score of 75, and Joyce ranked third with 73. After a second interview, first Johnson was chosen, but then, because of affirmative action considerations, Joyce got the job. Johnson sued, contending that he was better qualified. In 1982 a judge ruled that Johnson had been a "victim of discrimination." The Reagan administration joined attorneys for Johnson and appealed to the Supreme Court.[31]

Justice William Brennan, in writing for the Court, put its stamp of approval on voluntary employer action designed to break down old patterns of race and sex segregation. " 'Given the obvious imbalance in the skilled craft category' in favor of men against women, Brennan said, 'It was plainly not unreasonable . . . to consider the sex of Ms. Joyce in making the promotion decision.' " Brennan called the affirmative action plan "a moderate, flexible case by case approach to effecting a gradual improvement in the representation of minorities and women in the agency's work force."[32] Justice Antonin Scalia responded with a scathing dissent emphasizing the burden that falls on the "Johnsons of the country," whom he called "the only losers in the process."[33]

THE COURT AND THE PUBLIC ARE DIVIDED
ON AFFIRMATIVE ACTION

The Supreme Court remained divided on affirmative action, and by a bare majority the Court supported affirmative action for purposes of hiring and promotion, but not to determine layoff lists. A Gallup poll conducted in June 1987 following the *Johnson* decision showed that the public also continued to be divided on the issue of affirmative action and that the majority of those polled continued to be opposed (see Table 1).

Eight years in the White House allowed President Reagan to accomplish, with judicial appointments, what he was not able to do with judicial arguments. When Supreme Court justices retired, he used his power of appointment to add

Table 1   Affirmative Action Ruling

	APPROVED	DISAPPROVED	NO OPINION
National	29%	63%	8%
Democrats	37	54	9
Republicans	22	74	4
Independents	27	64	9
Men	26	66	8
Women	32	59	9
Whites	25	67	8
Blacks	56	34	10
Hispanics	46	47	7

Source: George Gallup, Jr., "Little Support for High Court Ruling on Hiring," *San Francisco Chronicle*, June 15, 1987.

conservatives Sandra Day O'Connor and Antonin Scalia to the bench—and he appointed conservative William H. Rehnquist to be chief justice. Even so, as we have seen, affirmative action programs continued to win majority Court approval through 1987. Then, however, when Justice Powell, the "swing" vote, retired, and Reagan replaced him with conservative Anthony M. Kennedy, the Court was packed for the next affirmative action case.

On January 24, 1989, the Supreme Court announced its decision on the *Richmond v. Croson* case. The Court ruled, 6–3, that a 1983 Richmond, Virginia, ordinance that channeled 30 percent of public works funds to minority-owned construction companies violated the Constitution. Justice O'Connor, who wrote the majority opinion, argued that "laws favoring blacks over whites must be judged by the same constitutional test that applies to laws favoring whites over blacks"—namely, that classifications based on race are suspect and have to be scrutinized very carefully.

In scrutinizing this case, O'Connor did not see the necessary evidence of past discrimination that would justify using race-based measures. Black people made up 50 percent of the Richmond population, she noted, and although there was a "gross statistical disparity" between "the number of prime contracts awarded to minority firms and the minority population of the city of Richmond," still, she argued, this case does not "constitute a prima facie proof of a pattern of practice of discrimination." The appropriate pool for comparison is not the general population but the "number of minorities qualified to undertake the task," and O'Connor pointed out that the city did not know exactly how many minority business enterprises (MBEs) there were in the relevant market who were qualified to undertake prime or subcontracting work in public construction projects. Even if there were a low number of MBEs, she argued, maybe it was not because of discrimination but because of "black career and entrepreneurial choices." "Blacks may be disproportionately attracted to industries other than construction."[34]

Justice Thurgood Marshall, in his dissent, found it "deeply ironic" that the majority did not find sufficient evidence of past discrimination in Richmond,

Virginia, the former capital of the Confederacy. "Richmond knows what racial discrimination is; a century of decisions by this and other Federal courts has richly documented the city's disgraceful history . . . ," he wrote, and Marshall defended, again, the use of race-conscious measures to redress the effects of prior discrimination.[35]

The *Richmond* case did not end the debate, but perpetuated the uncertainty surrounding affirmative action plans. Now such plans could stand only if they could survive strict judicial scrutiny—for example, if they were adopted to eliminate "patently obvious, egregious discrimination that can be linked to the deliberate acts of identifiable parties." Mere numerical disparities would not be enough. Experts predicted that the lower courts would be flooded with challenges to affirmative action by white plaintiffs.[36]

OTHER CASES THAT INFLUENCED AFFIRMATIVE ACTION

On June 5, 1989, the court again decided a case that would affect affirmative action policy. In *Wards Cove Packing v. Atonia*, the court ruled, 5–4, that plaintiffs who are not employers have the burden of proving whether a job requirement that is shown statistically to screen out minorities or women is a "business necessity." The case redrew the ground rules unanimously established by the Court in 1971, which prohibited not only employment practices *intended* to discriminate but also practices that had discriminatory *impact*.

The plaintiffs in this case were nonwhites, Filipino and Alaskan native cannery workers who were channeled into lower paid unskilled jobs. Noncannery jobs were filled by the company with predominantly white workers who were hired in Washington and Oregon. With these statistics showing disparate impact, and consistent with precedent, the lower court asked the salmon canneries to justify, on grounds of "business necessity," the business practice of flying in whites for managerial jobs and hiring local nonwhites to work in the cannery. Justice Byron White, writing for the majority, overturned eighteen years of precedent. He said that the cannery business did not have to prove anything. It was up to the nonwhite cannery workers to disprove the company's claim that there was no discrimination.

Justice John Paul Stevens, in his dissent, called the decision "the latest sojourn into judicial activism," accusing the majority of "[t]urning a blind eye to the meaning and purpose of Title VII. . . ."[37]

One week after the *Wards Cove* decision, the court dealt an even more lethal blow to affirmative action. In *Martin v. Wilks*, five members of the court ruled that whites may bring reverse discrimination claims against judge-approved affirmative action plans. This meant that consent decrees, which settle many discrimination suits and had been thought to be immune from subsequent legal attack, were now fair game.

The *Martin v. Wilks* case had its roots in the early 1970s, when a local chapter of the National Association for the Advancement of Colored People

(NAACP), supported by the federal government, sued the city of Birmingham, Alabama, on the grounds that blacks were being discriminated against in hiring and promotion in the city's fire department. Several years later a settlement was reached, although the union representing the "almost all white work force" objected to the settlement at the hearing.[38] The Federal District Court "approved the settlement and entered a consent decree under which blacks and whites would be hired and promoted in equal number until the number of black firefighters approximated the proportion of blacks in the civilian labor force." A few months later, fifty white firefighters sued the city claiming discrimination. The Federal District Court dismissed the suit. In 1987 the Eleventh Circuit Court overturned that dismissal, a decision inconsistent with those of every other circuit court, and reinstated the white firefighters in the city of Birmingham; a group of black firefighters appealed to the Supreme Court.

Chief Justice William Rehnquist wrote the majority opinion, in which he agreed with the Eleventh Circuit Court, arguing that a decree could be binding only on parties who had been part of the original lawsuit. "Outside groups" could not be required to join such a suit, and if they were not bound by the decree, they could sue. Justice Stevens's dissent pointed out that the Court's decision "would subject large employers who seek to comply with the law by remedying past discrimination to a never-ending stream of litigation and potential liability. He called the results 'unfathomable' and 'counterproductive.' "[39]

RESPONSES TO THE COURT DECISIONS

These decisions of the Court stimulated two important responses. First, across the country, lawsuits were filed by white male workers who now had standing in the Court to allege that they had suffered reverse discrimination because of affirmative action programs, even programs that were court-imposed or that resulted from full trials. The effects were felt from San Francisco[40] to Birmingham.[41] The second important response to the Court's decisions came from Congress.

For six months, civil rights organizations and their congressional allies worked together to prepare legislation that would basically reverse three of the Supreme Court decisions, two that related to affirmative action, the *Wards Cove* case, "in which the Court ruled that . . . the plaintiff has the burden of proving that an employer had no business reason for a practice with discriminatory effects," and the *Martin v. Wilks* case, "in which the Court held that Court-approved affirmative action plans can be challenged as reverse discrimination. . . ."[42] The proposed legislation would also reverse another civil rights (but non–affirmative action) case, *Paterson v. McClean Credit Union*, "in which the Court ruled that an 1866 law prohibiting racial discrimination in contracts applies only to hiring agreements, not to on-the-job discrimination."[43]

The civil rights bill's sponsors, Senator Edward Kennedy (D-MA) and Representative Augustus Hawkins (D-CA) were confident about getting the majority necessary to pass the law. The challenge, which kept them negotiating behind closed doors, was to line up the sixty Senate cloture votes needed to shut off debate and to get the sixty-seven votes to guarantee override of a possible presidential veto. This civil rights bill, because it dealt with more subtle issues like "burden of proof" and "right to sue," was not as "sexy" as, for example, the Voting Rights Act, and the fear was that the supporting public might be less attentive to its fate.[44] Nevertheless, the White House watched closely.

At the end of May 1990, reporters were describing the "tough test" faced by the Bush administration. Although the president originally had warned he would veto the civil rights bill, by spring he was backing off from his threat. There seemed to be two reasons for his change of heart. First, it appeared that many Republicans in the Senate were ready to break with the White House to support the bill. The president's veto might not be sustained. The second reason for the president to look for compromise was his concern about his reelection. President Bush was eager to court the African-American vote in 1992; in mid-1990, he had a 56 percent black approval rating and was the most popular Republican president among blacks since Dwight Eisenhower.[45] A compromise on the civil rights bill seemed likely. Thus, in 1990 it appeared that a committed pro–civil rights core in Congress and a pragmatic White House would help important elements of affirmative action to survive. But in the fall of 1990 President Bush vetoed the civil rights bill, and Congress was unable to override his veto. That December, Robert Allen, chairman of AT&T, arranged a private dinner between top business and civil rights leaders. A coalition of two hundred top CEOs, the so-called Business Roundtable, voted to continue these talks, and both sides agreed to have lawyers meet to try to "hammer out their differences." Saving affirmative action and the civil rights bill now seemed probable.

The Bush administration, however, was unhappy with the prospect of such a compromise. Preparing for the presidential campaign of 1992, GOP strategists believed that a Republican anti–affirmative action position would be very effective and that a compromise bill would dilute the Republican political advantage on the quota issue. Therefore, the White House proceeded to destroy the business civil rights negotiations. Roundtable members were warned that their talks undermined business support for the president's version of a civil rights bill, and Chief of Staff John Sununu personally drummed up opposition among smaller companies. The White House campaign was blunt and vicious. Even Robert Allen came under personal attack from conservative columnist Paul Gigot in the *Wall Street Journal* because of his involvement. The participants who had seemed so hopeful buckled under the political pressure.[46]

AFFIRMATIVE ACTION: A WOMAN'S ISSUE

The aim of affirmative action is the redistribution of benefits and opportunities. Has the program benefited women?

According to the Department of Labor guidelines, starting in April 1982, women were to be included in the special class or "protected class" benefiting from compensatory policies. Note, however, that in all the Supreme Court landmark cases except the *Johnson* case, women were not the protected class directly benefiting from the affirmative action programs in question. Thus, even with the Department of Labor guidelines, there is no guarantee that women, as a protected class, will be included in affirmative action pools, which are up to each employer to define.

Industrywide figures consistently have painted a mixed picture for employed women under affirmative action. For example, Goldstein and Smith analyzed minority and female employment changes in over 74,000 separate companies between 1970 and 1972. They compared contractor and noncontractor companies with a presumption that federal contractors are more likely to conform to affirmative action goals. What they found surprised them.

Although, as expected, black males did economically better in employment in contractor companies between 1970 and 1972, so did *white males*. The big losers during these years were white women. Between 1970 and 1972, before the OFCC revised guidelines included women, white women not only showed no employment gains, they showed significant employment losses. In fact, white women's losses were equal in magnitude to the significant gains made by white males.[47]

Under the revised guidelines, it appears that the effect of including women in the federal affirmative action program, as a protected class, is mixed. From 1967 to 1980, for white women, "[r]ough stability prevailed over this period in their wages relative to white men," according to Smith and Welch. Sociologist Paul Burstein suggests an interesting explanation, rarely considered by economists, to account for why white women have not experienced a large wage advance under the 1972 guidelines. As a group, their "seeming decline" in income is probably due to the steady influx of relatively inexperienced female workers into the labor force. Women as a group are better off, but their average income drops.[48] The story on wages for black women is different. Between 1967 and 1980 the largest wage advances were achieved by black women, who went from earning 74 percent of the wage of similarly employed white women in 1967 to almost complete racial parity in 1980.[49] It has been suggested that "part of the reason for nonwhite women's gains . . . may be their having been so badly off initially that their jobs and incomes could improve considerably without posing any real threat to the normal workings of the economy."[50]

In a National Bureau of Economic Research paper, Jonathan Leonard studied the effectiveness of affirmative action for the employment of minorities and women.[51] Focusing on the period between 1974 and 1980, he also compared *contractor and noncontractor* establishments. Leonard compared the mean employment share of targeted groups and controlled for establishment size, growth region, industry, occupation, and corporate structure. He found that members of protected groups grew faster in contractor than in noncontractor establishments, 3.8 percent faster for black males, 7.9 percent faster for other minority males, 2.8 percent for white females, and 12.3 percent for black females.[52] This suggests that affirmative action programs benefit black women and tend to help white women, though not as much as they benefit minorities.

When Leonard focused on the effect of compliance reviews—that is, the role they played over and above that of contractor status—he found that they advanced black males by 7.9 percent, other minority males by 15.2 percent, and black females by 6.1 percent. It *retarded* the employment growth of whites (including white women). Thus, he concluded, "*with the exception of white females*, compliance reviews have had an additional positive impact on protected group employment beyond the contractor effect."[53] His data also show that white women were not benefiting from affirmative action when it comes to promotions.[54]

Leonard suggests an explanation for why white women's position in contractor companies has not improved significantly compared to noncontractor companies. It is that these women have so flooded the employment market that they have been hired in *both* contractor and noncontractor companies. As he says, "female [employment] share" has "increase[d] at all establishments because of the supply shift. . . ." Thus, his comparison of contractor and noncontractor hiring does not show the general large increase in white women hired. His explanation seems plausible considering the clear increase in the number of women employed, which is reflected by Bureau of the Census data for the period between 1970 and 1980.[55]

Although it appears that not all women have benefited directly from affirmative action, there are many specific cases where women (including white women) have directly benefited from an affirmative action approach. Affirmative action, with its emphasis on numbers and parity, can indirectly benefit women (including white women) because it inevitably shifts our focus from rhetoric to results. Thus, in some areas, such as academic admissions (which falls under Title IX protection), public scrutiny was all that was necessary to make possible a large redistribution of places to all women. Quoting McGeorge Bundy, Wilkinson wrote, "Since 1968 the number of women entering medical schools has risen from 8 percent to 25 percent of the total. A parallel increase has occurred in law schools. No constitutional issue is raised by this dramatic change, . . . the women admitted have had generally competitive records on the conventional measures."[56]

Even though they score competitively, I am arguing that affirmative action has helped these women get admitted to professional schools by focusing public attention on admissions criteria and admission results. In this context let us remember a Charlotte Perkins Gilman line in a poem that focuses on Socialist change. "A lifted world lifts women up," she wrote.

Thus, there is a mixed answer to the question, "Does affirmative action benefit women?" Nonwhite women seem to have most clearly benefited directly from the program, but all women may be benefiting indirectly. Might affirmative action be a women's issue for reasons other than women's benefits?

Perhaps affirmative action could be seen as a woman's issue, in the tradition of social feminism, because it calls for a fairer distribution of social benefits. Of course, I am not suggesting that women be insensitive to the catalogue of arguments, some of them practical, that have been made against affirmative action.[57] What I would suggest is that women (and men) be wary of falling into the trap of characterizing affirmative action as the "opposite" of a merit system. It is not. After all, proportionality is even used to select justices on the Supreme Court, where there may be a Jewish seat, a Southern seat, a black seat, and now a woman's seat.[58]

The major issue raised by affirmative action is not merit but redistribution. Allan Bakke's arguments were made against a special program benefiting minorities. Over and over he raised the flag of "fair competition," but Davis Medical School had another special program, which Bakke did not complain about—the Dean's special admissions program "under which white children of politically well-connected university supporters or substantial financial contributors have been admitted in spite of being less qualified than other applicants, including Bakke."[59] Thus, the Bakke issue is not, and never was, special programs. The issue is who will be benefiting from these special programs—and that is a matter not of merit but of politics.

NOTES

1. See Allan P. Sindler, *Equal Opportunity: On the Policy and Politics of Compensatory Minority Preferences* (Washington, DC: American Enterprise Institute for Public Policy Research, 1983).

2. See Jonathan S. Leonard, "The Effectiveness of Equal Employment Law and the Affirmative Action Regulation," Working Paper No. 1745, NBER Working Paper Series, National Bureau of Economic Research, November 1985 (unpublished).

3. See Thomas Sowell, *Civil Rights: Rhetoric or Reality?* (New York: William Morrow, 1984), and James E. Jones, Jr., "The Bugaboo of Employment Quotas," *Wisconsin Law Review*, 5 (1970).

4. Daniel C. Maguire provides the most complete compendium of practical "problems" in *A New American Justice* (New York: Doubleday, 1980).

5. This, to the credit of its author, is the focus of Daniel C. Maguire's book cited in note 4.

6. Arval A. Morris, "Affirmative Action and 'Quota' Systems," Commentary, 26 Ed. *Law Report*, 1985.

7. David H. Rosenbloom, *Federal Equal Employment Opportunity Politics and Public Personnel Administration* (New York: Praeger, 1977), p. 60; see also James E. Jones, "Twenty-one Years of Affirmative Action: The Maturation of the Administrative Enforcement Process under the Executive Order 11,246 as Amended," *Chicago Kent Law Review*, 59 (Winter 1982); Paul Burstein, *Discrimination, Jobs, and Politics*, (Chicago: University of Chicago Press, 1985), pp. 8, 13.

8. U.S., Federal Register, March 6, 1961, 26, pt. 2: 1977

9. Rosenbloom, *Federal Equal Employment Opportunity Politics*, pp. 67–69.

10. Jones, "Twenty-one Years," p.f. 72.

11. *U.S. Federal Register*, 30, pt. 10: 12319

12. In *U.S. v. Local 189*, United Papermakers and Paperworkers, 290F2d 368, and Crown Zellerbach Corp., 282F Supp. 39 (E. D. La. 1968) "the government sought an injunction against the union's interference with the company's contractual obligations under Executive Order 11,246. . . ." Ibid., p. 83.

13. There are many who criticize the way affirmative action has been implemented. For an overview, see Leonard, Working Paper No. 1745, and Leonard, "Affirmative Action as Earnings Redistribution: The Targeting of Compliance Reviews," *Journal of Labor Economics*, 3 (3) (July 1985), pp. 380–384; see also James P. Smith and Finis Welch, "Affirmative Action and Labor Markets," *Journal of Labor Economics*, 2 (April 1984), pp. 285–286, 298.

14. Leonard, Working Paper No. 1745, p. 4.

15. Sowell, *Civil Rights* p. 41.

16. Judith Hole and Ellen Levine, *Rebirth of Feminism* (Quadrangle/New York: New York Times Book Company, 1971), p. 46; see also Morris Goldstein and Robert Smith, "The Estimated Impact of the Antidiscrimination Program Aimed at Federal Contractors," *Industrial and Labor Relations Review*, 29 (4) (July 1976).

17. Interview with Joseph Hodges, assistant re-

gional director, Office of Federal Contract Compliance, U.S. Department of Labor, Region IX, February 6, 1987.

18. See, for example, Joann S. Lublin and Andy Pasztor, "Tentative Affirmative Action Accord Is Reached by Top Reagan Officials," *Wall Street Journal*, December 11, 1985, p. 4; and Robert Pear, "Rights Chief Assails Hiring Goals as Failure," *New York Times*, November 1, 1985, p. 19.

19. Lublin and Pasztor, "Tentative Affirmative Action Accord."

20. Kenneth B. Noble, "Labor Dept. Aide Quits in Protest Over 'Lip Service' to Jobs Rights," *New York Times*, January 21, 1987; see also "Job-Bias Official Quits Labor Post," *Washington Post*, January 21, 1987.

21. Interview with Paul Grossman, head of the Attorney's Division, Office for Civil Rights, U.S. Department of Education, Region IX, February 6, 1987.

22. Christopher F. Mooney, S.J., *Inequality and the American Conscience* (New York: Paulist Press, 1982), p. 5.

23. J. Harvey Wilkinson III, *From Brown to Bakke: The Supreme Court and School Integration* (New York: Oxford University Press, 1979), p. 255.

24. Ibid., p. 301. Since Justice Powell was the "swing" vote, "An irony of Bakke, wrote Washington attorney and civil rights activist Joseph Rauh, was that 'Affirmative action was saved by a conservative Southern justice.'"

25. Mooney, *Inequality*, p. 101.

26. Ibid, p. 103.

27. United States Commission on Civil Rights, *Toward an Understanding of Stotts*, Clearinghouse Publication 85, January 1985, p. 2.

28. Ibid.

29. Wygant v. Jackson Board of Education in *United States Law Week*, 54 (45) (May 20, 1986), pp. 4480f.

30. Ibid, p. 4489.

31. David G. Savage, "Landmark Ruling Upholds Job Preferences for Women," *Los Angeles Times*, March 2, 1987, pp. 10, 22.

32. Ibid, p. 22. See also "Caveats Reversed in Workplace Equality," Insight, *Washington Times*, April 27, 1987, pp. 8–12.

33. Ibid, "Caveats Reversed."

34. Linda Greenhouse, "Court Bars Plan Set Up to Provide Jobs to Minorities," *New York Times*, January 24, 1989, pp. 1, A12; Sandra Day O'Connor, "Excerpts from Court Opinions in Voiding of Richmond's Contracting Plan," *New York Times*, January 24, 1989, p. A12.

35. Thurgood Marshall, "Excerpts," Ibid., p. A12.

36. Linda Greenhouse, "Signal on Job Rights," *New York Times*, January 25, 1989, pp. 1, A9.

37. Linda Greenhouse, "Court, Ruling 5 to 4, Eases Burden on Employers in Some Bias Suits," *New York Times*, June 6, 1989, pp. 1, A24; "Excerpts from Court Opinions about Job Rights," *New York Times*, June 6, 1989, p. A24.

38. Linda Greenhouse, "Court 5–4, Affirms a Right to Reopen Bias Settlements," *New York Times*, June 13, 1989, p. A7.

39. Ibid.

40. Martin Halstuk, "White Cops' Suit Alleges Bias in S.F. Promotions," *San Francisco Chronicle*, September 26, 1989, p. 1.

41. Ronald Smothers, "Ruling on Firefighters Is Debated in Alabama," *New York Times*, June 14, 1989, p. A18.

42. Susan Rasky, "Rights Groups Work on Measure to Reverse Court's Bias Rulings," *New York Times*, December 30, 1989, p. A11.

43. Ibid.

44. Ibid.

45. Larry Martz, Ann McDaniel, and Bill Turque, "Bush's Pledge: 'I Want to Do the Right Thing,'" *Newsweek*, May 28, 1990, pp. 20, 21.

46. Bob Cohn and Thomas M. DeFrank, "A White House Torpedo," *Newsweek*, April 29, 1991, p. 35.

47. Goldstein and Smith, "Estimated Impact."

48. Burstein, *Discrimination*, p. 148.

49. James P. Smith and Finis Welch, "Affirmative Action and Labor Markets," *Journal of Labor Economics*, 2 (2) (April 1984).

50. Burstein, *Discrimination*, p. 150.

51. Leonard, Working Paper No. 1745.

52. Ibid., p. 10.

53. Ibid., p. 11.

54. Ibid., p. 17.

55. See, for example, a study by Cynthia M. Taeuber and Victor Valdisera, *Women in the American Economy*, Current Population Reports, Special Studies Series P-23, No. 146, U.S. Department of Commerce, Bureau of the Census, p. 23, which focuses on occupations with major employment gains for women and shows that in many of the male-dominated fields, the percentage of women employed rose sharply.

56. Wilkinson, pp. 262–263.

57. The best list of arguments against affirmative action is in Maguire, *A New American Justice*, pp. 31–39.

58. Wilkinson, *From Brown to Bakke*, p. 269.

59. Charles Lawrence III, "The Bakke Case: Are Racial Quotas Defensible?" *Saturday Review*, October 15, 1977, p. 14.

Affirmative Action and Combat Exclusion: Gender Roles in the U.S. Army

Richard D. Hooker, Jr.

Come now, and let us reason together.

ISAIAH 1:18

The issue of women in combat, thought to be resolved by the demise of the Equal Rights Amendment and the conservatism of successive presidential administrations in this decade, is riding the crest of continuously evolving social mores and changing views of sexual politics. Changes in definitions of sex roles and the removal of many traditional barriers to women in the U.S. Army and the other military services ensures that this emotional and confrontational issue will not go away soon.

This article contrasts the Army's affirmative action policy with the exclusion of women from combat roles. Current policies may provide grounds for challenges to the combat exclusion rule, but some evidence suggests that combat readiness and full gender integration may not be fully compatible goals. A reassessment of current policies may be needed to clarify the relationship between the twin priorities of maximum combat readiness and maximum opportunity for women. The answers to these and related questions may profoundly affect not only the long-term nature of military service in the United States, but the civil–military relationship itself.

This is a revised version of an article that appeared in *Parameters*, December 1989, published by the U.S. Army War College. Reprinted with permission.

Captain Richard D. Hooker, Jr., is an instructor in the Social Sciences Department at the US Military Academy.

CURRENT POLICY

Current Army assignment policies for women are based on Title 10 of the U.S. Code, Section 3012, which gives the secretary of the Army the authority to set personnel assignment and utilization policies for all soldiers. Unlike the case of the Navy and the Air Force, there are no statutory restrictions that prohibit the employment of female soldiers in combat. However, in an effort to ensure a measure of consistency with sister services, Army assignment policies parallel those in the rest of the Department of Defense by restricting women from serving in positions requiring routine exposure to direct combat.[1]

Current policies concerning women in the Army are a product of the rapid expansion of women in the force beginning in the early 1970s. Two significant events were primarily responsible. The first was congressional approval of the Equal Rights Amendment (ERA) in March 1972. The second was the end of the draft in 1973, which caused an immediate decline in the number of qualified males joining the force.[2] Although ratification of the ERA ultimately foundered,[3] legislation was passed in 1975 opening the service academies to women, and soon after the Women's Army Corps was disestablished and women were integrated into male promotion lists.[4]

In 1977 the secretary of the Army issued a combat exclusion policy prohibiting assignment of women to the combat arms. Problems were quickly identified, since women in some other specialties often collocated with combat units and were exposed to virtually identical measures of risk:

> The rapid growth of women in the Army took place without adequate planning and analysis. . . . There was no established policy of putting the right soldiers in the right jobs based on physical capacity to meet the job requirements. Also, the Army had not made a thorough analysis of where women should serve on the battlefield.[5]

In May 1981 the Army implemented a temporary leveling off of female accessions at 65,000—the so-called Woman Pause—"to permit a review of policies and programs and to determine the effect that the use of women may have on combat effectiveness and force readiness."[6] A policy review group was established to study these issues. Its report was issued on November 12, 1982, establishing the Direct Combat Probability Coding system that is still in use. Many of the assumptions and conclusions[7] outlined in the 1982 Women in the Army Policy Review continue to guide Army policy today.

U.S. Army policy as of 1989 was that "women will be assigned in all skills and positions except those which, by doctrine, mission, duties of the job, or battlefield location involve the highest probability of direct combat with enemy forces."[8] Direct Combat Probability Coding (DCPC) is the mechanism used to assess and identify those positions closed to women. The DCPC process assigns each position in the Army a ranking from P1 to P7 based on the probability of *routine* engagement in direct combat. Only those positions coded P1 are closed to women. This policy, which is periodically reviewed and updated,[9] is referred to informally as the "combat exclusion" rule. In 1988 the DCPC process was amplified through the "risk rule":

> The risk rule states that *noncombat* units should be open to women unless the risk of exposure to direct combat, hostile fire, or capture is equal to or greater than that experienced by associated *combat* units in the same theater of operations.[10]

At the present time, approximately 750,000 positions in the Total Army[11] can be filled by either sex.[12] Eighty-seven percent of enlisted military occupational specialties (MOSs), 91 percent of warrant officer positions, and 96 percent of officer specialties are open to women.[13] Females make up 11 percent of the active force, filling 11,110 officer positions out of 91,443 overall, 435 warrant officer positions out of 14,971, and 72,389 enlisted positions out of 654,537.[14] Today, women are represented in every career management field except infantry, armor, and special operations.

The promulgation of a unified promotion system has been accompanied since its inception by an affirmative action program designed to compensate for the effects of "past personal and institutional discrimination" which may have operated to the disadvantage of female soldiers. This program encompasses minority as well as female-specific promotion and assignment issues. It is intended to counteract the effects of latent or residual discrimination by ensuring that female soldiers enjoy promotion and assignment potential commensurate with their representation in the force. Board instructions include the following guidance to panel members:

> [Discrimination] may manifest itself in disproportionately lower evaluation reports, assignments of lesser importance or responsibility, etc. Take these factors into consideration in evaluating these [soldiers'] potential to make continued significant contributions to the Army. . . . The goal is to achieve a percentage of minority and female selections not less than the selection rate for the number of [soldiers] in the promotion zone (first time considered category). . . . [P]rior to adjournment, the board must review the extent to which it met this goal and explain reasons for any failure to meet this goal in the report of [soldiers] recommended for promotion.[15]

But what exactly is meant by "affirmative action"? The concept is both an outgrowth of and a response to the civil rights movement of the 1960s. Affirmative action goes well beyond the establishment of equality of opportunity to ensure equality of *result*. In the interest of vigorously moving to correct past injustices, the federal government in general and the armed forces in particular have embraced the *preferment* of insular groups that in the past have suffered from institutional discrimination.[16]

As a group, women in the Army have enjoyed greater promotion success than men for almost a decade.[17] Individually, some less well qualified candidates have inevitably been selected for promotion and command—an unavoidable price, perhaps, of a necessary and just commitment to the achievement of parity, but one with unpleasant side effects just the same. It is this phenomenon that gives rise to the charge of reverse discrimination, most keenly felt by individuals who believe they possess equal or superior qualifications but nevertheless lose out to female or minority peers for promotion or command selection. Although personnel managers avoid using the term *quota* in favor of *goal* or *objective*, board results consistently confirm that promotion rates for women meet or exceed the targets set by the Department of the Army.[18] At least from an institutional perspective, the Army has lived up to its promise to provide equal promotion opportunities for women by implementing an aggressive and comprehensive affirmative action agenda.

Affirmative action has generated a momentum all its own. While some advocates are critical of policies that inhibit career opportunities for women in *any* way, expansion of career fields and access to previously closed opportunities and positions in the last decade has been impressive by any standard. Few Western military establishments come close to matching the level of participation of American women in the armed forces, as the figures cited above demonstrate. Pressures continue to build, nevertheless, for realization of a gender-neutral Army in the near future.

JUDICIAL INTERVENTION

The courts have led the way in recasting traditional approaches to employment of women in the Army. Case law that arose in the 1970s in the areas of equal protection and gender discrimination provided much of the language and rationale later used to advance the cause of expanded participation for women in the military. It was only in 1971 that the Supreme Court for the first time invalidated a state law on grounds of sex discrimination.[19] In this early phase, gender discrimination cases employed a relatively lenient standard of review. A "rationality" test was made to determine whether the statute in question had been applied in an "arbitrary or irrational" manner. If a reasonable relationship could be demonstrated between a state interest and the statute intended to effect it, intervention by the federal courts was unlikely.

> The two sexes are not fungible. . . . [I]t is only the "invidious discrimination" or the classification which is "patently arbitrary [and] utterly lacking in rational justification" which is barred by either the "due process" or "equal protection" clauses.[20]

In *Frontiero v. Richardson*,[21] a landmark 8–1 ruling with implications that ranged far outside its immediate military compass, the Supreme Court invalidated federal statutes allowing married Air Force males to draw quarters allowances for their wives but requiring service females to prove dependency on the part of their husbands. Although the Court in *Frontiero* narrowly avoided granting "suspect" classification to gender discrimination cases (which would have justified the highest and most searching review[22]), the legal status of military women as equal partners to their male counterparts was firmly established.

Frontiero was quickly followed in 1974 by a series of class action suits filed in California challenging all-male policies at the service academies.[23] Charging sex discrimination and denial of equal protection of the laws by preventing access for women to training, educational and career opportunities in the military, the plaintiffs (the aspiring candidates were joined in the action by their congressmen) sued to open the naval and air force academies to women the following year.[24] The case was decided against the plaintiffs in the U.S. District Court for the District of Columbia in June 1974, but moved on appeal to the U.S. Circuit Court of Appeals.

The appellate court moved slowly, probably in the knowledge that legislation was brewing in the Congress that could decide the issue without embroiling the courts in such a heavily political matter. Despite Department of Defense testimony strongly opposing the proposed legislation,[25] resolutions in the House and Senate calling for open admission to the academies passed easily. On October 8, 1975, President Ford signed Public Law 94-106, mooting the legal challenges still pending in the courts. The following July, women for the first time joined the entering classes at the air force, naval, and military academies.

As if to further demonstrate its commitment to the principles of affirmative action for women in the military, the Court in 1975 upheld a federal statute that allowed female naval officers twice passed over for promotion to remain on active duty through the thirteenth year of service. Male officers under the same conditions were involuntarily released from service following the second nonselection for promotion.[26] Although patently establishing a different standard for women in the Navy, the Court felt strongly that servicewomen were operating under reduced opportunities for promotion and that judicial intervention was needed to correct what it saw as inherently biased personnel policies.

The mid-1970s saw the Court move toward a more stringent standard of review with *Craig v. Boren*.[27] Though the case did not arise in a military context (at issue were Oklahoma statutes governing legal drinking ages for 3.2 beer), *Craig* raised the threshold of acceptable government action in gender-related cases by requiring the government to prove a *substantial* relationship to an *important* state interest to justify a gender classification—a much more difficult and exacting task for legislators and policymakers.[28] Henceforth, a *reasonable* connection between means and ends would not suffice. Court deference to congressional and presidential autonomy in areas relating to the military began to decline. Throughout this period and in the years since, federal courts in a series of decisions continued to broaden the rights of women in the military, often setting aside (though not completely abandoning) the traditional deference to Congress and the Executive Branch in areas of military policy.[29]

In *Crawford v. Cushman*[30] the courts held that substantive constitutional claims against the military were justifiable and struck down mandatory discharge regulations for pregnancy. *Owens et al. v. Brown*[31] eliminated blanket restrictions against sea duty for women in the Navy. In *Dillard v. Brown et al.*[32] challenges to regulations governing sole parents in the service were ruled reviewable by the courts. And as recently as 1986, the courts in *Hill v. Berkman et al.* asserted the right of the judiciary to exercise "jurisdiction to review the classification of a position as combat or combat-supported."[33] Where earlier government claims that pregnancy, sole parent status, and other similar factors degraded readiness had been accepted as "rational," the courts now moved boldly to substitute their own judgment in determining the effects of gender-related phenomena on military efficiency.

Against this backdrop, *Rostker v. Goldberg*[34] surfaced in the federal courts. The case involved a fourteenth Amendment equal protection challenge to Selective Service legislation exempting females from registration for the draft. Originally introduced in 1968 by males opposed to the draft, the issue had been rejected by the courts eleven times.[35] Goldberg's challenge had languished in the courts since 1973 owing to the end of the draft and draft registration in the Ford administration, only to be resurrected by Carter's call for registration. On July 18, 1980, the Third U.S. Circuit Court of Appeals accepted Goldberg's arguments and invalidated federal draft registration, scheduled to begin days later. However, the court did not order the government to amend its registration policy to include women as a remedy. Instead, it ordered cancellation of registration for both sexes![36]

Rostker quickly moved to the Supreme Court following an injunction blocking the lower court's ruling. Some felt that the creation of a gender-neutral military establishment was imminent. One Carter official testified before the Congress that he saw no more difference between men and women in terms of military service than he did between blue-eyed and brown-eyed people.[37]

Drawing back from the precipice opening before it, the Court accepted the contention of the Congress that female registration was unnecessary as long as the purpose of the draft was to create a pool of combatants:

> [Congress] determined that any future draft . . . would be characterized by a need for combat troops. [The] purpose of registration, therefore, was to prepare for a draft of *combat troops*. Women as a group, however, are not eligible for combat.[38]

Citing Congress's greater expertise in matters of national defense as well as the government's compelling interest in raising and supporting armies, the Supreme Court ruled against the plaintiffs in upholding the constitutionality of female exemption from registration and the draft. At this critical juncture, deference to Congress returned as a guide to judicial resolution of a crucial and controversial civil–military issue.

How can we interpret these seemingly contradictory signals from the courts? A steady succession of court victories has validated the transfer of private-sector women's rights into the military sphere. Many barriers long thought to be relevant to the efficiency and readiness of the armed forces have fallen or are under increasingly heavy challenge through direct or indirect judicial intervention.[39] For the fundamental issues of direct participation of women in combat and registration and conscription of women, the courts have continued to defer to the legislative and executive branches as the ultimate guardians of the war-making power. Yet even here the courts have asserted their right to review and, ultimately, to intervene.

NORMATIVE APPROACHES

Few issues in the areas of civil rights and civil–military relations are as value-laden or as controversial as those involving the role of women in the armed forces. Advocates on both sides find it difficult to address these issues calmly and without emotion. Nevertheless, objectivity and balance are needed to maintain an appropriate perspective on this most difficult of issues. What are the dominant arguments defining the continuum of debate on gender roles in the U.S. Army and in the military as a whole?

Proponents of a gender-neutral military establishment envision the participation of women in all phases of military life, to include membership in and command of "combat" organizations such as maneuver battalions and brigades, naval warships, and fighter and bomber squadrons. They rely heavily on legal arguments borrowed from the civil rights and feminist movements to attack gender distinctions as inherently discriminatory or violative of fundamental constitutional guarantees of equal protection and due process. One central tenet is lack of opportunity for promotion to the highest grades, traditionally reserved for officers possessing combat specialties. Another is a declining pool of eligible male volunteers, which can be offset by recruiting larger numbers of females into previously closed specialties.

Because expanded roles for women in the military have been accompanied by defensive weapons training as well as doctrinal requirements for transient exposure in forward areas, it is often argued that traditional distinctions between combat and noncombat or combat support roles have become blurred or are no longer meaningful. Technological advances in nuclear and conventional weaponry, accompanied by a proliferation of rear area threats, buttress this claim. Integrated military training in precommissioning schools, in officer and enlisted initial entry or basic courses, and in many service schools is often cited as proof that no practical distinctions exist between male and female performance in basic combat tasks.

Although these individuals and organizations do not always claim to represent the views of the majority of women in the United States, they insist that the right of *individual* women to pursue fulfilling and rewarding careers in the military cannot be abridged by "traditional" views of sexual roles that overstate sex differences and devalue female strengths and capabilities. Differences in physical capacity or behavior patterns are believed to be largely irrelevant or distorted by bias in the structure of test instruments or interpretation of test data.[40] Sexual issues[41] that do not lend themselves easily to this interpretation can be solved, it is argued, by the application of better, more equitable leadership and training programs.[42] Finally, advocates for gender neutrality in the military posit an irrebuttable presumption that opposition to their views is proof of sexual bias.[43] Thus, they can frequently seize the moral high ground and force their opponents to respond reactively and defensively.

It is important to note that this perspective is not confined to fringe elements or to small but vocal groups operating on the periphery of the policymaking apparatus. Many women (and not a few men) in each service support a more gender-neutral approach, a point of view that tends to dominate service literature on the subject.[44] Their views enjoy widespread currency and support in the academic, media, and legal communities. This movement is no mere exercise in advocacy. It represents a powerful and broad-based constituency with considerable prospects for eventual implementation of its views.

Opponents of combat roles for women focus on two essential themes. The first is the effect on readiness and efficiency of sexually integrated combat units and the impact of a female presence in the "fighting" components. The second is the social impact of female mass casualties which would surely follow commitment of a fully integrated military force to combat under modern conditions.[45]

For "traditionalists," the argument that physical, psychological, or social/cultural differences are irrelevant to military efficiency is risible. They cite medical evidence that documents male advantages in upper body strength, cardiovascular capacity, lean muscle mass, and leg strength to demonstrate significant differences in physical capacity.[46] Physiological research suggesting a higher incidence of injury in training for women augments this thesis.[47] Emphasis on the *aggregate* effect of women in the force is stressed, for while the physical capacity of individual females may equal or exceed that of the male mean, they are sparsely represented among the population. Reduced physical capacity, primarily a factor in tasks requiring heavy lifting or stamina, is predictable when females are compared to males according to this view.

For this school, psychological, social, and cultural factors are inextricably embedded in the physical differences between the sexes. They are much harder to quantify, but it is argued that their influence is nonetheless profound. While sexual roles have been greatly redefined in the last twenty-five years, sexual role differentiation remains central to our way of life. Combat exclusion proponents insist that sexual behavior traits, whether genetic (inherited) or environmental (learned), cannot be wished away. Their potential impact on the performance of combat units must be factored into the equation.

Crime statistics are often used to demonstrate that female participation in violent crime is dwarfed by that of males—implying much higher levels of aggression for men. Biomedical and genetic research supports the hypothesis that sex-role characteristics are by no means purely environmental or social/cultural products.[48] These and other studies are believed to complement what is perhaps the most strongly held normative assumption of all: that in the aggregate, females lack the aggressiveness and psychological resistance to combat-generated stress of males and are therefore less suited for the rigors and demands of extended combat.

An important factor, not to be overlooked according to advocates of more traditional roles for female soldiers, is the effect of female presence on the fragile psychological basis that is the foundation of cohesion and esprit in traditionally all-male combat units. Thus it is argued that sexual integration of these units, even with females screened for physical capacity, would destroy or impair fighting efficiency by introducing elements such as protectiveness, sexual attraction, social role inversion, and leader–follower conflict based on gender stereotypes, among others.[49]

While this assumption is dismissed by combat exclusion opponents as sexist, or at most curable with good leadership and proper training, it is frequently asserted by combat veterans familiar with the unique psychological stresses and demands of the battlefield.[50] They insist that the psychological "chemistry" of combat units is regulated and defined by adherence to and reinforcement of the traditional sex roles of warrior and protector. To dilute this crucial but delicate balance by adding females merely to promote feminist values of full equality—values that do not reflect the aspirations of women as a group—would destroy the sexual identity that lies at the root of the combat ethos.

OBSERVATIONS

Affirmative action in its broadest sense commits the armed forces to policies that ultimately collide with the combat exclusion rule. Because no official attempt is made to articulate the basis for excluding women from combat beyond vague references to "the implied will of Congress," it is difficult from an institutional perspective to mount a reasoned defense against those who move for full sexual integration of the military. Indeed, evolving policies on women in the Army already embrace most of the arguments of those who advocate a gender-neutral force.

For example, current policy does not restrict females from any career field or position because of physical requirements. Although the 1982 policy review recommended "matching the soldier to the job" on a gender-neutral basis using physical demands analysis during medical screening, such testing is conducted on an "advisory" basis only—leaving final determination of acceptability to recruiters already pressed to fill recruiting quotas.[51]

> [Physical capacity] testing is done at the MEPS (Military Entrance and Processing Station) and we don't even get involved. The same test is given regardless of the MOS . . . [and] in two years I've never had a recommendation for a rejection yet. The bottom line is, if they have the minimum smarts and can pass the physical, I sign them up. That's what I get paid for.[52]

In 1976 the General Accounting Office (GAD) notified Congress of emerging concerns that women were being assigned to positions "without regard to their ability to satisfy the specialties' strength, stamina, and operational requirements."[53] Company-grade commanders of integrated units report identical problems in the force today—thirteen years later:[54]

> Although I had upwards of seventy women in my unit I could not employ many in the MOSs they held due to their inability to perform the heavy physical tasks required. So I used them in headquarters or administrative jobs. . . . Complaining to higher headquarters wasn't really an option. These things were considered "leadership" problems.[55]

Assignment of female soldiers without regard to their physical ability to do the job can only degrade unit readiness and damage both self-esteem and successful integration of the female soldiers affected.

Current policy also admits of no potential impact on readiness or efficiency because of other gender-related factors. Of nineteen areas identified as possible areas of concern, only pregnancy made the cut as a female-specific issue. The rest, which included fraternization, assignment and management of military couples, sole parenting, sexual harassment, professional development, attrition and retention, and privacy and field hygiene issues, among others, were classified as "institutional" matters and referred to appropriate Army staff agencies for resolution.[56] In short, they were dismissed as having little relevance to the formulation of overarching policies governing utilization of women in the Army.

It would be unfair as well as inaccurate to say that all of these factors pose insurmountable problems that cannot be coped with in many, if not most, unit environments. It is just as inaccurate, however, to say that they are irrelevant to combat readiness and efficiency. Perhaps no bright line exists to show where fairness and equity should give way to prudence and necessity. Still, the question must be asked—and, more important, answered.

WOMEN IN COMBAT REVISITED: LESSONS FROM THE GULF WAR

Just as Operation Just Cause, the Panama invasion, generated intense debate on the subject of women in combat, so, too, has Operation Desert Storm revived and intensified political activity surrounding this contentious issue. What exactly did we learn from the Desert Storm experience, and how should it affect policies regarding the role of women in the military?

In broad terms, existing policies in place at the time seemed to work well. Women deployed alongside their male counterparts and performed their assigned duties well. Women served in all military occupational specialties except those relating to direct combat. Some women, such as female transport helicopter pilots and air crew, ground radar specialists, and truck drivers, came under fire or served in close proximity to the enemy. A very small number were injured or killed in training or operational incidents, and one was captured. None, however, participated in direct armed combat with the enemy.

Some problems were identified that caused concerns for military commanders. The number of women who could not deploy to the combat theater because of medical problems, pregnancy or sole parent responsibilities was significantly higher than that of men. Units continued to experience the same incidence of pregnancy for female service members in the combat theater as in stateside, peacetime conditions—despite rigorous sanctions, strict segregation of sleeping accommodations, and confinement to unit areas. These women were evacuated to the United States. In some cases, military couples were required to deploy to the Gulf simultaneously on short notice, causing severe family disruption and the extended absence of both parents.

Advocates for the elimination of all remaining combat exclusions for women cited the Desert Storm experience as proof that the time is now ripe for total integration of women throughout the force. Opponents point out that, while existing policies were apparently validated (although some adjustments based on lessons learned may be in order), the case for women in direct ground combat roles is no stronger than before. The strong showing of women in combat support roles reinforced the viability of widespread use of women in the military, but Desert Storm provided no opportunity to test, for example, the public's readiness to accept large numbers of female fatalities or amputees or its willingness to sanction involuntary conscription of women into direct combat roles— an inevitable corollary to the elimination of combat exclusion policies.

What happens next? As this is written, Congress apparently intends to permit (though not require) women to serve as combat pilots in attack aircraft, and the Senate has voted to allow women to serve in maneuver combat roles on a test basis. Two outcomes from the Gulf War are possible. One is that the experience of women serving in the Gulf has created a political momentum for mandatory use of women in direct combat. The other is that the immediate postwar euphoria, which is stimulating such intense activity on the issue, will subside. Time will tell which it will be, and which will best serve the real, but not always complementary, interests of equity and security.

SUMMARY

In the military as elsewhere, resolution of competing claims involving constitutionally protected rights is an exercise in line-drawing. Here the first imperative for any armed force—the maximum possible level of combat readiness and efficiency—stands in potential conflict with bona fide institutional desires for equal opportunity. Evolving policies have predictably attempted to define these twin imperatives as mutually supportive, not mutually exclusive. Since the end of the Vietnam War, the U.S. Army has repeatedly demonstrated its commitment to the fullest possible range of opportunities for women in the force. Yet nagging contradictions persist.

If, for example, it is the implied will of Congress that women not serve in direct combat, then doctrinal proliferation of females in forward areas[57] in the absence of a clear delineation between combat roles and support roles confuses the issue. Congress and the courts may find it impossible to sustain what may *appear* to be an increasingly artificial distinction. Risk of death or capture is, after all, a function of position on the battlefield as well as unit mission.

Despite judicial support for ever-broadening female participation in the military, a healthy deference to the leading role of the executive and legislative in military matters still exists. By dismissing most gender-related factors as irrelevant to military efficiency, defense policymakers have reduced the arguments against total gender neutrality to one: popular opinion. As the record shows, popular opinion often carries little weight with federal judges concerned to protect individual freedom and opportunity. There must be substance to the combat exclusion rule or it will surely fall.

The organizational structure of military units is highly flexible and can adapt to many of the changes that necessarily accompany the expansion of women in the Army. This should not be confused with a priori assumptions equating equal opportunity with gender-irrelevancy in terms of battlefield performance. The price of error, however well-intentioned, could be fatal.[58]

Expanded opportunities for women have enhanced the quality of the service, binding it closer to the lives of the people and aspirations of the society it serves. The contributions and professional dedication of female soldiers serving throughout the force now make sex-based distinctions in many areas unsustainable. Many barriers have fallen, revealed as discriminatory obstacles without a rational basis. To the extent that sexual integration and overall combat efficiency are found to be in harmony, there can be little excuse for restricting female participation.

Sexual differentiation nevertheless remains a fact of life. The differences between men and women can be muted, compensated for, and even exploited to enhance military performance—up to a point. It is dangerous to assume, however, that physiological, psychological, cultural, and social distinctions rooted in gender are meaningless on the battlefield.

There is a substantive and important difference between those units whose primary purpose is direct, sustained ground combat and those that support them. In combat, ground maneuver units will continue to suffer the heaviest casualties, place the heaviest demands on the physical abilities of soldiers, and endure the highest levels of psychological trauma and stress. At the sharp end of the force, sexual differentiation may matter very much indeed. The combat exclusion rule reflects this basic premise as a matter of policy. Without a clear articulation of its basis in logic and fact, a task of important and immediate consequence, a gender-neutral Army could be imminent.

NOTES

1. Army policies are, however, more liberal in permitting women to serve in combat zones and forward areas of the battlefield. Information paper provided by representatives of the Human Resources Division, Office of the Deputy Chief of Staff for Personnel, Headquarters, Department of the Army, March 10, 1989, hereinafter cited as "HRD/ODC-SPER."

2. In the decade of the 1970s the number of women in the U.S. military increased by 350 percent. Jean Yarbrough, "The Feminist Mistake: Sexual Equality and the Decline of the American Military," *Policy Review* (Summer 1985), p. 48.

3. Despite a congressional extension of the ratification deadline, the amendment fell three states short of ratification. See Jo Freeman, "Women and Public Policy: An Overview," in Ellen Boneparth (Ed.), *Women, Power and Policy*, (New York: Pergamon, 1982), p. 55.

4. Jeanne Holm, *Women in the Military* (Nevato, Calif, Presidio Press, 1982), p. 276.

5. Discussion paper, "Assimilation of Women in the Army: Problems and Lessons Learned," February 17, 1988, HRD/ODCSPER.

6. HQDA Letter 616-81-1, Office of the Adjutant General, Subject: "Women in the Army Policy Review," dated May 11, 1981.

7. A significant exception is the Review Group's recommendation that "all soldiers [be] matched to their job through demonstrated physical capability at least equivalent to that required of the job" through gender-neutral physical demand analysis (also known as MEPSCAT) administered at the reception station. See U.S. Department of the Army, *Women in the Army Policy Review*, ODCSPER, November 12, 1982, pp. 5–6 (hereinafter cited as *WITA Policy Review*). MEPS-CAT evaluation is conducted as an "advisory" exercise only. In practice it is not used solely to deny a recruit entrance into a career management field for which he or she is otherwise fully qualified.

8. Ibid.

9. The latest such review, a secretary of defense–directed study of women in the military released in January 1988, approved the opening of a further 11,138 positions to both male and female soldiers on a gender-neutral basis. Tom O'Brien, "New Jobs Open to Women," *Soldiers*, February 1989, p. 10.

10. Emphasis in the original. *Report of the Secretary of Defense to the Congress on the 1990/1991 Biennial Budget* (Washington: U.S. Government Printing Office, January 9, 1989), p. 104.

11. "Total Force" includes the Army Reserve and National Guard units and positions as well as the active force.

12. O'Brien, "New Jobs," p. 10.

13. Ibid.

14. Data provided by Major Karen Habitzreuther, Women in the Army Policy Action Officer, HRD/OD-CSPER, September 29, 1989.

15. Representative sample of guidance for Army promotion boards, provided by representatives of Promotions Branch, U.S. Total Army Personnel Command (PERSCOM), ODCSPER, March 1989.

16. Henry J. Abraham, *Freedom and the Court*, 5th ed. (Oxford, Oxford University Press, 1988), p. 517.

17. Carolyn H. Becraft, "Personnel Puzzle," *U.S. Naval Institute Proceedings*, April 1989, p. 44.

18. Female representation in grades above 07 remains very limited because of the dominance of the combat arms at those levels and because expansion of female soldiers throughout the rest of the force is still a relatively recent phenomenon.

19. *Reed v. Reed*, 404 U.S. 71 (1971).

20. *Gutierrez v. Laird*, 346 F. Supp. 289 (1972).

21. 411 U.S. 677 (1973).

22. To date, suspect classification remains solely reserved for cases involving alienage or race. In practical terms, governmental action imposing important distinctions between identifiable groups can be "fatally" compromised by the heightened standard of judicial review applied to suspect classifications. See Gerald Gunther, *Individual Rights in Constitutional Law*, 4th ed. (Mineola, NY: Foundation Press, 1985), p. 254.

23. *Edwards et al. v. Schlesinger*, 377 F. Supp. 1091 (1974) and *Waldie et al. v. Schlesinger*, 377 F. Supp. 1091 (1974).

24. Albert P. Clark, "Women at the Service Academies and Combat Leadership," *Strategic Review*, 5 (Fall 1977), p. 66.

25. A high percentage of academy graduates were commissioned into naval warfare specialties, combat flying positions, and maneuver combat arms closed to women. Clark, "Women at the Service Academies," p. 67.

26. *Schlesinger v. Ballard*, 419 U.S. 498 (1975).

27. 429 U.S. 190 (1976).

28. Abraham, *Freedom and the Court*, p. 507.

29. See Yarbrough, "The Feminist Mistake," p. 48.

30. 531 F. 2d 1114 (1976).

31. 455 F. Supp. 291 (1978).

32. 625 F. 2d 316 (1981).

33. 635 F. Supp 1228 (1986).

34. 453 U.S. 57 (1981).

35. Holm, p. 373.

36. Registration had been revived as part of the government's reaction to the invasion of Afghanistan and was to begin in a matter of days. Interestingly, the Carter administration had vigorously opposed congressional initiatives to resurrect registration only the year before. Holm, *Women in the Military*, p. 348.

37. Yarbrough, p. 49.

38. Emphasis in the original. Mr. Justice Rehnquist writing for the majority, cited in Gunther, *Individual Rights*, p. 321.

39. In some cases policies have been changed through statute or by executive decree in anticipation of their eventual invalidation by the courts. Previous restrictive policies in areas such as pregnancy, fraternization, sole parenting, commissioning programs,

promotion and retention, assignment, and service benefits have felt the impact, directly or indirectly, of judicial reach.

40. "We question the validity of much of the research on women conducted by the military. We believe there is a clear bias against women. . . . The assumption was made that women cannot withstand stress, are not ready for awesome responsibility, and that they cause problems. Can an institution with these biases be trusted to do objective research?" (Carol C. Parr, National Organization for Women, speaking in testimony before the Subcommittee on Priorities and Economy in Government, Joint Economic Committee, Congress of the United States, September 1, 1977.)

41. Such as higher incidence of training injuries, for example.

42. "The Army must objectively analyze female capabilities . . . and avoid irrelevant comparisons with male soldiers. I strongly believe that healthy women properly led, trained, equipped, and motivated are capable of filling any Army position, including those from which they are presently excluded." (Robert L. Nabors, "Women in the Army: Do They Measure Up?" *Military Review*, 62 (October 1982), 60).

43. One such example is James Webb, former secretary of the Navy and author of a controversial article based on his personal experiences in ground combat and critical of expanded roles for women in combat units. In the wake of controversy following publication of the article, Webb was quickly fired from the faculty of the U.S. Naval Academy. See James H. Webb, "Women Can't Fight," *Washingtonian*, Spring 1979.

44. This is not, however, to say that most males in the armed forces support combat roles for women. For examples of military literature sympathetic to combat roles for women see Barry J. Coyle, "Women on the Front Lines," *U.S. Naval Institute Proceedings*, April 1989, pp. 37–40, and Michael A. Andrews, "Women in Combat?" *Military Review*, 59 (July 1979), pp. 28–34.

45. It is true that under current policy many female casualties would be incurred in a mid-or high-intensity conflict. Modern estimates continue to project, however, that just as in World War II, Korea, and Vietnam, the overwhelming majority of casualties would be sustained in the combat arms, specifically in the ground maneuver arms of infantry and armor/cavalry. The difference in potential impact on society between the two scenarios is highly significant and should not be viewed as one and the same.

46. The 1982 *WITA* study reported the following measurements of median physical capacity for women as compared to men: leg extensor strength—65 percent; upper body strength—58 percent; trunk flexor strength—68 percent; aerobic capacity—78 percent;

lean body mass—75 percent. See *WITA Policy Review*, p. 2–15.

47. One study reported a 54 percent incidence of injury sustained by females in an eight-week basic training cycle, with an average training loss of thirteen days. See Dennis M. Kowal, "Nature and Causes of Injuries in Women Resulting from an Endurance Training Program," *The American Journal of Sports Medicine*, 8 (4) (1980), pp. 265–268.

48. In virtually all societies where statistics are kept, male participation in violent crime exceeds that of females on the order of 9:1. Sex-role differentiation is reflected in differences in brain configuration between the sexes in all mammals (including humans), while laboratory experimentation confirms that artificial variation in hormone levels produces profound behavioral changes in "normal" sexual and social behavior. "The Sexual Brain," *Science Journal*, Public Broadcasting Service, April 13, 1989.

49. The point here is not so much whether concepts such as sex-role identification or protectiveness are legitimate. It is whether they predominate in the society from which soldiers are drawn. Clearly this appears to be so. To eliminate such behavioral distinctions, particularly in the compressed training cycles common in wartime, would appear to be a truly daunting task—particularly if they have physiological and psychochemical determinants as well as strictly social ones.

50. See Webb, *Women Can't Fight*.

51. Telephone interview with then-Captain Karen Habitzreuther (see n. 14), April 5, 1989.

52. Interview with USAREC (U.S. Army Recruiting Command) company commander, April 13, 1989.

53. GAO Report FPCD-76-26, "Job Opportunities for Women in the Military; Progress and Problems," cited in *WITA Policy Review*, pp. 1–6.

54. Interview with a recent commander of a 280-member logistics unit in the United States.

55. Interview with a company-grade logistics commander.

56. *WITA Policy Review*, pp. 1–14.

57. While female pilots cannot be assigned to attack helicopter units, they may, for example, fly troops forward of friendly lines in assault helicopters such as the UH-60 Blackhawk (Habitzreuther interview, April 5, 1989).

58. It is difficult to see how unrestricted female participation in the military can be reconciled with current laws regarding conscription. In a national crisis it would be hard to argue that women should be exempted from involuntary combat service if they were already serving on a volunteer basis, without granting males the same legal protections.

8

WOMEN ACTIVISTS: ATTITUDES, TACTICS, AND CHANGE

We have thus explored the issue of women in politics. We began with a theoretical component; moved to political attitudes, voting, and elections; looked at women and government; and continued with an analysis of women and national policy. We began with theory and conclude this volume with practice. In our concluding chapter, we look at three essays that concern women who have gone beyond merely reading about politics to becoming involved in some aspect of the political process.

The editor's essay explores Virginia Foster Durr's contributions to the civil rights movement in the Deep South, using the theoretical framework of leadership as outlined by James MacGregor Burns. Ms. Durr worked behind the scenes for many years in efforts to eliminate the poll tax and bring about the right to vote for all Americans. She also supported the civil rights movement by giving aid and encouragement to many civil rights activists, including Rosa Parks and the Montgomery, Alabama, bus boycotters. Ms. Durr worked as her husband's legal secretary in support of many civil and human rights cases. She further opened her home in Montgomery, Alabama to many civil rights workers who traveled to and from Alabama, and provided them with room, board, and other support. Individuals who stayed in the Durr home included the Kennedys, Tom Hayden, and C. Vann Woodward.

We then move from an analysis of one woman's activism to a look at leaders of anti–nuclear weapons groups in the United States and Great Britain. Glen Sussman examines the extent to which gender-based differences exist among political actors involved in a salient contemporary issue—nuclear weapons. Sussman uses survey data gathered from anti-nuclear weapons activists in the two countries to compare political attitudes and policy preferences. He also analyzes participation levels by these political activists—looking at both conventional and unconventional political actions. His findings are then discussed against the backdrop of the so-called gender gap which has received much publicity in recent political literature.

The final article is a study of two anarchist feminist groups. There are many approaches to the study of organizations, in both the private sector and the public sphere. But the study of specific women's groups at the grass-roots level is still an area that has not been fully explored. We do know that the women's consciousness-raising groups of the 1960s and early 1970s represented attempts to build alternative organizations.

In her essay, Kathleen P. Iannello identifies a modified consensual structure in which routine decisions are made by a few and critical decisions are made by the entire group membership. Other important characteristics of these model organizations include the following: (1) recognition of ability or expertise rather than rank or position, (2) the notion of power as the ability to accomplish or achieve goals (as opposed to the idea of power as domination), and (3) clarity of goals, which are arrived at through a consensual process. Let us further examine this grassroots approach to the study of organizations.

Virginia Foster Durr:
An Analysis of One Woman's
Contributions to the Civil Rights
Movement in the South

Lois Lovelace Duke

INTRODUCTION

Scholars have long acknowledged that the records do not always adequately show the significant contributions made by reformers responsible for progressive and social change in our society. Even when many of these individuals are identified, it is not uncommon for the documented accounts to list accomplishments superficially, for example, historical data may be cited to refer to achievements that are stated in a mere sentence or two.

Even when many leaders who work for political and social change are referenced in the literature the role of women has generally been overlooked by research scholars.[1] James MacGregor Burns notes that "This leadership bias persists despite the political influence of the likes of Eleanor Roosevelt, Golda Meir, Indira Gandhi, or Margaret Thatcher."[2] Susan Carroll notes that, even when women have appeared in leadership positions, their role frequently has been portrayed as insignificant, whereas the leadership function of their male counterparts is not only well documented, but accepted as natural.[3]

This study explores the significant contributions made by Virginia Foster Durr in bringing about social change far beyond that reflected in the available literature. Ms. Durr worked behind the scenes for many years in efforts to eliminate the poll tax and bring about the right to vote for all Americans. She also supported the civil rights movement in the South, giving support and encouragement to many civil rights activists, including Ms. Rosa Parks and the Montgomery, Alabama, bus boycotters. She worked to advance the social and

Lois Lovelace Duke is an associate professor of Political Science at Clemson University.

This article originally appeared in *Current World Leaders*, Vol. 34, No. 6, December 1991. Reprinted with permission.

civil rights of all individuals, particularly blacks in the Deep South. This study assesses Ms. Durr's political activism in an attempt to gain a better and more comprehensive understanding of her contributions to society, in general, and her accomplishments for U.S. Blacks, specifically.

In retrospect, scholars reflect that the civil rights movement could never have occurred without the leadership of dedicated persons who were willing to risk personal safety, chastisement by other members of Southern society, and many other sacrifices. The leaders of the movement had experienced a level of consciousness raising such that their actions supported the cause and served to mobilize the actions of others. This interaction between leaders and followers has been theoretically defined by Burns as representing transactional and/or transforming leadership.[4]

In order to understand more fully the accomplishments and contributions of Virginia Foster Durr, we shall extend Burns's concepts of leadership to the appeals made by Ms. Durr, and others like her, to those who followed. Consequently, Burns's theoretical framework will provide insight into the motivation of these dedicated leaders who contributed to the civil rights movement.

Burns argues that leadership involves making something happen that would not otherwise take place.[5] He further stipulates that leadership is not to be equated with coercive power. Instead, leadership must mobilize while power coerces. And, in order to mobilize, the leader must be cognizant of the followers' needs and goals—goals that represent the values and the motivation—the wants and needs, the aspirations and expectations of both leaders and followers. Leadership thus has less to do with power as domination than with power as enablement.[6]

For Burns, enablement occurs when motivation is joined with purpose. According to Burns, purpose is an "absolutely central value,"[7] and "all leadership is goal-oriented."[8] Motive and intent are essential elements in political behavior, people respond to purpose, and leaders must clarify choices for potential followers.[9]

In the flow of events, leadership is a creative and independent force, one that works through holding out the promise of purpose to potential followers.[10] Coercion is thus only one form of power. Power is also exercised when purpose motivates people to act in concert instead of going their separate ways. In Burns's words, "purpose and power are commingled."[11] Burns contrasts leadership with coercion because he sees politics as more than a strategic struggle between contending interests.

Burns's theory emphasizes leader–follower interaction. He remarks that "the most powerful influences consist of deeply human relationships in which two or more persons engage with one another."[12] Burns explains that people learn "by shared experiences and interacting motivations."[13] Therefore, leadership can and does serve as a catalyst for a compelling cause and an inspired body of followers. Leadership involves the activation of followers and their resources so as "to realize goals independently or mutually held by both leaders and followers." This mobilization occurs by arousing, engaging, and satisfying the motives of followers.[14]

Burns argues that transactional leadership entails modal values—means or procedures that enable transactions to occur that otherwise might not take place. As he observes with regard to "the classic seat of transactional leadership"—legislative bodies: "Leadership is necessary for the initiating, monitoring, and assured completing of transactions, for settling disputes, and for storing up political credits and debits for later settlement."[15] Burns regards transactional leadership as the most common form of leader–follower interaction.[16]

According to Burns, transforming leadership, though more complex, is more potent. The transforming leader recognizes and exploits an existing need or demand of a potential follower. But beyond that, the transforming leader looks for potential motives in followers, seeks to satisfy higher needs, and engages the full person of the follower.[17] Burns's concept of transforming leadership characterizes mobilization as transcending "the claims of the multiplicity of everyday wants and needs and expectations, to respond to the higher levels of moral development, and to relate leadership behavior—its roles, choices, style, commitments—to a set of reasoned, relatively explicit, conscious values."[18]

Full mobilization involves two simultaneous "transformations"—one within the individual from self-involvement to public involvement and the other among individuals as they reshape their particular and disparate goals into a shared social purpose. Scattered efforts give way to a unified effort, and, as Burns sees it, individuals put more of themselves into a higher purpose than they do into an ordinary, everyday purpose.

In setting forth Burns's concept of leadership, this research frames the contributions made by Ms. Virginia Foster Durr within the theoretical components of Burns's theory. Ms. Durr is one of many "invisible decision makers" who worked quietly behind the scenes to transform society. As Burns observed, "heroic, transcending, transforming leadership excites the previously bored and apathetic; it recreates a political connection with the alienated; it reaches even to the wants and needs of the anomic and shapes their motivation."[19] Ms. Durr made such a contribution to the civil rights movement.

CONTRIBUTIONS

Ms. Durr has been an activist and civil rights worker most of her adult life. She has made significant contributions to the advancement of all civil liberties to include the following:

1. As a young woman in Birmingham, she conceived and organized two major projects to relieve Depression-era suffering: She talked local dairies into donating milk for distribution to the poor instead of pouring the milk not sold into gutters, and she planned free concerts in the city auditorium using the local firemen's and policemen's bands.

2. Later, after moving to Washington, D.C., she became an activist in the movement to do away with the poll tax. She later led this effort as vice-chair of the National Committee to Abolish the Poll Tax.

3. After returning to Alabama to live in 1951, she worked as her husband's legal secretary in support of many civil and human rights cases. She further opened her home (providing room, board, and other support) to many civil rights workers who traveled to and from Montgomery, Alabama.

EARLY LIFE

Virginia Foster Durr is the daughter of the former Anne Patterson and Dr. Sterling Foster, a Presbyterian minister. She was born shortly after the turn of the century and reared in Birmingham, Alabama. Virginia was exposed to social and literary circles characteristic of the well-established upper socioeconomic milieu in the South. Her sister, Josephine, who later married Hugo Black, attended Sweet Briar College in Virginia.

Ms. Durr was sent to a finishing school in New York and attended the National Cathedral School in Washington, D.C. She attended Wellesley College for two years, but because of family finances had to return to Birmingham. Even though the family experienced financial difficulties about this time, Ms. Durr spent a year making her debut into Birmingham's society.[20] Ms. Durr then secured a job at the county bar association's law library working for $25.00 per month. She later moved up to the position of law librarian, which paid $150.00 per month.[21]

Ms. Durr describes her growing-up years as a time in which she was encouraged to be attractive, to have a lot of beaus, and to get married.[22] She expressed the sentiment that she could "only become involved in social and political issues after she was safely married."[23]

Ms. Durr met Clifford Judson Durr, her future husband, at church. She describes a terrible pressure by her family to get married. After a year's courtship, Virginia and Clifford were married in 1926. Clifford had been a Rhodes scholar and head of a fraternity at the University of Alabama. At the time of the marriage he was affiliated with a corporate law firm in Birmingham.[24]

Ms. Durr describes her first years as a newlywed in Birmingham as a period in which she was active in the Junior League, in the church, and in a bridge club.[25] By the early 1930s, however, people started losing their jobs in Birmingham. She explains how as more and more individuals became unemployed, there were more and more beggars coming to the doors for food and handouts.[26]

Ms. Durr reports that it was at about this point in her life that she sensed what was really going on in her social environment. She describes how the poverty of the Depression years made her keenly aware of social and economic injustices within U.S. society. She relates how her level of consciousness was raised to the point that she felt she must take action. And she further describes how she knew that, in turn, she must persuade others to follow her. Burns describes this purposeful awakening of individuals such that changes can be made in the political, social, cultural, and economic environment. Thus, when the leader sees that change must and should be made, he or she convinces others to follow. Ms. Durr did this.

She convinced the Junior League to sponsor a project to provide milk that would be donated to the people instead of being thrown out. She worked diligently to convince the local dairies to cooperate with the project; initially they were concerned with the fear that people would not buy milk when they knew they could get it free. Later, Ms. Durr coordinated free band concerts and sing-alongs for the entire community, using the local firemen's and policemen's band. She describes this period as one in which many families had nothing, not even ten cents for a movie.[27]

MOVE TO WASHINGTON, D.C.

The Durrs moved to Washington, D.C., in 1933 when Cliff took a job as corporate lawyer with the Reconstruction Finance Corporation.[28] He later was affiliated with the Federal Communications Commission. Roosevelt had taken office in March 1933 and they arrived in Washington in April 1933. The Durrs resided in Washington for sixteen years; it was during this period that Ms. Durr's social awareness and concern for the betterment of her fellow Americans developed fully.

She cites three major influences on both her and her husband during their Washington years. The first was the Roosevelts and the Roosevelt administration. As she describes the move to Seminary Hill in Washington (so named because this area of Washington was where the Virginia Episcopal Theological Seminary was located), "We were the first New Dealers on Seminary Hill. . . ."[29] Second, she worked as a volunteer for the Women's Division of the National Democratic Committee. During this time, the committee was involved in projects that included the 50/50 plan (a move to make all Democratic committees 50 percent women and 50 percent men) and a study of the South that revealed the poll tax to be a major problem.[30] Finally, Ms. Durr met important members of the Washington community through her sister, Josephine, and Josephine's husband, Hugo Black, who introduced the Durrs to prominent politicians and other members of the government in Washington.

THE SOUTHERN CONFERENCE FOR HUMAN WELFARE
AND THE POLL TAX

Ms. Durr participated in the first meeting of the Southern Conference for Human Welfare in Birmingham, Alabama, in November 1938. She attended as a delegate from the Women's Division of the Democratic National Committee. The meeting grew from an informal group of young Southerners who were working in the New Deal, called the Southern Policy Committee. This informal group met for dinner once or twice a month to discuss the South. During these meetings, a formal report had been developed looking into the agricultural, industrial, and economic problems of the South. (The report was titled "Report on Economic Conditions of the South."[31])

Ms. Durr describes the Southern Conference as being attended by about 1,500 individuals from all over the South; the group was made up of blacks and whites, labor union people, and New Dealers. She relates how Bull Connor, Birmingham's chief of police, warned the participants that they would be jailed if they broke the segregation laws of Alabama. As a result, the workshops of the conference were held in various churches and other community buildings in order to comply with the segregation laws.[32]

It was during this time that Ms. Durr experienced some of the challenges faced by the transforming leaders described by Burns. She had to confront the animosity and hostility of the Deep South's traditional regional and cultural milieu. This society was a segregated one based on the color of one's skin. She bravely attended these meetings in predominantly black churches and community buildings, knowing that her actions spoke for an integrated society in a part of the country known for its distinctively segregated culture. She knew she was working for social change frowned on by most of the white community. However, Ms. Durr was looking beyond her everyday wants and needs to a higher level of what was morally right. She did not sacrifice her goals for the sake of expediency. Burns describes this in his concept of the transforming leader.

The conference conducted meetings on rights for the U.S. laborer. There were resolutions presented on the right to organize and to get credit, and on the elimination of the poll tax. The main concern, however, according to Ms. Durr, was the right to vote. She said, "I concentrated on the poll tax and on getting women to vote."[33] After returning to Washington, Ms. Durr continued her efforts to eliminate the poll tax, including working as a volunteer on a special committee established to eliminate the poll tax. The committee put out newsletters, supported legislation, and lobbied on the Hill.[34]

In August 1941 the special committee to eliminate the poll tax was separated from the Southern Conference and established as the National Committee to Abolish the Poll Tax. Support for the new committee came from the labor unions, the NAACP (National Association for the Advancement of Colored People), the Negro Elks, church organizations, and the Council of Negro Women (referred to by Ms. Durr as Mrs. Mary McLeod Bethune's Organization).[35] Ms. Durr served as vice-chairman of the National Committee to Abolish the Poll Tax and chairman of the Washington Committee of the Southern Conference. As she describes her activities: "In the poll tax fight, we were working to get legislation passed through the Senate and the House to remove the poll tax requirement for federal elections. Congress had the right in federal elections to do away with things like that, we thought. We tried to organize grass-roots support. We sent out letters and newsletters and had meetings and speakers all over the country. The unions and all other organizations that were part of the committee took up the cause. It became a tremendous issue. Though I had a pretty large family by that time, I did some speaking. I lobbied and raised money and went to meetings and just worked and worked. Cliff thought it became an obsession with me. The children would say, 'Oh, poll tax!' "[36]

Ms. Durr relates how Claude Pepper of Florida introduced the bill to abolish the poll tax in the Senate in 1941; he did so year after year. The Committee also got support in the House as far as introducing legislation and getting it through the House. The bill always failed in the Senate, where it was filibustered by Southern senators.[37] As Ms. Durr recounts, "We did make the poll tax a national issue and we did abolish the poll tax for veterans." The poll tax was finally abolished by the Twenty-fourth Amendment to the Constitution in 1964.[38]

The last year the Durrs were in Washington, D.C., Clifford Durr went into private law practice there. One of his first cases was a loyalty oath case that generated a great deal of publicity. The case involved a man from Texas who had been fired because he was found to be disloyal; he allegedly belonged to the Washington Book Store, said to be a Marxist bookshop. Durr had the man reinstated to his job; subsequently, Durr handled other loyalty oath cases. Because of this, Ms. Durr felt the big corporations that might have retained her husband elected not to do so. Ms. Durr supported and assisted her husband during the research and preparation of the briefs in these cases.[39]

RETURN TO ALABAMA

The Durrs returned to Alabama in 1951, and Clifford opened his law practice in Montgomery in 1952. Ms. Durr served as her husband's secretary, and Clifford became involved in a number of civil rights cases representing individuals who had been beaten up in jail or who had been charged exorbitant interest rates on loans. Ms. Durr explained that her husband worked through the head of the NAACP in Montgomery, E. D. Nixon, and Aubrey Williams, who had become the editor of the *Southern Farmer*, in getting referrals.[40]

After their return to Alabama, Ms. Durr participated in a group that decided to integrate two groups of United Church Women. As she explained, previously there had existed two organizations, one black and one white. Even though the white group sponsored black speakers, who would be invited to have lunch with them, the white group had not allowed the black United Church Women to attend the white United Church Women's meetings. A group of the women banded together and formed an integrated prayer group; they always met in black churches. According to Ms. Durr, the church was the first organization to integrate in Montgomery.[41]

The group of church women stayed together until an incident in which a countergroup, whose members were fighting desegregation, took down all of their auto license numbers and published the names, telephone numbers, and addresses of everyone at the church women's meeting in a newspaper. After this, the women began to receive harassing telephone calls. After that, Ms. Durr explained, the group never met.[42] The formal group did not meet on a regular basis in the black churches because many of the members were fearful of possible violent action against them. However, Ms. Durr describes how the women responded. They started meeting in individual homes on a more informal basis with smaller groups of women, both black and white. Ms. Durr led the women as they worked together to alter this long tradition of separating the races. She and her family faced tremendous social pressures as word of her involvement in this movement spread throughout the community.

For example, Ms. Durr describes how her actions brought reproach within her own family circle. Even though she had the support of Clifford, her husband, and her immediate family, other relatives did not support her overt actions on behalf of civil rights for the blacks. She relates how she was ostracized in Montgomery's social circles, how her children were treated cruelly by other children in the community, and how she and her family were snubbed in church and at civic and community events. One has to remember that this was a Deep South society in which even the water fountains were labeled "white" and "black" in order to comprehend fully the strength of this leader as she fought for societal change amid criticism and harassment from many of her friends and peers. Burns describes such persistence, courage, and sacrifice on the part of transforming leaders.

BUS BOYCOTT IN MONTGOMERY

Ms. Durr reported that by the time of the bus boycott in Montgomery in December 1955, she had come to know many of the black leaders in Montgomery. Dr. Martin Luther King, Jr., had just taken over as minister of the Dexter Avenue Baptist Church. Ms. Durr had also met Mrs. Coretta Scott King at a black funeral; during 1954 and 1955, Ms. Durr developed a close relationship with Ms. Rosa Parks. Ms. Durr had recommended Ms. Parks for a scholarship to attend the integrated Highlander Folk School in Tennessee for two weeks.[43]

Ms. Parks resumed her job as a seamstress at the Montgomery Fair when she returned from the Highlander School. According to Ms. Durr, Ms. Parks's working environment consisted of a small, overheated room in which the heavy pressing irons added to the heat. Also, according to Ms. Durr, Ms. Parks suffered from chronic bursitis in her shoulder.[44]

Ms. Durr recounts how Ms. Parks had complained to her many times about the city buses. According to various accounts, a company rule dictated that fares must be deposited in the coin box beside the driver, but that black passengers had to board the bus from the rear. Therefore, blacks had to get on in the front of the bus, drop their coins in the designated box, and then get off in order to reboard the bus from the rear. According to Ms. Durr, Ms. Parks had complained many times that bus drivers would wait until blacks had paid their money and left the bus to run around to the rear door to get in, then slam both front and rear doors and drive off.[45]

On the evening of Thursday, December 1, 1955, Ms. Parks was riding the bus home. She was sitting in the row of seats directly behind the section marked "Whites Only." Accounts reveal that on runs where few, if any, white passengers got on, blacks could sit anywhere, except in the first ten seats. However, if more whites boarded the bus, drivers would order the blacks to move and give up their seats.[46]

On this particular afternoon, Ms. Durr recounted how Ms. Parks described how the bus was full of blacks when some more white men boarded. The bus driver turned around and said, "Nigger, move back." But Ms. Durr stated that Ms. Parks refused to move. The bus driver called the police, and Ms. Parks was arrested and taken to jail.[47]

Ms. Durr stated that when she and her husband arrived home from the law offices at about 5 p.m. that day, they received a call from E. D. Nixon, the NAACP leader, who informed them of Ms. Parks's arrest. When Nixon had attempted to find out Ms. Parks's status, the police would tell him nothing. Mr. Durr contacted the jail and was told that Ms. Parks had been booked on the city segregation ordinance. Nixon came up with the bail money and the Durrs went with him to post the bond.[48]

The Durrs later met with Ms. Parks, her husband, her mother, and Nixon. It was decided that Ms. Parks would challenge the bus ordinance on constitutional grounds; Fred Gray, a lawyer for the NAACP in Montgomery, would represent her. Clifford Durr agreed to assist, but the lawyer of record would be Gray.[49]

In the meantime, the black community united. Nixon contacted the Reverend Ralph Abernathy of the First Baptist Church and the Reverend H. H. Hubbard, head of the Baptist Ministerial Alliance. Others included in the initial planning of the collective action were the Reverend L. Boy Bennett, head of the Interdenominational Ministerial Alliance, which included all the other Protestant groups; Ms. Jo Ann Robinson, a member of the Alabama State College faculty and head of the Women's Political Council, a black civic group; and Dr. Martin Luther King, Jr. The group met at the Dexter Avenue Baptist Church and agreed on a one-day bus boycott. Dr. King volunteered the use of his church mimeograph machine to make 7,000 copies of the following flyer for citywide distribution. It read:

> Don't ride the bus to work, to town, to school, or any place Monday, December 5. Another Negro woman has been arrested and put in jail because she refused to give up her bus seat. Don't ride the buses to work, to town, to school, or anywhere on Monday. If you work, take a cab, or share a ride, or walk. Come to a mass meeting, Monday, at 7:00 P.M., at the Holt Street Baptist Church for further instruction.[50]

The one-day bus boycott was successful. The black community further united at the subsequent meeting, agreed on the name Montgomery Improvement Association (MIA) for a permanent organization, and elected Dr. King president. The organization used volunteer drivers and car pools, created a network of dispatch and pick-up points throughout Montgomery, encouraged those who could to walk, and accepted donations in the form of money, new vehicles, and offers from the white community for various means of support and assistance.[51] Ms. Durr relates how she and her husband developed close relationships with the black community during this time. She describes how she had come to realize that she could not really form true personal friendships in the black community unless she interacted on an equal basis with Ms. Parks and other black women, many of whom were servants in white homes. Thus, Ms. Durr worked not only with the black leaders but also with a multitude of the black followers in this movement. She recounts how, as the boycott dragged on, she struggled to keep the movement and the motivation alive. She recalls also that it was during this period that elements of both the black and white communities began to work together as the boycott continued. Thus, she inspired and led individuals across the two cultures. She communicated with those around her and led them to commit to the movement as well. She remembers how she encouraged those who became discouraged, both black and white, and how she worked to mobilize support across all levels of the community as the struggle for equality of human rights stretched before her.

The boycott lasted one year (December 1955–December 1956). During this period, more than 100 leaders of the MIA were arrested and found guilty of an old law that prohibited boycotts; the home of Dr. King was damaged by a bomb; and attempts were made to frighten the volunteer drivers using such tactics as petty harassment, being given tickets for speeding, and in some cases even being arrested and taken to jail. Also during this time, the black community brought action through the courts questioning the constitutionality of the segregation laws and the bus ordinance.

However, Ms. Durr never waivered in her fight to bring about social change. She always kept the ultimate and original goal of racial equality at the forefront as she continued to motivate those black people in the community who were abused and mistreated. She recalls how she and her husband reached the point where they were lending their many black clients money rather than making it themselves. She remembers the enormous number of mostly black clients who could never pay them anything. Ultimately, the state and local laws requiring segregation on buses were declared unconstitutional by the Supreme Court.[52]

SUPPORT TO THE CIVIL RIGHTS MOVEMENT IN THE 1960s

During the 1960s the Durrs befriended and supported the Freedom Riders, representatives of the Student Nonviolent Coordinating Committee (SNCC), and other sympathizers with the civil rights cause. Their home was always open to individuals traveling to and from Montgomery and en route to Mississippi in support of the movement. Individuals who stayed in the Durr home included the Kennedys, Tom Hayden, Jim Forman, and Dr. Horace Mann Bond, Julian Bond's father. Ms. Durr recounts one particular incident during the summer of 1965, prior to the Selma march. She recalled: "I came home and soon began to get telephone calls from people who were coming to Selma. The first call was from C. Vann Woodward, the Sterling professor at Yale. He and Lou Pollak, dean of the Yale Law School, were coming down and they wanted to know if they could get a bed at our house. Tom Emerson's son, who was also a great friend of ours and a professor at Yale Law School, stayed at our house. Then

John Beecher called from San Francisco. He was with a San Francisco paper that engaged him to cover the Selma march. Carl Braden came in with an Episcopal preacher, and then a group called the Brotherhood came down. The house was just full of people, absolutely full. I spent all my time making coffee and frying bacon and eggs for them."[53]

LATER YEARS

Ms. Durr still resides in Montgomery, Alabama, in a modest home on Cloverdale Drive. She has long since moved from the family's larger, old antebellum-style home at the corner of Felder and Court, located in what is called Montgomery's Garden District. She remains quite active for a woman her age. As she reflects on her role in the massive social change that has taken place during her lifetime, she expresses only two regrets: (1) the fact that more blacks are not as politically active today as she would like; for example, she referred to the low voter turnout among the black community and how she hopes this will be reversed; (2) her regret that, because of the many hardships inflicted on the Durr family as a result of her and her husband's stance on the civil rights issues, all of her three daughters dislike the city of Montgomery; all the girls attended school out of the South.[54]

Ms. Durr sums up her reaction to the role she played in the civil rights movement in this manner: "I never even thought about what role I was playing at the time. I was just trying to get the next thing done, whether it meant getting out a brief or getting the next meal on, just trying to get through the next thing that had to be done."[55]

DURR'S LEADERSHIP AND CONTRIBUTIONS TO CHANGE

James MacGregor Burns categorized leadership as transactional or transforming.[56] He maintains that transactional leadership occurs when one person takes the initiative in making contact with others for the purpose of an exchange of valued things. Transformational leadership, on the other hand, occurs when one or more persons engage with others in such a way that leaders and followers raise one another to higher levels of motivation and morality.[57]

Burns holds that both forms of leadership can contribute to human purpose. However, he maintains that transformational leadership is more concerned with end values, such as liberty, justice, and equality. He cites grass-roots leaders, such as parents, teachers, and peers, as far more pervasive and widespread in their role as transforming leaders than we generally recognize. He offers as a test of their leadership function their "contribution to change."[58]

Virginia Durr is a grass-roots leader who contributed to social change in this country. As Burns advocates, we need to restore the role of purposeful leadership to theories of history. In so doing, we will be able to look at history from the bottom up and not merely from the top down.[59]

This research points up such a need also. If scholars analyzing great leaders over time focus on those unassuming individuals who worked quietly and diligently at the grass-roots level to bring about progressive change, then not only men but also women will be categorized as the "great ones." Leaders, including Virginia Foster Durr, will then be recognized for the significant contributions they have made and can make on a personal, grass-roots level. Virginia Foster Durr, who was influenced by the Roosevelts, the Kennedys, the Johnsons, and the Kings, is representative of one woman who can and did influence government and the political process.

Ms. Durr had a specific purpose and goal. These were shared with others who had similar goals through interaction and exchange. She worked with other civil rights activists to bring about social, cultural, and political change in the Deep South. As Burns points out, two simultaneous "transformations" occurred in Ms. Durr's life and experiences: one within her as an individual, from self-involvement to public involvement, and the other among individuals as she helped reshape their particular and disparate goals into a shared social purpose. She was willing to make sacrifices then and now as she continues to fight for civil rights causes and equality for all races.

NOTES

1. Susan J. Carroll, "Feminist Scholarship on Political Leadership," in Barbara Kellerman (Ed.), *Leadership: Multidisciplinary Perspectives* (Englewood Cliffs, NJ: Prentice-Hall, 1984), p. 143.

2. James MacGregor Burns, *Leadership* (New York: Harper & Row, 1978), p. 50.

3. Carroll, "Feminist Scholarship," p. 143.

4. Burns, *Leadership*, pp. 18, 23.

5. Burns, *Leadership*; William K. Muir, *Police: Streetcorner Politicians* (Chicago: University of Chicago Press, 1977); Aaron Wildavsky, *The Nursing Father: Moses as a Political Leader* (Tuscaloosa: University of Alabama Press, 1984), p. 188; Clarence N. Stone, "Transactional and Transforming Leadership: A Re-Examination," Paper presented at the annual meeting of the American Political Science Association, September 1990.

6. Paul E. Peterson, *City Limits* (Chicago: University of Chicago Press, 1981), p. 148; Stone, "Transactional and Transforming Leadership," p. 2.

7. Burns, *Leadership*, p. 13; Stone, "Transactional and Transforming Leadership," p. 3.

8. Burns, *Leadership*, p. 455; Stone, "Transactional and Transforming Leadership," p. 3.

9. Burns, *Leadership* pp. 12, 119, 437; Stone, "Transactional and Transforming Leadership," p. 3.

10. Burns, *Leadership*, p. 20; Bryan D. Jones, "Causation, Constraint, and Political Leadership," in Bryan D. Jones (Ed.), *Leadership and Politics* (Lawrence: University Press of Kansas, 1989), pp. vii, 9–10; Jameson W. Doig and Erwin C. Hargrove, " 'Leadership' and Policy Analysis," in Jameson W. Doig and Erwin C. Hargrove (Eds.), *Leadership and Innovation* (Baltimore: Johns Hopkins University Press, 1987); Stone, "Transactional and Transforming Leadership," p. 3.

11. Burns, *Leadership*, p. 438; Stone, "Transactional and Transforming Leadership," p. 3.

12. Burns, *Leadership*, p. 11; Stone, "Transactional and Transforming Leadership," p. 3.

13. Burns, *Leadership*, p. 448; Stone, "Transactional and Transforming Leadership," p. 4.

14. Burns, *Leadership*, pp. 425, 18; and Stone, "Transactional and Transforming Leadership," p. 5.

15. Burns, *Leadership*, p. 344; Stone, "Transactional and Transforming Leadership," p. 6.

16. Burns, *Leadership*, p. 4; Stone, "Transactional and Transforming Leadership," p. 6.

17. Ibid.

18. Burns, *Leadership*, p. 46; Stone, "Transactional and Transforming Leadership," p. 7.

19. Burns, *Leadership*, p. 137; Stone, "Transactional and Transforming Leadership," p. 8.

20. Information for this paper comes primarily from personal interviews with Ms. Durr and from Hollinger F. Barnard, Ed. *Outside the Magic Circle*, (Tuscaloosa: University of Alabama Press, 1985).

21. Barnard, *Magic Circle*, pp. 3, 65.

22. Ibid., p. 66.
23. Ibid.
24. Ibid., p. 20.
25. Ibid., p. 74.
26. Ibid.
27. Ibid., p. 77.
28. Ibid., p. 85.
29. Ibid., pp. 89–94.
30. Ibid., pp. 101–115.
31. Ibid., pp. 116–134.
32. Ibid.
33. Ibid.
34. Ibid.
35. Ibid., pp. 152–170.
36. Ibid., p. 157.
37. Ibid., pp. 152–170.
38. Ibid., p. 162.
39. Ibid., pp. 221–229.
40. Ibid., pp. 241–253.
41. Ibid., pp. 241–253.
42. Ibid.

43. Ibid., pp. 274–288.
44. Ibid., pp. 278–279.
45. Ibid.; Janet Stevenson, *The Montgomery Bus Boycott, December 1955* (Franklin Watts, 1971), p. 1.
46. Stevenson, *Bus Boycott*, p. 1.
47. Barnard, *Magic Circle*, p. 279.
48. Ibid., pp. 279–280; Stevenson, *Bus Boycott*, pp. 1–8.
49. Barnard, *Magic Circle*, p. 281.
50. Stevenson, *Bus Boycott*, pp. 11–15.
51. Ibid., pp. 19–31.
52. Ibid., pp. 32–61; Barnard, *Magic Circle*, pp. 281–288.
53. Barnard, *Magic Circle*, pp. 289–325.
54. From personal interviews with Ms. Durr on January 23 and January 30, 1988.
55. Barnard, *Magic Circle*, p. 337.
56. Burns, *Leadership*, pp. 4, 19–20.
57. Ibid.
58. Ibid., pp. 426–427.
59. Ibid., p. 442.

American and British Trends in Gender Differences: A Comparison of Anti–Nuclear Weapons Activists

Glen Sussman

During the past few years, scholarly attention has been directed at the "gender gap" in political attitudes and behavior. Indeed, in the United States as well as other postindustrial democracies, women have become increasingly politicized.[1] Recent studies of the United States and Great Britain, for instance, have indicated that gender-based political differences are in evidence in both countries, particularly in the domain of war and peace issues[2] and in the participatory sphere.[3] During the past decade, a popular movement opposed to nuclear weapons as a deterrent emerged to challenge political authorities. Given the fact that women have played an integral part in this movement,[4] it is important to assess women's role in public policy issues.

Research into gender and politics demands scholarly attention as particular issues become salient to women and men who may decide to engage in political action. As Marianne Githens argues:

> What is now needed is a new research agenda focusing on what women define as political and what they see as appropriate political behavior within this context. To achieve this, methodological tools, frameworks and concepts to pursue such an investigation must be developed.[5]

Most studies of political orientations and behavior tend to focus on *mass* level data. Further investigation is needed at the *activist* level to explore the extent to which gender-based differences are in evidence. As citizens in postindustrial democracies are being confronted with complex policy issues, it is important to

Glen Sussman is an assistant professor of political science at Morningside College.

This project was supported by a Summer Research Fellowship from University House, The University of Iowa, and the Office of Grant and Research Development, Washington State University.

examine the characteristics of an attentive group of women and men who engage in the process of organization and mobilization of public opinion.

The study reported here is based on two data sets gathered in a mail survey of leaders of anti–nuclear weapons groups conducted in the United States and Great Britain in 1984–1985.[6] A variety of directories and handbooks were employed to gather lists of organizations and their leaders.[7] The design of the survey and its implementation employed the guidelines set forth in Dillman's "total design method,"[8] resulting in a response rate of 63 percent for U.S. activists ($n = 263$) and 65 percent for British activists ($n = 305$). The breakdown of respondents by gender was similar in both national settings—namely, 40 percent women and 60 percent men.

The first objective of the study centered on selected aspects of the nuclear issue. Two sets of measures were employed to tap political orientations and policy preferences. The first set of survey items concerned orientations toward (1) the United States and the Soviet Union and (2) the role of détente and deterrence as means to reduce the risk of nuclear war. Second, respondents were asked to select from a list of policy options the "most desirable" and the "most feasible" means to move toward denuclearization.

The second objective of this study was an investigation into participation levels. Activist women and men were first asked to indicate their level of conventional participation. Conventional participation is defined as "activities that are accepted by the dominant political culture."[9] This measure employed commonly accepted survey items. The level of participation for each conventional act was determined by a four-point scale anchored at one end by (1) "often" and at the other end by (4) "never."

In order to assess the political resources available for access into the policy process, the Barnes and Kaase[10] multi-item survey scale was used to determine the level of approval for unconventional types of political action. Eight unconventional political acts were measured using a five-point scale anchored at one end by (1) "strongly approve" and at the other end by (5) "strongly disapprove."

GENDER CONSIDERATIONS, POLITICAL ORIENTATIONS, AND POLICY PREFERENCES

Threat Perception

Gender-based political orientations for three categories in the nuclear domain—(1) threat perception, (2) nuclear arms race, and (3) means to reduce nuclear risk—are presented in Table 1. In the first case, addressing threat perception, it is the United States that elicits gender-based concern. Gender differences among U.S. activists vary depending on the *source* of the perceived threat. Compared with their male counterparts (6 percent), activist American women (17 percent) viewed the United States as posing a potential military threat to eastern Europe, an area long considered important to Soviet security interests. Moreover,

Table 1 Comparison of Political Orientations by Gender (in percentages)

Political Orientation	AMERICAN ACTIVISTS		BRITISH ACTIVISTS	
	Men	Women	Men	Women
Threat perception				
United States threat to eastern Europe:				
Likely	5.6	16.5	21.5	30.2
Not likely	94.4	83.5	78.5	69.8
	100.0	100.0	100.0	100.0
Soviet threat to western Europe:				
Likely	4.4	6.8	1.8	6.5
Not likely	95.6	93.2	98.2	93.5
	100.0	100.0	100.0	100.0
Nuclear arms race				
United States perpetuates the nuclear arms race:				
Agree	94.7	94.6	95.0	94.7
Unsure	5.3	5.4	1.6	2.5
Disagree	0.0	0.0	3.4	2.6
	100.0	100.0	100.0	100.0
Soviet Union perpetuates the nuclear arms race:				
Agree	79.3	73.6	75.0	60.5
Unsure	11.8	19.1	12.5	31.6
Disagree	8.9	7.3	12.5	7.9
	100.0	100.0	100.0	100.0
Means to reduce risk				
Détente reduces nuclear risk:				
Agree	82.6	72.1	85.0	78.1
Unsure	7.2	13.5	7.5	6.6
Disagree	10.2	14.4	7.5	15.3
	100.0	100.0	100.0	100.0
Deterrence reduces nuclear risk:				
Agree	24.5	10.2	5.7	11.4
Unsure	11.9	12.0	13.9	3.5
Disagree	63.6	77.8	80.4	85.1
	100.0	100.0	100.0	100.0

female activists in the United States are decidedly more concerned about U.S. actions in Europe than about Soviet actions. Cross-nationally, gender variation is also evident among British activists. Almost one-third of the activist British women demonstrate distrust of the United States, compared with about one out of five of their male counterparts. As far as the Soviet threat to western Europe is concerned, gender differences among both U.S. and British activists are negligible.

Nuclear Arms Race

Government officials, activists, and citizens have debated the issue concerning which of the two superpowers—the United States or the Soviet Union—is more responsible for perpetuating the nuclear arms race. In addressing the extent to which the United States and the Soviet Union are viewed by U.S. and British activists as responsible for encouraging nuclear competition, we find cross-national similarities and differences. Among both U.S. and British activists, little differentiation in political views is evident with regard to the United States. In the case of the Soviet Union, however, gender-based variation is manifested. Both activist U.S. and British men demonstrate more concern with the Soviet role in the nuclear arms race than do their female counterparts. Notwithstanding a minor gender difference among U.S. activists, the gap is considerably wider among activist British men, who are clearly more sensitive to Soviet actions than are British women (75 percent to 61 percent, respectively).

Means to Reduce Nuclear Risk

In seeking to reduce tensions and, more important, the likelihood of a nuclear conflict, the United States and Soviet governments have pursued two important policies—namely, détente and deterrence. Détente can be characterized as a means of relaxing tensions between two political actors.[11] Deterrence can be defined as a threat to discourage an opponent from taking military action by demonstrating that the consequences of such behavior outweigh the benefits.[12]

The data presented in Table 1 show that, while activists in two national settings view détente as producing a peaceful environment and reducing the prospects for nuclear conflict, this view is held more strongly by male activists in both countries. Moreover, the American female cohort is conspiciously different regarding this policy initiative. The rate of "don't know" responses among activist American women was twice that of the other three social groups. Perhaps they are less certain of the value of détente, or perhaps they are less informed about the meaning of this particular policy concept.

Nuclear Deterrence

During the last forty years, nuclear deterrence has been at the foundation of Western security. During the 1980s, however, domestic opposition to a nuclear-based deterrent created divisive political relations both within countries and between the governments of North America, western Europe, Australia, and New Zealand. For example, in the United States local communities have declared themselves nuclear-free zones; at the state level, nuclear freeze referenda have passed in several state legislatures.[13] Nationally, nuclear freeze legislation was debated but defeated in the U.S. Congress.[14] In Great Britain, both interparty and intraparty divisions were evident in political party debates as the Labour party in the early to mid-1980s committed itself to unilateral nuclear disarmament—to be implemented in the event Labor gained a majority in the British Parliament.

It is clear that the policy of nuclear deterrence is at the center of public debate. Are gender-based differences in evidence on this most important question?

Given the antinuclear orientation of the survey's respondents, it is not surprising to find that a majority in all four social groups are opposed to nuclear deterrence. Gender differences in Great Britain are small, with women a bit more critical of deterrence than men (85 percent to 80 percent, respectively). However, gender-based variation is more conspicuous among U.S. activists. In fact, when assessing responses on this survey item across all four social groups, U.S. male activists are the anomaly. They are quite distinct compared with both their female counterparts and British activists. Activist American men (25 percent) are twice as likely as activist American women (10 percent) and two to four times as likely as British activists to agree that deterrence reduces the risk of nuclear war. On this particular survey measure, activist American men appear to replicate to some extent the more "aggressive" attitudes on foreign policy and war and peace issues found among men in the U.S. mass public.

Range of Nuclear Policy Options

Public debate over contemporary nuclear politics has produced a range of policy options, including a nuclear freeze, various forms of arms reductions, and elimination of nuclear arms. Given the changing nature of Soviet–American relations under Gorbachev, including the Intermediate Nuclear Forces (INF) treaty among others, nuclear arms control has received renewed attention. How have U.S. and British activists viewed nuclear policy options, and to what degree, if any, do women and men differ? The distribution of the policy preferences of U.S. and British activists is presented in Table 2, which includes responses to both the "most desired" policy option and to what these activists consider to be the "most feasible" to achieve.

Analysis of the four "desirable" policy options reveals distinct gender-based differences among only the U.S. activists. In fact, what is most conspicuous about these policy options is that a similar majority of British men and women prefer the most radical policy—unilateral disarmament—with differences evident only among the three other policy options. As far as the American group is concerned, however, half of the activist women are clearly more in favor of unilateral disarmament, compared with only one-third of the activist men. Taken in conjunction with the results concerning nuclear deterrence, these findings suggest that activist American men are conspicuously different from activist American women and from British activists, male and female.

Moving from what is preferred to what is considered practical to achieve, a noticeable shift in orientation is evident. Notwithstanding preference for more demanding forms of nuclear arms control, U.S. activists, both women and men, are less optimistic about what is realistically attainable. Regardless of gender, a fairly similar majority of U.S. activists see a nuclear freeze as the most feasible goal to be achieved. The most conspicuous pattern regarding these policy options

Table 2 Comparison of Policy Preferences by Gender (in percentages)

MOST DESIRABLE

Policy	AMERICAN ACTIVISTS		BRITISH ACTIVISTS	
	Men	Women	Men	Women
Unilateral disarmament	35.2	49.9	61.4	61.1
50 percent mutual reduction	38.8	28.7	22.8	13.9
10 percent annual mutual reduction	13.3	9.6	13.9	22.2
Freeze at current levels	12.7	11.8	1.9	2.8
	100.0	100.0	100.0	100.0

MOST FEASIBLE

Policy	AMERICAN ACTIVISTS		BRITISH ACTIVISTS	
	Men	Women	Men	Women
Unilateral disarmament	6.5	5.0	19.4	16.2
50 percent mutual reduction	11.5	9.0	13.5	6.3
10 percent annual mutual reduction	25.4	26.0	17.4	10.8
Freeze at current levels	56.6	60.0	49.7	66.7
	100.0	100.0	100.0	100.0

is the gender gap among British activists. Whereas activist British women *desire* unilateral disarmament—a more demanding form of nuclear arms control—67 percent (compared with only 50 percent of the men) indicate that the best that can be achieved is the nuclear freeze—the least demanding policy alternative.

The responses among British women raise the question of their sense of efficacy. Compared with their male counterparts, they appear to be more pessimistic in their appraisal of what goals can be achieved.

A GENDER GAP IN POLITICAL PARTICIPATION?

The impact of gender on political participation in countries where egalitarian norms are emphasized will now be explored. How can activist women and men in the United States and Great Britain be characterized in terms of political participation? Political participation can be divided into conventional and unconventional types of action. Conventional participation assumes many forms, both passive and active. Although men have been more active in the past than women across the range of participation activities, in recent years activism has increased among women. To what extent, if any, do activist women and men differ in this participatory domain?

A quick scan of the data in Table 3 indicates that the participation gap slightly favors activists U.S. women, whereas variation is in evidence among British activists. Among the passive types of conventional participation for U.S. activists, gender-based variation is small but consistent across all four types of participation. Among British activists, the gender gap is manifested by type of activity. Activist British women and men rely on different sources of political information, with men leaning toward the print media and women apt to use the broadcast media. The most striking finding is gender-based variation in voting behavior. Activist British women engage in this participatory mode to a greater extent than their male counterparts.

Conventional participation also includes increasingly demanding forms of political involvement. Once again, activist U.S. women exhibit a higher level of political involvement than men across all four modes of participation. The gender gap in political influence, attendance at political meetings, and political communication is small, but it favors activist women. Moreover, in electoral campaigns, a distinct participatory gap is in evidence. Indeed, women (76 percent) play a very active role compared with men (59 percent), suggesting that they see this mode of political involvement as a means to exert political influence.

Gender-based differences are less explicit for British activists than for American activists. Clearly, activist British women and men show a strong inclination to influence other people. Both are also equally committed to attending political meetings. However, gender-based differences favoring British women emerge in two areas. British women (89 percent) are more likely to contact public officials and are also more likely to campaign for a candidate (42 percent) compared with their male counterparts. Overall, the conventional participatory

Table 3 Comparison of Passive and Active Types of Participation by Gender (in percentages)*

Participation	AMERICAN ACTIVISTS		BRITISH ACTIVISTS	
	Men	Women	Men	Women
Passive				
Read about politics in the newspaper	100.0	100.0	97.2	93.9
Watching political programs on television	83.6	84.7	85.4	88.6
Discuss political affairs	98.2	100.0	100.0	97.4
Vote in political elections	94.8	97.3	87.7	96.5
Active				
Try to influence other people	97.7	99.1	96.1	92.3
Attend political meetings	85.8	88.3	77.5	78.0
Contact public officials	90.7	93.7	79.3	88.6
Campaign for a candidate	59.4	75.7	34.1	42.1

Note:

*Table entries are the percentage participating often or sometimes.

differences favoring activist women found in this study add to contemporary research about increasing female political action among the electorate in the United States[15] and, to a lesser degree, in Great Britain.[16]

Most analyses of levels of political involvement direct attention to conventional modes of behavior. The preceding discussion has examined the degree to which participatory similarities and differences are found among activist women and men in the United States and Great Britain. We now turn to unconventional modes of political behavior to provide a broader picture of the political resources available to influence political authorities.

The relationship between gender and eight types of unconventional political acts is presented in Table 4. These "disruptive" activities may well be employed when disagreement occurs over the public policy issue agenda—specifically, political priorities—in this case, security policy. The findings reported here indicate that, overall, activist U.S. women and men exhibit shared characteristics. As one moves up the unconventional participation scale to more disruptive types of activities, American women and men are fairly similar—except in their attitudes toward petitions, demonstrations, and boycotts. These activities gain more approval among women, whereas men are more inclined to approve of damaging property and other similar types of action.

Among the British group, women and men are fairly similar to their U.S. counterparts as one examines nonelectoral types of political activities. Gender-based differences are most conspicuous on three measures—petitions, blocking traffic, and painting slogans. Women approve of these types of activities more than men do; men were more likely to approve of damaging property. The use of violence is rejected as a viable means of political action by virtually all activists.

Whether or to what extent one approves of or engages in specific types of political action may depend on how effective one considers a particular act—and how committed one is to a public policy goal. Clearly, the legitimacy of certain acts may also be a consideration in order to receive the support of rather than alienate the larger polity.

The results set forth herein suggest that unconventional participatory actions are considered legitimate political resources by activist women and men in two national settings. Approval scores for the unconventional political acts indicate that female activists clearly are not passive citizens but are quite likely to approve of various types of "disruptive" political acts. Moreover, taken in conjunction with the overall level of conventional activism, a more diverse political action repertoire appears to be identified with activist women, particularly in the United States.

SUMMARY

Public policy problems, including nuclear deterrence, are becoming increasingly salient to citizens in postindustrial democracies. On the basis of survey findings, gender differences in nuclear attitudes appear to be more relevant for U.S.

Table 4 Comparison of Approval for Unconventional Participation by Gender (in percentages)

Type of Participation	AMERICAN ACTIVISTS			BRITISH ACTIVISTS	
	Men	Women		Men	Women
Sign petitions:					
Approve	94.2	99.1		88.9	100.0
Unsure	4.1	0.9		5.6	0.0
Disapprove	1.7	0.0		5.5	0.0
	100.0	100.0		100.0	100.0
Lawful demonstrations:					
Approve	97.6	100.0		97.7	100.0
Unsure	1.2	0.0		0.6	0.0
Disapprove	1.2	0.0		1.7	0.0
	100.0	100.0		100.0	100.0
Boycotts:					
Approve	88.7	94.5		83.5	80.6
Unsure	9.5	4.6		11.4	16.7
Disapprove	1.8	0.9		5.1	2.7
	100.0	100.0		100.0	100.0
Occupying buildings:					
Approve	60.4	61.6		66.4	64.0
Unsure	21.6	21.2		17.0	24.3
Disapprove	18.0	17.2		16.6	· 11.7
	100.0	100.0		100.0	100.0
Blocking traffic:					
Approve	62.5	62.7		65.9	77.5
Unsure	17.3	17.3		16.5	18.9
Disapprove	20.2	20.0		17.6	3.6
	100.0	100.0		100.0	100.0
Painting slogans:					
Approve	57.8	57.5		50.0	56.6
Unsure	16.3	18.9		17.6	16.8
Disapprove	25.9	23.6		32.3	26.6
	100.0	100.0		100.0	100.0
Damaging property:					
Approve	16.7	11.1		22.2	10.5
Unsure	14.8	18.5		18.8	22.9
Disapprove	68.5	70.4		59.1	66.6
	100.0	100.0		100.0	100.0
Using violence:					
Approve	1.8	1.8		3.4	0.0
Unsure	5.5	3.6		1.7	2.8
Disapprove	92.7	94.5		94.9	97.2
	100.0	100.0		100.0	100.0

activists than for their British counterparts. Most important are cross-national and gender differences regarding nuclear deterrence and policy preferences to reduce the nuclear threat. Compared with activist women, U.S. men are more likely to see the value of nuclear deterrence and less inclined to support unilateral disarmament—the most far-reaching type of policy option. In contrast, male and female British activists exhibit similar attitudes regarding these issues. Compared to British men, however, activist British women are less inclined to believe that far-reaching arms control measures can be achieved.

In the area of political participation, we have found that gender differences exist in both countries, but more so in the United States. In the United States, the level of participation among activist women is similar to or greater than that of activist men. By contrast, gender differences are less apparent among British activists. Activist British women, however, are conspicuously more participatory than their male counterparts in the areas of electoral politics and several unconventional modes of political action.

The empirical evidence presented here suggests that, in both the United States and Great Britain, gender differences exist among one set of political participants involved in a contemporary public issue. The findings reported here also demonstrate the salience of women's political activism across a variety of participation modes. At least at the *activist* level, the *style* of gender politics may be changing. If the woman of the 1950s was considered passive, our findings confirm the rise of the activist woman of the 1980s. Contemporary and future issues on the public agenda may well reflect women's policy preferences as these are translated into political action. Women may indeed constitute a potentially powerful force for change in postindustrial democracies.

NOTES

1. Carol Mueller (Ed.), *The Politics of the Gender Gap* (Beverly Hills, CA: Sage Publications, 1988); Keith Poole and L. Harmon Zeigler, *Women, Public Opinion and Politics* (New York: Longman, 1985); Susan Welch, "Sex Differences in Political Activity in Britain," *Women and Politics*, 1 (1980), pp. 29–46.

2. Robert Shapiro and Harpreet Mahajan, "Gender Differences in Policy Preferences: A Summary of Trends from the 1960s to the 1980s," *Public Opinion Quarterly*, 50 (1986), pp. 42–61; Pippa Norris, "The Gender Gap in Britain and America," *Parliamentary Affairs*, 38 (1985), pp. 192–201.

3. Joni Lovenduski and Jill Hills (Eds.), *The Politics of the Second Electorate* (London: Routledge & Kegan Paul, 1980), pp. 8–32, 33–51.

4. Werner Kaltefleiter and Robert Pfaltzgraff, *The Peace Movements in Europe and the United States* (New York: St. Martin's Press, 1985), p. 192.

5. Marianne Githens, "The Elusive Paradigm: Gender, Politics and Political Behavior," in Ada Finif-

ter (Ed.), *Political Science: The State of the Discipline*, (Washington, D.C.: American Political Science Association, 1983), p. 492.

6. The author would like to thank Brent Steel, who helped develop the questionnaire, distributed and collected the British surveys, and prepared the British dataset for computer analysis.

7. Melinda Fine and Steven Peter (Eds.), *The American Peace Directory 1984* (Cambridge, MA: Ballinger, 1984); Housmans Diary Group (Ed.), *Housmans Peace Diary 1985* (London: Housmans, 1985); Andrew Wilson, *The Disarmer's Handbook* (New York: Penguin, 1983).

8. Don Dillman, *Mail and Telephone Surveys: The Total Design Method* (New York: Wiley, 1978).

9. Margaret Conway, *Political Participation in the United States* (Washington, DC: Congressional Quarterly, 1985), p. 3.

10. Samuel Barnes and Max Kaase (Eds.), *Political Action* (Beverly Hills, CA: Sage Publications, 1979).

11. John Spanier, *American Foreign Policy since World War II*, 9th ed. (New York: Holt, Rinehart & Winston, 1983), p. 178.

12. Charles Kegley and Eugene Wittkopf, *American Foreign Policy*, 2nd ed. (New York: St. Martin's Press, 1982), p. 89.

13. William Sweet, *The Nuclear Age* (Washington, D.C.: Congressional Quarterly, 1984), p. 220.

14. Douglas Waller, *Congress and the Nuclear Freeze* (Amherst: University of Massachusetts Press, 1987).

15. Sandra Baxter and Marjorie Lansing, *Women and Politics*, rev. ed. (Ann Arbor: University of Michigan Press, 1983).

16. Vicky Randall, *Woman and Politics*, 2nd ed. (Dobbs Ferry, NY: Macmillan Education Ltd., 1987).

A Grassroots Approach to Change:
Anarchist Feminism
and Nonhierarchical Organization

 *Kathleen P. Iannello*

Since the early 1920s, but with particular intensity in the 1970s, the feminist movement has sought to affect public policy toward women in a number of important ways. The approach we are most familiar with and receives the most press coverage and public attention has been that of liberal feminists. The liberal feminist approach to changes in public policy has been aimed mainly at the federal level of U.S. government such as work toward enactment of an Equal Rights Amendment (ERA), a legislative goal yet to be realized, as well as legislation concerned with pay equity, child care and reproductive freedom.

There are other approaches that receive less mention in the news, but work just as hard at changes in public policy with regard to women. All feminists work in some way toward the reduction or elimination of male domination, or patriarchy. However, some feminists argue that the solutions of liberal feminism are not enough. These include anarchist feminists, who lend support to liberal feminist initiatives but in their own actions initiate a bottom-up or grass-roots approach.

Anarchist feminists examine, through a more broadly focused approach, forms of organization that provide unequal access to economic, political, and social resources.[1] They argue that, "power originates in, and is transmitted through" these organizational structures which they define as centralized, hierarchical forms.[2]

Because many organizations are centralized and/or hierarchical, the real issue has less to do with specific forms of power or domination than with the nature of power itself. Therefore, anarchist feminists argue that the primary goal is to eliminate power, even though ". . . power relationships are supported

Kathleen P. Iannello is an Assistant Professor of Political Science at Gettysburg College.

by an ideology which refuses to consider any other alternative to them."[3] Further, they argue that elimination of patriarchy is only a first step toward this goal. "Anarchist feminism works to end all forms of inequality, beginning (but not ending) with patriarchy."[4]

The way to begin this task, they argue, is to build "alternative forms of organization alongside the institutions of the larger society."[5] By alternative forms of organization, they mean groups in which leadership positions are rotated and responsibility is shared among group members. In doing so, they attempt to "eradicate all the structural factors that create and maintain leaders and followers."[6] This is something that must be practiced on a daily basis, they argue, and not put off while waiting for larger social change. "For social anarchists . . . the revolution is a process, not a point in time; and how one lives one's daily life is very important. People don't learn that they can live without leadership elites by accepting socialist ones; they do not end power relationships by creating new ones."[7] Instead, there must be a redefinition of power—a qualitative change. This means a change from *power as domination* to *power as the ability to accomplish or achieve goals*: empowerment.

ANARCHIST FEMINISTS AND POWER

Anarchist feminists believe that:

> Creating political change requires that we set up organizations based on power defined as energy and strength, groups that are structured, not tied to the personality of a single individual, and whose structures do not permit the use of power to dominate others in the group. At the same time, our organizations must be effective in a society in which power is a means of making others do what they do not wish to do.[8]

The women's consciousness-raising groups of the 1960s and early 1970s represent an attempt to build alternative organizations. According to Jo Freeman's account of their experiences, they succeeded in raising consciousness but not in operating in nonhierarchical ways. As Freeman indicates, there was a kind of "tyranny of structurelessness," in that lack of structure gave way to the development of informal leaders—individuals who gained power due to media attention or personal characteristics.[9] Such leaders were not chosen by the group and thus could not be removed by the group. Lack of a leadership process created a kind of tyranny—unaccountable leadership.

In the years since, it appears that some women's groups have come to learn that nonhierarchy does not mean nonstructure. Combining the concept of nonhierarchical *structure* with theories of empowerment, anarchist feminists may be contributing something new to existing theories of organization.

TOWARD A MODIFIED CONSENSUAL MODEL

Anarchist feminists argue that the development of alternative forms of organization as a method of political and social change "can occur only in practice." They argue further:

> While our alternative institutions cannot fully succeed so long as we live in a society based on private profit rather than public good—a society in which work and human development are polar opposites—feminist organizations provide a framework within which to experiment. The organizations we build are an integral part of the process of creating political change and, in the long run, can perhaps serve as proving grounds for new institutions.[10]

Next, we will examine two feminist organizations that have attempted to build and maintain nonhierarchical structure. Both organizations exist in the same small New England city and are similar in size but differ in services performed and explicit goals. They are referred to here by ficticious names: the feminist peace group and the women's health collective.

Methods used to study these organizations were qualitative. Information was gathered through two years of personal observation of organization meetings, including special committee meetings and special projects/events, tape-recorded personal interviews averaging one hour in length of a cross-section of approximately thirty women drawn from both organizations, and the reading and researching of documents related to the history and operation of the organizations.

FEMINIST PEACE GROUP

This organization describes itself as a group of feminist activists working for disarmament and social justice in its immediate community and the world. It is a part of a larger women's peace organization that has branches in nations around the world. The local branch formed in the spring of 1983. They describe themselves as "feminist activists who were seeking a diverse, effective and explicitly feminist women's peace group. . . . [We] embrace feminism as the most effective and comprehensive analysis of our political, economic, social, and military institutions. We see the rule of men over women as the model for other forms of dominance and oppression. And we strive for a radically different society which values cooperation, nonviolence, nurturance and spiritual integrity."[11]

The organization, which has a mailing list of over 100, relies on three categories of members:

1. Active members, who participate in project groups and retreats
2. Supporting members, who attend events and participate in telephone trees
3. Sponsoring members, who provide financial support for projects and actions

The approximately fifteen active members meet once a month; they also divide into a number of project groups, which, they say, "allow us to divide responsibility and to work easily with new people."[12] The project groups offer a way for the organization to involve and assimilate new members. They view the project groups as a way of dealing with a growing membership—the groups allow them to maintain a system of shared decision-making and leadership roles. All group decisions are made through consensus, which means that all members present at meetings must agree or, at least, not object to decisions being made. Meetings are "facilitated" by members on a rotating basis. Both the meeting agenda and the decision about who will facilitate are determined in the first few minutes of every full meeting.

THE WOMEN'S HEALTH COLLECTIVE

This organization describes itself as a "modified collective" numbering approximately fifteen member/workers. The organization's focus is on women's reproductive health. It was formed in 1972 by community members as a nonprofit organization "in response to the need for safe, legal abortion services for . . . women." Its mission statement indicates the goals of the organization as follows:

> To provide high quality, cost-accessible, health care for and by women that includes but is not limited to gynecological and abortion services.
>
> To empower women by informing them medically and politically and by training women health workers.
>
> To be a woman-operated business striving for consensual power-sharing and equality of worker input in major policy decisions.
>
> To have our business structure be seen as a working model for other interested groups.[13]

Over the years of existence, the health collective has gone through two major organizational/structural changes. At the time of its inception, the organization was established with a staff that made decisions about the day-to-day operation of the clinic. There was a separate (outside) board made up of community members, which met with the staff every two weeks to make major policy decisions. As the staff members explain, "This was helpful in the beginning, as a broad range of experience and opinions were needed."[14] By the end of the first two years, however, the board has become what the staff described as a "technical legality," and it was dissolved.

At this point the full staff became the board as well, and all staff members participated in all decision making, according to consensus. The staff/board met weekly at that time and made all routine as well as critical policy decisions, including the hiring of staff and the determination of salaries. At this point in their development, the staff decided that all salaries would be the same for all members. In terms of jobs/tasks, as they explain:

The philosophy of the collectivity involves the idea that each staff member should ideally be trained to do any given task. Most staff members rotate positions of counselor, coordinator and phone counselor. Training programs are arranged for staff to learn more specialized tasks such as lab work, administrative skills and physician assistant skills.

After nearly ten years of operating in this fashion, the health collective once again changed or modified its structure. Members indicate that there were two major reasons for a change:

1. A need to make the "business" of the organization more efficient
2. A need to recognize, through position and salary, the expertise of certain members

The structure that recently developed out of these needs is one in which there are currently three coordinators who have responsibility for areas such as personnel, medical, and business. These tasks have been delegated to them by the full staff. The women in the organization describe how the coordinator positions evolved from the expertise certain women brought with them when they joined the clinic. For instance, one member, who had worked in another medical organization, brought with her knowledge of medical protocol. She eventually became the medical coordinator.

It is also important to note that when expertise is lost through the departure of a member, the position the member held is dissolved. For example, a woman who brought "political and communication" skills to the organization became outreach coordinator. When she left the organization, the outreach coordinator's position was dissolved. Although coordinator positions do not rotate, coordinators do make an effort to share knowledge and information with the rest of the group. Although this new structure brought with it some differentiation as to position and salary, the full staff still makes policy decisions in these areas. The full staff now meets once a month to consider critical policy questions, with routine decisions delegated to coordinators.

FEMINIST MODELS

The Feminist Peace Group

Within the feminist peace group, nearly all of the active membership, as defined earlier, were interviewed. Of these, every individual expressed the commitment to nonhierarchical structure. This group represents the highest degree of ideological commitment or strength of political ideals, and is an interesting model of nonhierarchy. The three groups of members provide a network of communication and support that hinges on each member's ability to contribute to the organization—whether that contribution is simply monetary, communicative, or an investment of time. Within the active group, ability and interest are recognized through the various project groups. An example is a media project called "redirection." This group designed a series of radio ads against the development and sale of war toys. They also developed a follow-up telephone survey to attempt to measure the influence of the ads on the local community. Some of the project groups have been in existence since the beginning of the organization, while new ones have been created and old ones dissolved. The membership of the project groups changes with the shifting interests and abilities of the overall group membership. The organization has also recruited new members simply by sparking interest in the community through specific projects such as the media project described above.

One difficulty for this organization has been related to what they called the "housekeeping" chores, which include collecting member dues, distributing monies raised through grants and other means, keeping the membership list and organization files, and preparing two yearly social/informational public events. In the past, these tasks simply fell to those interested and willing to do them. As member interests and energies have been more focused toward the project groups, however, those falling into this category have numbered fewer. The active membership decided that a project group would be formed to deal with these housekeeping tasks. Members who placed themselves within this group were those who did not want to make a larger time commitment to other project groups. In other words, the development of this group provided active members yet another option of participation that best reflected their abilities at the time. That housekeeping became a problem for this group underscores the fact that every organization has a number of tasks that must be tended to in order to keep the organization functioning. This is important in that some aspect of the organization's operating procedures must speak to this issue. This may be a reason that some collectivist groups fail: they lack the *structure* to deal with basic operating problems or needs.

THE WOMEN'S HEALTH COLLECTIVE

Within the women's health collective, as in the feminist peace group, nearly all workers/members were interviewed. Of these, approximately three-quarters expressed a strong commitment to nonhierarchical structure. Those who did not, however, expressed commitment to working in an entirely female-run business. When asked to explain this response, individuals indicated that they were looking for a female-managed business because they expected to find a supportive work environment, more flexible working hours, and co-workers who really understood the individual's needs both inside and outside the work environment. In short, these individuals listed many of the values behind feminist ideology as described in the work of Gilligan and others.[15] None of these women were opposed to the kind of structure the health collective utilizes. However, some of them were surprised, upon being hired, to find that they would need to learn about consensus decision making in order to work within this group.

As with the feminist peace group, one of the most significant aspects of the women's health collective is the recognition of ability or expertise within the membership. This organization went through more than ten years of experimentation with structure, and is still experimenting. Their development of the coordinator positions reflects this recognition. It can be viewed as a model of organization in which expertise is recognized without the creation of hierarchy. Coordinators are *delegated* responsibility from the entire staff. Yet, they also have a responsibility to educate the remaining staff in a specific area of routine work, such as medical protocol. This is a model of nonhierarchy that demonstrates the concept of empowerment, in that organization members become enriched or gain personal power through the expertise of others. The development of expertise in this organization may be more critical than in the peace group because of the external constraints. The health collective is a business that must deal with external hierarchies of the marketplace and of both the medical and the political world. For them, the development and sharing of expertise may be much more a matter of survival than it is for the peace group, which is a volunteer organization with less specific goals.

UNIQUENESS OF THE STRUCTURE

One of the most significant aspects of these organizations, and the most important finding of this study, is the structure (see Figure 1). This is evident in the way the women of the peace group and those of the health collective make decisions. First, they are keenly aware of the distinction between *critical* and *routine* decisions. Decisions that are critical have the potential for changing the direction of the organization. Those that are routine are important to the operation of the organization on a daily basis but are not likely to raise significant questions about changes in overall policy. Within the literature of organizations, Selznick discusses the distinction between critical and routine decisions.[16] Although it is an important distinction, it certainly is not new. But what is new is the way in which feminists have structured organizations in light of this distinction.

In both the peace group and the health collective, critical decisions are reserved for the entire membership of the organization, and routine decisions are delegated horizontally. For example, in the peace group the project groups make routine decisions. In the health collective it is the coordinators and their respective committees who make decisions about problems they are close to and have information about. It is recognized that routine decisions have the potential for becoming critical. In the event that they do, they are reconsidered by the entire group.

What is unique about the structure of these anarchist groups is that everyone is involved in making critical policy. In hierarchical organizations, only those at the top, with varying degrees of input from lower levels, make critical policy. Additionally, in these anarchist groups, routine decisions are delegated horizontally to those who have an interest in making them. Although such delegation can involve additional responsibility, authority, and expertise, it does not result in a superordinate—subordinate relationship.

In the peace group, some rotation of members according to tasks helps

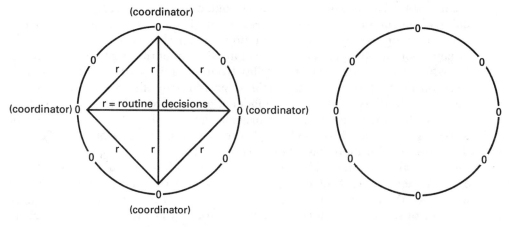

Modified Consensual Organization
Routine decisions are made inside
the circle, critical decisions are
made on the circle.

Consensual Organization
All decisions, critical and
routine, are made on the circle.

Key: 0 represents organization members.
Lines on the circles and within the circle
represent paths of communication within
the organization.

Figure 1 Consensual and Modified Consensual Organization

to ensure that hierarchy does not develop. Because it is a volunteer organization, the peace group can afford the organizational costs involved in retraining members in new areas. By contrast, the health collective decided that it could not afford those costs and therefore relied more on the process of the organization, including trust among members, to avoid the development of hierarchy.

Thus, although the most important defining element of these structures is the reserving of critical decisions for the entire membership and the delegation of routine decisions to the few, other aspects of the internal environment are important to the maintenance of nonhierarchical structure. These aspects are best described by the term *process*, which includes the concepts of consensus, empowerment, and emerging leadership. Without the trust among members that is fostered through consensus decision making and the conscious effort to avoid domination, hierarchy would be difficult to avoid. In this way, the political ideals of the members and the ideological commitment to nonhierarchy are vitally important.

A MODIFIED CONSENSUAL STRUCTURE AND FEMINIST GROUPS

From the study of these anarchist feminist groups, a modified consensual structure has been identified. Again, the most important defining element is the *outward*, not downward, delegation of routine decisions to the few and the reserving of critical decisions for the entire membership. Other important elements of the model include the following:

1. Recognition of ability or expertise rather than rank or position
2. The notion of empowerment as a basis of consensual "process"
3. Clarity of goals, which are arrived at *through* this consensual process.

It was found that a number of organizations like the peace group and the health collective exist throughout the country. These groups have not received the attention that was given to the women's consciousness-raising groups of the 1960s and 1970s.

One important point is that the peace group and the health collective began as simple consensual structures. They have experienced the problems of other consensual structures and moved forward. Further research into groups like these in the United States would enhance the current literature on the women's movement and contribute further to our understanding of political change through grass-roots approaches.

NOTES

1. Lydia Sargent, *Women and Revolution* (Boston: South End Press, 1981), p. 116.

2. Ibid., p. 115.

3. Ibid., p. 116.

4. Ibid., p. 116.

5. Ibid., p. 114.

6. Ibid., p. 116.

7. Ibid., p. 114.

8. Nancy Hartsock, "Staying Alive," in Alison M. Jaggar and Paula S. Rothenberg, *Feminist Frameworks*, (New York: McGraw-Hill, 1984), p. 273.

9. See Jo Freeman, *The Politics of Women's Liberation* (New York: Longman, 1975).

10. Hartsock, "Staying Alive," p. 271.

11. Organization mission statement, Feminist Peace Group, pp. 1–2.

12. Ibid., pp. 1–2.

13. Organization mission statement, Women's Health Collective, p. 1.

14. From a history of the Women's Health Collective.

15. See Carol Gilligan, *In a Different Voice* (Cambridge, MA: Harvard University Press, 1982).

16. Philip Selznick, *Leadership in Administration* (New York: Harper & Row, 1957), p. 56.

FURTHER READING

DECKARD, BARBARA SINCLAIR. *The Women's Movement.* New York: Harper and Row, 1979.

EISENSTEIN, HESTER. *Contemporary Feminist Thought.* Boston: G.K. Hall, 1983.

EISENSTEIN, ZILLAH R. *The Radical Future of Liberal Feminism.* New York: Longman Press, 1981.

EVANS, SARA. *Personal Politics.* New York: Knopf, 1979.

FERGUSON, KATHY E. *The Feminist Case against Bureaucracy.* Philadelphia: Temple University Press, 1984.

FREEMAN, JO. *The Politics of Women's Liberation.* New York: Longman, 1975.

FRIEDAN, BETTY. *The Feminine Mystique.* New York: Dell, 1964.

GILLIGAN, CAROL *In a Different Voice.* Cambridge, MA: Harvard University Press, 1982.

GREENBERG, EDWARD S. *Workplace Democracy.* Ithaca, NY: Cornell University Press, 1986.

HARTSOCK, NANCY. "Political Change: Two Perspectives on Power," *Quest* (Summer 1974).

HARTSOCK, NANCY. "Staying Alive," in Alison M. Jaggar and Paula S. Rothenberg (Eds.), *Feminist Frameworks.* New York: McGraw-Hill, 1984.

LOVE, NANCY. *Dogmas and Dreams.* Chatham, N.J.: Chatham House, 1991.

MARTIN, PATRICIA YANCEY. "Rethinking Feminist Organizations." *Gender & Society* (June 1990).

MILLETT, KATE. *Sexual Politics.* New York: Doubleday, 1970.

ROTHSCHILD, JOYCE and J. ALLEN WHITT. *The Cooperative Workplace.* New York: Cambridge University Press, 1986.

SARGENT, LYDIA. *Women and Revolution.* Boston: South End Press, 1981.

SCOTT, RICHARD W. *Organizations.* Englewood Cliffs, NJ: Prentice-Hall, 1981.

SELZNICK, PHILIP. *Leadership in Administration.* New York: Harper & Row, 1957.

TONG, ROSEMARIE. *Feminist Thought.* Boulder, CO.: Westview Press, 1989.

REFERENCES _____

JAMES DAVID BARBER and BARBARA KELLERMAN (Eds.), *Women Leaders in American Politics* (Englewood Cliffs, NJ: Prentice-Hall, 1986).

LAWRENCE BAUM, *American Courts: Process and Policy*, 2nd ed. (Boston: Houghton Mifflin, 1990).

SANDRA BAXTER and MARJORIE LANSING, *Women and Politics: The Invisible Majority*, rev. ed. (Ann Arbor: University of Michigan Press, 1983).

KAREN BECKWITH, *American Women and Political Participation: The Impacts of Work, Generation, and Feminism* (Westport, CT.: Greenwood Press, 1986).

MARTIN BINKIN and SHIRLEY BACH, *Women and the Military* (Washington, DC: Brookings Institution, 1977).

EARL BLACK and MERLE BLACK, *Politics and Society in the South* (Cambridge, MA: Harvard University Press, 1987).

CAROLINE BLACKWOOD, *On the Perimeter* (New York: Penguin, 1984).

MARTHA BLAXALL and BARBARA REAGAN (Eds.), *Women and the Workplace* (Chicago: University of Chicago Press, 1976).

JANET BOLES (Ed.), *American Feminism: New Issues for a Mature Movement*, Special Issues of *The Annals* (May 1991).

ELLEN BONEPARTH and EMILY STOPER (Eds.), *Women, Power, and Policy: Toward the Year 2000*, 2nd ed. (Elmsford, NY: Pergamon, 1988).

SUSAN BROWNMILLER, *Against Our Will: Men, Women and Rape* (New York: Bantam, 1975).

NANCIE CARAWAY, *Segregated Sisterhood: Racism and the Politics of American Feminism* (Knoxville: University of Tennessee, 1991).

SUSAN CARBON, (Guest Ed.), *Judicature*, Special Issue of *Women in the Judiciary*, 65 (6) (December–January 1982).

SUSAN CARROLL and WENDY STRIMLING, *Women's Routes to Elective Office* (New Brunswick, NJ Eagleton Institute, 1983).

SUSAN J. CARROLL, *Women as Candidates in American Politics* (Bloomington: Indiana University, 1985).

JOAN CARVER, "The Equal Rights Amendment and the Florida Legislature," *Florida Historical Quarterly*, 60 (4) (1982), pp. 455–481.

WILLIAM H. CHAFE, *Paradox of Change: American Women in the Twentieth Century* (New York: Oxford University Press, 1991).

CAROL A. CHRISTY, *Sex Differences in Political Participation: Processes of Change in Fourteen Nations* (New York: Praeger, 1987).

PATRICIA HILL COLLINS, *Black Feminist Thought* (Cambridge, MA: Unwin Hyman, 1990).

ALICE COOK and GWYN KIRK, *Greenham Women Everywhere* (Cambridge, MA: Pluto Press, 1983).

BEVERLY B. COOK, LESLIE F. GOLDSTEIN, KAREN O'CONNOR, and SUSETTE M. TALARICO, *Women in the Judicial Process* (Washington, DC: American Political Science Association, 1988).

LAURA L. CRITES and WINIFRED L. HEPPERLE (Eds.), *Women, the Courts, and Equality* (Beverly Hills, CA: Sage Publications, 1987).

ROBERT DARCY, SUSAN WELCH, and JANET CLARK, *Women, Elections, and Representation* (New York: Longman, 1987).

BARBARA SINCLAIR DECKARD, *The Women's Movement: Political, Socioeconomic, and Psychological Issues* (New York: Harper & Row, 1983).

KAREN DeCROW, *Sexist Justice* (New York: Vintage, 1974).

CARL N. DEGLER, *At Odds: Women and the Family in America from the Revolution to the Present* (New York: Oxford University Press, 1980).

IRENE DIAMOND, *Sex Roles in the State House* (New Haven: Yale University Press, 1977).

DEBRA DODSON (Ed.), *Gender and Policy-Making: Studies of Women in Office* (New Brunswick, NJ: Center for the American Woman and Politics, 1991).

LOIS LOVELACE DUKE (Ed.), "Women in American Politics," *Journal of Political Science*, 17 (1, 2) (Spring 1989).

HESTER EISENSTEIN, *Contemporary Feminist Thought* (Boston: G. K. Hall, 1983).

ZILLAH R. EISENSTEIN, *The Radical Future of Liberal Feminism* (New York: Longman, 1981).

CYNTHIA FUCHS EPSTEIN, *Women in Law* (New York: Basic Books, 1981).

SUSAN ESTRICH, *Real Rape* (Cambridge, MA: Harvard University Press, 1987).

SARA M. EVANS, *Personal Politics: The Roots of Women's Liberation in the Civil Rights Movement and the New Left* (New York: Knopf, 1979).

SUSAN FALUDI, *Backlash: The Undeclared War against American Women* (New York: Crown, 1991).

SONDRA FARGANIS, *The Social Reconstruction of the Feminine Character* (Lanham, MD: Rowman & Littlefield, 1986).

KATHY E. FERGUSON, *The Feminist Case against Bureaucracy* (Philadelphia: Temple University Press, 1984).

JANET A. FLAMMANG (Ed.), *Political Women: Current Roles in State and Local Government* (Beverly Hills, CA: Sage Publications, 1984).

MICHEL FOUCAULT, *Power/Knowledge: Selected Interviews and Other Writings 1972–1977* (New York: Pantheon, 1980).

DIANE FOWLKES, *White Political Women: Paths from Privilege to Empowerment* (Knoxville: University of Tennessee Press, 1992).

JO FREEMAN, *The Politics of Women's Liberation* (New York: McKay, 1975).

———, "Feminist Activities at the 1988 Republican Convention," *PS: Political Science and Politics*, 22 (1) (March 1989), pp. 39–47.

———, "Women at the 1988 Democratic Convention." *PS: Political Science and Politics*, 21 (4) (Fall 1988), pp. 875–881.

BETTY FRIEDAN, *The Feminine Mystique* (New York: Dell, 1964).

———, *The Second Stage* (New York: Summit Books, 1981).

JOYCE GELB and MARIAN LIEF PALLEY, *Women and Public Policies*, 2nd ed. (Princeton, NJ: Princeton University Press, 1987).

IRWIN GERTZOG, *Congressional Women* (New York: Praeger, 1984).

CAROL GILLIGAN, *In a Different Voice: The Changing Political Attitudes of American Women* (Cambridge, MA: Harvard University Press, 1982).

MARIANNE GITHENS and JEWEL L. PRESTAGE (Eds.), *A Portrait of Marginality: The Political Behavior of the American Woman* (New York: David McKay, 1977).

NANCY LORING GOLDMAN, *Female Soldiers: Combatants or Noncombatants?* (Westport, CT: Greenwood Press, 1982).

LESLIE F. GOLDSTEIN, *The Constitutional Rights of Women: Cases in Law and Social Change* (Madison: University of Wisconsin Press, 1988).

LINDA GORDON, *Heroes of Their Own Lives* (New York: Viking, 1988).

EDWARD S. GREENBERG, *Workplace Democracy* (Ithaca, NY: Cornell University Press, 1986).

BERNARD GROFMAN, and AREND LIJPHART, *Electoral Laws and Their Political Consequences* (New York: Agathon Press, 1986).

BERNARD GROFMAN, AREND LIJPHART, ROBERT B. MCKAY, and HOWARD A SCARROW, *Representation and Redistricting Issues* (Lexington, MA: Lexington Books, 1982).

DONNA HARAWAY, "A Manifesto for Cyborgs," *Socialist Review*, 80 (1985).

BARBARA HARFORD and SARA HOPKINS (Eds.), *Greenham Common* (Scranton, PA: Quartet Books, 1984).

SUSAN M. HARTMANN, *From Margin to Mainstream: American Women and Politics since 1960*. (New York: Knopf, 1989).

NANCY HARTSOCK, *Money, Sex, and Power: Toward a Feminist Historical Materialism* (Boston: Northeastern University Press, 1983).

MILDA K. HEDBLOM, *Women and Power in American Politics* (Washington, DC: American Political Science Association, 1988).

JEANNE HOLM, *Women in the Military* (Novato, CA: Presidio Press, 1982).

BELL HOOKS, *Talking Back* (Boston: South End Press, 1989).

———, *Yearning* (Boston: South End Press, 1990).

JEFFREY C. ISAAC, *Power and Marxist Theory: A Realist View* (Ithaca, NY: Cornell University Press, 1987).

ALISON M. JAGGER, *Feminist Politics and Human Nature* (Lanham, MD: Rowman and Allanheld, 1983).

M. KENT JENNINGS AND BARBARA G. FARAH, "Ideology, Gender, and Political Action: A Cross-National Survey," *British Journal of Political Science* (April 1980), pp. 219–240.

M. KENT JENNINGS AND RICHARD NIEMI, *Generations and Politics* (Princeton, NJ: Princeton University Press, 1981).

JOHN JOHNSON AND CHARLES KNAPP, "Sex Discrimination by Law," *New York University Law Review* (October 1971).

LOUISE B. JOHNSON, *Women of the Louisiana Legislature* (Farmerville, LA: Greenbay Publishing, 1986).

LYNDON B. JOHNSON SCHOOL OF PUBLIC AFFAIRS, *Local Government Election Systems* (The University of Texas at Austin, Policy Research Project Report 62, 1984).

SPENCER KIMBALL AND HERBERT DENENBERG (Eds.), *Insurance, Government, and Social Policy* (Homewood, IL: Richard D. Irwin, 1969).

JEANE KIRKPATRICK, *The New Presidential Politics: Men and Women in National Politics* (New York: Russell Sage Foundation, 1976).

———, *Political Woman* (New York: Basic Books, 1974).

ETHEL KLEIN, *Gender Politics: From Consciousness to Mass Politics* (Cambridge, MA: Harvard University Press, 1984).

MIRRA KOMAROVSKY, *Women in College* (New York: Basic Books, 1985).

BARBARA E. KOVACH, *Sex Roles and Personal Awareness* (Lanham, MD. University Press of America, 1990).

FRANK P. LE VENESS AND JANE P. SWEENEY (Eds.), *Women Leaders in Contemporary U.S. Politics* (Boulder, Co: Lynne Rienner, 1987).

JEAN LIPMAN-BLUMEN, *Gender Roles and Power* (Englewood Cliffs, NJ: Prentice-Hall, 1984).

HILARY M. LIPS, *Women, Men and the Psychology of Power* (Englewood Cliffs, NJ: Prentice-Hall, 1981).

AUDRE LORDE, *Sister Outsider* (Freedom, CA: Crossing Press, 1984).

NANCY LOVE, *Dogmas and Dreams* (Chatham, NJ: Chatham House, 1991).

STEVEN LUKES, *Power: A Radical View* (New York: Macmillan, 1974).

RUTH B. MANDEL, *In the Running: The New Woman Candidate* (New Haven: Yale University Press, 1981).

KATE MILLETT, *Sexual Politics* (New York: Doubleday, 1970).

MARTHA MINOW, *Making All the Difference: Inclusion, Exclusion, and American Law* (Ithaca, NY: Cornell University Press, 1990).

BRIAN MITCHELL, *Weak Link* (Washington, DC: Regnery Gateway, 1989).

CHRISTOPHER F. MOONEY, S.J., *Inequality and the American Conscience* (Ulster Park, NY: Paulist Press, 1981).

CAROL MUELLER, "Feminism and the New Woman in Public Office," *Women and Politics*, 3 (Fall 1982), pp. 7–21.

CAROL MUELLER (Ed.), *The Politics of the Gender Gap* (Beverly Hills, CA: Sage Publications, 1988).

ALBERT J. NELSON, *Emerging Influentials in State Legislatures: Women, Blacks, and Hispanics* (New York: Praeger, 1991).

SUSAN MOLLER OKIN, *Justice, Gender, and the Family* (New York: Basic Books, 1989).

KAREN ORREN, *Corporate Power and Social Change: The Politics of the Life Insurance Industry* (Baltimore: Johns Hopkins University Press, 1974).

SHANE PHELAN, *Identity Politics* (Philadelphia, PA: Temple University Press, 1989).

KEITH T. POOLE and L. HARMON ZEIGLER, *Women, Public Opinion, and Politics: The Changing Political Attitudes of American Women.* (New York: Longman, 1985).

HANNAH PITKIN, *The Concept of Representation* (Berkeley: University of California Press, 1967).

VICKY RANDALL, *Women and Politics: An International Perspective* (Chicago: University of Chicago Press, 1987).

Report of the New York Task Force on Women in the Courts (New York: Unified Court System, Office of Court Administration, March 1986).

SARA E. RIX (Ed.), *The American Woman: A Status Report* (New York: Norton, 1986, 1988, 1990, 1992).

HELEN ROGAN, *Mixed Company* (New York: G. P. Putnam's Sons, 1981).

RONNA ROMNEY and BEPPIE HARRISON, *Momentum: Women in American Politics Now* (New York: Crown Publishers, 1988).

DAVID H. ROSENBLOOM, *Federal Equal Employment Opportunity Politics and Public Personnel Administration* (New York: Praeger, 1977).

PAULA S. ROTHENBERG, *Racism and Sexism* (New York: St. Martin's Press, 1988).

JOYCE ROTHSCHILD and J. ALLEN WHITT, *The Cooperative Workplace* (New York: Cambridge University Press, 1986).

WILMA RULE and JOSEPH F. ZIMMERMAN, *U.S. Electoral Systems: Their Impact on Women and Minorities* (Westport, CT: Greenwood, 1992).

VIRGINIA SAPIRO, *The Political Integration of Women: Roles, Socialization and Politics* (Champaign: University of Illinois Press, 1983).

LYDIA SARGENT, *Women and Revolution* (Boston: South End Press, 1981).

ELMER ERIC SCHATTSCHNEIDER, *The Semisovereign People* (Troy, MD: Dryden Press, 1960).

RICHARD W. SCOTT, *Organizations* (Englewood Cliffs, NJ: Prentice-Hall, 1981).

LYNNE SEGAL, *Is the Future Female?* (New York: Peter Bedrick Books, 1987).

PHILIP SELZNICK, *Leadership in Administration* (New York: Harper & Row, 1957).

ALLAN P. SINDLER, *Equal Opportunity: On the Policy and Politics of Compensatory Minority Preferences* Washington, DC: (American Enterprise Institute for Public Policy Research, 1983).

ELIZABETH ANNE STANKO (Ed.), *Judge, Lawyer, Victim, Thief* (Evanston, IL: Northwestern University Press, 1986).

DOROTHY MCBRIDE STETSON, *Women's Rights in the U.S.A.: Policy, Debates, and Gender Roles* (Pacific Grove, CA: Brooks/Cole, 1991).

ABIGAIL M. THERNSTROM, *Whose Vote Counts? Affirmative Action and Minority Voting Rights* (Cambridge, MA: Harvard University Press, 1987).

DOROTHY THOMPSON, (Ed.), *Over Our Dead Bodies: Women Against the Bomb* (New York: Virago Press, 1983).

ROSEMARIE TONG, *Feminist Thought,* (Boulder, CO: Westview Press, 1989).

———, *Women, Sex, and the Law* (Lanham, MD: Rowman & Allanheld, 1984).

LAURENCE H. TRIBE, *Constitutional Choices* (Cambridge, MA: Harvard University Press, 1985).

ELIZABETH VALLANCE, *Women in the House: A Study of Women Members of Parliament* (Atlantic Highlands, NJ: Athlone Press, 1979).

MARCIA LYNN WHICKER and JENNIE J. KRONENFELD, *Sex Roles: Technology, Politics, and Policy* (New York: Praeger, 1986).

J. HARVEY WILKINSON III, *From Brown to Bakke: The Supreme Court and School Integration* (New York: Oxford University Press, 1979).

Women's Rights Law Reporter, Special Issue: Women and the Judiciary, 9 (2) (Spring 1986).

JOHN F. ZIPP and ERIC PLUTZER, "Gender Differences in Voting for Female Candidates: Evidence from the 1982 Election," *Public Opinion Quarterly,* 49 (1985), pp. 179–197.

CONTRIBUTORS _____

Todd W. Areson, a local government consultant in Richmond, Virginia, studies policy management, organizational, and intergovernmental issues facing localities and their state associations of elected and appointed officials. He has extensive experience directing university–local government consortia at all three levels of the intergovernmental system.

Ruth Bamberger, professor of political science, Drury College, teaches courses in American Politics and Political Philosophy. She has researched public policy developments in the private insurance industry in the states and federal government.

Linda L. M. Bennett, associate professor of political science, Wittenberg University, Springfield, Ohio, teaches courses on the U.S. presidency, Congress, public policy, and research methodology. Her publications include articles on the gender gap and on citizen involvement and participation, and a book on education policy systems at the state level.

Steven E. Bennett, professor of political science, University of Cincinnati, Cincinnati, Ohio, teaches courses on elections in the United States, political participation, public opinion, and research methodology. His publications include articles and books on American mass belief systems, political apathy, political information, and political participation.

The Bennetts are the co-authors of several articles on American political behavior and *Living with Leviathan: Americans Coming to Terms with Big Government* (Lawrence: University Press of Kansas, 1990).

Diane D. Blair, professor of political science, University of Arkansas, Fayetteville, Arkansas, teaches courses in U.S. national government, state and local government, and politics in literature. She has written extensively on Arkansas politics and government, state politics, and women in politics.

Lewis Bowman is an adjunct professor at the University of North Texas, Denton, Texas. His research and teaching interests are U.S. politics, political parties, and interest groups and he is currently co-directing a multistate research project about political party activism in the South.

Charles S. Bullock III is the Richard B. Russell Professor of Political Science at the University of Georgia. He received his Ph.D. from Washington University, St. Louis, and has done research on Congress, civil rights, and policy implementation. He is the co-author of *Law and Social Change* (1974), *Racial Equality in America* (1975), *Coercion to Compliance* (1976), *Public Policy and Politics in America*, 2nd ed. (1984), *Public Policy in the Eighties* (1983), *Implementation of Civil Rights Policy* (1984), and *Government in America* (1984). Bullock is a past president of the Southern Political Science Association. He has served as chair of the Legislative Studies Section of the American Political Science Association. He is on the editorial boards of the *Journal of Politics* and *Social Science Quarterly*. In 1991 he received the William A. Owens Creative Research Award.

Barbara Burrell, Honorary Fellow, Women's Studies Research Center, University of Wisconsin and Research, Wisconsin Survey Research Laboratory, UW-Extension, has taught courses on political parties, legislative and presidential politics, and women and politics. She has written on women as candidates for state and national office.

Nancie E. Caraway is a feminist scholar and political theorist from Hawaii who is currently living and working in Washington, D.C. She teaches courses in multiculturalism, feminist theory, women and politics, the politics of popular culture, and the politics of media/film. She is an assistant professor of government at the American University and continues to be stimulated and engaged by her daring young female and male feminist students.

Cal Clark, professor of political science, University of Wyoming, Laramie, Wyoming, teaches classes on political economy, research methods, and East Asia. He is the author of *Taiwan's Development*, co-author of *Women in Taiwan Politics*, and *Flexibility, Foresight, and Fortuna in Taiwan's Development*, and co-editor of *North/South Relations, State and Development*, and *The Evolving Pacific Basin*.

Janet Clark, professor of political science, University of Wyoming, Laramie, Wyoming, teaches classes on U.S. politics, women and politics, and state and local government. She is the co-author of *Women, Elections, and Representation, Women in Taiwan Politics*, and *The Equality State*; the editor of *Women & Politics*; and past president of the Western Social Science Association and the Women's Caucus for Political Science.

Elizabeth Adell Cook teaches in the government department of Georgetown University. She has written several articles on feminist consciousness and is the co-author of *Between Two Absolutes: Public Opinion and the Politics of Abortion*. Her research interests include public opinion, electoral behavior, and gender politics.

Iva Ellen Deutchman, associate professor of political science, Hobart and William Smith Colleges, teaches courses in U.S. politics, political behavior, and gender politics. She has written extensively on feminist theory and gender and state legislatures, and is currently doing comparative work on gender in Australia and the United States.

Victor F. D'Lugin, associate professor of politics and government, University of Hartford, West Hartford, Connecticut, teaches courses in political theory, U.S. political thought, public law, and women's studies. He has written on Jung and political theory and on the politics of the gay and lesbian civil rights movement.

Lois Lovelace Duke is an associate professor of political science at Clemson University and author of many pieces on women and politics and on U.S. national government, including the recently co-edited volume with James MacGregor Burns, William Crotty, and Lawrence Longley, *The Democrats Must Lead: The Case for a Progressive Democratic Party*. In addition, her research interests include mass media and politics and state and local government. She is a recent past president of the Women's Caucus for Political Science: South and is a current member of the board of the League of Women Voters, Clemson, South Carolina.

Joanne V. Hawks, director of Sarah Isom Center for Women's Studies, University of Mississippi, teaches courses on the history of Southern and American women and on the role of women in society. With Carolyn Ellis Staton, she has researched and written articles on women in Southern legislatures from the 1920s to the present.

Captain Richard D. Hooker, Jr., is a career Army officer and assistant professor of political science at the U.S. Military Academy, where he teaches courses in government and executive politics. He holds master's and doctoral degrees from the University of Virginia and has written widely on strategy, tactics, and social policy issues in the military.

William E. Hulbary, associate professor of political science in the Department of Government and International Affairs, University of South Florida, Tampa, Florida, teaches courses in political behavior, U.S. politics and research methods, and statistics. His research and writing focuses on political behavior, political parties, and political socialization.

Kathleen P. Iannello, assistant professor of political science, Gettysburg College, Gettysburg, Pennsylvania, teaches courses in public policy, U.S. politics, and women and politics. She has recently written a book on women's organizations and consensual decision making entitled *Decisions without Hierarchy* (New York: Routledge, 1992).

Malcolm Jewell, professor of political science at the University of Kentucky in Lexington, teaches in the areas of legislatures and political parties. He has written extensively about legislative elections and representation, primary elections, and political parties, particularly at the state level.

Roberta Ann Johnson is a professor of politics at the University of San Francisco. She has a B.A. degree (magna cum laude, Phi Beta Kappa) from Brooklyn College, and her M.A. and Ph.D. degrees from Harvard University. From 1980 to 1985 she was a technical assistance specialist in the Office for Civil Rights, U.S. Department of Education. She has published numerous articles on minorities, women, the disabled, and civil rights–related topics, including a book, *Puerto Rico: Commonwealth or Colony?* (New York: Praeger, 1980).

Anne E. Kelley, associate professor of political science in the Department of Government and International Affairs, University of South Florida, Tampa, Florida, teaches courses in political parties and interest groups, Florida politics, and U.S. political theory. Her research and writing focuses on Florida politics, political parties and interest groups, and women and politics.

Susan A. MacManus is professor and chair of the Department of Government and International Affairs at the University of South Florida, Tampa. Her research interests include urban and minority politics, public policy analysis, and public budgeting and finance. Her articles on women and politics have appeared in the *Journal of Politics, the Western Political Quarterly, the Social Science Quarterly, the Urban Affairs Quarterly, Women & Politics,* and the *Journal of Political Science.* Her most recent book, *Doing Business with Government* (1992), includes discussions of the difficulties female business owners have contracting with governments at all levels.

Elaine Martin, associate professor of political science, Eastern Michigan University, Ypsilanti, Michigan, teaches courses in judicial politics, women in politics, and public administration. She has published extensively on the subject of gender and the judiciary, and is now at work on a book: *Distinguished Women: Voices from the Bench.*

Wilma Rule is an adjunct professor of political science at the University of Nevada, Reno. She has published articles on majority and minority women's opportunity for election to local and national legislatures. With Joseph F. Zimmerman, State University of New York, Albany, Professor Rule is co-editor of *U.S. Electoral Systems: Their Impact on Women and Minorities* (Westport, CT: Greenwood, 1992) and *Electoral Systems in Comparative Perspective: Their Impact on Women and Minorities* (Westport, CT: Greenwood, forthcoming).

Carolyn Ellis Staton, professor of law, University of Mississippi School of Law, teaches courses on sex discrimination, school law, and evidence. With Joanne V. Hawks, she has researched and written articles on women in Southern legislatures from the 1920s to the present.

Gertrude A. Steuernagel, associate professor of political science and Coordinator of Women's Studies at Kent State University, Kent, Ohio, teaches courses in women and politics, political theory, and women's studies. She writes on women and political participation and on feminist political theory. She is co-editor of *Foundations for a Feminist Restructuring of the Academic Disciplines.*

Glen Sussman, assistant professor of political science, Old Dominion University, Norwolk, Virginia, teaches courses in Congress and the president, media and politics and parties and elections. He is currently working on a comparative survey research project studying media coverage of state legislatures.

Joan Hulse Thompson, assistant professor of political science, Beaver College, Glenside, Pennsylvania, served as an American Association of University Women Educational Foundation Fellow at the Congressional Caucus for Women's Issues in 1983–1984. She was an American Political Science Association Congressional Fellow in 1985–1986.

Marcia Lynn Whicker is a professor in the Department of Public Administration at Rutgers University, Newark. She has taught and conducted research in the areas of U.S. government and institutions, the presidency, gender roles, public policy, and public administration.

Thomas A. Yantek is an associate professor of political science at Kent State University, Kent, Ohio. He teaches and does research in the areas of U.S. politics, political economy, and research methodology. His research has appeared in journals such as the *American Journal of Political Science, the Western Political Quarterly,* and *Polity.*